CHURCHILL AND EMPIRE

CHURCHILL AND EMPIRE

A PORTRAIT OF AN IMPERIALIST

LAWRENCE JAMES

PEGASUS BOOKS
NEW YORK LONDON

CHURCHILL AND EMPIRE

Pegasus Books LLC
80 Broad Street, 5th Floor
New York, NY 10004

Copyright © 2014 by Lawrence James

First Pegasus Books hardcover edition June 2014

ISBN: 978-1-60598-569-5

10 9 8 7 8 6 5 4 3 2 1

Printed in the United States of America
Distributed by W. W. Norton & Company, Inc.

To Martha and Vivian James

CONTENTS

ACKNOWLEDGEMENTS

My greatest thanks are to my wife, Mary, for her encouragement, patience and enthusiasm during the preparation and writing of this book. Thanks are also due to my sons, Edward and Henry James, Ruth James, Alan Samson, Andrew Lownie, Lucinda McNeile, Holly Harley, Hannah Lissaman, Michael Rudd, Dr Martin Edmonds, Dr Tim Congdon, Ian Bradley, Professor Nick Roe and Dr Jane Stabler, Rupert Boulting, Dr M. D. Anderson, Trevor Royle, Debbie Usher, A. N. Wilson, Percy Wood, and Andrew Williams. All have given invaluable advice and suggestions. I am also indebted to Viv Hawkes for generous help in the preparation of the manuscript. I owe a similar debt to the late Dan Thomas, Peter Muil and Justin Wells for their forbearance and kindness in assisting and guiding me through the mysteries of information technology. Further plaudits for generosity of spirit and help are due the staffs of the Bodleian Library, the India Records Office, Rhodes House Library, the Imperial War Museum, the Middle East Centre, the National Library of Scotland, the National Archives, the Vere Harmsworth Library and St Andrews University Library, in particular Lynda Innocent and her colleagues.

Like Churchill I am unhappy about changes made to place and country names, so I have kept Burma and Persia throughout the text.

INTRODUCTION

This book is about a subject that has been overlooked or discreetly sidelined in Churchillian literature: his ardent and unswerving faith in the British Empire. His imperial vision was at the heart of his political philosophy. What Churchill called Britain's imperial 'mission' was both his lodestar and the touchstone which he applied to policy decisions when he was First Lord of the Admiralty, Secretary for War, Colonial Secretary and Prime Minister. Throughout his political career he was convinced that, together, the Royal Navy and the Empire were the foundations of British global power and greatness. Imperial Britain was, he believed, uniquely qualified to further progress and enlightenment throughout the world.

As Churchill repeatedly insisted, the Empire was a precious asset, not just for Britain, but for civilisation as a whole. It existed in a Hobbesian universe in competition with other predatory empires whose ambitions and anxieties led to the First and Second World Wars, which were imperial conflicts in which all the protagonists were fighting to safeguard and extend territory and influence. This was so in 1914 and again in 1939, when the British Empire was directly threatened by Italy and Japan and indirectly by Nazi Germany. All three powers were engaged in imperial wars of conquest whose objectives included the elimination of British influence in the Mediterranean and Middle East and the annexation of British colonies in Africa, the Far East and the Pacific.

Throughout the Second World War, imperial geo-political considerations were, I have argued, always uppermost in Churchill's mind whenever he had to make major strategic decisions. In both world wars and the inter-war years, he was also concerned with external and internal ideological challenges to imperial security. The danger posed by Pan-Islamism was the overriding reason why Churchill threw himself so enthusiastically behind the Gallipoli campaign in 1915. Likewise and with equal zeal, he backed military intervention to reverse the Russian revolution because he feared that Bolshevik subversion would undermine British power in the Middle East and Asia.

Churchill's imperial preoccupations are central to understanding him as a statesman and a strategist. The kernel of his imperial creed was simple, enduring and frequently reiterated in his speeches, journalism and writing of history. The British Empire embodied the enlightenment of Western civilisation and, therefore, was a force for the redemption and regeneration of mankind. It was integral to that 'civilisation' which Britain was defending between 1940 and 1945. In Churchill's imagination, its enemies included Lenin, the tribesmen of the North-West Frontier, Hitler and, during the Cold War, Stalin.

Churchill loved the Empire with the same intensity as he loved individual liberty and the principles of parliamentary democracy. His two mistresses were incompatible, for the Empire withheld freedom and the right to representation from nearly all its subjects. This contradiction was overridden by the unwritten contract by which the governed forfeited their freedom in return for a humane, fair government which kept the peace and set its subjects on the path towards physical and moral improvement. Sophistry came to his rescue when, during the war, an American journalist asked him about Indian protests against imperial rule. Churchill wondered which Indians she had in mind. Were they the American Indians who languished in reservations and whose numbers were dwindling, or were they the Indian subjects of the British Raj who were thriving and whose numbers were rising.

Churchill's Empire was never static: he regarded it as an evolving organism, although he was determined to frustrate any development that, however remotely, would diminish Britain's status as a world power. Anxieties on this account as much as his personal loathing for Hinduism impelled him to wage a prolonged political campaign against Indian self-government during which he contemplated ruling India by force, a policy that seemed to contradict his essential humanitarianism.

I have traced the roots of Churchill's essentially liberal imperialism to his birth, upbringing and early political education. He was part of the patrician elite of late-Victorian Britain and was imbued with that high-minded altruism which distinguished so many young men from his background. Public life was public service and a chance to do good, and the Empire offered abundant opportunities; Churchill's heroes were the soldiers who pacified frontiers and tamed their wild inhabitants, the engineers who built railways across deserts and the district commissioners who brought stability to areas of endemic disorder and governed their inhabitants with a firm and even hand.

By his mid-twenties, Churchill had absorbed the current racial dogma that identified the Anglo-Saxon race as uniquely qualified to rule and share the blessings of a civilisation. American on his mother's side, he convinced himself that the United States was psychologically and morally a perfect partner in this global enterprise. This conceit dominated his wartime and post-war dealings with America and made him enemies in both countries. American statesmen and soldiers were repelled by the notion of using their country's power to prop up the British Empire and their counterparts resented their country's subjection to American interests.

Churchill stubbornly refused to countenance the possibility of any divergence in interests and objectives between Britain and America. He clung tenaciously and often in the face of reality to his grand vision of the British Empire and the United States sharing the responsibility for guiding the world towards a happier future.

These are topics and themes that I have explored and interwoven in a narrative that follows the chronology of Churchill's career from the Battle of Omdurman in 1898 until his resignation as Prime Minister in 1955. Domestic matters have been included only when they intruded on Churchill's imperial preoccupations. There was of course no boundary between imperial and foreign policy since, as Churchill always insisted, Britain was a global power only because she possessed a vast territorial empire and a huge navy. At various stages and in order to place the subject within a wider historical context, I have paused to examine the nature of the British and other empires and the ideologies that were contrived to legitimise them.

Wherever possible I have avoided the academic and political post mortem that followed the death of imperialism and empires. A forensic exercise has mutated into a rancorous debate over the virtues and vices of the old empires that shows no signs of flagging. To an extent, public rows about the nature of vanished supremacies have some relevance to the modern world since great powers are still trying to impose their will on weaker nations; the inhabitants of Tibet, Chechnya, Iraq and Afghanistan can be forgiven for believing that the age of empires has not yet disappeared. One by-product of the post-imperial debate over empires has been the growth of an ancestral guilt complex which has taken root in Britain. This *angst* adds nothing to our understanding of the past, which it distorts by imposing contemporary concepts and codes on our ancestors.

In writing this book I have endeavoured to navigate a passage between the extremes of triumphalism and breast beating. I have avoided drawing up a debit and credit with, say, the Amritsar massacre balanced against the establishment of a medical school at Agra. The quantification of one bad deed against a good one achieves nothing beyond reminding us that virtue and vice co-existed within the Empire, as it does in every field of human activity. As for Churchill, I hope that readers who feel the need to judge him will do so according to the standards he set for himself and the Empire.

PART ONE

1874–1900

Jolly Little Wars:

Omdurman

General Sir Herbert Kitchener, commander-in-chief of the Anglo-Egyptian army in the Sudan, loathed all journalists and in particular Lieutenant Winston Churchill of the 4th Hussars. He had joined Kitchener's staff in the summer of 1898 to witness the last phase of the campaign against the Khalifa Abdullahi and report on its progress for the *Morning Post*. Kitchener had objected strongly to Churchill's appointment, but he had been outwitted by Lady Randolph Churchill, who had enlisted her high society friends and charmed elderly generals at the War Office to procure her son's attachment to Kitchener's staff. Her success was galling since Kitchener, the son of a retired army officer with modest means, had had to rely on his own merit and hard graft to gain advancement.

Yet the general and his unwelcome staff officer had much in common. Both served and believed passionately in the British Empire and each was an ambitious self-promoting egotist. The general knew that a glorious victory in the Sudan would propel him to the summit of the Empire's military hierarchy. The subaltern treated imperial soldiering as the means to launch a political career. In the previous year he had fought on the North-West Frontier of India and had written an account of the campaign that had impressed the Prince of Wales and the Prime Minister Lord Salisbury. For Churchill, the Sudan war was an opportunity to acquire another medal, write another book and remind the world that he was a gallant, talented and capable fellow who deserved a seat in the House of Commons. Voters were susceptible to what he later described as the 'glamour' of a dashing young officer who had proved his mettle on the frontiers of their Empire.

On 2 September 1898, Kitchener was about to deploy 23,000 British and Sudanese troops and a flotilla of gunboats against more than twice that number of Sudanese tribesmen commanded by the Khalifa on a plain a few miles north of Omdurman. Kitchener proceeded cautiously. European armies in the tropics did not always have things all their own way. Two years before, the Italians had been trounced at Aduwa by an Abyssinian host, admittedly equipped with some modern weaponry. Churchill knew this and the night before a battle a brother officer noticed that he was 'less argumentative and self-assertive than usual'. He voiced anxieties about a night attack which could easily have tipped the odds in favour of the Khalifa.[1]

The Khalifa relied on the fervent Islamic faith of his warriors who, thirteen years before, had defeated a modern Egyptian army, broken British squares, stormed Khartoum and cut down the commander of its garrison, General Gordon. At Omdurman the Dervishes stuck to their traditional tactic of frontal assaults by spear and swordsmen. The Krupp cannon and Nordenfelt machine-guns captured from the Egyptians were left behind in the arsenal at Omdurman, although some tribesmen carried obsolete rifles. Discipline, training and overwhelming firepower gave Kitchener the advantage in a conventional battle. Artillery, Maxim machine-guns and magazine rifles created a killing zone that was theoretically impassable.

Attached to an outlying cavalry picket, Churchill watched with amazement the advance of the Sudanese horde which stretched back over two miles of desert. The oncoming mass of camelry, horsemen and infantry with their white jibbahs, banners, drums, war cries and sparkling spear points aroused his historical imagination. Was this, he wondered, how the army of Saladin must have appeared to the Crusaders? The spectacle was filmed from the deck of the gunboat *Melik* by the war artist Frederick Villiers in the knowledge that scenes of the battle would fill cinemas across the world. Sadly, his cine camera was knocked over by a shell case and his footage was lost. It was left to photographers, artists and journalists like Churchill to satisfy the British public's craving for vivid images of the Battle of Omdurman.

Kitchener's lines were protected by a zeriba, an improvised hedge of prickly mimosa branches. No Dervish ever reached it. At 3,000 yards the attackers were hit by shells, at 1,700 by Maxim fire and at 1,500 by rifle volleys. A scattering of survivors got to within 500 yards of their enemies, although Churchill was struck by the suicidal courage of 'one brave old man, carrying a flag' who got within 150 yards of the zeriba. Successive onrushes came to the same end. 'It was a terrible sight,' Churchill thought, 'for as yet they had not hurt us at all, and it seemed an unfair advantage to strike thus cruelly when they could not reply.' His feelings were shared throughout the army. Corporal George Skinner of the Royal Army Medical Corps observed that: 'Nothing could possibly stand against such a storm of lead, in fact no European would ever think of facing it in the daring way these fanatics did.' Over 10,000 Dervishes were killed and an unknown number died from their wounds.

The Khalifa's army began to disintegrate and Kitchener was determined to deny it any chance to regroup. A pursuit was ordered and Colonel Roland Martin and four squadrons of the 21st Lancers were instructed to harass the flanks of the Dervishes who were fleeing towards Omdurman, the Khalifa's capital. After advancing one and a half miles the horsemen encountered what was thought to be a party of about 150 skirmishers who were covering the Sudanese line of retreat. Roland's horsemen came under fire and he ordered a charge to drive off the tribesmen. 'The pace was fast and the distance short,' Churchill recalled. Suddenly and to their horror the riders found themselves galloping pell-mell into a dried-up wadi, crammed with over a thousand Dervish spearmen and cavalry. 'A score of horsemen and a dozen bright flags rose as if by magic from the earth. Eager warriors sprang forward to anticipate the shock,' Churchill wrote afterwards. With a 'loud furious shout' the horsemen crashed into their adversaries and there was a bloody scrimmage in which the Dervishes hacked and slashed their enemies. At last they were on equal terms, sword against sword and lance against spear. Churchill, who had proclaimed to his family and brother officers his ardent desire for the risks of the battlefield, preferred to have the odds in his favour. He had armed himself with the most up-to-date technology, a ten-shot Mauser automatic pistol, with which he killed at least five tribesmen before riding out of the mêlée.

The lancers extricated themselves, rode on, halted, dismounted and scattered the tribesmen with carbine fire. Out of the 320 men who had charged, 20 had been killed, 50 wounded and 119 horses were lost, casualties which provoked the future Field Marshal Haig to accuse Colonel Roland of criminal recklessness with other men's lives. Churchill thought otherwise; the 21st Lancers had shown splendid bravery. His judgement was shared by Queen Victoria, who honoured the Lancers with the title 'The Empress of India's Own', and by the press and the public. Omdurman may have been a victory for modern, scientific warfare, but the lancers' charge was signal proof that the British soldier was more than a match for the Dervish on his own terms. 'My faith in our race and blood was much strengthened,' Churchill wrote afterwards.[2] He never forgot the charge and until the end of his life would enthral anyone who cared to listen with his recollections of those terrifying few minutes.

Imperial glory was followed by imperial shame. Injured Dervishes were left to die a lingering death on the battlefield, or were shot and bayoneted. Kitchener's subordinate Major John Maxwell organised death squads to eliminate prominent supporters of the Khalifa during the occupation of Khartoum. Hitherto, Churchill had admired Kitchener as a good general even if, as he privately admitted, he was 'not a gentleman'. His callousness after the battle appalled a young man with a quasi-religious faith in a humanitarian Empire, as it did many of his fellow officers and that section of the public which mistrusted imperialism.

Churchill confided to his mother that the victory at Omdurman was disgraced by 'the inhuman slaughter of the wounded'.[3] There were rows in the press and the Commons, but the government rallied to Kitchener, who received a peerage and a gift of £30,000. He proceeded onwards and upwards to become commander-in-chief first in South Africa in 1900 and then in India. On the outbreak of war in 1914 he was appointed Secretary of State for War. The nation had an almost mystic faith in the imperial hero who had defeated the Sudanese and the Boers. Posters showing his martial moustache, staring eyes and accusatory finger helped persuade a million young patriots to enlist.

Churchill too did well out of Omdurman. He wrote another bestseller, *The River War*, and made his formal political debut by unsuccessfully contesting Oldham as a Conservative in July 1899. His version of Omdurman glossed over the mistreatment of the wounded which had so distressed him at the time, although his readers' memories and consciences may have been stirred by his bald statement that, after Omdurman: 'All Dervishes who did not immediately surrender were shot or bayoneted.' In the Sudan and elsewhere, momentary brutality was soon redeemed by the benefits of imperial government. Many years afterwards, Churchill flippantly recalled the wars of conquest of his youth: 'In those days, England had a lot of jolly little wars against barbarous peoples that we were endeavouring to help forward to higher things.'

The Battle of Omdurman brings Churchill's imperial creed into sharp focus. It was another victory for the British Empire and, it went without saying, another stride forward for civilisation. The two were synonymous for Churchill. This is what he declared on the hustings at Oldham and would continue to say for the rest of his life. The British Empire was a dynamic force for the regeneration and improvement of mankind. It brought peace to areas of chronic instability, it provided honest and just government, it invited backward peoples to enrich themselves by joining the modern world of international trade and investment, and it offered the blessings of Europe's intellectual and scientific enlightenment to all its subjects. It also made Britain a world power. In the last chapter of *The River War*, Churchill reminded readers that Omdurman had secured Britain's grip on the Nile and the Red Sea and facilitated the expulsion of the French from a strategically vital region.

Omdurman had been an exhilarating experience for Churchill the romantic and Churchill the historian. He was already steeped in history and he believed that he could identify its primal impulses and where they were leading mankind. The battle had been one of those moments of high drama which appealed to Churchill's sense of the theatre of great events. They were the raw material for the rich and evocative style of prose which he was already cultivating. Here, from *The River War*, is his account of an incident in the 1885 Sudanese campaign in which a British square is attacked by Dervishes:

Ragged white figures spring up in hundreds. Emirs on horses appear as if by magic. Everywhere are men running swiftly forward, waving their spears and calling upon the Prophet of God to speed their enterprise. The square halts. The weary men begin to fire with thoughtful care. The Dervishes drop quickly. On then, children of the desert!

War fascinated Churchill. In 1898 it still had an afterglow of Napoleonic glamour which, he was shrewd enough to realise, was about to fade away for ever. 'The wars of the peoples', he predicted in 1900, 'will be more terrible than those of the kings.' Of course he was right. Many of his brother officers, including Haig, would command armies in the trenches, fighting the industrialised warfare of the masses and mass casualties. At Omdurman, Churchill experienced a battle that could still be considered as glamorous, not least because it contained an episode which epitomised (in the imagination if not the reality) all the romance of war, a cavalry charge. Churchill thought that he had been very lucky to have taken part in such a stirring anachronism.

Churchill's history was always selective. Lingering over the slaughter after Omdurman would at the very least have compromised the moral elements in his wider imperial vision. He was discovering the power to control history and, through his version of it, harness it to promote his own version of Britain's imperial destiny. His accounts of the 1897 Malakand campaign, the Sudan war and early operations during the Boer War of 1899 to 1902 commanded national attention. They also established Churchill's reputation as a pundit on the art of war who understood the military mind and had mastered the technicalities of strategy and tactics. His authority in such matters was enhanced by his graphic prose and dazzling rhetoric. Churchill understood and implicitly believed in Disraeli's aphorism 'It is with words that we govern men'. At every stage of his career, he wrote compelling histories which described the events he had witnessed and, most important of all for an ambitious politician, how he shaped them. The results were subjective, occasionally misleading and always gripping.

War was part and parcel of imperialism. Territory was acquired by victories and imperial rule was sustained by the use of maximum force whenever resistance occurred. Yet, as Churchill came to appreciate, the expediencies of the battlefield drove exasperated commanders to jettison those moral codes which, he believed, defined Britain as an agent of civilisation. Writing home in 1897 after a bout of hard fighting on the North-West Frontier, he mentioned that the Pashtun 'kill and mutilate' captured or injured men, and that in retaliation 'we kill their wounded'. He added that he had not 'soiled my hands' with such 'dirty work'.[4] Here and at Omdurman, Churchill had had a foretaste of the predicaments he would later encounter as a minister responsible for the actions of frustrated and vengeful subordinates who suspended the moral principles which he believed were the foundations of the Empire.

He'll Be Prime Minister of England One Day:
A Subaltern's Progress

Churchill's presence at Omdurman was an outcome of his carefully calculated plans to get himself elected as a Conservative to Parliament, where he was confident that his merit would quickly propel him on to the front benches. He had taken an eccentric course, for soldiers, particularly young ones, were rare in the Commons. Other young Tories of his background who shared his ambitions followed the conventional trajectory that passed through Eton and Oxford, which was then the nursery for aristocrats with political aspirations. This path had been taken by Winston's father, Lord Randolph Churchill who, after graduating, had been provided in 1874 with the seat of Woodstock, which was still in the gift of his father, the sixth Duke of Marlborough.

This road was closed for Churchill. He passed through two preparatory schools and then to Harrow where his talents remained undetected. Churchill showed no interest in or capacity for what he later called 'those combinations of Latin words and syllables which are perhaps as useful or harmless a form of mental training as youth can receive'. In 1889, when he was fifteen, Churchill's schoolmasters relegated him to Harrow's army class, a refuge for dunces flummoxed by parsing and gerunds. These deficiencies were overlooked by Sandhurst, whose entrance exams were less rigorous than those of Oxford and Cambridge, although the army was considered a proper and honourable profession for men of Churchill's background.

Churchill's imperial education was informal and far more stimulating than that offered by his schools. It had begun when he was five and had been captivated by the vivid engravings in the illustrated weeklies of scenes from the 1879 Zulu War. Firm-jawed Tommies faced what he remembered as 'black and naked' Zulus armed with assegais. At his first prep school Churchill had followed the fortunes of the expedition sent in 1884 to rescue General Gordon from Khartoum. He envied another pupil who had received a gift of tin soldiers dressed in the new khaki uniforms which were worn in the desert. Churchill soon amassed his own miniature armies and engaged his younger brother Jack in battles, always taking care that his forces had greater numbers and better equipment.

Churchill's boyhood Empire was an intriguing land of the imagination, filled with excitement and opportunities for adventure. It was the Empire of G. A. Henty's schoolboy fiction in which plucky lads displayed their resourcefulness and won the respect of the natives through their courage and sense of fair play. They were needed, for, during the last quarter of the nineteenth century, Britain was engaged in a new bout of overseas expansion, fighting campaigns of conquest and consolidation across Asia and Africa. Like Henty's young heroes, Churchill was keen to participate and risk his life for the Empire.

In January 1894 he was commissioned into the 4th Hussars, a fashionable and dashing regiment in which rich, blue-blooded officers were expected to ride hard and relax extravagantly. With considerable reluctance and apprehension, Lord Randolph agreed an allowance to cover his son's indulgences. So far, Winston had shown none of those virtues cherished by Victorian parents and pedagogues. He had been a rumbustious boy who possessed an enormous curiosity, a vibrant imagination and an independence of mind and spirit, qualities his education had been contrived to suppress. Moreover, the young Churchill chose to obey authority out of respect rather than duty.

Sandhurst tempered his waywardness and he congratulated himself on having been 'mentally, morally and physically improved' by what he had learned there. His grandmother the Duchess of Marlborough reported that the College had done wonders for Winston, who had quietened down and become 'nice mannered', although she was displeased to discover that he smoked cigarettes. They were soon replaced by cigars.

A photograph of Churchill in his elegant hussar's uniform with its gold lace shows an insouciant and perhaps disdainful young beau sabreur destined for the polo field and ready to throw himself into the raffish life of a mess which was a martial version of P. G. Wodehouse's Drones Club. Yet his mind was already set on two immediate objectives. One, worthy in a soldier, was to make a reputation for courage on the battlefield, and the other, uncommon for cavalry subalterns, was to study history, economics and political philosophy. Both would assist Churchill to follow his father into politics and succeed where he had failed so disastrously. Lord Randolph, once the brightest star in the Conservative firmament, had burned himself out politically and physically. Since his resignation from Lord Salisbury's cabinet in 1886, he had wandered in the political wilderness and by 1894 he was clearly dying. There is a valid case to be made that his son was desperate to vindicate his memory and perpetuate his populist but unorthodox programme of 'Tory Democracy'. Acutely aware of his ancestry, Churchill may also have wanted to resuscitate the genius of the Churchills which had remained submerged since the death of the first Duke of Marlborough in 1722.

Churchill exploited his family's social and political connections for all they were worth in his attempts to place himself in the field of fire. His mother's string pulling secured him leave from his regiment to visit Cuba as a war correspondent covering the islanders' rebellion against their Spanish rulers. In August 1896 an imperial campaign beckoned and he badgered his mother to mobilise 'her influential friends' and 'those who would do something for me for my father's sake' (Lord Randolph had died the year before) and arrange him a posting to Rhodesia [Zimbabwe], where the Ndebele had risen against the British South Africa Company.[1]

Despite his father's erratic career, the Churchill name still counted for something in Conservative circles. Marlborough money was available to fund his election expenses and all that was needed was a chestful of medals and, in his own words, Churchill would be ready to 'beat my sword into an iron despatch box'. He boasted to his brother officers of the glittering future that lay ahead of him. Some were taken in, although his bumptious self-confidence often grated on the nerves of a caste which traditionally prized reserve and understatement. Major Aylmer Haldane, who met Churchill in India in 1897 and again in South Africa in 1899, was among those impressed. His friend seemed set to become the Secretary of State for India 'before long'. Their commanding officer at Ladysmith, General Sir George White, once pointed Churchill out and remarked: "That's Randolph Churchill's son Winston: I don't like the fellow, but he'll be Prime Minister of England one day.'[2]

Imperial campaigning was a godsend for Churchill's friable finances. 'The pinch of the matter is that we are so damn poor,' he complained to his mother, who allowed him £400 a year. It failed to cover his annual outlay in India and she reproached him for his fecklessness: 'If you had any grit and are worth your salt you will try to live within your means.' The trouble was, as he realised, that they were both spendthrifts; there was a painful equation between his £100 polo pony and her £200 ballgown. Relief came with Churchill's posting to the Malakand Field Force in September 1897 which had been arranged by a family friend, the force's commander, General Sir Bindon Blood.

During the next three years Churchill achieved solvency. He boasted that his journalism and campaign histories had earned him £10,000, some of which was spent easing the rigours of campaigning.

When he landed at Durban in October 1899, his baggage included 18 bottles of whisky (a lifelong taste which he had discovered on the North-West Frontier), 16 of St Emilion and 6 of thirty-year-old brandy. Churchill did not have the opportunity to enjoy his portable cellar, for within four weeks he had been taken prisoner by the Boers after the ambush of an armoured train near Chieveley in Natal.

He and the train's commander Major Haldane were conveyed to a prison compound for officers in Pretoria, from which Churchill famously escaped. His fellows officers were uneasy about his flight, which, they feared, would antagonise the Boers and make them tighten their hitherto relaxed security. 'You are afraid', was Churchill's response, 'I could get away any night.' Audacity, which included an element of carelessness about the fate of others, paid off and the immense publicity his escape attracted helped secure his election for Oldham in 1901. He had been extremely lucky, for the thrilling story of his flight from Pretoria to Laurenço Marques in Portuguese Moçambique had been a heartening distraction from the cheerless newspaper reports of British reverses on every front in South Africa. During 1900 the tide turned against the Boers and Churchill returned to the front line as an officer in a volunteer cavalry regiment and journalist.

A Dog with a Bone:

Lieutenant Churchill's Imperial World

Churchill announced his single-minded devotion to the British Empire and his views on its place in the scheme of things in his first political speech, made to the local Tory Primrose League during their annual fête in the grounds of Cannington Hall in Somerset in 1897. It was Jubilee year and so he reminded his rural audience of 'the splendour of their Empire' and the value of the Royal Navy. Battleships, dominions and colonies made Britain a great power and together were the guarantee that 'our flag shall fly high upon the sea' and that our 'voice shall be heard in the councils of Europe'. Finally, he invoked Britain's 'mission of bringing peace, civilisation and good government to the uttermost end of the earth'.[1]

The Empire was a responsibility that had to be taken seriously by everyone. In June 1899, Churchill told the electors of Oldham that: 'The consciousness of dominion over subject races must alone increase the self-respect of every Englishman. Be he rich or be he poor, or whatever his fortune may be *noblesse oblige* has a meaning to every man of British birth.'[2] This assertion was rooted in his father's Tory Democracy, which had been a programme for national regeneration largely invented by Lord Randolph to make his party attractive to the newly enfranchised working classes. Tory Democracy was a blend of social reform (at Oldham Winston announced his support for old-age pensions), Disraelian one-nation Conservatism and patriotism.

It was in the name of Tory Democracy that Churchill invited the millhands and shopkeepers of Oldham to think of themselves as bound by that essentially aristocratic notion of '*noblesse oblige*' by which a landlord had moral obligations to his tenants. Churchill's Empire was an accumulation of overseas estates and it was the duty of every Briton to see that they were well managed and that their inhabitants were well treated. This was why he would later refer to Britain as an

'Imperial Democracy'. In a wider context this national responsibility was what Rudyard Kipling called the 'white man's burden' in a poem written in 1900 to prepare Americans for their imperial duties to the people of the recently annexed Philippines.

The United States was shouldering part of a global burden. Its weight was unevenly distributed between nine other imperial nations which possessed colonies in Asia, Africa, the Caribbean and the Pacific. They were Britain, France, Italy, Germany, Russia, Japan, the Netherlands, Spain and Portugal and, by 1900, their combined empires covered 85 per cent of the world's surface. This partition of the globe had been under way for the past four hundred years and had always been accepted as natural, legitimate and, on the whole, desirable for both rulers and ruled.

Churchill's British Empire was a paradigm which set a noble example to the world. It contrasted favourably with the unloved and brutal Spanish administration of Cuba, which he briefly visited in 1895. Afterwards, he remarked that under British rule the island would have evolved into a 'free and prosperous' country with just laws and a Cuban cricket XI that might have played at Lord's. Moreover, and this would have pleased both Churchill and the voters of Oldham, Cuban cigars would have been exchanged for Lancashire cottonware.

The British Empire was the largest empire. In 1900 the red bits on the world map added up to 1.8 million square miles which were home to 294 million people, nearly two-thirds of whom were Indian. There were over 13 million British colonists, most of whom were first- or second-generation immigrants who had settled in Canada, Newfoundland, Natal, Cape Colony, Australia and New Zealand. The white dominions were the British Empire's greatest success story to date. They had started their lives as outlets for Britain's and Ireland's surplus (and often unwanted) population and, within one hundred and fifty years, the fledgling settlements had evolved into stable, sophisticated, modern democracies. All had thriving and expanding economies based upon minerals and agriculture. Britain was fed and clothed by the dominions. Since 1885 Canadians had converted 775,000 square miles of prairie into the world's largest wheatfield and, by 1900, four million Australians shared a continent with 54 million sheep whose fleeces supplied the woollen mills of Yorkshire. Growth on this scale was a magnet for capital and British investors poured money into railways, banks and harbours. The dominions were fiercely loyal and a military asset. In 1885 units of Canadian and Australian volunteers had joined the Sudan expeditionary forces and larger contingents from all the dominions fought in the Boer War.

British imperial diversity was a product of geography and history. Territories had been occupied and in some cases settled for a wide variety of economic, political and strategic reasons. From the seventeenth to the early nineteenth centuries profit had been the driving force behind expansion and it had led to the conquest of the West Indian sugar islands and the annexation of Singapore and Hong Kong. The big money was to be made in India and its ruthless pursuit transformed the East India Company from a commercial enterprise into a political and military power obsessed with regional security and stability. In the 1750s the Company had begun to conquer territory and establish a network of alliances with tractable or cowed local princes. In the process, three political principles were established which would be repeatedly applied elsewhere in the Empire: never temporise with local opposition; apply superior force whenever prestige was in jeopardy; and make as many friends as possible among the indigenous elite. These stratagems worked and, by 1849, Britain had total mastery of the sub-continent. Although he doubted the existence of God, Churchill found it possible to represent Britain's accumulation of territory as the workings of a benign Providence and evidence of a unique destiny to improve the world.

India was Britain's prize possession. Its piecemeal subjugation had transformed an industrial nation with a powerful navy into a global superpower. India gave Britain status, wealth and a reservoir of soldiers. Their wages were paid by the Indian government and they could be deployed anywhere in the world. In 1877 Disraeli ordered Indian troops to be shipped to Malta to checkmate the Russian threat to Constantinople. In return for manpower and prestige, the British gave Indians an administration which was humane and just. School and college syllabuses were contrived to open the Indian mind to the European intellectual and scientific Enlightenment. Lessons in history, political philosophy and English law might qualify Indians to rule themselves at some date in the far distant future, which was the goal of the Indian National Congress founded in 1885. The notion of Indian self-government was always abhorrent to Churchill. His two years in India had implanted in his mind an unshakeable conviction that a thousand or so British administrators and a garrison of 60,000 British and 150,000 Indian soldiers were all that stood between the sub-continent and a holy war between the Hindu majority and Muslim minority.

India's greatest gift to Britain was prestige, a truism which Churchill would repeat throughout his political career. Prestige was hard to quantify with any precision, but it mattered enormously for all the imperial powers. Its magic bewitched politicians, newspaper proprietors and voters in Britain, America and the Continent. Perceptions of national prestige facilitated the grafting of imperialism on to the intoxicating nationalisms that had emerged among the middle and working classes during the middle decades of the nineteenth century. It was, therefore, relatively simple for politicians, journalists and lobbyists to claim that their country's status in the world would be enhanced by the accumulation of overseas territories and the frustration of other powers with similar motives.

British prestige was buttressed by India and the Royal Navy. Maritime supremacy had made the creation of the British Empire possible and remained the key to its survival. So long as Britannia ruled the waves, Britain's overseas commerce, investment and widely dispersed territories were safe, which had been the historic lesson of the seventeenth- and eighteenth-century wars against the Netherlands, France and Spain. 'Command of the sea is everything,' Churchill told his mother in 1896 and, with variations, this assumption remained a favourite theme of his speeches for the next thirty years. Of course it made sense since, as he was so fond of saying, Britain was an *island* nation. As he once observed, 'our lives, our liberties, our peaceful industry and our democratic progress' ultimately rested on 'naval supremacy'.

Commanding the seas was an expensive and complex business

which presented Britain with a series of geo-political problems. Battlefleets and squadrons relied upon a string of fortified harbours, dockyards and coaling stations across the world. Gibraltar and Malta made the Mediterranean a British lake. Halifax (Nova Scotia), Hamilton (Bermuda), Freetown (Sierra Leone), the Falkland Islands and Simon's Bay (near Cape Town) dominated the Atlantic and Aden, Bombay, Singapore, Sydney and Hong Kong secured the Red Sea and the Indian and Pacific Oceans. These outposts and the warships they served gave Britain the ability to transport troops anywhere in the world; the Royal Navy protected the transports which carried dominion forces to South Africa between 1899 and 1902.

Wherever British maritime supremacy appeared to be in jeopardy governments took fright. In 1854 Britain (backed by France) invaded the Crimea to besiege and demolish the Russian naval base at Sebastopol. Its existence challenged the Royal Navy's dominance in the eastern Mediterranean which made it easy for Britain to overawe the Ottoman Sultan. The opening of the Suez Canal in 1869 created new strategic fixations which led to the conquest of Egypt in 1882 and the imposition of a government under the thumb of British bureaucrats. Alexandria became a British naval base and a British garrison guarded the Canal.

The *coup de main* against Egypt did not produce peace of mind for Britain's diplomats and strategists. They pored over maps and decided that the safety of one waterway was permanently endangered by another, the Nile. Whoever controlled the river controlled Egypt and so, in 1896, Kitchener began his conquest of the Sudan. Further south, Britain occupied Uganda and secured the headwaters of the White Nile. And just in time, for a tiny French detachment commanded by Commandant Jean-Baptiste Marchand had marched across central Africa (he travelled by bicycle) and camped at Fashoda on the Upper Nile. He was politely evicted by Kitchener, who turned up on a gunboat with superior forces. The cavalry charge of Omdurman had been one incident in a sequence of intrigues, campaigns and annexations stretching back over sixteen years and whose underlying purpose had been the security of the Suez Canal. The effort and expense (the Egyptian Treasury footed part of the bill) were justified in terms of imperial communications and, of course, naval supremacy.

*

Churchill's study of Gibbon's *Decline and Fall of the Roman Empire* and Admiral Mahan's *The Influence of Sea Power upon History* had taught him that successful empires always needed to be ready to defend themselves. Empires were transitory phenomena which could succumb to internal stresses, failures of willpower and stronger, predatory rivals. All these factors had contributed to the decline of the Spanish, Portuguese and Ottoman Empires which, by 1900, seemed to be in irreversible decay. The future of the Austro-Hungarian Empire (the only one confined to Europe) also looked uncertain thanks to clamorous nationalist movements in its Polish, Czech and Balkan provinces.

By contrast, three old imperial powers, Britain, France and Russia were healthy, virile and hungry for new lands, as were four newcomers, Germany, Italy, the United States and Japan. All were competitors in a race for Asian and African territory, which had been gathering pace since the early 1880s, when Britain's occupation of Egypt had alerted other powers to the need to claim as much as they could as fast as possible. Contemporaries explained this rush for land in terms of Darwin's evolutionary theories. The fittest and most adaptable of the great powers would survive and grow stronger at the expense of the enfeebled. Britain had what was commonly called 'the lion's share', which aroused the jealousy of its rivals. As Churchill observed in 1899, 'the position of England among the nations is the position of a dog with a bone in the midst of a hungry pack.'[3]

There was still some meat available, but it was being gobbled up quickly. After a brisk, one-sided war in 1898 the United States had acquired Cuba, Puerto Rico and the Philippines from Spain. Japan had snatched Formosa [Taiwan] from China and, after defeating Russia in 1905, prepared for further penetration of Manchuria and the annexation of Korea. During 1912 and 1913, Greece, Serbia, Romania and Bulgaria seized the Ottoman Empire's outlying Balkan provinces and Italy invaded its last North African possession, Libya. At the same time, Germany was contemplating the purchase of Portugal's African colonies of Angola and Moçambique, and Russian strategists were preparing for a pre-emptive coup to seize Constantinople and the Straits.

The British Empire was never directly imperilled by these developments. American, Japanese, Italian and German annexations were tolerated, for they did not infringe British interests and were the consequence of the perfectly legitimate aspirations of those nations. Such leeway could never be allowed to Russia, which had been Britain's rival in the Near East and Asia throughout the nineteenth century. Since the time of Catherine the Great, Russian armies had been thrusting southwards and eastwards, first towards the Black Sea, then into the Caucasus and, from 1830 onwards, into Central Asia. Its independent khanates were subjugated and newly built railway lines carried more soldiers further eastwards towards China. Seen from London and Calcutta, the tracks that snaked across Central Asia towards the Persian and Afghan frontiers directly threatened India. By 1880 Russian armies could, theoretically, be transported to Afghanistan from where they could launch a mass invasion of the sub-continent. At the very least, British prestige would be severely jolted by an incursion and scaremongers predicted that the Russian arrival would encourage popular uprisings across India.

British fears were fuelled by the periodic outbursts of various Russian generals who boasted that one day the Czar's armies would conquer India. This was the vodka speaking. The ramshackle logistics of the Russian army and the extreme unlikelihood that the Afghans would permit it to pass through their country made the venture a gamble in which the odds were stacked against Russia. Nevertheless, the mere hint of any Russian interest in Afghanistan provoked a massive armed response, designed to persuade the Afghans that Queen Victoria was to be more feared than the Czar. Afghanistan was invaded in 1838 and again in 1878, but each time the British withdrew, leaving its inhabitants badly mauled but still defiant. For the next thirty years British intelligence officers played the 'Great Game' in the Himalayas, snooping for signs of imminent Russian aggression. Their fears and activities were portrayed in Rudyard Kipling's novel *Kim* which appeared in 1901 and had been written as a warning to the British public of the danger to India.

In that year the concentration of most of Britain's white troops in South Africa prompted a fresh bout of hysteria, which was made worse by Whitehall war games based on the hypothesis that a Russian army reached the Khyber Pass. It was calculated that Czar Nicholas II could deploy 180,000 men on the Afghan frontier. If he did, then the Empire's manpower (including Indians, Australians and New Zealanders) would be stretched to breaking point and might not reach the front in time to repel the Russians.[4] Informed guesswork by staff officers as to the course of an Anglo-Russian war took on board the possibility that Britain's other major imperial rival, France, might join in the fight. At one fell swoop a Franco-Russian armada would attack the Suez Canal and isolate Britain from all its Asian, Far Eastern and Australasian possessions. This was ridiculous, since the Franco-Russian alliance of 1892 would only be activated if one of the signatories was attacked by two or more powers, but then reason seldom intruded into Admiralty and War Office plans for future wars. France had nothing to gain from involvement in a war to help Russia conquer India and there was no advantage for Russia in fighting Britain in support of French claims to the Sahara Desert. Flying the tricolour over sandy wastelands was a matter of national pride to French right-wing nationalists and Anglophobes who clamoured for war during the confrontation at Fashoda. Their hullabaloo was ignored by the level-headed French Foreign Minister Théophile Delcassé who feared that a conflict with Britain over who owned the Nile would be a one-sided affair in which the Royal Navy would cripple France's overseas trade, cut off its colonies and, perhaps, annex them. An Anglo-French war in 1898 would be a repeat of the Seven Years, Revolutionary and Napoleonic Wars in which France had lost nearly all its colonies.

The outcome of Fashoda fitted a contemporary diplomatic pattern by which disputes between the great European powers over the ownership of stretches of desert, jungles and coral islands were settled by diplomacy, despite the ritual snarling and sabre-rattling by chauvinist newspaper editors and politicians. Talks were convened, lines drawn on maps and national honour was satisfied. To an extent, Churchill stood aloof from the Cassandras; like his father he thought that Russia was entitled to Constantinople and the Straits and, for a time, he considered that Germany should extend its empire in Africa. Hungry powers were dangerous and their appetites deserved to be satisfied so long as British possessions and interests were not jeopardised. The French could have the Sahara, but not the Nile.

*

Economic impulses played a significant part in the rush for land. Those on the left, most notably Lenin, mistakenly imagined that capitalism was in a crisis that was driving the industrialised nations to acquire new markets, resources and outlets for surplus capital. This was so, but only to a very limited extent. Most of the investment which flowed out of Europe avoided newly annexed colonies and went towards stable nation states such as Canada, Australia, South Africa, Argentina and Russia. All possessed dynamic economies and were, therefore, safe bets. Canny investors in London knew that they would get good returns from, say, Argentinean railways which conveyed meat and grain to Buenos Aires for shipment to European markets. French financiers felt the same way about investing in Russian industrial ventures.

Newly acquired territories in the tropics aroused little enthusiasm in Europe's money markets simply because the investment risks were too great. Nevertheless, optimists predicted bonanzas of the kind which had occurred in South Africa after the discovery of diamonds in 1870 and gold in 1885. There were plenty of rumours of minerals in the still largely unexplored and newly annexed colonies in the African interior, but sound money never followed hearsay. In 1905 the *Economist* urged its readers to be wary of 'nebulous' tales of ores allegedly waiting to be mined in Central Africa. Such warnings were hardly needed; *The Stock Exchange Official Intelligence* for the previous year contained a list of British colonial enterprises which were moribund, slithering into insolvency, or kept afloat by government subsidies. Typical was the Rhodesia Railway Company (founded in 1893) which was a million pounds in the red, had never paid a dividend and was dependent on an annual subsidy of £35,000 paid by the British government and the British South Africa Company.

State subsidies propped up all of Germany's new colonies which, in 1914, contributed one per cent to the country's gross national product. In 1913 the French taxpayer picked up a bill for £425,000 to pay the wages of 350 white officers and 4,000 black askaris whose job it was to police the 669,000 square miles and estimated ten million inhabitants of French Equatorial Africa. One wonders how effectively they performed their duties in the region adjacent to Joseph Conrad's

Heart of Darkness, or, more importantly, what returns France received from their exertions. Britain too had its colonial backwaters that struggled to get by on taxation raised from impoverished populations. In the early 1900s the revenues of British Honduras and the Gambia were just £50,000 each and barely met the costs of their administration. Education in the Seychelles was funded entirely by sales of the colony's postage stamps to collectors.[5]

Colonial economic growth was slow and fitful. During the first decade of the twentieth century, Malayan tin and rubber were making profits, as were oil wells in the Dutch East Indies [Indonesia]. Elsewhere, there were thin pickings, although they did not stop imperial enthusiasts from predicting a glittering future for new colonies. Churchill was among the optimists; after his East African tour in 1908, he felt confident that 'piece goods *made in Lancashire*' would soon cover the 'primordial nakedness' of the Kikuyu and Masai. How these subsistence farmers and stock-raising nomads would find the cash to pay for their cotton shirts was, as yet, unclear.

While Churchill was fighting frontier wars and starting his political apprenticeship, each of the imperial powers was fulfilling what they claimed were their national destinies. It was a form of vanity with a strong quasi-religious element which suggested that Providence favoured certain nations and turned its back on others, usually because they lacked the requisite moral qualifications to rule others.

French imperialists puffed their country's '*mission civilisatrice*', while German imperialists praised their countrymen's superior culture and efficiency, which made them ideal colonists, unlike the grasping British who were just after a quick profit. A capacity to rule others had become part of national self-esteem and a source of self-congratulation, particularly in Britain. These arguments justified the occupation of territories, the subjection of their inhabitants and their integration into economic systems that favoured their rulers.

These arrangements included the imposition of linguistic supremacy with school and university syllabuses which used the language of the imperial power, an important feature of the British, French, German, Russian and American empires. Indian schoolchildren studied Shakespeare and Milton, Senegalese learned about the heroic

Gauls and the American high school system was transported to the Philippines.

Local cultures and religious rites that were judged barbaric or subversive were uprooted or placed under tight supervision. Imperial overlordship also required the adoption of imported legal codes, or the redrafting of indigenous ones. Wherever possible and in the interests of stability, the imperial powers made a point of integrating new regimes with traditional sources of secular and spiritual authority. Britain, France and Russia made accommodations with their Muslim subjects by which the state respected and safeguarded Islam so long as its princes and clergy cooperated with the imperial authorities. Domestic slavery, common in Muslim states and the tribal polities of West and Central Africa, was outlawed and its extirpation was widely advertised as proof of the humanitarianism of the imperial powers.

The intended result was always the same. The cobwebs of ignorance and superstition were swept away and the subjects of the new empires were taught to admire and emulate the achievements and virtues of their rulers. In 1897 Churchill hoped that 'educational changes' in India would gradually extinguish the Hindu 'faith in idols of brass and stone' and so pave the way for the emancipation of the Indian mind.

Planned and unplanned social changes occurred in many regions under imperial rule. Frenchmen and Italians were encouraged to settle in Algeria, where they were offered the most fertile lands, and over one and a half million Russian peasants and artisans were transplanted into Central Asia. Local labour shortages provided the stimulus for other migrations. After the Japanese annexation of Korea in 1910, 700,000 Koreans were forcibly transported to work in Japanese factories and mines. Within the British Empire, thousands of Indians were tempted to work as labourers on the sugar plantations in the British West Indies after the end of slavery there in 1838. Smaller numbers of Indians were induced to work as navvies on the Uganda railway sixty years later. Many stayed on after its completion and, during his 1908 visit to East Africa, Churchill was impressed by the thrift and industry of the Indian traders who had shown an 'economic superiority' over the indigenous blacks. He was, however, worried that the Indians would teach the Africans 'evil ways', by which, presumably, he meant forming groups to campaign for political rights and legal parity with Europeans, as was happening in South Africa.[6]

In the third part of his *History of the English-Speaking Peoples*, which was published in 1957, Churchill wrote of the Britain of his youth as occupying the 'summit of the civilised world'. The prevailing wisdom, to which he subscribed, was that some races had proved themselves better at mastering their environment than others. Their capacity to do so dictated their place in what Churchill and many of his contemporaries regarded as a layered, racial hierarchy. Some races had distinctive qualities. British officers in India, including Churchill, talked themselves into believing in the innate courage of 'warrior races' such as Sikhs and Gurkhas, which was replicated by the Hausas of West Africa. Racial definitions often tended to perpetuate ludicrous prejudices; during the First World War a military intelligence officer insisted that the genetic 'instability' of the Maltese made them highly susceptible to enlistment by German spies.[7]

Churchill swallowed these surmises. In 1901, he told the Commons that the 'fighting races' of India and the Sudanese askaris respected and admired British officers who, it went without saying, were all gentlemen. German officers in East Africa [Tanganyika] were not, according to a later intelligence report from a British officer in Nyasaland [Malawi]. They won few hearts because they lied to the natives and were not sportsmen, preferring to command their askaris to kill big game with volleys, rather than stalk them alone.[8] The African instinctively recognised a cad.

Churchill had grown up in a world in which the majority of people were governed by foreigners, an arrangement of which he approved, so long as their rule was humane. By 1900 the imperial dispensation of power was deeply entrenched, largely unchallenged and appeared to be permanent, at least for the foreseeable future. He had absorbed the contemporary ideology which legitimised empires as the engines of progress that were adding to the sum of human happiness. Strangely, for a man who had studied history and was guided by it, Churchill failed to understand that, like other historical phenomena, empires were transient. For a variety of reasons, they flourished, decayed and passed away, and, in 1900 there were pessimists who wondered whether what seemed to be an overstretched British Empire would follow this pattern. Churchill rejected this possibility; throughout his career he spoke and acted as if the British Empire was unique in that it had a peculiar permanence.

PART TWO

1901–1914

4

An Adventurer:
Questions of Character

There were striking parallels between Churchill's political and military careers. The thrusting and flamboyant subaltern became the fearless, ambitious and self-promoting MP who was always game for a fight. He fought to win and, therefore, was a good man to have on your side and his career flourished accordingly.

His performances in the Commons and on the hustings were spell-binding displays of analysis, argument and waspish humour. Churchill was a tigerish debater and there were moments when listeners could be forgiven for imagining that the speaker was again a young cavalryman who galloped at his opponents and floored them with a few deft strokes of his sabre. His spontaneity was sometimes misleading, for his speeches were always painstakingly prepared and rehearsed.

In 1901 Churchill had been elected as a Conservative on the liberal wing of a party in which he was never wholly comfortable. In his early speeches, he voiced his unease, once accusing the Tories of disregarding working-class voters and neglecting 'the improvement of the condition of the British people'. This indifference, he argued, had encouraged the growth of class warfare, evidence of which was the emergence of the Labour Party, which Churchill loathed. He also had private misgivings about the Conservative leadership which he once confided to his mother. Arthur Balfour, who became Prime Minister in July 1902, was a 'lazy, lackadaisical cynic' and Lord Curzon the Viceroy of India was 'the spoiled darling of politics – blown with conceit – insolent from undeserved success – the typification of the superior Oxford prig'.[1]

Like his father, Churchill had the knack of goading monochrome and pompous political hacks, irrespective of their political allegiance. One of his earliest targets was his fellow Tory St John Brodrick, the stolid Minister of War. Using his recent experience in the Boer

War, Churchill denounced his cheese-paring measures which had deprived the army of adequate equipment and endangered soldiers' lives. It was the first of Churchill's attacks on the bureaucratic mind which abhorred imagination, venerated the proprieties of form and preferred procrastination to action. Furthermore, as his behaviour on the Conservative benches showed, Churchill did not subscribe to that sterile canon which elevated blind allegiance to a party and its leader as public virtue. He judged arguments on their merits rather than submitting them to the litmus test of official party dogma.

Impatience and frustration hastened Churchill's departure from the Tories. It was an imperial issue which had finally prompted Churchill to ditch them in 1904. During the previous year they had fallen out with each over whether or not Britain remained a Free Trade nation. Dissidents led by the former Liberal Radical Joseph Chamberlain argued that Free Trade was responsible for present economic stagnation and made British products vulnerable to its more competitive rivals, Germany and the United States. In place of Free Trade, Chamberlain proposed a system of imperial preference to create an imperial free trade zone. Tariffs would be imposed on foreign imports, including food, and the money raised would fund a far-reaching programme of social regeneration and colonial investment.

Churchill was unconvinced. He stood by old economic shibboleths contained in Adam Smith's *The Wealth of Nations* which had provided his and earlier generations with the formula that had been the key to Britain's economic power and prosperity, Free Trade. It had delivered cheap imports and, through competition, stimulated efficient methods of production. The results were sound profits, full employment, high wages and cheap food. All had been self-evident during the heyday of Britain's industrial growth, but, by 1900, the good times had passed and the economic future looked unpromising with slumps alternating with booms. Unemployment spiralled and social tensions intensified. Both would disappear, if, as Chamberlain argued, Britain treated its Empire as an economic asset.

Churchill the Free Trader disagreed and launched an offensive against Chamberlain and the Tariff Reform League. Its protectionist measures would not reinforce imperial bonds, for the 'gossamer threads of Empire' were already 'pliant as elastic' and as 'tense as steel', which had been amply proved by the recent dominion war effort in South Africa. India, Churchill believed, would be alienated by prohibitions on its imports and exports. As for raising cash for social reform, it was nonsense to imagine that dominion goodwill in the form of favourable trading arrangements could be bought by bribes taken from the pockets of the 'poorest of our own population', who would be further squeezed by higher food prices. Turning on the former manufacturer Chamberlain and his industrialist backers, Churchill argued that their case was permeated by a demeaning 'commercialism which seeks to run the British Empire as if it were a limited liability company'.

Chamberlain had started a civil war within the Conservative Party and given Churchill the opportunity to restart his career in more ideologically congenial company. With hindsight, it could be argued that he had never been a Tory at heart, but had entered the party out of filial devotion and dynastic tradition. Free of this obligation, he had at last found himself in congenial company. As he told an enthusiastic audience in Manchester's Free Trade Hall, he was now in a party which considered that 'the condition of a slum in an English city is not less worthy of the attention of statesmen and of Parliament than a jungle in Somaliland'. There were loud and extended cheers.

Churchill had backed a winner. In December 1905 Balfour resigned and in the general election of February 1906 the Liberals won a landslide victory.

Humbugged:
The Colonial Office 1905–1908

Churchill was delighted by Sir Henry Campbell-Bannerman's offer of the Under-Secretaryship of State for the Colonies in December 1905. The Prime Minister had qualms about appointing a young man in a hurry and some Liberals questioned the sincerity of his recent conversion. But in Churchill's favour were his political flair, eloquence and recent wartime experience of South Africa, whose future stability was a major preoccupation for the new ministry. Once behind a desk, Churchill revealed how he could channel his energy, adapt to humdrum routines and cope with petty and tiresome human and administrative problems. Churchill worked hard, mastered complex subjects and argued his department's case cogently at the despatch box. When he left the Colonial Office in April 1908, he believed that he had performed his duties well and characteristically said so.

Early apprehensions as to Churchill's temperamental suitability to office were offset by his rock-like senior partner, the ninth Earl of Elgin, the Colonial Secretary. Elgin was an archetypal aristocratic public servant: he was high-minded, industrious, aloof and taciturn. In private, he was a countryman more interested in forestry than in the London-based social world of politics. As Viceroy of India between 1894 and 1899, Elgin had built railways and vainly attempted to avoid punitive frontier campaigns, which he deplored. His commonsense would balance Churchill's foolhardiness and occasional flights of fancy. The pair did not always see eye to eye, but there was mutual respect and Elgin often refused to give way to Churchillian charm or petulance. 'These are my views,' Churchill once wrote on a memorandum. 'But not mine,' remarked Elgin with his usual terseness, and he got his way.

Elgin and Churchill were served by a small staff of sixty civil servants whose analyses and recommendations provided the raw material for ministerial decisions. Like Elgin, these men were

Oxford or Cambridge classicists and could be somewhat sniffy about Churchill, the autodidact who was once unaware that what he imagined as his original ideas were in fact those of Aristotle.[1] Officials and ministers shared another form of snobbery, that of a sophisticated, metropolitan elite for colonial politicians who were shifty and had larrikin manners. There was also a general mandarin impatience with native races who seemed forever susceptible to all kinds of collective insanity, chiefly religious. When Jan Smuts, a lawyer-turned-Boer general and co-leader the Transvaal *Het Volk* [The People] party, visited London in 1906, one colonial official remarked that he had 'all the cunning of his race and calling'. Sayyid Muhammad Ibn Hassan the Somali resistance leader was simply the 'Mad Mullah'.

Headstrong and wayward colonial administrators were another departmental bugbear. Some lost their nerve and others panicked, causing embarrassment to the government and tarnishing the reputation of the Empire at home and abroad. Churchill gave short shrift to these miscreants. He secured the sacking of Sir James Swettenham the Governor of Jamaica after he had publicly insulted an American admiral whose sailors had helped in relief operations after a local earthquake. Telegraphic communication had reduced but not eliminated the capacity of the man-on-the-spot to get himself and his masters into a pickle.

In terms of overall colonial policy, Churchill had always been sympathetic to the Liberal brand of imperialism with its strong emphasis on the moral responsibilities of Empire. Britain was a benevolent and compassionate trustee for its colonial subjects who were entitled to the same legal protection as Britons. The colonies provided an opportunity for the application of traditional Liberal values and the world would take note of how a humane nation ruled others without compromising its own high moral standards.

In 1905 the leading Liberal Imperialists H. H. Asquith, Sir Edward Grey and R. B. Haldane dominated Campbell-Bannerman's cabinet, but they had to contend with a residual hostility to imperialism from the radical wing of their party. In the past many Liberals had been unhappy with the concept of empire which, for all its good intentions, rested on the denial of individual liberty.

Following Gladstone's cue, Liberal critics of the British Empire summed up imperialism as the coercion of the weak by the strong and identified its prime beneficiaries as big business and glory-seeking generals and proconsuls. Imperialism, in particular the Conservative variety, was leading the country astray by persuading the masses that conquering and ruling other peoples' countries were the true measure of Britain's greatness, rather than its moral rectitude and love of freedom.

During the 1890s questions about the nature and future of British imperialism entered the political arena. The Tories declared themselves the natural party of Empire, determined to keep Britain ahead of its rivals in the race for colonies. Those who objected were dismissed as 'Little Englanders' and accused of lacking patriotism and vision. Soon after he had parted company with the Tories, Churchill alleged that they had spent the past ten years insinuating 'a want of patriotism' to everyone who had disagreed with them. Yet chauvinism had proved a Tory trump card. Outbursts of mass jingoism marked the first phase of the Boer War and reached fever pitch with the spontaneous street celebrations after the relief of Mafeking in May 1900. Four months later, the Tories wrapped themselves in the Union Jack and won the 'Khaki' election during which they claimed that all Liberals were open or covert pro-Boers.

Churchill and the Liberal Imperialists were disturbed by this cynical manipulation of patriotism. War and the willingness to wage it in the face of the slightest provocation had become integral to Tory imperial policy. There had been frontier wars in India, Nigeria, the Gold Coast [Ghana] and, in 1903, the invasion of Tibet, which Churchill denounced. 'What parity is there between the delinquencies of Tibet and the revenge of Great Britain?' he asked Glaswegian Liberals in November 1904. 'We have done wrong, we have taken life without justification'; there were cheers. As Churchill spoke, British forces were engaged in another fruitless and expensive campaign to subdue Somaliland. What was to be gained, he asked some years later, from the conquest of 'a country valueless to all except the wild inhabitants who live in it, and to them it is dearer than life'.[2]

These conflicts were overshadowed in terms of costs and casualties by the Boer War which had ended in May 1902. It had been fought to establish British paramountcy in South Africa which required the extinction of the Boer republics of the Transvaal and Orange Free State. The former produced a quarter of the world's supply of gold, which made cynics wonder whether the war had really been waged to protect British investments. Churchill saw the war as the unavoidable outcome of a power struggle in which Britain had no choice but to fight and 'curb the insolence of the Boer' although he admired their patriotism and was not afraid to say so during his maiden speech.

Both sides had claimed provocation, which was true enough. Nevertheless, the intrigues of the Colonial Secretary Joseph Chamberlain, Britain's High Commissioner in Cape Colony Sir Alfred Milner and the diamond magnate Cecil Rhodes plainly showed that they were prepared to stop at nothing, even war, to get their way. At the very end of 1895 and with the tacit connivance of Chamberlain and British officials in Cape Town, Rhodes had plotted a *coup de main* against the Transvaal. Troopers from his private army the British South Africa Company Police rode to Johannesburg, where they mistakenly imagined they would join forces with local insurgents drawn from the non-Boer, gold-mining community. The Jameson Raid was a fiasco, but this did not prevent the Tory press from praising the patriotism of Rhodes and the daring of Jameson and his filibusterers. Their exploits were put to verse by Alfred Austin the poet laureate who once defined bliss as reading newspaper reports of British victories overseas.

Anti-imperialists were shocked. Journalist J. A. Hobson conjured up a conspiracy theory that alleged that control of Britain and its Empire had been hijacked by a coterie of financiers and newspaper proprietors keen to enrich themselves. The backstairs influence of these schemers had propelled Britain into the Boer War to safeguard their share portfolios. This fantasy was believed by Little Englanders, socialists and anti-Semites (some of the guilty moneybags were Jewish) and was later elaborated on by Marxist historians.

By no stretch of the imagination did capitalism benefit from the Boer War. It had inflicted enormous damage to the infrastructure of South Africa and caused the mass dislocation of its population. Agriculture and mining were disrupted; Transvaal's gold exports fell from £16.4 million in 1898 to £7.3 million in 1902. Perhaps most frightening of all, the war had profoundly unsettled the black majority, who were showing signs of restlessness. Blacks had played a significant part in what has been wrongly described as a white man's war; they laboured for both armies and were hired by the British as armed frontier guards and scouts. In remote districts of the Transvaal, independent bands of Zulu partisans harried Boer forces. During peace negotiations in 1902, Boer representatives demanded that once the war was over, they should be allowed to keep their rifles to defend themselves against the blacks.[3]

South Africa was in a mess and its political and economic reconstruction had been placed in the hands of Milner. He was a dedicated servant of the British Empire, possessed a formidable administrative mind and believed that the best solutions to political problems were imposed from above by men of his intellectual eminence. Milner knew best and mistrusted democracy and compromise. He had set his heart on the creation of a united, self-governing South Africa in which the majority of whites were emotionally and politically attached to Britain and the Empire. This too was Churchill's dream; during a brief visit to the United States in 1900 he told journalists that once the war was over South Africa would emerge as a united, self-governing dominion like Canada.

To accomplish this the Boers first had to be persuaded to forgive and forget. Churchill knew that this would be a very difficult and slow process. During the war he had praised them for their dogged defence of their independence, customs and identity. Military defeat did not dissolve Boer patriotism. Falling back on their Calvinism, the Boers treated their recent misfortunes as a penalty imposed by a stern Jehovah for their collective sins. Like the Old Testament Jews, the Boers saw themselves as a chosen race and pinned their hopes on Divine mercy and a future deliverance. All was not lost. In 1905 the Cape politician J. X. Merriman reflected a resurgent optimism when he wrote: 'Milners may come and Milners may go, but Afrikanerdom, in the wide sense of the word, is not to be broken.'

Hopes for the future could not exorcise the horrors of the war from the historic memory of the Boers. Churchill appreciated this and, when his colleagues were discussing plans for granting independence to the Transvaal in 1906, he reminded them that 20,000 Boer women and children had died from diseases in camps into which they had been herded by the British army during the second phase of the war.[4] This measure, combined with the burning of farms and the destruction of crops and livestock had been instigated by the commander-in-chief Kitchener in order to deprive Boer guerrillas of supplies and intelligence. By May 1902 there were 117,000 Boer women and children behind barbed wire and an unknown number of their black slaves.[5] The whole ghastly business caused revulsion at home and a wave of anglophobia across Europe and America, but Kitchener was concerned with results and did not give a damn for public opinion.*

Milner believed that he could bypass the antipathy of half a million Boers by contriving constitutions for the Orange Free State and the Transvaal which were tilted in favour of a minority of what he called the 'politically British' voters. His ruses included fixing the franchise qualification to exclude poor, landless Boers, attracting British immigrants with promises of land and including Rhodesia with its 15,000 settlers in his projected South African union.[6] The sums did not add up and, when Churchill arrived at the Colonial Office, there was no blueprint for the future of the old Boer republics which were still technically British colonies.

South African nationalists gave a guarded welcome to the Liberal government, although J. X. Merriman feared that the Liberal Imperialists were as inclined towards 'arrogant meddling' as the Conservatives had been. He was wrong: the new ministry wanted a quick, negotiated settlement and accepted the principle of one [white] man, one vote and were ready to dispel Boer anxieties about their national identity.

Milner's activities in South Africa provided the Colonial Office with another headache: the welfare and future of the estimated 52,000 Chinese indentured labourers currently working in the goldmines.[7] The High Commissioner had allowed the mining companies to recruit these workers to offset a shortfall in the black and white labour force that was impeding gold production. Both Alfred Lyttelton

---

* The 1941 Nazi propaganda film *Ohm Krüger* showed one of these camps with Churchill as its commandant. This film was being shown in South African cinemas as late as the 1960s.

Conservative Colonial Secretary and star cricketer (W. G. Grace called him 'the champagne of cricket') and Milner's successor Lord Selborne approved this measure.

They had made a gross miscalculation, for they had delivered the Liberals a cause with which to arouse the moral conscience of the nation. In simple language of political polemic, the Conservatives had condoned 'slavery' (Churchill used the word in several speeches) and turned a blind eye to systematic brutality. The Chinese coolies were confined to compounds, where company-enforced celibacy was alleged to have driven them to mass sodomy. Flogging was the normal punishment and it was inflicted frequently and wantonly without a murmur from local officials who were answerable to the Colonial Office.

The mistreatment of the Chinese coolies in the Transvaal ignited passions similar to those which had been generated in France a few years before by the Dreyfus affair. Conservatives accused the Liberals of exaggeration, of seeking to sabotage the recovery of South Africa's economy and whipping up class hatred against the rich in general. The Liberals responded by orchestrating public indignation. Enslaved to a handful of city moneybags, the Tories had turned a blind eye to slavery and dragged Britain's name through the mud. During his December 1905 election campaign in Manchester, Churchill hired men dressed as coolies (presumably with pigtails) who were driven through the streets by slave-drivers wielding whips. This early version of agitprop street theatre helped to win him the seat. It was one of the rare occasions in which a colonial issue had a powerful and direct impact on a domestic election.

Repatriation of the Chinese had been part of the Liberal manifesto, and Elgin and Churchill had to devise ways to implement this policy. Selborne and the men-on-the-spot were uncooperative and Churchill soon discovered their callous indifference to the maltreatment of the coolies. One case came to Churchill's attention in October 1906 after the Colonial Office had demanded a transcript of the trial of one R. H. Witthauer, whom a magistrate had acquitted of thrashing a coolie. Chinese evidence had been ignored, as was Witthauer's boast of how he beat coolies. Churchill was appalled by a 'meagre and unsatisfactory' report, which he summed up as 'tissue of falsehood'.

He and the Colonial Office had again been 'humbugged by the officials on the spot'. Cruelty had gone unpunished, justice had been denied and Empire had been tarnished in the eyes of its humblest subjects. Churchill wanted to make more of this case, but his colleagues did not. He sadly minuted: 'However as everyone seems to relish this treatment, I feel unable to undertake a crusade.'[8]

Nevertheless, it was the fervent hope of Elgin and Churchill that the restoration of responsible government in the Transvaal and Orange Free State would relieve the Colonial Office of such wearisome local problems as the repatriation of the Chinese. Negotiations proceeded swiftly and a constitution that enfranchised all white males was agreed. The Afrikaans language was assured parity with English, and Boer traditions and culture were guaranteed protection. These were important matters to the Boers who, after three hundred years separation from their home country the Netherlands, had developed their own distinctive national identity. This was acknowledged in 1906 and with it the tacit assumption that the Boers could never have the same emotional ties to Britain as say Australians. Nevertheless, Churchill believed that the arrangements made for the self-government of the Transvaal and the Orange Free State would generate goodwill towards the British Empire. He was confident that, over time, Boer cooperation would become loyalty. His hopes were justified by the example of Canada, where sensitive treatment had won over the French Canadians whose dislike of Britain had been as bitter as that of the Boers.

Elections held in January and February 1907 gave the *Het Volk* party a small majority in the Transvaal and the *Orange Unie* party won a landslide in the Orange Free State, where Christian de Wet, the former Boer kommando general, became Prime Minister. Afrikanerdom was reviving. There were compensations for Britain, for there was every reason to believe that opinion in the former Boer republics was swinging towards combining with Cape Colony and Natal to form a Union of South Africa. The Liberal spirit of conciliation was turning old enemies into new comrades.

Churchill had contributed to the evolution and implementation of a policy that had seemed to conciliate Boer nationalism without injuring imperial interests. A friendly or at least compliant South Africa was necessary for the security of the Cape route to India; Suez Canal charges were steep and it was foolhardy to imagine that it could always be kept open, come what may. Independence for the Orange Free State and the Transvaal had far-reaching consequences, not only for South Africa but for the Empire as a whole. Through patience and a willingness to understand historic grievances, a way had been found to appease local nationalism without endangering imperial solidarity. For the rest of his life Churchill was extremely proud of the South African settlement, which was signal proof of a tolerant Empire that had within it the capacity to generate goodwill between former enemies.

Tractable British Children:
More Native Questions

Like all self-governining dominions, the Tranvaal and Orange Free
State were legally free to deal with their native subjects as they
saw fit. This was good news to the Colonial Office, which had found
itself squeezed by two inflexible pressure groups. On one side were
representatives of the South African white population which sought
to perpetuate the unconditional subordination of the negroes. On
the other were the predominantly Christian lobby groups in Britain
which had close links with the Liberal Party and demanded humane
treatment for native populations everywhere. This was why in March
1906 Churchill found himself answering a Parliamentary question
about the use of the sjambok [a rhino-hide whip] on black servants
in the Transvaal and Orange Free State.[1] Such enquiries and the spirit
behind them were resented by South Africans as examples of what
J. X. Merriman called 'the benevolent and ignorant interference of
England'.[2]

According to the 1904 census there were 1.1 million whites and
3.4 million blacks in South Africa. Their present subjection was
the consequence of an extended sequence of wars during the first
eighty years of the nineteenth century and the local consensus was
that, if controls were slackened, the negro would rise against his
masters. The 'kaffirs', as whites disdainfully called the blacks, were
indispensable to the South African economy as workers in the mines,
in agriculture and the service industries. Smuts wanted these helots to
become consumers, who would be sucked into the labour market by
discovering new 'wants'.[3] Yet buying the white man's clothes, crockery
and furniture would not transform the status of the negro. Their own
experience and that of southern states of America convinced South
Africans that negro inferiority was genetic, permanent and would
never be changed by contact with Europeans.

Pleading for even minimal black rights would have been

incompatible with the spirit of Anglo-Boer conciliation. When peace had been signed in 1902, Kitchener had solemnly affirmed that Britain would perpetuate 'the just predominance of the white race', a pledge that satisfied the most basic need of the Boers. The demands of realpolitik clashed with the wishes of the humanitarian lobby in Britain, but its voice was weaker than in the past. Fifty or so years before, it was widely believed that the negro occupied the lowest rung of the racial ladder, but missionaries and their domestic supporters argued that he could easily move upwards with a helping hand from Europeans.

Racial attitudes had subsequently hardened and Churchill echoed the modern view of the global racial dispensation when he spoke of 'the gulf which separates the African negro from the immemorial civilisations of India and China'. This did not mean that the black man should be exploited or mistreated. Rather, Churchill argued, he should be left alone and undisturbed. 'Large reservations of good, well watered land' should be found where 'the African aboriginal, for whom civilisation has no chance, may dwell secluded and at peace'.[4]

Neither isolation nor peace was on offer for black men in South Africa. Racial dogma and economic imperatives condemned them to tight supervision under a legal system which denied them the rights of Europeans. However regrettable, this fact was no longer the concern of Britain. The Transvaal and the Orange Free State had become self-governing dominions and a part of what was now becoming known as the 'Commonwealth'. It was axiomatic that dominions took care of their own affairs through elected assemblies. This independence was a source of immense pride and the dominions objected to any form of interference, however well intentioned, from Britain.

In 1906 Elgin and Churchill broke the rules when they tentatively criticised the racial policies of Natal. Early in February two white police officers were murdered near Pietermaritzburg in Natal and, as Churchill later told the Commons, their Zulu assailants 'dipped their spears' in their victims' blood. Panic, paranoia and bloodlust successively seized a colony in which 904,000 blacks outnumbered 97,000 whites. With the approval of the local assembly the governor, Colonel Sir Henry McCullum, declared martial law, imposed press censorship and mobilised the militia. Twenty-two suspects were arrested and later tried by courts martial which sentenced twelve to be shot. Zulu resistance spread and within a few weeks Natal was faced with a widespread insurrection.

During the first stage of the campaign the Colonial Office was closely informed about developments. Elgin and Churchill were prepared to steady the nerves of the Natalians by ordering a battalion of the Cameron Highlanders to Pietermaritzburg to act as a strategic reserve. By late March, both men were alarmed by the precipitate and violent reaction of the local authorities and they cabled the governor with pleas for the 'utmost caution', asked for transcripts of the trials, called for a suspension of the executions and recommended retrials in the civilian courts. This was blatant interference in the internal affairs of a dominion, but Elgin and Churchill argued that it was legally justified. Imperial forces were serving in Natal and, at some later date, the Crown would have to issue an indemnity to the militia officers who had passed the death sentences. Natal would have none of this. The governor and the assembly simultaneously threatened to resign and gave the go-ahead for the shootings, which were carried out on 2 April.

Alarm bells rang in other dominions. There were protests from Australia and New Zealand who insisted that the Colonial Office had overstepped the mark. There was also a predictable outcry from the Transvaal, Orange Free State and Rhodesia, and an angry row in the Commons. A Tory repeated the false rumour that white women and children had been massacred and another insisted that the settlers in Natal knew best how to handle the natives and should be left to get on with the job. Churchill back-pedalled, arguing that Britain did have some moral responsibility, but that he was now satisfied that the courts martial had been fair. He concluded by accusing the Tories of making political capital out of the crisis, which provoked uproar.

There had been some discussion in the Commons about the causes of the uprising. Blame was laid on Natal's poll tax, a levy which was in large part intended to push Zulus towards the cash economy by forcing them to find paid work in the mines. There were attempts to link the insurgency to the subversive doctrines of messianic, African 'Ethiopian' churches. Lord Selborne the High Commissioner in the

Cape suspected that the root of the trouble was a surplus of 'lusty' and 'idle' Zulu males with time on their hands, which chimed in with the Natalian view that the blacks in general were becoming truculent. Liberated from the Colonial Office, the Natal government launched a punitive campaign which dragged on into July. 'No prisoners were taken ... dum-dum [expanding] bullets were extensively used,' recalled one participant.[5] Police and militia columns burned villages, looted and summarily flogged hundreds of Zulus. Mohandas Gandhi, an Indian barrister with strong imperial sympathies who had joined an ambulance unit, was forbidden to treat wounded Zulus. 'This was no war', he wrote later, 'but a manhunt.'[6] The statistics said it all: 3,000 blacks were killed and 4,000 were rounded up for internment while government forces suffered less than twenty dead.

Churchill was incensed by what he called the 'disgusting butchery of the natives'. He was desperate to intervene and 'bring this wretched colony – the hooligan of the British Empire – to its senses'. He vainly hoped that the Colonial Office could somehow restrain 'our colonists (*who so thoroughly understand native war*) from killing too many of them'. When the Natal government requested permission to deport twenty-five ringleaders to Mauritius or St Helena, Churchill took a close interest in their welfare and was shocked to find that their diet in captivity was fit only for 'the lowest animals'. After the war, when Elgin proposed to give a medal to the 7,000 participants in the campaign, Churchill objected, calling it a 'silver badge of shame'. Elgin defended his decision with words that would have ominous echoes later in the century: the medal would be 'worn by men who did their duty in obedience to their orders, and did it well'.[7]

Natal's vile punitive war had offended Churchill's humanity and sense of justice, but there was nothing he could do about it, which no doubt added to his fury. Their early reactions strongly suggested that the dominions would not tolerate any infringement of their sovereignty and Britain could not afford a quarrel because of the disturbed international situation. For the past ten years Anglo-German relations had become increasingly fraught and Britain's old bogey Russia had just completed a railway line whose terminus at Kushk was just five hundred miles from Kandahar. If war broke out in Asia or in Europe, British strategic plans depended on dominion manpower. A third of the Empire's 65 million white inhabitants lived in the dominions They were already contributing to the imperial defence budget (Natal gave £35,000 a year) and, if a war broke out, they would be expected to give men, as they had done during the Boer War. This hard fact of life was understood by Churchill, who, in 1901, had admitted that Britain could not wage 'great wars' without 'the entire forces of the Empire'.

During the autumn and winter of 1907–8 Churchill undertook an extended imperial progress in what was then an eccentric belief that it was invaluable for officials based in Whitehall to have a first-hand knowledge of the colonies and their inhabitants. He briefly visited Malta, Cyprus and Somaliland, and spent a longer time touring Kenya and Uganda. His narrative of the journey, together with his opinions on future colonial policy, were published in the *Strand Magazine* and he sent a cascade of memoranda and reports to his colleagues in London, much to their annoyance. Churchill also hunted big game and went on a pig-sticking safari in pursuit of Kenyan warthogs in the company of Lord Delamare, the fiery-tempered tribune of the colony's white settlers. Churchill was endeavouring to create a uniform, humane and coherent native policy for the African colonies and to contrive ways in which they could be developed and pay their own way. His views on the treatment of native populations had been made clear during the Natal uprising and were vehemently repeated in June 1907 after a nasty incident in Nairobi. Captain Ewart Grogan, a former explorer and president of the Colonists' Association, had flogged three Kikuyu servants in front of the law courts for jolting a rickshaw and cheekiness to white ladies. Kenya's governor, Colonel J. Hayes Sadler, was determined to prosecute Grogan and was strongly backed by the Colonial Office. Elgin thought that such brutality would stir up native unrest and for Churchill its punishment was a matter of high principle. He wrote:

We must not let these few ruffians steal our beautiful and promising protectorate away from us, after all we have spent on it ... This House of Commons will never allow us to abdicate our duties towards the natives – as peaceful, industrious, law-abiding folks as can be found anywhere.[8]

The 'ruffians' were a section of Kenya's white immigrants. They totalled about 4,000 and included some unsavoury characters. A young officer Richard Meinertzhagen was disgusted to find the Nairobi mess of a King's African Rifles battalion filled with men loafing in their pyjamas, drunkards, officers who boasted about their native mistresses, a homosexual and misfits banished from British regiments. These ne'er-do-wells complemented the civilian 'poor whites' who lowered European prestige in the eyes of the natives and the Colonial Office was considering plans for their forcible deportation.

Settler farmers presented another, less tractable problem: whether or not Kenya would become a white man's country. As Churchill discovered on his arrival, the white community was fractious and prone to grouse about local officials, the natives and Indian immigrants. The economy was stagnant, a large number of white farmers were on the verge of bankruptcy and in London the government was preparing to fund their repatriation.[9] Kenya was not yet a magnet for settlers; there was a trickle of Boers from South Africa and Colonial Office offers of fertile lands to Jewish settlers had recently been turned down by the Zionist movement after its representatives inspected the colony.

Kenya's economic future depended on cash crops raised on large-scale, white-owned farms in the temperate and fertile Ukamba and Naivasha districts. So far, these enterprises had foundered because of the unwillingness of the natives to become labourers. As Churchill explained to a gathering of native chiefs, the government would guarantee enough land to support their people, but they had to find work. 'No man has the right to be idle', Churchill insisted, 'and I do not excuse the African.' Churchill the romantic was impressed by natives in their splendid tribal dress and body paint and was saddened by chiefs in white man's cast-offs.[10]

At the same time as urging Africans to become labourers and consumers, Churchill was apprehensive about their long-term future at the hands of their masters, once a new economic order had been installed. The black man could easily descend into the same degraded helotry endured by his counterparts in South Africa or, for that matter, Mississippi. Churchill warned that: 'It will be an ill day for these native races when their fortunes are removed from the impartial and august administration of the Crown and abandoned to the fierce self-interest of a small white population.' For the time being the welfare of these 'light-hearted, tractable British children' was guaranteed, Churchill consoled himself, by the stamina and dedication of the young men of the colonial service. Rulers over vast areas, collectors of taxes and enforcers of justice, these officials deeply impressed Churchill whenever he met them. They were the 'guardians' of the rights of Africans and would protect them from exploitation.[11]

Churchill's experience of Kenya confirmed his earlier impressions of the omnipotence of the Empire. In India in 1897 he had been filled with wonderment by the smooth-running machinery which enforced the Pax Britannica in the remotest regions. Frontier tribesmen rebelled, telegrams passed to and fro between London, Simla and Peshawar, reinforcements were summoned and they, their ammunition and supplies were conveyed by steamships and trains to forward camps. All this was beyond the comprehension of the Pashtun, but in Kenya, Churchill was glad to find the natives were already conscious of a chain of authority which stretched upwards from the district commissioner ('the man of soldiers and police') to a hidden and awesome power. 'They wonder what that mysterious force can be and marvel at its greatness,' he wrote approvingly.[12]

By contrast to Kenya, the future of Uganda seemed assured and full of promise. Churchill was enchanted by the country, its nominal ruler the Kabaka, his court, ministers and 'parliament' which made laws. There was British supervision, but the progress of the Ugandans (200,000 were literate), guided by British missionaries, vindicated the arguments of what Churchill called the 'negrophiles' at home. He even wondered whether this demi-paradise might benefit from 'State Socialism'.[13] Churchill expanded on the wonders of Uganda when he returned home and addressed the National Liberal Club. 'Clothed, cultured, educated natives' inhabited a garden of 'exuberant fertility' which, like the rest of Britain's African colonies, possessed an enormous potential for growing cotton, rubber, timber and hemp.

Colonial self-sufficiency could only be achieved by building railways. They required investment by the state, as did the creation of the agencies necessary to promote economic growth. Soon after his return to England, Churchill proudly told the British East African

Association that the Colonial Office had allocated an annual budget of £60,000 for veterinary services in Kenya and plans were in hand for forestry and agricultural departments to assist white farmers. This was all to the good, but it could not mask the fact that colonial projects were not attracting significant capital from private sources.

Churchill had misgivings about the racial question in East Africa. Indian settlers, who had helped build the railways, were proving their 'economic superiority' to the natives as entrepreneurs and he speculated on the emergence within Kenya of a black working class, an Indian middle class and a white upper class.[14] This was not altogether desirable and, in any case, Churchill was far from certain whether the white settlers would wither under the climate and eventually drift back to Britain.

Indian immigrants in South Africa occupied a racial limbo between white and black, and the former were determined that Indians should never enjoy parity with Europeans. Mohandas Gandhi reflected the widespread resentment of Indians in South Africa who, in his words, thought themselves 'insulted and degraded as if they belonged to a barbarous race'. This was how they were treated by the Transvaal administration which, in 1906, demanded the fingerprinting of all Indians as part of their official registration. In November Gandhi came to London with a delegation to protest against this affront and he found plenty of sympathy on moral grounds among politicians and officials who rightly guessed that humiliation of Indians in South Africa would have political repercussions among Indians on the sub-continent.

On 28 November Gandhi laid his case before Churchill at the Colonial Office. Indians were loyal and wanted nothing more than the rights of British subjects, an argument which must have struck a chord with Churchill, as it did with many prominent Liberals. As Churchill had already recognised, the trouble was the rigid racial code of the Boers, which rested on the authority of the book of Genesis and was, therefore, beyond debate or compromise. With the independence of the Transvaal and Orange Free State due in a few months, Britain could not afford a row over racial policy, so Churchill plumped for procrastination. 'Delay this' was his response to Gandhi's appeal.[15] Gandhi felt cheated and returned to the Transvaal to initiate a campaign of passive resistance against the fingerprint law which, unsurprisingly, was soon endorsed by the newly elected government in Pretoria.

Once again, the overriding need for strategic security and dominion unity had compelled Churchill to compromise his ideals. Injustice to Indians was outweighed by the need to maintain the goodwill of the Transvaal, which would help speed up the creation of a new dominion, the Union of South Africa. It was inaugurated in 1910 and proclaimed as the triumphant fruition of conciliatory Liberal policies which Churchill had endeavoured to implement.

Self-congratulation was premature, for Boer attachment to the British Empire proved to be brittle. Soon after the outbreak of war in 1914, 5,000 Boers under de Wet launched a pro-German rebellion, which was crushed by the Prime Minister, Botha. In 1917 Lord Buxton the Governor-General of South Africa warned an MI5 officer that surveillance and internment of Germans within the dominion would provoke massive Boer hostility, even, he predicted, a civil war. Anti-war groups were sympathetic to Germany and there were many politicians and ministers who reviled Botha as a traitor.[16]

Shortly before he left the Colonial Office, Churchill used an address to supporters of colonial missions to put the case for the Liberal brand of imperialism he had pursued in office. He praised the efforts of missionaries in Uganda and assured his listeners that the moral impulses behind the Empire were strong and healthy. 'British influence', he promised, 'will continue to be a kindly and benignant influence over subject races.' 'We shall be found,' he concluded, 'wherever we are, trying to do justice in this world, and trying also to point to a more perfect justice in the world to come.'[17]

This was rousing stuff and, as far as Churchill was concerned, contained a strong element of truth. He had striven to uphold his personal ideals, but had painfully learned that they sometimes had to be diluted or set aside in the interests of political expediency. Nevertheless, he felt sure that 'liberal principles', including his own paternalism, were now pervading the Empire. In theory at least, he was at ease with the principle of extending responsible government to those who deserved it. After his brief visit to Malta he expressed sympathy with the demands of 'an ancient and intelligent community' for local self-government. He was not offended by Cypriot calls for 'Enosis' [Union with Greece] during his visit to the colony.[18]

In the months after his return from Africa, Churchill was becoming more and more concerned with the application of Liberal principles to the pressing problems of domestic unemployment, poverty and social unrest. He spent the next three years coping with these at the Board of Trade and Home Office before becoming First Lord of the Admiralty in October 1911.

Breathing Ozone:
The Admiralty, October 1911–March 1914

Churchill became First Lord of the Admiralty on 23 October 1911. He was now one of the most powerful men in the Empire with responsibility for the fighting efficiency of the Royal Navy, the defence of Britain, the external security of its Empire, and the protection of its overseas trade and investments. As a member of the Committee of Imperial Defence (CID) Churchill enjoyed his first taste of a highly stimulating and addictive activity: strategic planning.

His mind and temperament, though not his temper, fitted Churchill for this task. As a schoolboy he had waged make-believe wars with toy soldiers who did whatever he wished; now he was the master of a vast fleet whose ships did the same. Then and later he found this power deeply gratifying, for, by his own reckoning, Churchill possessed an innate genius for waging war. He believed that he had the knack of understanding the broad picture without losing sight of mundane minutiae, and he was proud of his strategic insights. His mind was quick, open to fresh ideas and imaginative. These qualities disturbed professional officers and civil servants whose training had made them suspicious of the unconventional and unfamiliar.

Tantrums, bitter rows and clashes of personality were inevitable and occurred whenever Churchill found himself preparing for a war, or fighting one. At the Colonial Office, Sir John Hopwood, a starchy under-secretary with a pedestrian intellect, had warned Lord Elgin that Churchill was 'most tiresome to deal with and will, I fear, give trouble – as his father did'.

Churchill entered the Admiralty in the wake of an international crisis which, it had been feared, might trigger a European war. In July 1911, a German gunboat the *Panther* had anchored off Agadir on the Atlantic coast of Morocco. Its arrival was another of Wilhelm II's provocative and characteristically cloven-hoofed gambits contrived to demonstrate that Germany was prepared to overturn the global status quo whenever its interests or ambitions were ignored. This time the Germans wanted further concessions at the expense of the French in Morocco. France refused to be bullied, as did Britain, which was unnerved by the prospect of Germany securing a potential naval base five hundred miles south of Gibraltar.

The Kaiser was also testing the *entente cordiale*, an arrangement concluded in 1904 by which Britain and France had agreed to settle their outstanding colonial disputes and promised future diplomatic cooperation. The confrontation over Agadir proved that the bond between the two powers was strong: in a speech to City financiers at the Mansion House, David Lloyd George the Chancellor of the Exchequer warned that Britain would never repudiate its position as a great power nor allow itself to be relegated to the role of a bystander in international affairs. The Germans blinked and then backed off in the face of Anglo-French solidarity.

Churchill was a passionate Francophile. As a schoolboy he had visited Paris where his father showed him the black-shrouded statue of Strasbourg and explained to him that this monument symbolised the provinces of Alsace and Lorraine, which had been surrendered by France after its defeat by Prussia in 1871. Young Winston understood the emotions that underpinned the French desire for 'revanche' and he sympathised with them. He was also stirred by the historic France, the nation of 'La Liberté' and 'La Gloire'. Its spirit had been revealed to him in 1907, when he had watched the summer manoeuvres of the French army at Metz. Wonder-struck, he watched 'the great masses of the French infantry [in blue coats and red trousers] storming a position, while the bands played the Marseillaise', and he remembered that 'by these valiant bayonets the rights of man had been gained and that by them these rights and also the liberties of Europe would be faithfully guarded'. By contrast a visit to the German army's manoeuvres two years later filled him with foreboding; the grey-uniformed soldiers were, he thought, 'a terrible machine'.

Yet Churchill had distanced himself from those Germanophobes in Britain who were busy working themselves into a lather about the expansion of the German navy and predicted an unavoidable war between Britain and Germany. They were, he had alleged in 1908, a tiny but noisy band of lunatics comfortable in the knowledge that they would not be called upon to fight the battles. Churchill also pleaded for tolerance towards Germany's overseas ambitions. Addictions to the German 'tropical plantations' and 'coaling stations' would never, he asserted, 'alter the destiny of great communities like Canada, Australia, South Africa and India'. The British and German Empires could co-exist peacefully.

Immediately after the Agadir crisis, and a few weeks before he took charge of the Royal Navy, Churchill was admitted into the secret world of the ministers and strategists who were preparing exigency plans for a future European war. He joined the Committee of Imperial Defence (CID), where he discovered that Britain had been preparing to fight on the side of *entente* powers, that is France and Russia, against the Triple Alliance of Germany, Austria–Hungary and Italy. There was no formal alliance, but the committee heard of the arrangements that had already been made for Anglo-French cooperation in the event of a war which were revealed with characteristic fluency by General Sir Henry Wilson, the Director of Operations at the War Office. French military intelligence was aware of the outlines of the German Schlieffen Plan by which a million German troops would deliver a swift offensive through Belgium and north-eastern France. Within forty-two days Paris would be encircled and an outflanked and fragmented French army would be destroyed piecemeal. The French General Staff imagined that with British reinforcements the German advance could be halted, leaving the bulk of the French army free to launch its counter-attack (Plan 27) through Alsace and Lorraine towards the Rhine. The German High Command knew about Anglo-French plans, but were confident that the tiny British Expeditionary Force [BEF] would neither impede the invasion nor prevent the destruction of the French army.

Sir Henry's account of how the war would unfold was lucid and contrasted with the fumbling delivery of the First Sea Lord Admiral Sir Arthur ('Tug') Wilson. Wilson had refused to allow the fuss over Agadir to interfere with his sport, and he had gone off to Scotland to shoot grouse, taking with him the Royal Navy's war plans, which were in his head. It was one of the more bizarre quirks of modern history that a falling grouse might have stunned the sixty-nine-year-old Admiral, and left the fleet temporarily without orders if the Germans had launched a surprise attack across the North Sea. Tug Wilson's performance before the CID had been dreadful. Everyone, including Churchill, admired the doughty old sailor – he had won a VC in the Sudan defending his Gatling gun from Dervishes – who embodied all the virtues of the Royal Navy and rather too many of its faults. He was nudged sideways, which was probably for the best since the CID intended the fleet to remain on the defensive unless the German battlefleet emerged from its bases at Wilhelmshaven and Kiel. A strategy of waiting, watching and ferrying an army to France ran against the grain for men like Wilson and a service that fostered an offensive spirit and prized audacity; they dreamed of a second Trafalgar which would knock out the German navy and demonstrate beyond question that Britannia ruled the waves. It was one of Churchill's main tasks to win the wholehearted compliance of the navy to what, in essence, was a passive role.

The Prime Minister Asquith and his cabinet believed that Churchill's vigour and strength of character would give the navy the forceful and decisive leadership needed to maintain the tempo of its modernisation and, when necessary, to impose his will on the hidebound prima donnas who inhabited its upper echelons. He did what was expected of him with characteristic brio; in the next eighteen months he spent one hundred and eighty-two days at sea on board the Admiralty steam yacht the *Enchantress,* inspecting ships, shore stations, dockyards and fuel depots. He watched naval exercises, toured aerodromes, learned to fly himself and had the impudence to offend naval etiquette by canvassing the opinions of junior officers and ratings. His temerity offended Sir John Hopwood (now at the Admiralty) who complained about it to George V, a former naval officer much preoccupied with service protocol.

Churchill's total immersion in every aspect of the navy was accompanied by a sustained assault on its arthritic bureaucracy (which included a department for distributing cutlasses to warships) and an unyielding insistence that old systems and methods had to be jettisoned and new technology welcomed. His manner was often impatient and his tone was acerbic. Admiral Sir John Jellicoe the

Second Sea Lord thought that the articulate Churchill unnerved tongue-tied officers, of whom he was one. He echoed the widespread resentment of other senior officers who regarded the First Lord as an amateur who was 'quite ignorant of naval affairs'.[1]

Churchill's methods were harsh, but essential. The Royal Navy had entered the twentieth century with a mindset firmly rooted in the age of Nelson. Officers accustomed to behaving as autocrats on the bridge grew into overbearing admirals who treated even the mildest censure as insubordination. Prickliness and arrogance were inevitable by-products of the peculiar ethos of the Royal Navy. Professional pride lay at its heart and it was fortified by the know-ledge of the navy's illustrious history. The navy had saved Britain from invasion during the Napoleonic Wars and its victories had helped engineer Napoleon's final overthrow. In what the Emperor had once called a contest between an elephant and a whale, the beast of the oceans had come out on top. Every sailor understood this and so, of course, did Churchill, the political champion of maritime supremacy.

Past and present were an unbroken thread. As a thirteen-year-old midshipman, John Fisher the future First Sea Lord had listened in 1854 to stories about life under Nelson's command told by Admiral Sir William Parker, the commander-in-chief at Plymouth. This sense of historic continuity stretching back to the heroic age of Trafalgar and an accompanying aura of superiority gave the Royal Navy a confidence and *esprit de corps* which, its officers believed, were the key to winning battles. Tug Wilson would have thought so. Yet minds focused on former glories tended to accept old ways as the best. Change and innovation were distrusted; at the first sight of a new Royal Navy airship in 1911, an elderly admiral exclaimed: 'It is the work of a lunatic.'[2]

The lunatic was Admiral Sir John Fisher who had been First Sea Lord between 1904 and 1910. He was a jaunty, cocksure egotist who loved dancing and was suspected of having Oriental blood which explained his allure to blue-blooded ladies. Jealous and envious enemies (he had plenty) within the higher ranks of the service thought him a bounder. He had a careless tongue and spoke his mind brusquely and with an utter indifference to the consequences of his words. His indiscretions were more than compensated for by his demonic energy, open mind and penetrating intellect.

Fisher's task was to reform and modernise the Royal Navy. He proceeded on the assumption that it was technically unfit to fight a modern war and that its high command was overstocked with elderly officers whose brain cells had atrophied through lack of use. King Edward VII, the Conservative government and its Liberal successor gave Fisher a free hand with some trepidation, and he set to work on the navy guided by what he called his three 'Rs' – 'Ruthless, Relentless, Remorseless'. Their application led to a sweeping cull of redundant warships, mostly gunboats deployed on foreign stations, and the creation of a new class of fast, well-armoured and heavily gunned capital ships. The first HMS *Dreadnought* was completed in October 1906 and made all other battleships obsolete. More followed and were complemented by another novel class of warship, the battlecruiser, which was a hybrid with the broadside of a dreadnought and the speed of a cruiser.

New ships were needed to fight a new enemy. Fisher had convinced himself that Britain would have to fight Germany in the near future and eliminate the German battlefleet in an engagement somewhere in the North Sea. Inspired by the news of how, in 1904, the Imperial Japanese Navy had launched a pre-emptive attack which had destroyed the Russian Far Eastern fleet at Port Arthur, Fisher suggested that the Royal Navy should follow suit and deliver a surprise attack on the German base at Wilhelmshaven. 'My God, Fisher you must be mad,' declared Edward VII, but the First Sea Lord's outburst caused alarm in Berlin.

The architect of the new German battlefleet, Admiral Alfred von Tirpitz, did not want a war with Britain. He had started to build a new German navy virtually from scratch in 1895 so that it could match those of France and Russia and prevent them from interrupting the food imports upon which Germany depended. After 1898 Tirpitz adopted a new objective: to create an enlarged navy that would be the servant of Germany's *weltpolitik*, whose objective was to turn the nation into a global superpower, strong everywhere and with a colonial empire appropriate to its new status. In theory, a big, modern German battlefleet concentrated in bases between 350 and

450 miles (less than twenty-four hours' sailing time) from Britain's eastern coastline would create sufficient apprehension in Britain to persuade its government to treat Germany's international pretensions with benevolent sympathy. If a war broke out, the sheer size and close proximity of the German battlefleet would deter Britain from throwing in its lot with France and Russia.[3]

Tirpitz's big threat in the North Sea was stiffened by smaller but equally frightening threats in the Pacific. During 1901 and 1902 German naval staff busied themselves with plans for operations using the German squadron based at Tsingtao on the Chinese coast. German cruisers would blockade Australia and harry British shipping in Malayan waters.[4] A report filed in 1908 by the naval attaché in Berlin hinted at further depredations on the Empire. German naval officers were talking airily about obtaining new colonies in East and West Africa and coaling stations on Ascension Island, St Helena, Mauritius and the Seychelles. There were also sinister hints that German warships would succour a nationalist uprising in Ireland.[5] In all likelihood this was empty braggadocio, but since Germany was laying down more and more battleships, such information had to be taken seriously. From the day he arrived at the Admiralty, Churchill interpreted the German naval programme as a direct threat to the British Empire which, he believed, could never survive the loss of maritime supremacy.

Tirpitz's gamble failed. His squadrons of modern battleships failed to produce a cowed, tractable Britain whose government was content to be a passive onlooker in world affairs. Britain's reaction to Tirpitz's navy was to lay down more battleships, cover its flanks and find friends. Japan was the first. In 1902 a defensive alliance was agreed by which Britain promised support in the event of a Franco-Russian war against Japan and the Japanese pledged to back Britain against France and Russia. Japan also took over imperial defence commitments in local waters, which allowed Britain to transfer warships from the China and Pacific stations to European waters. There was disquiet in Australia and New Zealand at what seemed an abdication of imperial responsibilities.

By the time that Churchill entered the Admiralty, the Anglo-German race had taken a new and very dangerous turn. Before the launching of HMS *Dreadnought* Britain had a comfortable lead in orthodox battleships since it had begun with a head start. Ironically, the warship designed to blast conventional battleships off the seas meant that Britain and Germany were back under starter's orders for a fresh race. Each competitor now strained every financial muscle to get as many dreadnoughts and battlecruisers off the stocks as quickly as possible. Von Tirpitz's original vision of a ratio of two German to three British battleships seemed well within Germany's grasp and he intended to achieve parity by 1920.

Another, subsidiary naval race had started in 1909 when Italy and Austria–Hungary began laying down dreadnoughts. Both were allies of Germany and Churchill suspected that Austria–Hungary's naval programme had been instigated by Germany to put pressure on Britain in the Mediterranean.[6] Admiralty Intelligence correctly calculated that, within six years, Italy would have five dreadnoughts and Austria–Hungary four. Britain's command of the Mediterranean would be imperilled and imperial communications jeopardised, although there was a strong likelihood that Italy and Austria–Hungary would use their new battleships to pursue their own imperial rivalry in the Adriatic, the Aegean and Eastern Mediterranean. Nonetheless, Churchill had to contend with the possibility that the Royal Navy might have to fight a war on two fronts. The German battlefleet had transformed the North Sea into another vulnerable imperial frontier and the balance of naval power in the Mediterranean was tilting against Britain.

Churchill's overall view on the navy and its future wartime role had been shaped by his reading Alfred Mahan's *The Influence of Sea Power upon History* which had been published in 1889. Mahan was an American admiral whose theories were based upon his interpretation of the world wars of the eighteenth and early nineteenth centuries. He argued that Louis XIV's and Napoleon's efforts to secure paramountcy on the Continent had been ultimately frustrated by Britain's control of the seas that surrounded western and southern Europe. Britain was an island geographically positioned to dominate the commercial seaways of the western Atlantic, the English Channel, the North Sea, and the Baltic. It was able, therefore, to concentrate its fleet against those of

Spain, France, the Netherlands and Denmark, either individually (which was always preferable), or whenever their navies combined as the French and Spanish had before Trafalgar. Mahan concluded that command of European waters was the key to continental and, it went without saying, world power. He was also a social Darwinist, and this would have added to his appeal to Churchill, for he believed in the gospel of the unending struggle for land and status among the great powers.

Mahan provided Churchill with a philosophy of seapower. Fisher filled his ears with suggestions as to how it might be applied and, most importantly, how British seapower could be made unassailable through the application of modern science and technology. Churchill had first come under Fisher's spell in 1907, when they were both taking a holiday at Biarritz. They spent an afternoon and evening in an animated conversation which encompassed dreadnoughts, submarines, Nelson, the seizure of Borkum Island off the Friesland coast as a forward naval base, and the Bible, a subject closer to Fisher's heart than Churchill's. Churchill had found a soulmate, and at the Admiralty he made himself the conduit for Fisher's ideas. Fisher left office in 1910, hounded out by a cabal of stick-in-the-mud admirals headed by Admiral Lord Charles Beresford, a brave, reactionary and intensely jealous officer and Tory MP who fancied himself a second Nelson.

Fisher's influence remained as strong as ever, thanks to Churchill's dependence upon his advice. He worshipped Fisher, who reciprocated by praising the new First Lord as 'a splendid friend' who was 'splendidly receptive'. Churchill responded with his own hyperbole, describing the septuagenarian admiral as 'a veritable volcano of knowledge and inspiration' and once telling him that 'contact with you is like breathing ozone'.[7] The old admiral became Churchill's technical guru. He pressed the First Lord to continue the conversion of the fleet to oil, and urged the beefing up of submarine flotillas in the teeth of opposition from many older admirals. Tug Wilson considered them 'underhand, unfair and damned un-English'. Yet the submarine's capacity to sink surface ships was repeatedly proved during fleet exercises and, by 1914, Churchill had decided to drop one battleship from his shipbuilding programme and spend the money saved on twenty submarines.[8]

Fisher also urged Churchill to invest in naval aviation. He rightly prophesied that aircraft would replace cruisers and destroyers as the 'eyes' of the navy and that they would be needed to defend naval bases and depots from aerial attacks. These were already being contemplated by the German navy according to an Intelligence report of 1912, which described a lecture given by a German naval officer. The speaker predicted that 'if we could succeed in throwing some bombs into their docks' the 'unwarlike' British would soon cave in. Flying by night, Zeppelins would take the war to Britain.[9] Churchill's island race was no longer protected by its moat.

Churchill was quick to grasp the danger to Britain of aerial bombardment. He ordered the construction of a chain of air bases along the east coast and, when war was declared, Churchill's new Royal Naval Air Service possessed fifty-nine seaplanes and fifty-two aeroplanes. He had a schoolboy's sense of wonderment about these new gadgets and made several accompanied flights. He soon learned enough to fly solo and was eager to do so, despite the pleas of his wife Clementine and his cousin, the Duke of Marlborough.

Aircraft based on the east coast of England and Scotland were integral to a naval strategy designed to defend imperial frontiers whose safety had hitherto been taken for granted, the North Sea and the English Channel. This fact of life created two problems. The first was strategic and demanded both the numerical and technical superiority of a British battlefleet which, henceforward, had to be confined to home waters. This necessity created the second problem: funding. Churchill needed money from the dominions to fund new capital ships which, he hoped to persuade their governments, would be deployed in the North Sea and Mediterranean.

Churchill's appeals for dominion assistance met with a mixed reception. Australia and New Zealand agreed to pay for two battlecruisers (HMAS *Australia* and HMS *New Zealand*) which were completed in British yards in 1912. *Australia* was destined for the Pacific as the flagship for the projected Australian navy. Its presence did not bring peace of mind for the two dominions, who remained nervous about the German squadron at Tsingtao and having their security dependent on the Japanese keeping their word. Churchill reminded them how much more vulnerable they would be if the Royal Navy was defeated in the North Sea. This was no comfort to the Australian and New Zealand governments.

Canada's Prime Minister Robert Borden agreed to foot the bill for three battlecruisers. Churchill wanted them to be named after Canadian provinces and become the backbone of an 'imperial squadron' to be stationed at Gibraltar. The Liberal opposition in Canada's Senate refused to approve funds for the ships. Borden remained optimistic, blaming the Senate's vote on isolationist elements within the Liberal opposition and the intensely parochial and curmudgeonly French community. Malaya's sultans were more generous and raised £2.5 million for a dreadnought HMS *Malaya* which was laid down in October 1913.

Churchill had been disheartened by the myopia and shilly-shallying of dominion politicians, in whom he suspected the lack of an altruistic imperial spirit. With some reluctance, he agreed in October 1913 to an imperial strategic conference to be convened in twelve months. 'It was high time', he wrote, 'that the Dominions had a true strategic conception on which the Empire is conducted impressed on them.'[10] The dominion prime ministers had already received a lesson in broad imperial geo-strategy during the 1911 Imperial Conference. It was delivered by Sir Edward Grey and was pure Mahan. British seapower, he explained, was the keystone of the Empire and, if it was dislodged or fractured, the dominions would be left isolated and exposed. The Foreign Secretary also explained Britain's perspective on the latest political and military developments in Europe. All strongly indicated that Germany's ultimate goal was domination of the Continent. The Kaiser was Napoleon reborn and, if he succeeded, then Europe's economic resources (and navies) would pass into German hands. Britain had to do everything in its power to prevent this, which meant meeting the theoretical German naval threat in the North Sea. Grey thought it unwise to refer to his government's commitment to the defence of France. A German victory in home waters would mean the catastrophe conjured up by Churchill in *The World Crisis*. 'The British Empire would dissolve like a dream; each isolated community struggling forward by itself; the central power of union broken ...'

One fact was emerging from the Admiralty's calculations; the

British Empire needed the French navy as much as France needed the British army. Long-term analyses indicated that by 1915 Britain would have thirty-four capital ships against Germany's twenty-three. This would give the Royal Navy's desired three to two advantage. In the meantime, the margin of superiority in the North Sea was disconcertingly narrow, even allowing for the fourteen mostly obsolescent battleships stationed at Gibraltar and Malta. If recalled in a crisis they would take between four and ten days to reach home waters.

The calculus of the Admiralty's staff officers forced Churchill and the cabinet to make a hard choice between imperial obligations and national security. Relocating the Malta squadron would involve enormous strategic risks since it endangered the sea lanes which ran through the Suez Canal. The Canal's strategic significance was about to become greater than ever, thanks to the navy's conversion to oil. A deal was being brokered between the Admiralty and the Anglo-Persian Oil Company by which the company would receive £2.2 million of government investment in return for 6,000 million tons of oil from its Abadan fields to be delivered over the next twenty years. This oil would be shipped through the Suez Canal.

Prestige was also at stake. Lord Kitchener, then High Commissioner in Egypt, warned that the disappearance of the Royal Navy's big ships from the Mediterranean would give an impression of weakness throughout the region. Fisher, who had served in the Mediterranean as commander-in-chief, shared Kitchener's neurosis about prestige and the dire consequences of its loss. 'Islam is the key to the British Empire,' asserted Fisher, and the departure of the battleships would be taken as a sign of weakness.[11] Churchill was unmoved; he imagined that Britain still had enough muscle to instil the requisite fear and respect.

The future place of the Mediterranean in Britain's naval strategy was resolved at a conference held in Malta at the end of May 1912, attended by Asquith, Kitchener and Churchill. Churchill's views prevailed. 'The return of the Malta squadron is absolutely indispensable,' he argued. Britain's bluff might soon be called by the dreadnoughts of the Italian and Austrian navies, although he was rightly sceptical as to whether these two powers would actually wage a joint naval war against Britain.[12] A hypothetic naval war for the mastery of the Mediterranean was now improbable, but, he argued, it was vital to concentrate every new and obsolescent capital ship that Britain could muster for the forthcoming 'great trial of strength' in the North Sea.[13]

The need to win this battle overrode all other considerations, including Britain's historic supremacy in the Mediterranean. Churchill won his case and the CID accepted that henceforward the defence of the Mediterranean would be shared with France under an agreement by which French battleships from Brest would stiffen the French squadron at Toulon in an emergency. French dreadnoughts would serve as a makeweight after the transfer of British capital ships to the Channel and the North Sea. So long as French goodwill lasted, the Mediterranean would theoretically remain a British lake. This bargain required Britain to take responsibility for the defence of the Channel and France's Atlantic coast in the event of Germany declaring war on France.

Always ready to suspect the worst where Liberal defence policy was concerned, the Conservative press was furious, accusing Churchill of handing over the protection of imperial interests in the Mediterranean to a nation with which we had an *entente* rather than a cast-iron alliance. Anger mingled with Francophobia. Churchill's dereliction of imperial duty was 'absolutely repugnant to the mass of Englishmen' roared the *Daily Express*. Another paper declared that his policy had 'marked the limits of what a self-respecting people should endure'.[14]

Naval policy had long generated a frenzied and bad-tempered public debate. Those who lived through the mid-twentieth-century nuclear arms race will need little imagination to appreciate the scaremongering and paranoia generated by the Anglo-German naval race. In Britain the arguments about how best to achieve the contemporary equivalent of dreadnought 'overkill' were periodically punctuated by the publication of novels about imaginary German invasions, written to make the flesh creep.[15] Erskine Childers's *The Riddle of the Sands* (1903) set the ball rolling with a thrilling account of how two English yachtsmen uncover a scheme to ferry a German army across the North Sea while the Home Fleet is distracted. Later plots adopted the 'bolt-from-the-blue' scenario of sudden amphibious attacks delivered without warning. The possibility that Germany might follow the dastardly example of Japan's surprise attack on Port Arthur in 1904 gave such fiction a chilling credibility.

After the war Churchill described his years in the Admiralty as a period when Europe was 'passing into the iron grip and rule of the Teuton and all that the Teutonic system meant'.[16] He was viewing pre-war Germany through the prism of the war and that not entirely fictional creation of Allied wartime propaganda, the barbaric Hun. Yet before 1914 Imperial Germany was widely seen in Britain as a cultured and civilised nation in the forefront of modern science and philosophy. It was a country where the middle and upper classes took their holidays, particularly when they required a spa to cleanse their digestive systems. There were warm social links between the British and German upper classes and the Kaiser appeared each summer at Cowes in nautical rig and joined shooting parties on northern grouse moors.

Early in 1914, the Kaiser's young brother Prince Heinrich of Prussia (an honorary Admiral of the Fleet in the Royal Navy) told the naval attaché in Berlin that there should exist a natural understanding between Britain and Germany because 'the other large European nations are not white men'.[17] What Churchill may have made of this is not known, but in July 1912 he had told the CID that he hoped Germany would never stoop so low as to discard the rules of civilised nations and launch a pre-emptive attack on Britain. Yet he had his doubts and instigated measures to detect and repel such an attack. Germany for its part had misgivings about an Anglo-French 'bolt from the blue'.[18]

Churchill seems to have been genuinely perplexed by the nature of Germany's long-term ambitions. He did not begrudge the Germans additional colonies, but he was profoundly disturbed by the existence of a battlefleet based less than a day's sailing away from the British coast. It was, he claimed, a 'luxury' for a power whose strength had traditionally rested on a large and efficient army. Appeasement offered an escape from the naval impasse, and in, 1912 and 1913, Churchill tentatively offered Germany a naval 'holiday' in which both nations suspended laying down battleships for two years. His suggestion was rejected. In March 1914, he told the Commons that it was perfectly legitimate for any power to build warships to guard its colonies and overseas trade, or further its international ambitions. This was not the case with Germany, for whom it was mere 'sport', whereas it was a 'matter of life and death' for an empire whose survival depended upon maritime supremacy. German determination to press ahead with its naval policy was, he concluded, an expression of malevolent hostility.

Invasion fears added to Anglo-German tension. There were moments when Churchill succumbed to these jitters and he once added to the alarmist literature on this subject with a draft of a short story in which the German army came ashore in East Anglia and advanced on London. Yet an Admiralty Intelligence analysis of the 1911 Italian seaborne expedition to Libya revealed that it had been a ponderous affair in which it had taken three weeks to ship 35,000 men across the Mediterranean and establish the necessary logistical arrangements for an inland offensive against tribal forces.[19] Furthermore, neither Germany nor Britain had any experience of large-scale amphibious operations, nor had their forces ever undertaken them as exercises.

Germany's resolve to pursue the naval race was flagging by 1914, but not as a consequence of Churchill's enlarged battlefleet. Russia, recovering from its defeat by Japan in 1905, was bent on the restoration of its status as a superpower. This required the modernisation of its army and navy: between 1909 and 1914 Russia's military budget soared from 473 to 581 million roubles. Much of the extra cash was spent on acquiring up-to-date technology and logistical systems with which Russia could exploit its superiority in numbers. The famous Russian 'steamroller' was getting a new engine to power its advance into Germany. The German General Staff suffered a severe attack of nerves and clamoured for more money. Pumping up the army's budget meant the diversion of funds from the navy, and so its programmes were put on hold. By 1913 the German navy found itself facing an enforced 'holiday'. In the end, it was the German army's ability to defeat Russia and France that would lay the foundations of *weltpolitik* and not the Imperial navy.

Britain had won the naval race by a good furlong; in 1914 the Royal Navy had twenty-four battleships and battlecruisers to Germany's sixteen. The margin was slimmer in light cruisers and Germany's ninety-six modern destroyers outnumbered the Royal Navy's seventy-six. Like everyone else, Churchill had presumed that numbers mattered, which, of course, they did, but so too did the thickness and distribution of armour plating and the quality of electrical circuits, guns and fire-control systems. All would be assayed during the war and the results were often disappointing.

Churchill had done an enormous service to the Empire during his term at the Admiralty. An independent thinker and, at times, imperious master, he had modernised the Royal Navy and prepared it for its wartime role. The combined genius of Churchill and Fisher was not, however, reflected in the naval command, which remained encumbered with officers, who, for all their dedication, lacked the Nelsonian spark.

These Grave Matters:
The Irish Crisis, March–July 1914

During March 1914 Churchill was distracted from his naval duties by a major imperial crisis: the resolution of the Irish problem. For the past forty years it had been clear that the overwhelming majority of Catholic Irishmen and women wanted to restore the independent Irish parliament in Dublin. The Protestant minority, chiefly concentrated in Ulster, objected violently. In the past, they had enjoyed economic, legal and political privileges which they had repaid with loyalty to the Crown and they dreaded Home Rule, for it would deliver them into the hands of the Catholics, whose historic memories of injustice and maltreatment had fused into a vengeful spirit.

Ireland was riven by ancient and implacable tribal and sectarian antipathies. They exploded in March 1912 when Churchill visited Belfast to put his government's case for Home Rule and was mobbed by thousands of rabid Protestants. Seven battalions of infantry and one of cavalry were needed to protect him from what must have been the most terrifying display of religious fanaticism he had experienced since his campaigns on the North-West Frontier and Sudan.

Churchill and the Liberals believed that, whilst Ireland could not be permanently dragooned into the British state, it could be integrated into the British Empire as a democratic dominion. It was a solution that appealed to Churchill, who looked forward to bringing Ireland 'into the circle of the British Empire'. Once part of the 'true and indissoluble union of the British Empire', the Irish, like the Boers, would abandon their traditional animosity towards Britain, and a sense of 'mutual goodwill' would induce Protestants and Catholics to live together in harmony just like Britons and Boers in South Africa.[1]

This prospect seemed increasingly distant in March 1914. Over the past two years, Ulster Unionists had formed a private army to resist the enforcement of the Home Rule Act, which was scheduled for September. Recently, the Catholics in the south had followed suit and it seemed likely that the inauguration of the Dublin parliament would be the catalyst for an Irish civil war.

There was a worrying English dimension to the Irish imbroglio. The Tories backed the Protestants to the hilt. They were convinced that Ireland was integral to the United Kingdom and that its political future was a purely domestic matter. Ireland could never be treated in the same way as say Natal or Newfoundland because the historic memory of oppression among the Gaelic-Catholic Irish could never be erased. The new state was bound to disengage from the Empire at the first opportunity.

Irish nationalists had always made common cause with the enemies of the Empire, in particular the Boers, whom they identified as a people like themselves struggling for independence. Some Irish nationalists had volunteered to fight alongside the Boers. Their example strengthened Tory resistance to Home Rule; the Irish might even attach themselves to Britain's foes as they had done during the 1798 rebellion when the insurgents had invited French troops into the country. By an astonishing paradox the Conservatives preferred Ireland to stay within the United Kingdom under conditions which a majority of Irish found intolerable, and simultaneously denied them a state within the Commonwealth that might have gone some way to appease their national aspirations.

For the Conservatives, the 1801 Act of Union was inviolate and every means possible should be used to preserve it. During the 1885 general election Lord Randolph Churchill had played what he called the 'Orange Card' and whipped up the visceral anti-Catholicism of the Ulster Protestants who were rallying around the slogans 'Home Rule equals Rome Rule' and, more ominously, 'Ulster will fight and Ulster will be right'.

Ulster was ready to fight again in 1912. Within two years 100,000 Protestant volunteers had joined the Ulster Defence Volunteers [UDV] and undergone rudimentary military training. Over 400,000 Ulstermen and women had signed a 'Solemn Covenant' by which they swore never to submit to a Dublin government. The Ulster Unionists also mobilised support among descendants of Northern Irish immigrants in the dominions; Orangemen in Manitoba formed a detachment pledged to fight in Ireland.

In Britain the Conservatives were cheering on the Ulster Unionists and the UDV. After three successive general election defeats, the party had found a cause that might be a winner with the voters, who were either indifferent or hostile to Irish self-government. The Tories, therefore, unfurled the Union Jack and resuscitated their old mantra that Irish self-government would mark the beginning of the end for the British Empire. The Union was the linchpin of the Empire and, therefore, sacrosanct.

Arthur Bonar Law, a dour Scotch-Canadian businessman who had succeeded Balfour as Tory leader, led the chorus of hate. At Tory rallies, he made speeches which endorsed armed resistance to Home Rule. Edward Carson, the hawk-faced Unionist MP for that isolated citadel of the Protestant ascendancy Trinity College Dublin, reassured the UDV that the British army was 'with us' and, therefore, would never fire on them. Within two years the Unionists had implanted the rhetoric of violence and civil war in the British political vocabulary.

Asquith's cabinet kept its nerve (just), and proceeded in the hope that a compromise might somehow be negotiated. The requisite goodwill proved elusive and, by March 1914, a settlement was as far off as ever. Ministers turned their attention towards the security of Ireland. If the Home Rule Act was to be implemented and an Irish civil war averted, then the army and the navy had to be ready to disarm the paramilitaries and uphold the supremacy of Parliament. The government had first to make its moral and political position clear, and this task fell to Churchill. Lloyd George believed that plain speaking from a politician with a reputation as a conciliator might calm tempers.[2]

In a speech delivered in Bradford on 14 March, Churchill's tone was caustic and his logic brutal and flawless. The conduct of the Ulster Unionists and their Tory allies had raised three fundamental issues: public order, the allegiance of the King's subjects, and the absolute sovereignty of Parliament. The Liberals were ready to make concessions, whilst the Tories were bent on inciting a civil war, which he predicted would spread across the Irish Sea:

I am sure and certain that the first British soldier or coastguard, blue jacket or Royal Irish Constabulary man who is attacked and killed by an

Orangeman will raise an explosion in this country ... of a kind they [the
Conservatives] little appreciate, or understand, and will shake to the very
foundations the basis and structure of society.

By choosing to override the law rather than negotiate its amendment,
the Tories would reduce Britain to the 'anarchy of Mexico' which was
then engaged in a bloody civil war. They demanded the coercion of
four-fifths of Ireland's population, but howled 'sacrilege, tyranny and
murder' if anyone dared 'to lay a finger on the Tory fifth'. Bonar Law
and Carson had shown contempt towards Parliament which was 'the
supreme executive authority of this great state and Empire'. Churchill
ended with a challenge to the Unionists: 'Let us go forward together
and put these grave matters to the proof.' The Conservatives were
apoplectic: he had accused them of conniving at sedition and treason
and stolen their thunder in what was virtually an ultimatum from the
government.

   While Churchill was beating the war drum, the cabinet was taking
tentative steps to forestall an armed coup in Ulster. Intelligence
reports indicated that UDV units were planning to seize guns and
ammunition from unguarded Territorial Army depots. Their safety
required rushing troops north by the Dublin-to-Belfast line, which
was vulnerable to sabotage or a strike by railwaymen sympathetic to
the UDV. Churchill ordered four destroyers to make for southern
Irish ports and pick up troops, while a cruiser was instructed to stand
by off Carrickfergus. Ratings were instructed not to fraternise with
the local population. By 19 March troops were already being ferried
to the north.

   Churchill ordered the 3rd Battle Squadron of pre-dreadnought
battleships to steam from Arosa Bay near Cape Finisterre to Lamlash
Bay on the Isle Arran, less than three hours' sailing away from
Belfast. Asquith had approved this precautionary deployment, but
later distanced himself from the decision. Churchill boasted that
he had scotched a rebellion and he told General Sir John French
that the twelve-inch guns of the battleships would have Belfast 'in
ruins within twenty-four hours'.[3] This was gunboat diplomacy on a
grand scale; whereas a truculent Persian Gulf sheikh needed a single
warship to bring him to reason, the UDV and the Orangemen needed

five battleships. They cast anchor within a few days, but Churchill had made his point: the government would not shrink from harsh measures to uphold the law.

The application of a classic imperial remedy of last resort maddened the Unionists, who accused Churchill of trying to goad the Ulstermen into revolt. His ironclads were likened to the troops that marched out of Boston in 1775 to provoke the country people of Massachusetts into armed defiance. Moreover, Churchill's response seemed disproportionate to the threat. Yet, it was justified by a sheaf of alarmist intelligence reports from agents in Ulster who had been probing for evidence of a rebellion during the last week of March. These suggested, correctly, that the Ulster volunteers were covertly attempting to purchase rifles and machine-guns abroad, and that the 'roughest elements' might easily slip the leash. They had been conditioned to expect a fight, which many openly relished. Their middle-class and aristocratic patrons and leaders had become prisoners to their own bombast and might find themselves with no choice but to go ahead with a coup or face the anger of the rank and file. One intelligence report indicated plans for the declaration of a 'Provisional Government' in Belfast just before Home Rule became law.[4]

Unlooked for events at the Curragh Camp near Dublin had emboldened the paramilitaries and indicated that any armed coup might be feebly resisted by British forces. On 21 March a significant number of army officers had publicly announced that they would resign their commissions rather than command their units in operations to enforce Home Rule in the North.

The brunt of upholding the law fell to the 32,000 soldiers of the Irish garrison, two-thirds of whom were in the south. Their commander-in-chief General Sir Arthur Paget was called to London for discussions in Whitehall and he returned to Dublin imagining that he had the power to absolve pro-Unionist officers from their obedience to the Crown. He explained the political situation to senior officers at the Curragh Camp. Future operations against the UDV were a possibility, he informed officers, but those with kinsfolk in Ulster were told that they could discreetly slip away if they were ordered north, and that any officer who objected to these operations in principle was free to resign his commission. General Sir Hubert Gough, commander of the 3rd Cavalry Brigade, and fifty-seven of his officers immediately did so. More followed, which was to be expected, given the overwhelmingly Tory and Unionist sympathies of army officers.

On the following day Churchill sounded out Admiral Sir Lewis Bayly, the commander of the 3rd Battle Squadron, as to the loyalty of his officers. His reply was equivocal and hinted that sympathy for the Unionists would prove as strong in the wardroom as it was in the mess. Naval officers were, however, more circumspect than their army colleagues. While there were no dramatic confrontations, well-publicised threats of mass resignations or alarming newspaper headlines, a knot of naval officers placed their political sympathies before their loyalty to the Crown and confided to each other their intention of resigning rather take any part in still-hypothetical operations against Ulster. Some were ready to go further: junior officers serving with the 7th Destroyer Flotilla proposed to sail their ships to Belfast and Londonderry and place them at the disposal of Carson, the Unionist leader. By contrast, Commander Goodenough of the cruiser HMS *Southampton* had no second thoughts, remarking that his ship 'might have to go and bombard Belfast and that was that'.[5]

Military historians have sidestepped the political and legal aspects of this episode, which they have blandly dismissed as an 'incident' rather than a mutiny. Dissidence was excused on the grounds that Paget's remarks had been framed in such a way that officers imagined their honour had been impugned by being asked whether they would obey commands that were still notional. This is casuistry; while they did not actually refuse an order, the officers who resigned did so in the belief that they had the right to do so whenever they saw fit. Moreover, the dissidents were largely from the professional and landed classes and their utterances, coupled with those of their political allies, made it abundantly clear that their protest was also directed against all the policies of the Liberal government, which many believed reeked of socialism. The enforcement of Home Rule in Ireland was the last straw and a welcome pretext for Tories in messes and wardrooms to air their pent-up fury against the radicalism of a government that heavily taxed the rich and had recently curtailed the power of the House of Lords.

Churchill was shocked by the Curragh Mutiny, which he believed endangered the future security of the Empire. In a censure debate at the end of April, he speculated as to the chaos that would follow if the logic adopted by the Curragh officers was applied throughout the Empire. Would Egyptian and Indian NCOs be free to choose which orders they obeyed and which they ignored? Churchill also wondered how a signal public display of indiscipline by British officers might be interpreted in the war ministries of Europe.[6] Negotiations about Ireland's future dragged on and were only terminated by the outbreak of war on 4 August, when both sides agreed to a truce for the duration. A world war thus averted a civil war.

The Interests of Great Britain:
The Coming of War, July–August 1914

Churchill had long dreaded the outbreak of an industrialised war waged between the armies and navies of great powers. He had seen enough of modern firepower in the Sudan and South Africa to foresee that 'cruel and magnificent war' would be superseded by the 'cruel and squalid war' of the masses. It would definitely not be 'a gentleman's game'.[1] As the war progressed, his apprehensions were confirmed by the scale of the slaughter. By 1915, as he recalled in *The World Crisis*, he was already fearful of the damage that the war was inflicting on the 'structure of society' in Europe.

The ungentlemanly and unpredictable game of total war started unexpectedly in 1914 with the assassination of Archduke Franz Ferdinand and Archduchess Sophie by a Serbian terrorist in Sarajevo on 27 June 1914. The four weeks of international crisis and the war that followed have been widely described and dissected.[2] Suffice it to say that by the last week of July diplomacy had failed and civilian ministers in Austria–Hungary, Germany, Russia and France were compelled to abdicate their power in favour of their general staffs. Churchill had briefly hoped that what had suddenly become a helter-skelter rush to war might be halted by Europe's monarchs. This was mere fancy, for, like their ministers, Nicholas II, Wilhelm II and Franz-Josef were now in thrall to their respective high commands. Churchill too was part of this abrogation of civilian authority: on 27 July he began to issue the flow of signals that would put the Royal Navy on a war footing.

Military men were seizing the reins of power and their decisions were dictated by the war plans which they had been meticulously preparing for nearly a decade. Each war ministry was confident that it had concocted a formula that would bring the conflict to a swift and victorious end. General staff officers of all powers were united in their insistence that hesitation in the implementation of their plans would mean potentially fatal delays and that the engine of mobilisation could never work in neutral or reverse gears.

At every phase of the crisis each power was driven by an urge to assert the supremacy of its will. Prestige had to be upheld come what may and it would crumble at the first hint of irresolution. Russia leapt at the chance to prove that it was once again a virile superpower whose aspirations in South-East Europe were legitimate and exempt from diplomatic bargaining. Habsburg generals, most notably Conrad von Hötzendorf, welcomed an opportunity to give Russia's Balkan client Serbia a salutary knock, root out its terrorist cells and prove that Austria was the dominant regional power. At first, neither the hawks in Vienna nor St Petersburg imagined this localised trial of strength would lead to a world war. Continuing Russian military reforms, in particular the modernising of strategic railways which pointed westwards to the German frontier, were tilting the military balance against Germany. The prevailing view in Berlin was that it was better to fight Russia now rather than later, when it would be harder, perhaps impossible to defeat. The German High Command got exactly what it wanted: Russia began preliminary mobilisation on 25 July, which set the ball rolling. Germany's speedier and more efficient mobilisation began six days later.

Britain had no precast role in this crisis. It was outside the system of Continental alliances, although in terms of diplomacy it had consistently aligned itself with France and Russia. It had also held secret and tentative military discussions with them on hypothetical military and naval cooperation in a war against Germany. Britain's only concrete (and publicly known) commitment to the *entente* powers was a promise to keep the English Channel clear of German warships. Germany was never fooled by this pretence of neutrality, but its generals were confident that intervention by the British Expeditionary Force would not influence the result of the great battle for France.

Britain had secretly agreed to play a part in this battle, because the Committee of Imperial Defence had concluded that France's survival was vital for the future security of Britain and its Empire. After a period of intense political and strategic crystal-gazing, the committee concluded that a German victory would do untold damage to Britain. German supremacy on the Continent would be 'inimical to the interests of Great Britain' and the committee predicted that it would use its new power to annex Belgium and Holland and demand the surrender of French African colonies. It was taken for granted that Germany would confiscate French and Russian warships and so decisively swing the balance of world naval power against Britain.[3]

Churchill accepted these conclusions. On the whole they were sound, for, as will be seen later, Germany used its victories in the West and East to expropriate and exploit Belgian, Polish, Russian and Ukrainian territories and incorporate them within an economic zone whose sole purpose was to feed the German people and supply its industries with raw materials and workers. Final victory would bring further rewards. As late as September 1918 German imperialists were looking forward to the return of colonies that had been lost to the Allies as well as a share of their colonies in Africa.[4] Of course, by this time Britain, France and Italy also had detailed plans for the post-war annexation of former German, Austrian and Turkish possessions. The First World War was, therefore, a continuation of the global race for colonies.

Neutrality was not an option for Britain in 1914 in what was certain to become a contest in which every participant expected territorial dividends, not least as compensation for the sacrifice of lives and treasure. If Britain isolated itself from this war, then it would eventually be faced with two equally baleful consequences. On one hand, it would have to survive in a world dominated by an overmighty, land-hungry and hostile Germany. On the other, it would have to contend with Russia and France; whether as victors or losers, both powers were bound to revive their old colonial rivalries with Britain, the nation which had left them in the lurch. Russia in particular was bent on extending its power in Persia and fulfilling its old ambitions in the Near East, objectives that would have led to a collision with Britain. To crudely sum up the arguments for intervention: there was less to be feared from a victorious France and Russia than a victorious Germany.

This was the view of Asquith, Grey, Churchill and, after some last moment nudging by Churchill, Lloyd George. They agreed that the future security of the British Empire depended upon saving France from being defeated in a lightning offensive. The logic behind entering the war and the intelligence upon which it rested were largely unknown to the British public, which, during the first three weeks of the crisis, inclined towards neutrality.

Churchill had been mesmerised by dramatic events which seemed to possess a life force of their own. By the last week of July, he believed that a general war was imminent in which Britain would become involved. On 31 July he confided to Clementine that Germany 'cannot promise not to invade Belgium' and urged her to burn or lock up this indiscreet letter.[5] As a CID insider he knew that the Schlieffen Plan was the linchpin of Germany's strategy and that Britain was one of the nations which, over seventy years before, had guaranteed Belgian neutrality. Churchill, therefore, was fully aware that war was inevitable and he began mobilising the fleet.

On 27 July Churchill had sent telegrams to commanders across the world ordering them to place their ships on a war footing. There was no doubt as to the enemy. Admiral Sir Archibald ('Arky Barky') Milne was directed to concentrate the Mediterranean Fleet at Malta, to detach cruisers to discover the whereabouts of the German battlecruiser *Goeben* and the light cruiser *Breslau* and to shadow them. The commander-in-chief at Cape Town was instructed to track 'hostile' warships in local waters, since a war between the Triple Alliance (Germany, Austria–Hungary and Italy) and the Triple Entente (Britain, France and Russia) was 'by no means impossible'. On 28 July the cruiser *Dartmouth* was ordered to sail from Bombay and search for the cruiser *Königsberg* which was believed to have been at Dar-es-Salaam in German East Africa.[6]

At the same time, the machinery for home defence was being set in motion. The Home Fleet was ordered to its battle stations at Scapa Flow and Portland Bay. Seaplanes based along the East Coast were placed in readiness for reconnaissance flights over the North Sea and RNAS aircraft were ordered to be prepared to detect and repel German air raids on naval installations in the Thames estuary. Two Turkish battleships nearing completion on Tyneside yards were summarily commandeered at Churchill's orders for later transfer to the Grand Fleet. He was already considering offensive action and suggested to Asquith the occupation of a small island off the Frisian coast as a forward base for the close blockade of the German coast.

On 2 August, when hostilities between Germany and France had just begun, the government warned the former that its warships would be attacked if they approached the English Channel or the French Atlantic coast. Britain's entry into the conflict was now imminent and on the same day the Admiralty signalled commanders on all foreign stations to gather intelligence about German merchantmen and intercept all German telegrams.[7]

On 28 July Churchill told his wife he was appalled by the 'catastrophe and collapse' he was witnessing from his desk in the Admiralty, but added, 'I am interested, geared up and happy ... the preparations have a hideous fascination for me. I pray to God to forgive me for such fearful moods of levity.'[8] His adrenalin kept flowing; during the night of 3–4 August, when ministers gathered to await Germany's answer to the British ultimatum, Lloyd George was struck by Churchill's 'sense of purpose'. 'He was a happy man' whose face was bright and radiant as he outlined to his colleagues the arrangements he had in hand for mobilising the fleet.[9]

While Churchill had been ordering the fleet into its battle stations for a war against Germany, the cabinet was agonising over exactly how the conflict could be sold to the British people. A bizarre situation had developed, for Asquith, Grey and Churchill were fully aware that German invasion of Belgium was imminent and that, once it had started, the BEF would be shipped across the Channel to take up positions on the north-western flank of the French army. Ministers outside the CID, MPs, the press and the public were largely in the dark about these arrangements. All were being led to believe that Britain's mind had not yet been made up and would not be until there was definite evidence that German forces had entered Belgium. Churchill even indicated to Lloyd George that the Germans might still be dissuaded from undertaking an offensive against Belgium, which he knew was untrue.

What Asquith needed was the spontaneous explosion of public outrage which would inevitably follow the German advance into Belgium. It would justify an ultimatum to Germany and provide the

British public with an altruistic moral cause. In 1854 the people had been persuaded that the nation was fighting Russia as a champion of a bullied and cowering Turkey, which was in fact well able to look after itself. Again, in 1899 the Boer War had been sold as an exercise in national selflessness by defending the rights of European immigrants who had been denied political rights by the Transvaal government. The Schlieffen Plan provided a welcome pretext with which to arouse the moral indignation of the people and unite them behind the war.

The cabinet and nearly the whole of the Commons endorsed the government's ultimatum to Germany. War was declared on 4 August and Churchill afterwards pronounced it Britain's 'finest and worthiest moment'.

The mood of his colleagues was muted; they had secured a moral mandate for the war. Britain could now proudly claim to be fighting for the freedom of small nations and international law against a power which believed that military necessity gave it a mandate to trample on both. Germany had, after all, signed a treaty which guaranteed Belgium's frontiers and neutrality. A war in defence of ideals was infinitely more sellable than one waged for geo-political abstractions, chief of which was the premise that Britain and its Empire might not survive a German victory in France.

Within a week of the declaration of war, British propagandists were firmly entrenched on the moral high ground and were vilifying Germany as a brutish bully guided by the principle that might was right. This stereotype was tragically justified by the atrocities committed by German troops during the opening weeks of the war. Once dismissed as Allied inventions, the details of these outrages have been confirmed by recent research.[10] At least 15,000 buildings were destroyed, over 5,000 civilians murdered, including women and children, and untold numbers of women were raped by German soldiers. The German government excused its army's calculated terror on the grounds that Belgian and French civilians had sniped at its soldiers. This was a lie. These crimes were an expression of the philosophy of the German High Command which permeated all ranks of the German army in 1914 and for the rest of the war.

There were no rules or moral constraints in modern warfare; efficiency and remorseless willpower were the principles which dictated how a victorious war should be waged. Humanity, justice and morality were always subordinate to military necessity in Belgium and France (where a quick victory was desperately needed) and in the lands overrun by Germany in Eastern Europe.[11] Churchill soon understood this. On 29 August he told an American journalist that Britain was now 'at grips with Prussian militarism', which had been harnessed by 'the Prussian military aristocracy' to secure Germany 'a world-wide predominance'. If she achieved this, then the integrity and security of the Empire would be seriously, perhaps fatally endangered.

PART THREE

1914–1922

A War of Empires:

An Overview, 1914–1918

We have more or less forgotten the fact, self-evident at the time, that the First World War was an imperial conflict. With the exception of the United States, every power engaged was bent on accumulating land, economic advantage and influence. The four years of fighting were an extension of the late-nineteenth- and early-twentieth-century partition of the world by the great powers. Their objectives explain why the war was a sequence of interconnected campaigns in Europe, the Middle East, Asia, Africa and the Pacific. All were part of what Siegfried Sassoon percipiently identified as 'a war ... of conquest'.¹ He was a front-line soldier on the Western Front, a theatre on which British historians have focused, often in microscopic detail, with an emphasis on the myriad human tragedies of trench warfare and the proficiency of the generals who presided over it.

The Western Front was important, in so far as common strategic wisdom held that whoever won in this theatre would secure total victory. Yet from the winter of 1914–15 it was plain that the antagonists were evenly matched, a conclusion which was confirmed by the failed Allied and German offensives during 1916 and 1917. Early in 1916, Churchill's experience in the trenches as an infantry officer prompted him to confide to Clementine that victory was 'still in the grasp of our enemies'. Time was neutral throughout the war and, at least until the final fortnight of October 1918, its passage supported the view that neither the Allies nor the Central Powers could ever win an outright victory.

Pessimism on this score permeated the discussions of Lloyd George's coalition cabinet. He had come to power at the end of December 1916 and had to cope with a sequence of hammer blows which together added to the impression that the Allies might not win the war. The Passchendaele offensive failed disastrously and, in December 1917 the new Bolshevik regime in Russia threw in the sponge. In the following summer, ministers wondered whether France and Italy, both showing symptoms of exhaustion, would soon do likewise.

In the meantime the Central Powers fell on the disintegrating Russian Empire. The sheer scale of Germany's latent imperial ambitions was made frighteningly clear by the terms it imposed on the Bolsheviks in the Treaty of Brest-Litovsk, which was signed on 3 March 1918. The new and precarious Soviet state was forced to surrender what was left of Poland, Finland, the Ukraine and what are now Belarus, Latvia and Estonia. The Russo-German frontier now stretched from the Narva on the Baltic Sea to Sebastopol on the Black Sea. The puppet government of the Ukraine was compelled to oversee the export of the bulk of its grain harvest to Germany and Austria–Hungary.

Germany's new provinces were the springboard for an offensive towards the Caspian and the Caucasus intended to create a new German empire on the borders of Europe and Asia. Fifty divisions, including a large force of cavalry, advanced southwards and eastwards during the summer and autumn. German newspapers reported (probably truthfully) that these troops were welcomed as liberators from the Bolshevik tyranny.

Turkey joined in the scramble for Russia. It agreed an armistice with the Bolsheviks at the very end of 1917 and immediately afterwards Enver Pasha the Minister of War approved an offensive against what are today Georgia and Azerbaijan. Its aim was the creation of a new Turkish imperium whose foundations would be racial and religious. Muslims were promised protection from the atheist Bolsheviks and invited to join a new polity whose inhabitants would be united by their shared Turanian bloodlines. A novel form of empire had been invented based upon largely fabricated ethnic kinship between Turks and their former eastern neighbours.[2] As might have been expected, this premise required the extinction of anyone beyond the mystic bonds of ancestry and so the birth of the Pan-Turanian empire was marked by a fresh outbreak of massacres of Armenians and other Christians. The Germans were peeved by Turkish incursions into Georgia, which they wanted for themselves, but cooperated uneasily in a joint advance towards the oilfields of Baku. On at least one occasion, troops from the two armies fired on each other.

The Allies joined the scramble for Russia. Japan landed troops in Vladivostok in March with the stock annexationalist excuse that they were protecting their 'interests'. Within a few months, Japanese forces were edging inland towards Lake Baikal. Their activities disturbed Whitehall, where the Foreign Secretary Arthur Balfour wondered whether the Japanese would remain in Siberia, drily remarking that Japan might be the only power that emerged from the war 'with more money and territory' than it had at the beginning.[3] There was no chance of this, for British, American and Canadian units were quickly shifted into Siberia, again in defence of national interests.

What these might be was explained by a Canadian officer who observed that a 'wonderful opportunity' now existed for Canadian capitalists to buy up Russian companies for a bagatelle.[4] Enver Pasha had reached a similar conclusion, declaring in June that Turkey would claim legal rights to the lands it was now conquering in Russia and would insist on their recognition at some future peace conference. Like other leaders, he was pinning his hopes on the war ending in a draw and that armed occupation of an enemy's territory would prove a trump card in peace negotiations.

Those who masterminded Britain's war effort thought in acquisitive imperial terms. 'The British Empire is now fighting for its life,' declared Lord Kitchener the Secretary for War in November 1914. General Sir Douglas Haig, the commander-in-chief of the BEF between 1915 and 1918, agreed and convinced himself that he was the chosen agent of a Divine Providence whose grand design was the preservation of the British Empire. A trio of staunch imperialists, Bonar Law, Curzon and Milner, dominated Lloyd George's inner war cabinet. His new political secretariat included fervent imperialists like Leo Amery, the novelist John Buchan who had worked with Milner in South Africa, and Sir Mark Sykes, whose job it was to lay the foundations for British hegemony in the Middle East. Also on hand was General Smuts, a semi-official representative of the dominions, who amazingly believed that once Germany had lost her colonies, she had lost the war.[5]

As Prime Minister, Lloyd George forgot his old mistrust of

imperialism. In December 1917 he praised the recent capture of Jerusalem in the Commons and, revealingly, likened the piecemeal conquest of Palestine to Wolfe's capture of Quebec and Clive's victory at Plassey during the Seven Years War. Lloyd George reminded MPs that at the time these successes had been dismissed as mere 'sideshows', but they eventually paid a substantial imperial dividend.

Britain's campaigns of imperial conquest had begun the day after war was declared. The CID issued orders for amphibious offensives against German colonies in West Africa and encouraged Australian and New Zealand forces to seize German possessions in the Pacific as soon as possible. This was rapidly accomplished with the assistance of the Royal Navy, and a jubilant Australian newspaper proclaimed 'the foundation of a solid Australian sub-empire in the Pacific'. The cheering stopped after Sir Lewis Harcourt the Colonial Secretary warned that 'any territory now occupied must at the conclusion of the war be at the disposal of the Imperial [i.e. British] government'. He added another wet blanket: Australia's title to the Caroline and Marshall Islands could not be confirmed, because of pre-war promises to Britain's ally, Japan.[6] It was quite rightly assumed that Japan would expect some reward for protecting British Far Eastern and Pacific interests.

Germany's African colonies were also up for grabs. At the close of 1914, the deadlock on the Western Front was seen as an opportunity for the swift occupation of these isolated and weakly defended outposts. In January 1915 Sir Maurice Hankey ['Hanky Panky'] the influential Secretary to the War Council urged the transfer of troops to the German colonies in Africa to accelerate their conquest. Once in Allied hands, they would become vital assets 'when peace terms are discussed'.[7]

This was a superficially attractive prospect, but the government had to proceed cautiously, for Anglo-French imperial ventures were fraught with tensions. The former imperial rivals were never wholly convinced of each other's honesty and France's historic suspicion of British legerdemain and duplicity had never been dispelled by the 1904 *entente*. In West Africa, Britain had to avoid trespassing on areas coveted by its ally and, at the same time, the French had to be warned that there were regions closed to them. The War Office, therefore, politely refused French offers of Senegalese troops for the campaign in German East Africa, suspecting that local territorial concessions might turn out to be the fee for their hire. A tentative agreement was reached early in 1916, when the French withdrew claims to the spoils of East Africa, much to Britain's relief.[8]

French distrust of Britain was strongest over the Middle East. Historic memories which stretched back to Napoleon's invasion of Egypt in 1798 generated an almost paranoid fear that Britain would once again frustrate French regional ambitions, of which the most deeply cherished was the desire to possess Syria and the Lebanon.

The Allies were about to embark upon what one historian has perceptively called the 'War of the Ottoman Succession'. Britain was very quick off the mark; even before Turkey's declaration of war on 1 November 1914 the CID had drawn up plans for an immediate occupation of Basra to deny Turkey and Germany a terminus for the still incomplete Berlin-to-Baghdad railway. Anglo-Indian troops backed by warships tightened Britain's grip on the Abadan oilfields and persuaded the rulers of the Persian Gulf sheikhdoms that the King Emperor George V had replaced Sultan Mehmed V as their overlord and protector. By the end of 1914, an Anglo-Indian army was edging northwards into Mesopotamia, a region known to have considerable oil reserves. Its post-war status had yet to be decided, although its strategic position in relation to India made it unlikely that Britain would abandon it completely.

The Mesopotamian gambit unsettled the French, who were extremely prickly about any British activity that might, however remotely, infringe on their self-created rights in the Levant. Churchill understood this and took steps to appease French sensibilities in the area. In February 1915 he placed all naval operations in Lebanese and Syrian waters under the control of a French rather than a British admiral to avoid contention.[9] This was temporising, for at same time the Admiralty was drawing up exigency plans to deny France or any other power ports on the Syrian and Turkish coastlines.[10] In Cairo, a knot of senior civil servants and not-so-senior officers, including Sub-Lieutenant T. E. Lawrence, were scheming to forestall French plans for Syria. The older men had memories of Fashoda and were certain that, once the war was over, old regional animosities would be resuscitated.

This was a region where Russian ambitions also had to be satisfied. By the end of 1914, its demands for annexations at Turkey's expense had been rubber-stamped by France and Britain; these included Constantinople and the Straits. The Sykes–Picot agreement of 1916 allocated Kurdistan, Azerbaijan and Turkish Armenia to Russia. Italy too wanted to get its hands on a bit of the Levant. Its demands for a slice of the Anatolian littoral were high on a long shopping list delivered to the Allies during April 1915 as the price for joining them. Rome's overblown imperial ambitions also included the Dodecanese Islands, the independent kingdom of Abyssinia [Ethiopia] and small pockets of real estate in North and East Africa. The British cabinet was appalled by Italy's rapaciousness. Churchill denounced her as the 'harlot of Europe' and Fisher dismissed the Italians as 'mere organ-grinders! No use whatever'.[11] His last gibe was amply justified by the performance of Italy's generals.

Germany's overseas empire was an instant casualty of its policy of concentrating its fleet in the North Sea. On every other sea and ocean Britain was supreme and Germany's colonies were, therefore, isolated without any hope of receiving reinforcements or matériel from the homeland. Only in German East Africa was there serious resistance, brilliantly improvised by General Paul von Lettow-Vorbeck. South-West Africa was rapidly overrun by South African forces led by Louis Botha. He hoped that after the war it would be amalgamated into a greater South African state that would, in time, extend to Bechuanaland [Botswana], Rhodesia and Nyasaland. Like Australia, South Africa treated the war as an opportunity for empire building in its backyard.

German losses in the tropics were more than offset by substantial gains in Europe. Between 1914 and the end of 1916, German forces had secured Belgium, most of north-western France, Romania and a chunk of what had been Russia's western provinces, including much of Poland. The military authorities treated all these regions as if they were subservient dependencies: the relationship of the Belgians or the Romanians to their new overlords was close to that of the natives of Germany's pre-war African colonies to their masters. Harsh police states were installed, property was requisitioned and vast quantities of livestock and crops were confiscated and delivered to Germany. Artificial famines became common. Forced labour was widespread and men were conscripted for deportation to Germany, where they replaced industrial workers who were desperately needed at the front.[12] This pattern of exploitation would be repeated in the Second World War.

Centre and right-wing deputies in the *Reichstag* clamoured for the annexation of Belgium and looked forward to a happy time when, in the words of one German newspaper, 'superiority in Europe' would provide the opportunity for recovering and enlarging Germany's overseas colonies.[13] Such speculation fuelled Allied fears that a victorious Germany would repartition the world to their loss.

Churchill had preferred not to discuss Britain's imperial objectives in his wartime addresses. Instead, he portrayed the war as an apocalyptic contest between good and evil. It went without saying that Britain was on the side of light. He claimed that if Germany won then civilisation would be submerged under 'the tides of barbarism'. Humane, imperial government would be superseded by a brutal, global tyranny and he was fearful of what the Germans had in store for the people of India. This allegation was melodramatic, but understandable in the light of German exploitation of its occupied territories on the Continent and its connivance in the state-sponsored massacre of Armenians in the Ottoman Empire. Yet, in July 1917, he told voters in his Dundee constituency that British war aims were unsullied by greed or vengefulness. He changed his tune during the December 1918 general election when he promised voters that former German and Turkish territories would never be returned to their owners. To have even hinted otherwise would have been electoral madness, for the British people wanted the fruits of victory as due compensation for their huge sacrifice of blood and treasure.

Before the war, Churchill had repeatedly insisted that the Empire was vital for Britain's survival as a global power. He was vindicated by the mobilisation of imperial manpower and resources which were delivered into the hands of British ministers and generals. In 1914 just over a third of the Empire's white population of 65 million lived in the dominions and, by the end of the war, Canada, Newfoundland,

Australia and New Zealand had sent 1.2 million men to various fronts. India provided a further 1.4 million. Before 1918 a large proportion of these men were volunteers, many of whom imagined that they were on the threshold of an exciting but brief adventure. Whatever their motives, the dominion servicemen were essential to Britain's war effort on every front.

In August 1914 the dominions had thrown themselves wholeheartedly behind Britain in the conviction that its defeat would have unthinkable repercussions. There were often moving displays of patriotism: members of the New Zealand House of Representatives applauded their Prime Minister's promise of an Expeditionary Force and spontaneously sang 'God Save the King'. Canada agreed to a political truce and the opposition leader Sir Wilfrid Laurier declared that Britain was fighting for 'principles of liberty'. Within six weeks 32,000 Canadians had joined up for service in France. Max Aitken (the future Lord Beaverbrook), a Canadian businessman who had settled in Great Britain, where he was proprietor of the *Daily Express*, was overwhelmed by this display of imperial spirit. He appointed himself chief press publicist for the Canadian forces and promised Canada's Prime Minister Robert Borden that he would 'enshrine in contemporary history those exploits which will make the First [Canadian] Division immortal'.[14] Participation in the war was widely seen as defining the dominions in a historical sense: one New Zealand newspaper described the departure of its fighting men for distant fronts as having 'enriched our national tradition'.[15]

The flood of volunteers subsided during 1915, as it did in Britain. It had never been sufficient to meet the demands of the Allied generals in France, whose repeated reinforcement of failure and purblind refusal to recognise their mistakes led to futile offensives and spiralling casualty rates. Dead and crippled volunteers had to be replaced by conscripts. By 1916, the British and dominion governments were forced to introduce compulsory service and all found themselves in political quagmires of varying viscosity. The measure got through in New Zealand in August 1916 despite protests from the Labour Party and pacifists, the same groups that resisted conscription in Britain. Opponents of conscription in New Zealand and in Australia included a large number of men and women with Irish blood and strong nationalist sympathies who had been angered by the suppression of the Easter Rebellion in Dublin the previous April. Irish hostility to Britain extended to its Empire and was one reason why the Australians voted against conscription in two referendums in October 1916 and December 1917.

In an ingenious attempt to push through conscription in Canada, Robert Borden had enfranchised all women with close relatives serving in the forces. With more men in the army, the odds against their husbands and sons being killed or wounded decreased, or so it was argued. The slogan 'Vote to save your kin' helped win a general election and gave Borden the authority to enforce the Military Service Act on 1 January 1918. The upshot was a nasty shock which exposed the depth of anti-imperial feeling among the two million French Canadians, less than half a per cent of whom had yet enlisted. Most lived in Quebec and, like many other minorities, their nationalism tended to be resentful and insular. Resistance to conscription triggered large-scale riots in Quebec at the end of March 1918 in which there were at least 150 casualties. Order was reimposed by 6,000 English-speaking troops.[16]

The burden of the imperial war effort raised other questions of identity and allegiance within the dominions. Billy Hughes, Australia's Prime Minister and a trenchant champion of 'white' Australia, deliberately excluded men 'not substantially of European origin or descent' from conscription.[17] In 1914 a black volunteer from Cape Breton (perhaps a descendant of the ex-slaves who had fled to Canada after the American War of Independence) looked forward to 'killing Germans'. His offer was dismissed with a brusque: 'This is not for you fellows, this is a white man's war.' He and many others hoped that military service would enhance the status of blacks in Canada. Japanese Canadians vainly hoped that by joining up they would get the vote.[18] Racial barriers were slowly lowered in Canada thanks to the unending pressure for more recruits.

In May 1916 Churchill told the Commons that black men were now vital for the war effort. The recruitment of blacks had to be increased so that they could release white troops for service in France. He suggested that the new black army be concentrated in Egypt to keep order there and defend the Suez Canal from another Turkish offensive. Citing history to back his case, he drew the House's attention to the negro soldiers who had fought for 'freedom' as part of the Union army in the American Civil War.[19]

Freedom was a strange word to use in this context; did it mean merely freedom from German rule, or something wider? It was used again in July 1917, when King George V delivered a rousing address to black South African labourers at Abbeville: 'You ... form part of my great Armies which are fighting for the liberty and freedom of my subjects of all races and creeds throughout my Empire.' He concluded with a picturesque flourish, describing the carrying of supplies to the troops in the trenches as 'hurling your spears at the enemy'.[20]

The King and Churchill sincerely believed that the non-white population of the Empire enjoyed a form of liberty that would vanish if Germany won the war. This freedom was negative rather than positive; Indians and blacks were not free to choose how, by whom and under what rules they were governed. Yet, in theory, they were free from injustice and maltreatment, and could live peaceful and prosperous lives so long as they obeyed laws that had been framed in their interest. The young Zulus at Abbeville and their counterparts on other fronts were fighting for a benevolent imperialism that took care of them. This was an arcane but valid definition of freedom which George V and Churchill invoked. Yet, it was inevitable that coloured peoples drawn into a war ostensibly to safeguard 'freedom' would interpret the word differently.

Official propaganda did strike a sympathetic chord among the King's humblest subjects across the Empire. There was a genuine affection for Britain among many black soldiers from British Honduras [Belize] who were serving in Egypt in 1918, although it was eroded by the racial arrogance of British soldiers.[21] The black soldier's wartime experience of racial contempt is hard to quantify, but it did exist and contributed to the growth of colonial nationalism after the war. 'The black man should have freedom and govern himself in the West Indies,' demanded a black sergeant during a meeting called in December 1918 to protest against the replacement of black NCOs with white in the 9th battalion of the West Indies regiment.[22] All West Indian troops were immediately disarmed and the mutiny appeared to vindicate alarmist officials who had predicted that the heads of black men would be turned if they were allowed to fight in a white man's war. A new mood was abroad. After violent brawls between white and black seamen competing for berths on merchantmen in Glasgow in 1919, one black sailor declared: 'We are not Bolsheviks ... but we want to enjoy the freedom which is the basis of Great Britain.' The local African Races Association pertinently commented that black soldiers had fought alongside white 'to defeat the enemies of and make secure the British Empire'.²³

Black men won the white man's war in Africa. The protracted campaign in East Africa required two or three porters for every fighting man and wastage rates from disease were high. In all, just under a million carriers were recruited, a third of whom came from conquered districts of German East Africa. Roughly two-thirds of adult males in Nyasaland served as askaris or porters in what the latter called the war of *Thangata*; that is, 'work without benefit'.²⁴ Labourers for the vast base camps and storage depots in Egypt and France were hired in China, Egypt and South Africa. France imposed conscription on its West African colonies to provide 135,000 factory workers who filled the places of Frenchmen in the trenches. As in 1870, the French deployed Algerian and Senegalese troops in the front line.

Imperial subjects who volunteered for or were corralled into a war of empires were bound to ask questions about reciprocity. How would their exertions and sacrifices be repaid? Gandhi, who had become the leader of the Indian National Congress in 1915, believed that his country's war effort would prove beyond any doubt its loyalty to the Empire. This deserved to be repaid by political concessions that would accelerate Indian participation in government and, ultimately, full independence. There was some sympathy for this view in the war cabinet, although it was tempered by a greater apprehension about the pace of change and its conclusion. The former viceroy Lord Curzon took the line that concessions to the Congress Party would lead to the replacement of an impartial Raj by 'a narrow oligarchy of clever lawyers'.

Arab nationalists in Tunisia and Algeria echoed their Indian counterparts. In 1919 they asked to be allowed to speak for themselves at the Versailles Conference. They argued that: 'The Algero-Tunisian people has abundantly poured out its blood in the war; it has contributed to the deliverance of the invaded lands of France and Belgium.'[25] France reneged on this debt.

Churchill was both impressed and gratified by the scale of the imperial war effort. The Empire had given Britain the wherewithal to win a global war, and shared stresses and perils had reinforced imperial unity. In December 1918, Churchill told members of the London New Zealand Club that: 'Now we have got together, we have got to go on together.'[26] Over the past years, dominion prime ministers had attended sessions of the extended war cabinet, but, with the exception of Smuts, they were treated as observers rather than participants. What they had to say was often eccentric: Borden suggested that all of Britain's gains in Asia, Africa and the Pacific should be delivered to the United States, while Smuts proposed international control over the whole of Africa.[27]

After the armistice, the dominion prime ministers expected that their countries' steadfastness and losses had earned them the right to be treated as mature nations capable of thinking and speaking for themselves. It was time to say goodbye to nanny. On the last day of 1918, a reluctant cabinet allowed each dominion and India to have separate representatives at the forthcoming peace conference, rather than letting Britain act as their mouthpiece.

The war had shaken the political foundations of the Empire. The damage was not serious, but it was enough to cause alarm. Millions of the Empire's subjects, having been moved around the world and exposed to new ideas and experiences, began to ask questions about their place in the order of things.

I *Love* this War:

The Dardanelles and Gallipoli, August 1914–May 1915

Churchill was one of the principal architects of the Dardanelles and Gallipoli campaigns and their most stalwart champion. They were criticised by contemporaries and subsequent historians as a sideshow which was mismanaged and wasteful of manpower. Churchill stoutly denied these charges, pointing out that some of his detractors were perfectly happy to squander lives in France and Belgium for no advantage. As to the value of twin offensives against Turkey, if they had achieved their objectives they would have delivered the Allies mastery over the Middle East, opened seaborne communications with Russia and, perhaps, persuaded Bulgaria and Greece to declare war against the Central Powers.

Before looking at Churchill's motives for urging the Dardanelles offensive and his part in its direction, it is useful to pause and briefly look at his personal approach to the conduct of war. It was rather like that of Mr Toad to motoring. War was an intoxicant that offered irresistible opportunities for excitement and Churchill maintained that he had an intuitive knack for high command. Just as Toad saw himself as a heaven-born driver, Churchill thought of himself as a heaven-born *generalissimo*. He confessed his infatuation with war to Margot Asquith at a dinner party in Walmer Castle on 15 January 1915: 'My God! This, this is living history. Everything we are doing and saying is thrilling – it will be read by a thousand generations, think of *that*!! Why I would not be out of this glorious, delicious war for anything the world can give me ...' She noticed how his eyes 'glowed' when he said 'delicious', and afterwards he checked himself by hoping that his choice of such a sensual adjective had not been improper. Not long after, Clementine told Margot that 'inventing uniforms' was one of her husband's 'chief pleasures'.[1]

Even more revealing were Churchill's reactions to the awesome spectacle of the summer exercises of the French, German and British armies between 1906 and 1910. After watching these mock battles between masses of infantry, cavalry and artillery, he wished that he could somehow obtain some 'practice' in the manoeuvring of large forces. Mastering this art would be child's play, for 'I have the root of the matter in me'.[2]

Early in October 1914, he grabbed the chance to test this latent talent. He left his desk at the Admiralty and took personal charge of the 8,000 men of the Royal Naval Division which held the perimeter defences of Antwerp. Churchill proved a vigorous and pugnacious commander in the mould of Evelyn Waugh's Ritchie Hooke, but his heavily outnumbered force was compelled to withdraw after six days. The Tories, still rancorous about Churchill's part in the Ulster crisis, alleged that Antwerp was further proof of his recklessness, but it had its supporters. His defence of the port had been approved by Kitchener (now Secretary for War) and was later praised by General Sir John French, the commander-in-chief of the BEF.

Churchill returned to the Admiralty, where he was again working in harness with Fisher, who had been reappointed as First Sea Lord. Churchill had urged the appointment for selfish reasons. 'I took him because I knew he was old and weak,' Churchill later confided to Violet Bonham Carter.[3] He was mistaken in his belief that Fisher would allow him absolute control of the navy; the seventy-four-year-old Crimea veteran still had his willpower and, at least for the moment, his wits. Admiral Sir David Beatty, the commander of the Grand Fleet's battlecruiser squadron, predicted clashes of temper and temperament between 'two very strong and clever men, one old, wily and of vast experience, and one young, self-assertive with a great self-satisfaction, but unstable'.[4]

There was certainly a conflict of timetables. Fisher arrived at his office before eight, took a thin lunch and was back home in bed by nine. Churchill reached his desk by late morning, enjoyed a substantial lunch, took an afternoon nap, worked on and then ended his day with ample dinners during which, fuelled by champagne and brandy, he expounded his views on the war and his vital part in its direction. Brandy and cigars accompanied him to bed, where he busied himself with official papers until the early hours. A few of his annotations in red crayon reflected either flights of fancy or flagging concentration. Others were abrupt and pertinent: 'How did this mistake arise?' he angrily noted on a report that the cruiser *Warrior* had steamed in the wrong direction after having been ordered from Malta to Gibraltar.[5]

HMS *Warrior* was one of many warships being deployed in a cause which Churchill believed was vital: the reassertion of the Royal Navy's global supremacy and the restoration of imperial prestige. Both had taken a battering during the first five months of the war. The German squadron based at Tsingtao had wrought havoc in the Pacific. It evaded a hastily assembled force of Allied warships, including Japanese battleships, and this had compelled Churchill to postpone the sailing of convoys of troopships from Australia and New Zealand. The cruiser *Emden* sailed around the Indian Ocean, shelled Penang and sank a Russian cruiser and eighteen merchantmen before it was crippled by HMAS *Sydney* on 9 November. The main German force under Admiral Graf von Spee crossed the Pacific, encountered and destroyed a weaker squadron commanded by Admiral Sir Christopher Cradock off Cape Coronel on 1 November.

Coronel had been a signal humiliation which had to be avenged as quickly as possible. Churchill placed prestige before domestic security and, ignoring protests from Jellicoe, he detached three battlecruisers from the Grand Fleet to seek out and destroy von Spee's squadron. Two were sent to the Falklands, where they defeated the Germans on 6 December. Churchill was cock-a-hoop, for his gamble with the battlecruisers had paid off. On 15 February 1915, Churchill triumphantly informed the Commons that Britannia was now unchallenged mistress of the world's oceans and that the Empire was therefore safe and imperial manpower could be concentrated wherever it was needed.

Protected by the Royal Navy, a million men from Britain, the dominions and India had been shipped to various fronts since the start of the war. A tight blockade was beginning the slow strangulation of Germany's maritime trade. The navy had also achieved another success, unmentioned by Churchill, which played a highly significant part in the eventual Allied victory. The blockade isolated the Central Powers from the money markets of America. Starved of credit, they funded their war efforts by raising loans from their populations and printing money; chronic inflation and social unrest were the long-term result.

Not all MPs rejoiced with Churchill. Jeremiahs lamented the losses of warships and merchantmen to U-boats and mines. These multiplied after 4 February, when Germany declared an unrestricted U-boat campaign in which commanders were free to sink any merchant ship or liner without warning. In April 1915, Beresford, still nursing his old resentment against Fisher, privately told Asquith that Britain merely had 'partial control of the sea', because the sea lanes were not protected from submarines.[6] There was some truth in this since Churchill and Fisher had become distracted from the dangers posed by U-boats and mines. Since the first week of January, their minds had been focused on a grand naval operation designed to force the Dardanelles and compel Turkey to surrender.

The naval battle for the Dardanelles and the subsequent amphibious landings on the Gallipoli peninsula have become implanted in the national consciousness of Britain, Australia and New Zealand. Myth has prevailed, particularly in Australia, and it has been cruel to Churchill's reputation. Long before the final Allied evacuation on the last day of 1915, the soldiers at the front were blaming him alone for their misfortunes. On 10 August Colonel Fred Lawson of the Buckinghamshire Hussars wrote in his diary: 'I should very much like to have Winston tied to a pier here every morning at 9 o'clock when shelling commences, and watch him from the seclusion of my dugout.'[7]

The literature of the campaign is abundant and informative on technical matters and the experiences of those engaged in it.[8] These narratives have tended to extract the campaign from its political context, although the political and geo-strategic reasons for the Dardanelles and Gallipoli campaigns had a profound effect on their genesis, dictated the nature of the operations and underpinned the War Council's determination to press ahead with them for so long and in the face of multiple reverses. They must be understood to make sense of what happened on the battlefield and why.

Britain would have preferred not to fight the Ottoman Empire in 1914. A biddable Turkey was the natural ally of the British Empire and for the past hundred years its Middle Eastern provinces had provided a vast buffer zone which protected India and, later, the Suez Canal. A strong Turkey was the key to regional stability, which was why Britain had been prepared to tolerate the pre-war modernisation of the Turkish army by German staff officers. Bringing Turkey's armed forces up to date was part of a wider programme of modernisation that was being undertaken by the Committee of Union and Progress [CUP] which had taken power after the Young Turk revolution of 1908.

The 'Young Turks' were a band of deeply patriotic army officers in their thirties with a common vision of their country as a modern, European-style secular state cemented by a racially exclusive Turkish nationalism. Enver Pasha, whose office was decorated with portraits of Frederick the Great and Napoleon, was the guiding force behind the CUP and he persuaded his fellow ministers that a reborn Turkey would need an alliance with Germany in order to fend off its neighbouring predators, Russia and the Balkan states. Some of his colleagues favoured a Turko-British alliance, which made sense since in 1912 Britain had agreed to build two dreadnoughts for the Ottoman navy in Tyneside yards. These ships would give Turkey mastery over the Black Sea and checkmate Russia's well-developed plans for a *coup de main* against Constantinople. Closer British ties with the Ottoman Empire would, however, generate friction with Russia and, to a lesser extent, France, both of which had historic territorial ambitions in the Near East.

Britain's ambivalence encouraged Enver and the Interior Minister Talât Pasha to press for an alliance with the Central Powers, and their case was formidable. An Allied victory would mean the dismemberment of the Ottoman Empire, whilst an Allied defeat would lead to the restoration of Egypt and lands forfeited during the recent Balkan Wars.

An untoward event allowed the pro-German faction in the CUP to play its hand. On 10 August 1914 the German battlecruiser *Goeben* and the cruiser *Breslau* hove to off Cape Helles, having evaded pursuing British warships. The German commander Admiral Souchon asked for a Turkish pilot to guide his ships through the minefields of the Dardanelles. This was granted by Enver and the two vessels anchored off Constantinople. Permission was refused for British warships to pass Cape Helles, but a gung-ho Churchill was ready to send destroyers into the Marmora and beyond to torpedo the German ships. What amounted to a declaration of war against Turkey was overruled by the War Council. The *Goeben* and *Breslau* were subsequently transferred to the Turkish navy, a gesture of calculated generosity which contrasted with Churchill's recent and arbitrary confiscation of two Turkish battleships that were nearing completion in Britain.

The escape of *Goeben* and *Breslau* had been a black mark for the navy. Incompetence and faltering had blighted efforts to intercept them, which was unsurprising since the commander-in-chief of the Mediterranean Fleet Admiral Milne had once declared: 'They pay me to be an Admiral; they don't pay me to think.'⁹ He was disgraced and Fisher wanted him shot, as Admiral Byng had been in the eighteenth century for a similar lack of initiative and guts.

Milne's blunders contributed to Turkey's declaration of war on 28 October. The prevailing mood in Constantinople was bullish and expressed itself in a daring and aggressive strategy designed to challenge the regional power of Russia and Britain. Two large-scale offensives were planned against Egypt (which Britain formally annexed on 1 November) and across Turkey's eastern frontier into what is now Armenia.

Conventional warfare was, however, supplemented by a campaign of subversion intended to destabilise the British, French and Russian Empires. This began in Constantinople on 14 November, when, in the presence of the Caliph-Sultan Mehmed V, the *Seyüislam* proclaimed a worldwide *jihad* against the Allies. The senior cleric of the Ottoman Empire recited how, over the past century, these three powers had slaughtered Muslims, stolen their freedom, grabbed their lands and raped 'thousands of Muslim virgins'. Muhammad's living successor the Caliph now called upon all Muslims to launch a massive counter-attack and overthrow their infidel conquerors. Those who died would become martyrs and attain paradise. *Fatwas* were issued on the same day giving spiritual support for conscription throughout the Ottoman Empire.

This holy war was a Turko-German masterstroke and its

significance has been insufficiently understood. There were 170 million Muslims in the British, Russian and French empires and all of them had become potential enemies, which was why the *jihad* was of supreme importance in the planning of operations in the Near and Middle East. Large-scale subversion of the enemy's population was a new weapon, although it would be used again in 1917, when the German High Command arranged Lenin's passage to Petrograd. Pan-Islamism had an incalculable power to hurt the Allies: they could expect a chain of popular insurrections, terrorism, mutinies of Muslim troops and an upsurge in disorder in traditionally unruly regions. All were pinpricks, but they would divert white soldiers needed on other fronts. Recent history favoured the *jihad*, for there was still a deeply rooted and vibrant tradition of Muslim antagonism to colonial rule in North Africa, Central Asia, the Sudan, Northern Nigeria, Somaliland and the North-West Frontier of India. There were plenty of potential recruits for the Sultan's holy war.

An understanding of the implications of the *jihad* is essential in making sense of the Dardanelles offensive and explaining why Churchill was so unyielding in his support for it. Today the concept of the *jihad* is all too familiar. Al-Qaeda's attacks on New York and Washington in 2001 and similar outrages before and after have demonstrated the *jihad*'s potential as an instrument of war and its magnetic spiritual appeal to sections of the Muslim world, in particular the young. Recent events have also revealed the extraordinary power of the mosque for transmitting propaganda. In 1914 such knowledge was restricted to a small number of officials and soldiers with first-hand experience of India, the Middle East and parts of Africa. Churchill was one.

During the 1897 Malakand campaign he had been horrified by the strength of what he dismissed as Muslim 'superstition and credulity' and its power over men's minds. *Jihadic* sermons preached by mullahs dissolved the oaths of loyalty of Muslim sepoys who deserted to join their brothers in the faith.[10] Kitchener shared Churchill's experience of fighting holy warriors inspired by Islamic fervour. Likewise, Fisher's service in Asia and the Near East had made him conscious of the fissile, unpredictable and ever-present power of Muslim fanaticism. Before the war, he had warned that 'when Islam holds up its little finger, it's damned uncomfortable for us in Egypt, Persia and India'.[11] Just how it would do so and with what consequences were two great unknowns at the end of 1914.

Three policies offered themselves to the War Council: the appeasement of Muslim opinion, resolution in the form of a spectacular counter-stroke that would prove that the imperial ascendancy was unshakeable, or a blend of the two. Aggressive defiance was the instinctive response of soldiers (including Churchill) and proconsuls, for whom it was a matter of orthodoxy that any affront to imperial authority had to be met head on and crushed by superior force. This was the essential philosophy behind the Dardanelles expedition and it provided a motive stronger than the conventional strategic and diplomatic objectives cited in textbook accounts of the campaign.

Nonetheless, there was a place for appeasement, as Churchill recognised. As First Lord, he did all in his power to accommodate Muslim opinion and sensibilities. During November (the month of the annual *haj* to Mecca) he ordered the commanders of warships in the Red Sea not to fire on Turkish vessels conveying pilgrims, banned attacks on dhows flying the Turkish flag and forbade the shelling of Jidda and other Red Sea ports.[12] He was furious when the *Minto*, a small man-o'-war belonging to the Indian government, sank a dhow and put in at Jidda, which he considered acts of provocation.[13]

In November 1914 it was virtually impossible for British intelligence services to quantify the effect of the *jihad*, or to predict how it would be activated and where. The worst-case scenario was dramatically described at the beginning of John Buchan's thriller *Greenmantle* (1917) in which the fictional intelligence chief Bullivant warns: 'There is a dry wind blowing through the East, and the parched grasses await the spark. And the wind is blowing towards India ...' Ignition would be provided by a messianic Muslim holy man (Greenmantle) and the conflagration would spread across the Middle East towards India. Buchan knew what he was talking about: he was close to official circles and would eventually be employed by the War Office overseeing official propaganda. India was the prime target of the *jihad*: it was home to 66 million Muslims and a third of the Indian army were Muslims. Turko-German *jihadic* propaganda leaflets distributed on the Western Front urged Muslim soldiers to place their faith before their allegiance to an infidel King Emperor.

Some did, early in 1915, when two Muslim regiments mutinied in Rangoon and Singapore. The latter was a bloody affair in which the mutineers slaughtered their officers and randomly murdered European civilians. Interrogation of captured mutineers disclosed that several had been influenced by *jihadic* sermons in local mosques. Retribution was ferocious, with the mass public execution of twenty-one insurgents. The Indian government was understandably nervous. Its counter-propaganda emphasised the pledges of loyalty made by the All India Muslim League and prominent Muslim princes, including the Aga Khan.[14] Nevertheless, the Viceroy Lord Hardinge thought that the only truly effective antidote to the *jihad* would be to keep hammering the Turks in Mesopotamia and occupy Baghdad. He used the same argument in support of the Dardanelles campaign: a spectacular victory over Turkey would demonstrate to the Islamic world the impregnability and permanence of imperial power.

Egypt and the Suez Canal were endangered by *jihadic* propaganda. Pan-Islamic agitators made common ground with Egyptian nationalists, who were smarting from the recent deposition of the Khedive Abbas Hilmi and the imposition of direct British rule. During November 1914 there were intelligence reports that the Khedive, then an exile in Constantinople, was intending to return at the head of a Turkish army and be welcomed by his former subjects who had risen against the British. There was also intelligence of Turko-German agents doling out gold to the Sanussi in Libya in return for promises of raids into Egypt.[15] Faced with a Turkish advance towards the Suez Canal coinciding with a local nationalist uprising and a partisan war on his western frontier, the local commander Sir John ('Conkie') Maxwell pleaded with the War Office for reinforcements.[16]

Big alarms were augmented by smaller ones from various outposts across the Middle East. On the borders of Aden, a Yemeni sheikh swore he would obey the Caliph and fight the British because they intended to 'efface Islam'.[17] His zeal was exceptional, for an intelligence summary of August 1915 indicated that his fellow Arabs preferred a prudent neutrality which they would abandon only when it became clear whether Britain or Germany was 'the most powerful party'.[18]

Others were equally hostile to both powers. In southern Persia, where the German agent Wilhelm Wassmuss was busy whipping up anti-British feelings among local tribes, an intelligence officer wryly noted that they were as happy fighting each other as they were harassing the Bushire [Busher] garrison.[19]

Muslim credulity proved limitless and was easily manipulated by clerics working in harness with Turko-German propagandists. Rumour was their stock-in-trade. Sepoys in France wrote home with tales of Enver leading an army to Afghanistan and of Algerian troops refusing to fight for France. Widespread credence was given to the bizarre claim that the Kaiser had converted to Islam and had made the *haj* incognito. In one version of this fable he had yet to make his pilgrimage, but when he did he would be accompanied by his harem![20] Photos of shattered French and Belgian churches were displayed in the German press bureau in Constantinople in the hope that they would please Muslims and, in Haifa, the German consul was alleged to have told Palestinians that English and French women would be distributed among them as fruits of victory.[21] Pan-Islamic propaganda was unsophisticated, but then so was its audience.

Was the Empire really in danger? There was no clear answer, but one thing was certain: the *jihad* was a direct challenge to its prestige. This abstraction was a constant preoccupation of Churchill, Kitchener and that small body of men who ruled the Empire from desks in Whitehall or residencies in the tropics. All believed that history and their own experience had given them an arcane insight into the Oriental psyche: it instinctively revered hard power, applied confidently and remorselessly. The diplomat Harold Nicolson later defined prestige as 'power based on reputation' and, in the imperial context and the historic memory of the Empire's subjects, the essence of British power was superior military strength and the resolve to use it. The Sultan had called the bluff of imperial omnipotence by declaring a holy war and had called on Muslims to throw aside habits of fear, obedience and loyalty.

Had it succeeded, the Dardanelles campaign would have more than justified itself as a massive demonstration of British power that would resonate throughout the Middle East and Asia. The Sultan, his *jihad* and the only independent Muslim state would be swept away by the sheer might of the British Empire. This was why, in the autumn of 1915, Lord Curzon, a former viceroy, warned the war cabinet that the evacuation of the Gallipoli peninsula would do incalculable harm to British standing in India, Afghanistan, Persia and the Arab world. Kitchener felt the same way, as did the veteran French colonial commander General Gallieni, who feared that a retreat from Gallipoli could lose France Algeria and Morocco.[22]

The Ottoman Empire also offered pickings for all the Allied powers, who moved swiftly to stake their claims. Russia was first, with a demand for Constantinople to which the British agreed on 9 November, and then informed the French. Théophile Delcassé, the French Foreign Minister, acquiesced and, in return, secured Russia's approval for French claims to Syria and Cilicia.[23] Churchill warmly approved the fulfilment of what he thought to be a legitimate and laudable Russian ambition. As a young man he had written that if he had been Russian rather than English, 'I would never rest till I saw a Russian eagle floating over St Sophia'.[24] His father had felt the same way, which distanced him from orthodox Tory foreign policy, which was to keep the Russians bottled up in the Black Sea. During the Gallipoli campaign, some Tories grumbled that British lives were being thrown away for Russia's advantage.

The War Council was undecided about what Britain might claim. On 3 March 1915, when the naval operations in the Dardanelles were just beginning, Admiral Sir Henry Jackson, Churchill's chief of staff at the Admiralty, made a series of tentative proposals based solely on strategic imperatives. He wanted permanent naval bases at Lemnos and Aqaba on the Red Sea, and suggested the occupation of Alexandretta, which would put Britain in a position to sever rail communications between Constantinople and Syria, Mesopotamia and Arabia.[25] He judged these to be a fair return for Britain's investment of blood and money.

At the same time, Asquith was mulling over the future of the Ottoman Empire without much enthusiasm. According to his daughter, Violet Bonham Carter, his 'instinct' was against engrossing any more territory, since Britain already had 'as much as we could manage'. Yet because Russia and France were 'too greedy', it would be wise to take 'a wedge somewhere in self defence', perhaps in Mesopotamia. This slip of the tongue indicated that the Prime Minister imagined that old imperial rivalries would reappear after the war. He was, therefore, perfectly willing to accept Kitchener's and Churchill's demands for Alexandretta on strategic grounds, although there were bound to be difficulties with the French.[26] These did not deter the Secretary for War or the First Lord of the Admiralty, who approved preparations for an amphibious attack on Alexandretta.[27] The Turko-German high command suspected such an assault was imminent, but that its target would be Smyrna [Izmir].[28]

Churchill was closely engaged in every stage of the preparation and implementation of the Dardanelles offensive. He saw himself as not only the begetter but the guiding spirit of the venture. 'It is the biggest coup I have ever played for,' he told his friend and fellow enthusiast Captain Roger Keyes. Churchill set the pace of the campaign, vehemently pressing for it in the War Council and, once it was under way, injecting ginger into faint-hearted admirals.[29]

Throughout the planning and early phases of the offensive, Churchill acted as if he was in total and sole charge of the operations, leading from afar a great fleet and a great army engaged in a great enterprise that would change the course of history. He aired his private reveries to his guests after dinner at the Admiralty on 23 February. He was wearing 'dark green plush', presumably a smoking jacket, and was recovering from a bad cold, which had not depressed his spirits. Destiny beckoned, and he was 'thrilled at the prospect of the military expedition'. 'When the teeth of the situation had been drawn by the ships', then the army would march into Constantinople. Listeners might have wondered whether Churchill was dreaming of leading them in person, and in all likelihood they would have been right. He concluded: 'I think a curse should rest on me – because I *love* this war – I know it's shattering and smashing the lives of thousands and yet – I can't help it – I enjoy every second of it.'[30] Rupert Brooke was also touched by the romance and glamour of being part of the fall of Constantinople.[31]

Since the beginning of the war Churchill had been impatiently waiting an opportunity for a classic use of British seapower, and for several months he and Fisher had been peddling plans for a seaborne assault on either the German or Turkish coastlines. A proposal made in September 1914 for seizing the Gallipoli peninsula was squashed by the War Office on grounds of impracticability, the numbers of troops needed and the impossibility of obtaining the necessary surprise.[32] Undeterred, Churchill continued to ride what had become his hobby horse. He won support from Kitchener on the strategic grounds that an attack on Dardanelles would compel Turkey to withdraw men from the army that was being mustered for an offensive against the Suez Canal. On 2 January 1915, Russia added its weight to these demands with a request for a diversionary attack on the Dardanelles to relieve pressure on the Armenian front, where its forces were doing badly. They recovered within a month and inflicted a major defeat on the Turks at Erzurum.

Russia's plea for help was a godsend for Churchill. It gave him the chance not only to sell the idea of the campaign to his colleagues, but to instigate a plan of action. Throughout its genesis, there was what turned out to be a fatal uncertainty as to whether the fleet would rush through the straits like charging cavalry, or would proceed more slowly, destroying the shore batteries piecemeal with the army securing the northern shore of the Gallipoli peninsula. The latter plan was chosen. If this strategy worked, the Allies would gain 'a victory such as the war has not seen' that would overthrow 'a hostile empire' and mould the future 'destinies of nations', Churchill told his Dundee constituents on 15 March.

The campaign that followed has been outlined elsewhere and is beyond the scope of this book. So too is the political and military wrangling and buck-passing which led to the decision to evacuate the Gallipoli peninsula at the very end of 1915. Some points do, however, deserve attention here because of their influence on Churchill's future political career and, in particular, his attitude to strategic planning and the day-to-day conduct of operations during the Second World War.

It is important to remember that the Turko-German high command never shared the views of Churchill's critics. At the onset of the naval attack Turkish and German officers knew that, once Allied warships had broken through to the Sea of Marmora, Turkey would have to ask for an armistice.[33] Turkish naval officers expected a breakthrough, given the numbers of warships deployed by the Allies.[34]

These opinions delivered after the war to British naval intelligence officers strongly suggest that Churchill had been right to keep nagging local commanders about their inertia and hesitancy. Bad luck added to the problems, for Admiral Sir Sackville Carden (who had caught gyppy tummy after an overhelping of plum duff) was replaced on 16 March by Admiral Sir John de Robeck, an affable, stubborn mediocrity with brittle nerves. They snapped two days later after Turkish mines had sunk four pre-dreadnoughts. His chief of staff, Keyes, believed from that moment de Robeck 'ceased to exist' as 'a fighting admiral', and that Churchill was right to 'curse' him for what was tantamount to cowardice.[35]

Churchill castigated de Robeck, arguing that he still had sufficient warships for a fresh attack. He refused and settled down to wait for the arrival of the army. 'Much as one may like to obtain one's own glorification I prefer to go on my considered opinion and not be hurried,' he wrote.[36] No wonder Admiral Guido von Usedom, the German naval attaché, was astonished when de Robeck cancelled the offensive: 'The whole affair gave the impression of groping round without a plan' and gave rise to the belief 'that the enemy ... had been frustrated'.[37]

Unlike de Robeck, the Turko-German high command, including Mustafa Kemal Pasha (later Kemal Atatürk) chose not to loiter. They used the breathing space provided by de Robeck to continue to strengthen Turkish positions on the high ground above and beyond the beaches where Allied forces would eventually land. When they finally came ashore on 25 April, the Turks were well dug in. Within days the Allies were faced with a stalemate like that on the Western Front.

Here too the Allies were making no progress. Sir John French's spring offensive was an utter disaster on a scale beyond that of Gallipoli. There were losses of 50,000 without what a subsequent War Office analysis called 'compensatory gains'.[38] Morale in the War Council wilted and the knives were out for Churchill, whose passion and impulsiveness were grating on his colleagues. The Tory press weighed in on a politician who had long been the party's bane. H. A. ('Taffy') Gwynne, editor of the ultra-right-wing *Morning Post*, wrote privately to Asquith accusing Churchill of applying to the Dardanelles 'the same lack of study, the same desire to rush in without due preparation' that had been evident at Antwerp.[39]

Fisher was the first to jump ship; on 13 May he resigned in a tantrum that may have been a symptom of a general nervous collapse. He declared that he had always opposed the Dardanelles campaign, which was unwinnable and seriously weakened home defence by taking battleships away from the Grand Fleet. A cabinet crisis followed that was resolved by admitting the Conservatives to a coalition under Asquith. There was no room for Churchill, who was replaced by Balfour. 'I'm finished,' Churchill told Violet Bonham Carter. He was then a guest of the Asquiths and she noticed how he stood alone at the edge of a lawn overlooking a river bank, looking 'like Napoleon on St Helena'.[40]

Churchill's career had suffered a severe setback. The strategic decision to invade Turkey had been taken by the War Council (including Fisher) with French approval, but his relentless determination to achieve victory at all costs meant that he was an obvious scapegoat. He struck back forcefully, arguing that the offensive had been 'a legitimate war gamble' that could have succeeded if the necessary 'speed and vigour' had been applied at the right time. Churchill insisted that 'Energy and resolution' were all that were needed to fracture the Turkish defences on a front that was just ten miles wide.[41] They were absent, he claimed in *The World Crisis*, because 'military etiquette and military sensibilities' were inimical to 'flexibility and dynamism'.

The Dardanelles, coupled with Churchill's later experience on the Western Front during 1915 and 1916, gave him reason to mistrust the brains and backbone of professional soldiers and sailors. His misgivings were shared by Clement Attlee, the future Labour MP and Prime Minister, who had fought at Gallipoli and believed that in principle Churchill had been right. In 1965 he told a reunion of veterans that they had been engaged in 'an immortal gamble that did not come off ... Sir Winston had the one strategic idea of the war. He did not believe in throwing away masses of people to be sacrificed.'[42]

Gallipoli was a turning point in the history of the British Empire, although largely unnoticed at the time. A campaign undertaken to affirm imperial invincibility had been a humiliation; in 1916 the Ottoman government issued a postage stamp which showed the crescent of Islam imposed on the Dardanelles. Turkey had ended the hundred-year sequence of Muslim defeats at the hands of Britain, France and Russia. British prestige had suffered and would suffer again in April 1916, when Nurattin Pasha's counter-offensive in Mesopotamia ended with the siege of Kut-el-Almara, where 9,000 British and Indian troops surrendered.

They were abominably treated by the Turks, and a few survivors witnessed Turkish massacres of Armenians in 1918.[43] These had begun early in 1915, when the Russian invasion of eastern Turkey persuaded the CUP to destroy what it imagined was 'the enemy within'. In June, when the Russian threat had subsided but the Allies were fighting their way up the Gallipoli peninsula, Talât Pasha told a German naval officer that 'the Armenians are being more or less eliminated. That is hard but useful.' Turkey, he added, would be a better ally without internal enemies and it could safely 'cleanse' itself without fear of foreign intervention. At least 800,000 Armenians were murdered, some in specially built death camps.[44] To this day the Turkish government and Turkophile Western historians stridently deny the culpability of the Ottoman authorities.

By a strange paradox, the Armenian genocide had unexpected repercussions within the Ottoman Empire which turned out to be to Britain's short-term advantage and helped to recover imperial prestige. Devout Muslims had been horrified by the treatment of Armenian Christians, which seemed to confirm the impiety of the CUP (it had sanctioned the translation of the Quran from Arabic to Turkish) and its godless secularism. This sense of revulsion added to a wider Arab discontent and made it easier for Britain to secure a political victory that helped offset the loss of face after Gallipoli. During 1916 an alliance was agreed between Britain and France and Sharif Husain of Mecca, ruler of the Arabian province of Hijaz, who, like Mehmed V, claimed a pedigree which stretched back to Muhammad. Husain's endorsement of the Allies weakened the spiritual authority of the *jihad*. The political result was the Arab Revolt, which attracted both Muslims hostile to the regime in Constantinople and Pan-Arab nationalists whose aim was to create independent states in Arabia and Syria.

A pact of mutual convenience between Arabs who wanted to break away from the Ottoman Empire and the two powers who hoped to enlarge their own empires at Ottoman expense was riddled with contradictions. They broke surface violently after 1918 and were a headache for Churchill as Minister of War and Colonial Secretary. Pan-Islamic agitation continued during the war and became more menacing after 1918, when it merged with two other forms of populist anti-imperialism, nationalism and Bolshevism.

The Dardanelles had other imperial repercussions. The landings at Ari Burnu on 25 April and at Suvla Bay on 7 August have a hallowed place in the history and national consciousness of Australia and New Zealand. On both occasions, Australia and New Zealand Army Corps [ANZAC] troops fought alongside British and French forces and their courage and sacrifice were hailed by imperialists at home and in the dominions as proof of the bonds which held the Empire together. A month after Suvla Bay, the imperialist journal *The Round Table* echoed sentiments in Britain and Australia when it proclaimed that Australia 'is beginning to realise that she is fighting not only for the ideals common in the British Empire, but for her very life'. This was why young Australians were ready to die in Turkey.[45]

William Massey, the New Zealand Prime Minister, ordered all public employees to take half a day off work for a mass 'patriotic demonstration' after hearing news of the first ANZAC landing.[46] Two thousand three hundred Aussies and Kiwis were killed and ANZAC Day [25 April] remains a day of national celebration and mourning in Australia and New Zealand. Today, the places where ANZAC troops disembarked have become semi-sanctified, rather like Gettysburg, and are shrines for obligatory pilgrimages by young New Zealanders and Australians on world tours. Visiting sites that have been designated the 'Waterloo of Australasia' has become a tryst with a defining moment in national history and legend.[47]

Integral to the Gallipoli legend was the casting of Australian soldiers as victims. British generals were careless with the lives of young, ardent and brave Australians (they were equally cavalier with British and French lives) and what the official Australian war history called Churchill's 'excess of imagination, a layman's ignorance of artillery, and the fatal power of a young enthusiast to convince older and slower brains'.[48] Blaming Churchill was one strand in a conspiracy theory which insinuated that Australian patriotism had somehow been squandered or even betrayed.

Gallipoli certainly became part of Australia's self-image and was inviolate. Mild criticisms of the performance of Australian troops in the British official history of the campaign were deleted at the insistence of the Australian government in 1927. A reference to Australian stragglers and shirkers on landing beaches provoked the headline 'The Vilest Libel of the War' in the Sydney *Daily Guardian*.[49]

Pride and undercurrents of resentment mingled in the historical legacy of Gallipoli and they contributed to the strained and often acerbic relations between Churchill and Australia during 1941 and 1942. Sour memories of Gallipoli tinged the comments made in March 1941 by the General Officer Commanding the Australian Imperial Force in the Middle East, Lieutenant-General Sir Thomas Blamey. 'The fighting is the function of the Dominion troops,' he told the Australian Prime Minister, Robert Menzies, while British troops manned the lines of communication. He added:

Past experience has taught me to look with misgiving on a situation where British leaders have control of considerable bodies of first class Dominion troops while dominion commanders are excluded from all responsibility in control, planning and policy.

Menzies concurred and successfully urged Blamey's promotion which, he believed, would give great 'satisfaction' to the people of Australia, for it was 'a guarantee that our leader will have an effective voice at the right time'.[50] As everyone knew, no one had spoken up for the Aussies at Gallipoli and prevented their lives from being wasted by British ministers and dud generals.

Churchill's reputation had been badly bruised by his part in the Dardanelles and Gallipoli campaigns, which seemed to corroborate the old picture of him as a quixotic chancer who always wanted his own way and whose judgement was skewed. He was relegated to the Liberal backbenches after an interlude commanding a battalion on the Western Front. In July 1917 Lloyd George invited him to become Minister of Munitions, a post with abundant scope for his dynamic energy and administrative diligence, but which excluded him from the inner cabinet where strategic decisions were made.

This was frustrating for Churchill, and after the war he vented his feelings in *The World Crisis* where his judgements on the High Command had to be watered down by General Sir James Edmonds, the chief official war historian. Nonetheless, what escaped Edmonds's blue pencil picqued the brass hats. The Army Council grumpily commented that he had created 'the misleading impression of unthinking stupidity in the British higher command conveyed by picturesque phrases'.[51] Churchill's judgements have been supported by later historians and his own faith in his natural aptitude for grand strategy remained unshaken.

A Welter of Anarchy:

Churchill, the Empire and the Bolsheviks, 1919–1922

The precipitate collapse of the Austro-Hungarian, Bulgarian and Turkish war efforts in October and the first week of November 1918 took everyone by surprise. Five months before, Lloyd George's inner cabinet had been anxiously wondering how enough men could be found to defend the Western Front against German offensives during the following year. American manpower was now forthcoming, but not, ministers thought, in sufficient numbers to tilt the balance decisively. No one had yet foreseen that the Royal Navy's blockade of Germany was about to yield immense dividends: food shortages and inflation were worsening and, by October, public order began to dissolve with riots, strikes and a naval mutiny. The Kaiser's ministers faced two alternatives: a civil war or a truce.

It was one of the supreme ironies of the war that Germany's political and economic disintegration and the armistice signed on 11 November occurred at the time it was consolidating its grip on its new empire in Eastern and Western Europe. The chief condition of this armistice and that imposed on Turkey a week before was the withdrawal of all their forces from occupied territories. At a stroke each power was deprived of chips to cash in at the peace conference. The Turkish, German, Ottoman and Austro-Hungarian empires had been swept away by the war, and it seemed likely that the Russian would follow.

It was against this background that Churchill returned to the centre of the political stage. In January 1919 Lloyd George appointed him Secretary of State for War with ministerial responsibility for the Royal Air Force. For the next three years he worked on securing the peace, a task that turned out to be as slow and painful as winning the war had been. He knew what lay ahead, for, soon after taking office, he warned his Dundee constituents that 'Europe and a greater part of Asia were in a welter of anarchy'. Total war had left behind all kinds of detritus that had to be cleared away. Order had to be reimposed, economies repaired, debts repaid, peace treaties negotiated and conquered lands shared out among the victors. Defeated powers had to be taught a lesson, infant nations nursed and the Empire protected from a new species of enemy.

There was an abundance of wars to satisfy Churchill's penchant for deskbound generalship, for the restoration of a dislocated world produced a crop of conflicts. Between November 1918 and the end of 1921, the British army fought the Empire's foes in Russia, Ireland, the Middle and Near East and the North-West Frontier. French troops and tanks fought Arabs in Syria and Turkish armies fought Greek for chunks of Asia Minor. In Eastern Europe, Germans, Poles, Finns, Estonians and Lithuanians fought against Russian Bolsheviks, and Hungarians fought each other. The war to end all wars had been parent to a further four years of bloodshed.

Above all, and none of the Allied leaders who attended the Versailles Conference in January 1919 was sure how this could be accomplished, Bolshevism had to be confined within Russia, or, better still, snuffed out. For the next few months it seemed possible that the chilling events in Petrograd in October 1917 were about to be repeated in cities across Europe, the United States and Canada. The 'Red Scare' of 1919 was not a spasm of collective hysteria, rather it was a reasonable response to claims of the rulers of Soviet Russia who were predicting the impending overthrow of capitalism everywhere. Grigori Zinoviev, the head of Comintern (Communist International), boasted that the world revolution would be complete by the end of the year. He was wrong: the workers were crushed wherever they rose in arms and the police forces and intelligence agencies of the capitalist nations had no difficulties in ferreting out conspiracies and conspirators. Those with something to lose breathed again, but, as Churchill warned, respite was only temporary, for Soviet Russia remained a 'formidable and menacing' threat to stability everywhere.

High on the list of targets for Russian-inspired and -directed sedition was the British Empire. Superficially, it appeared robust and it was about to get a hefty share of the post-war spoils. Britain secured German East Africa, which was renamed Tanganyika, bits of

Togoland and a slice of the Cameroons in West Africa, Palestine and
Iraq. Australia and New Zealand swept up various Pacific islands,
and South Africa took over South-West Africa. Under unwelcome
pressure from President Woodrow Wilson, the new proprietors
of these regions held them under a mandate from the League of
Nations, which set standards of humane government and obliged the
mandate powers to initiate welfare and economic programmes for the
benefit of their new subjects. Seen from below, the new regimes were
indistinguishable from old-style colonial administrations.

New forces were, however, coming into play which questioned
the moral and political foundations for imperial overlordship. A
growing number of the mostly better-educated subjects of the British
Empire were showing often fissile dissatisfaction with their place in
the imperial order. Many had participated in a war for 'freedom' and
'justice', the words that had appeared on the condolence slips sent in
the name of George V to the families of men and women killed in
battle. The survivors had been given a medal inscribed 'The Great War
for Civilisation'. This was how Churchill had depicted the conflict,
but neither he nor the rest of Lloyd George's coalition cabinet had a
clear idea as to how these abstractions could be put into practice, or
whether it was desirable to do so.

One blueprint for a post-war global dispensation had been provided
by President Wilson's Fourteen Points. These rested on the assumption
that everyone in the world had a right to be part of a sovereign nation
state under a government of their choice. Self-government was the
key to universal human happiness and it was the duty of the Allies
to bring this about. Nothing was further from the minds of Lloyd
George, Clemenceau and Italy's Prime Minister Vittorio Orlando, all
of whom were haggling over the division of the empires of the Central
Powers. The prevalent view in the Foreign and Colonial Offices was
that the sanctimonious Wilson was meddling in matters that were
none of his concern and about which he knew nothing.

The trouble was that Wilson's Fourteen Points had been widely
disseminated by Allied propaganda agencies during the last months of
the war in an attempt to show that the Allies were on the side of liberty
and justice. War aims were taken as binding pledges by nationalists,
who suddenly found themselves equipped with a ready-made and,

they imagined, irrefutable ideology with which to challenge their masters. British officials were often flabbergasted by what seemed to be either impertinence or naivety. In 1918 General Sir Lionel Dunsterville, a veteran of the North-West Frontier, encountered the Persian nationalist leader Mirza Kuchuk Khan, whom he dismissed as an 'honest, well-meaning idealist' with a headful of dangerous thoughts. 'His programme', the general noted, 'includes all the wearisome platitudes that ring the changes on the will-'o-wisp ideals of liberty, equality and fraternity, "Persia for the Persians" and "Away with the Foreigners" are the obvious items.'[1] Persians of a like mind pinned their hopes on President Wilson and asked for their country to be represented at Versailles. This request was overruled at the insistence of Britain, which naturally objected to any international discussion of its paramountcy in Persia.[2]

Wilsonian doctrines were invoked in May 1919 by Sheikh Mahmud Barzinji, a Kurdish nationalist and self-styled 'King of Kurdistan', who told a British political officer that they gave his people the right to establish an independent nation rather than be corralled into the British-sponsored and predominantly Arab polity of Iraq. In May 1919, the embryonic Kurdish state was overturned by the troops and armoured cars of Sir Arnold Wilson, the civil administrator of Iraq. He was one of nature's authoritarians (he later joined Sir Oswald Mosley's blackshirts) and there were plenty of officials of his stamp scattered across the Empire whose instinctive reaction to any form of insubordination was to crack the whip and, if that did not do the trick, apply it vigorously. Their blinkered outlook and astringency often made matters worse and were an irritation for Churchill.

Churchill differed from the hardliners in that he saw the Empire as an evolving organism, which had to accommodate change in order to survive, but always under terms dictated by Britain. He accepted that Egypt and Ireland ought to receive a degree of autonomy so long as it never encompassed separation from the Empire.[3] Other politicians and administrators were less pliant and believed that Wilsonian principles were inimical to the idea of empire. The cabinet secretary Sir Maurice Hankey thought that the Fourteen Points 'struck at the roots of the British Empire all over the world'.[4] The former High Commissioner in Cairo, Sir Henry McMahon, told Milner that the anti-British insurrection in Egypt in March 1919 had been the direct result of the Wilsonian notion of 'self determination'.[5] Two years later a committee of staff officers and Foreign and Colonial Office mandarins concluded that 'the ideals of self determination ... and especially the declarations of President Wilson' had contributed substantially to the prevailing unrest throughout the Empire.[6]

The American president was a hero to anti-imperialists. An intelligence report on a plot to assassinate Lloyd George, Clemenceau and Wilson hatched in Switzerland in March 1919 included a revealing appeal by one of the conspirators, Satindra Das Gupta, an Indian Communist. He pleaded for the President to be spared, for 'Wilson is a nice man' who was being tricked by the enemies of 'the real liberty of the world'.[7]

This detail would have surely caught the eye of Churchill, who had always been and would remain an assiduous reader of all intelligence material, in particular decrypts of intercepted telegrams and wireless signals. Like Wellington, Churchill appreciated the immense strategic (and diplomatic) value of knowing what was happening, or about to happen on the 'other side of the hill'. An Indian Bolshevik's complicity in a plot to murder the Allied leaders must have confirmed what Churchill greatly feared: the malevolence, cunning and ruthlessness of Russia's rulers.

Lenin, Trotsky and Georgii Chicherin, the commissar for foreign affairs, sought the destruction of the British Empire and had said so frequently since the early days of the revolution. In December 1918, Lenin had called upon all the subjects of the world's empires to topple their rulers as part of the universal revolution. Two years later, and after British forces had waged war against the revolution and the British Treasury had bankrolled just about every counter-revolutionary warlord, Lenin declared: 'England is our greatest enemy. It is in India that we must strike them hardest.'[8]

A decrypt of an intercepted message sent in May 1920 from Chicherin to Leonid Krassin, head of the Russian trade mission in London, ordered him to take an unyielding line in negotiations since Britain was on the ropes. 'The situation in the East is a difficult one for England. In Persia they are almost helpless in the face of the revolution.

Disloyalty is increasing among Indian troops.' Fourteen months later, delegates to the Moscow Comintern conference learned that the world revolution was on course and making good headway. As ever, the British Empire was 'the most dangerous enemy to Soviet Russia and to the Third International', but it was vulnerable to subversion from within, for, as Chicherin predicted, 'no power can stop nationalism and Russia will exploit it'.[9] The struggle was going Russia's way, or so its propagandists claimed. In August 1921 the Tashkent edition of *Isvestia* reported that: 'The colonies are in a ferment. The peasants of Morocco, Algeria and India are in revolt.'[10] All anti-imperialists, whatever their political complexion, were the natural allies of Soviet Russia, which was willing to be their patron, paymaster and, wherever possible, their armourer.

Indian Muslims distressed by British backing for the dismemberment of the last, independent Muslim state, Turkey, were ripe for Soviet subversion. They detected an anti-Islamic bias throughout the negotiations at Versailles and were enraged when it became clear that Britain intended to abolish the caliphate.[11] These policies were pressed by the Turkophobe Lloyd George, whose indifference to Muslim opinion exasperated Churchill, and Edwin Montagu, the Secretary of State for India.[12]

Before and during the Third Afghan War of May 1919, Russia promised soldiers and arms to the Afghan government in its *jihad* against the British Raj, spread rumours that Britain planned to annex Afghanistan and claimed that its ruler, the Amir Amanullah, shared Lenin's faith in 'the principle of equality of all men and the peaceful union of all other nations'.[13] After the RAF bombed Kabul, local intelligence picked up a rumour that Russia was about to supply the Afghans with aircraft.[14] None appeared; all that the Afghans got were cheers of encouragement and sheaves of propaganda which reassured them that they were supported by their Muslim brothers in India and Egypt, many of whom were already fighting the British.[15]

Persian demands for an end to their country's subservience to Britain also attracted Soviet support. During the first half of 1920 military intelligence uncovered evidence of terrorists and agents flooding across the Persian border, spreading anti-British propaganda and forming revolutionary cells in Tehran. A renewed ideological offensive was reported at the end of the year, which was 'no longer carried by crude Bolshevik agents' but by 'Shia co-religionists of the Mohammedan malcontents in India who will have been poisoned by Bolshevik doctrines'.[16]

Moscow's propagandists magnified the power and persuasiveness of their campaign and its audience soon discovered that words were rarely, if ever, backed by practical assistance. Churchill took the Russians at their word and was convinced that they were waging a deadly clandestine war against the British Empire which involved the hijacking of indigenous nationalism and the harnessing of Muslim grievances. Lord Curzon, the Foreign Secretary, studied the intelligence reports and agreed. 'The Russian menace in the East', he warned the cabinet, 'is incomparably greater than anything else that has happened at any time to the British Empire.' Edwin Montagu, the Secretary of State for India, suspected Gandhi's passive resistance campaign of being manipulated by yet-to-be unmasked 'international revolutionaries'.[17] In March 1921 he informed the Commons that special intelligence units had been established in India to track down Bolshevik agents. One Tory MP piped up that Gandhi was plainly a Russian agitator who should immediately be gaoled.[18]

A shadowy and infinitely resourceful enemy made an ideal scapegoat. The waves of disorder that were sweeping through the Middle East and India were no fault of those who ran the Empire, but were rather the consequence of a conspiracy orchestrated in Moscow and undertaken by professional agitators. Gandhi and the Egyptian nationalist leader Sa'd Zaghul were simple souls who had been gulled by Russia, and their followers were either giddy students or criminals ready to profit from any breakdown in civil order.

Churchill proceeded on this premise. During 1919 and 1920, military intelligence reports provided him with ample evidence of Moscow's masterplan. Twenty Bolshevik agitators were uncovered in Constantinople and a Bolshevik propagandist ('a one-eyed man wearing a Bokharan costume') had been detected making his way to Kabul. The campaign of subversion was most intense in Persia, where guns were being smuggled across the border from Russia and where the Soviet legation was spreading details of social unrest in Britain. A defector revealed that his masters were willing to pay between six and ten pounds a month to Persian agitators and spies.[19] These and many other worrying revelations were proof of a systematic and sustained ideological war against the Empire.

Churchill ordered his subordinates to be watchful. After hearing that the newly formed Jewish Socialist Workers Party had been involved in the Jaffa riots in May 1921, Churchill instructed Sir Herbert Samuel, the administrator of Palestine, to determine how many recent Jewish immigrants from Russia were Bolsheviks. On hearing that the number was less than two hundred, he demanded their deportation. Interestingly, the culprits had been trying to seek Arab converts for a common, anti-British front.[20]

Many of these secret reports have only been released over the past thirty years and they have placed a fresh perspective on Churchill's policies towards Russia and his animus towards Bolshevism. His beloved Empire was facing a peril as great as, if not greater than, it had in 1914. 'After having defeated all the tigers and the lions I don't like being beaten by baboons,' Churchill told General Sir Henry Wilson, the Chief of Imperial General Staff, in April 1919 – 'baboons' being his favourite term for the Bolsheviks.[21]

Dissidents in India, the Near and Middle East were certainly aware of the power of the Russian bogey to panic the British into making compromises. London and Delhi's Bolshevik neuroses were cynically manipulated by the Amir of Afghanistan during peace negotiations in June 1919. He warned the Viceroy, Lord Chelmsford, that unless he was granted generous terms his country would succumb to Bolshevism. In April 1920, the newly elected Turkish national assembly in Ankara wired Moscow with the message that 'we agree to cooperate with the Russian Bolsheviks in their efforts to save the oppressed from imperialist governments'. Mirza Kuchuk Khan, whose views on Persian liberation had incensed General Dunsterville, was, in June 1920, calling himself the leader of the ominously named 'Revolutionary Committee of Persia' and boasting that he was the 'ally' of Russia. A petition delivered to Churchill during his tour of Palestine in March 1921 reminded him that 'Russia when it wakes up will have a word to say' about the injustice of Jewish settlements on Arab land.[22]

Such statements seemed to give substance to Churchill's darkest forebodings and stiffened his resolve to fight back. His reactions were exaggerated, for 'the baboons' made more noise than mischief. They did so in countries which had no socialist traditions and lacked a self-conscious industrial working class; the prerequisites for a Communist revolution in say Russia or Germany were absent in Egypt and India. As one Indian Communist complained in 1924, it was a nearly impossible task to create 'a class conscious proletariat' from widely scattered and illiterate peasants and workers who were 'under the surveillance of the police and the masters everywhere'.[23]

Churchill and his allies had been misled by an accidental conjuncture of post-war events. An intense barrage of Soviet propaganda had coincided with a sequence of anti-British protests and insurgency in northern India, Persia and Egypt and the half-hearted invasion of India by Afghanistan. All these activities were primarily concerned with squeezing local concessions from Britain. Afghani and Indian Muslims hoped to preserve the integrity of Turkey and the caliphate; Gandhi's Indian National Congress wanted the acceleration of measures for representative government and independence; and Egyptians wished to terminate Britain's protectorate over their country. Likewise, Persians wanted to tear up an unequal treaty imposed on their Shah by Britain in August 1919, despite its rejection by their Majlis [parliament]. None of these nationalist movements looked to Marxist-Leninism either for guidance, or as a model for their countries' future. Nevertheless, Churchill confidently asserted that the Bolsheviks were pulling the strings, once alleging that if Egypt was granted independence it might easily become Communist.[24]

Carry on like Britons:
Churchill's Russian War, 1919–1921

I n 1949, when the Cold War was gathering pace, Churchill looked
back on Britain's intervention in the Russian civil war and declared
that 'the strangling of Bolshevism at its birth would have been an
untold blessing'.[1] Between 1919 and 1921, he had been an inflexible
and, sometimes, almost hysterical supporter of a political infan-
ticide, which, he believed, would save civilisation from being overwhelmed by a barbarous ideology. His rhetoric reflected his fear and
fury: Russia had passed into a grisly limbo under 'a tyranny no Czar
could ever equal', a new 'Dark Ages' was approaching and 'Bolsheviks
hop and caper like troops of baboons amid the ruins of cities and the
corpses of their victims'. Churchill vowed to end their capering and,
simultaneously, stem the flow of virulent anti-imperial propaganda
which flowed from Moscow.

When he arrived at the War Office, Churchill found himself
in charge of what, superficially, seemed to be formidable armies
deployed on the periphery of Russia. In January 1919 there were
180,000 Allied troops in Russia, including 40,000 Czechs and about
400,000 counter-revolutionary (White) forces whom the Allies were
equipping with modern artillery, tanks and aircraft. There were also
growing contingents of Finns, Estonians, Latvians, Lithuanians,
Poles and Ukrainians for whom the collapse of the Czarist state had
provided a welcome opportunity to secure independence. Added
to these were various ethnic and religious groups in the Caucasus
and Central Asia who had hitherto been spectators to the upheavals
within Russia, but now wanted to manipulate them to break away
from Moscow's control.

All that was needed was an omnipotent political will to unite
these anti-Bolshevik forces and a coordinated strategy. Churchill
offered both in what he considered was an opportunity to dictate the
course of world history. For the next eighteen months, he stretched

his formidable assertive powers to their limit, cajoling and hectoring colleagues to support what quickly became his war. When one strategy foundered, he conjured up a replacement. His optimism in the face of multiple setbacks was breathtaking and, his opponents argued, a symptom of a deeply cracked judgement. The public was puzzled and sceptical; there was talk of 'Mr Churchill's Private War' and Beaverbrook's megaphone the *Daily Express* declared that Russia was not worth 'the bones of a single British grenadier'. The Labour *Daily Herald* denounced a war against the workers' state engineered by the 'Gambler of Gallipoli', which was to be expected from a paper kept afloat by Russian subsidies and whose foreign editor, William Ewer, was a Russian spy.

The mood of British forces in Russia was a blend of ennui, puzzlement and bitterness. 'We have been messed about like a flock of sheep,' complained men of a Royal Marine detachment who demanded their 'rights'. They spoke for hundreds of other frozen and disheartened soldiers and sailors stationed around Murmansk and Archangel. All were asking why they were there. Naval ratings under orders to sail to the Baltic in October 1919 refused to embark and their commanding officer was at a loss to explain the reasons for their mission. One rating darkly suggested that they were fighting for 'all the wealthy people in Britain'.[2] The previous April Sir Henry Wilson had warned Churchill that soldiers deeply resented postings to Russia. His response was a breezy personal message to units in North Russia, which urged them to 'Carry on like Britons fighting for dear life and dearer honour' and pledged that all would be home in time to see the harvest gathered. Cocksure patriotism did not do the trick and there were further mutinies among forces in northern Russia.

Britain's wartime allies were either lukewarm or indifferent to the Russian adventure. Isolationist pressure in the Senate compelled Woodrow Wilson to order the evacuation of American forces from Archangel once the spring thaw was under way. The Australian and Canadian governments refused to send contingents to a war that aroused deep hostility in their countries. For the first time, Britain had to confront the truth that the dominions were no longer pliant purveyors of manpower for whatever war London decided was in the Empire's interests. French resolve fell apart after its army met stiff resistance in the Ukraine and its Black Sea fleet mutinied. Bereft of allies, Churchill was driven to contemplate procuring Italian, Greek or even German assistance.

Desperate expedients were inevitable. The war of intervention was foredoomed, as Churchill admitted in a rare moment of realism soon after he arrived in the War Office. The armistice agreed three months before had been what he called the 'death warrant' for the Russian 'national cause', by which he meant the White armies. Allied troops had entered Russia during the spring and summer of 1918 to beef up the Whites in the hope that, if they won, Russia would re-enter the war. The panic passed and there was no Russian resurgence. This was now past history, but Churchill, attempting to whip up popular support for the intervention, declared in April 1919 that 'every British and French soldier killed during the last months of the war had been done to death by Lenin and Trotsky'.

Churchill soon discovered that Britain had become entangled with some deeply unpleasant Russian allies whose opinions and conduct provoked protests in the press and the Commons. In response, the cabinet issued an official denial that it was Britain's intention to restore the Romanov autocracy. This was true, but the thousands of former Czarist officers who fought with the White armies dreamed of a resuscitation of the old Russia. A restoration of the ancien régime was the avowed intention of the 5,000-strong Russia Corps fighting in Estonia; officers kept their former titles and talked openly about reinstating the old political and social order. Churchill thought highly of this division, but the Estonians who knew its men better likened it to the Czarist 'White Guard'.[3] Even more distressing and politically harmful was the anti-Semitism of the Whites, who blamed the Jews for the Revolution on the grounds that a substantial number of Bolshevik leaders were Jewish. Pogroms were widespread wherever the White armies marched and Churchill had to appeal directly to Generals Anton Denikin and Nikolai Yudenich to stop the massacres. His remonstrances were ignored.

During the spring of 1919 cabinet opposition to the Russian adventure increased. Nevertheless, Churchill battled on and convinced his colleagues that a final offensive in North Russia would give much-needed help to Admiral Aleksandr Kolchak's armies operating in that region. Churchill was full of martial enthusiasm; his order for the deployment of a new type of gas contained the minute, 'I should very much like Bolsheviks to have it.'[4] It was used but it did not kill as many Reds as he had hoped. He placed equal faith in new locally recruited contingents, including Bolshevik POWs. Churchill's vaunted Slavo-British Legion mutinied, murdering some of their officers, during an offensive that quickly ran out of steam at the end of July.[5] Measures were taken for the final evacuation of all units in Murmansk and Archangel in September to the satisfaction of Lloyd George who had been sceptical about the value of their presence from the start. Acting on his own initiative, a dejected Churchill grasped at a new straw by opening secret talks with the former Finnish regent Carl Gustaf Mannerheim in which he offered him £3 million in return for an attack on Petrograd.[6] The scheme came to nothing.

After the North Russian debacle, Churchill shifted his ground and concentrated on holding the line on the Russo-Persian border where, he contended, the Bolsheviks were directly threatening the Empire. Twice in March, he had alerted Lloyd George to the fact that the Bolsheviks were 'menacing Persia and Afghanistan' and that their 'missionaries are at the gates of India'. Changing tack, he reminded the Commons that the British presence was upholding the will of the infant League of Nations by preventing the spread of ethnic and religious conflicts in the region. In September he again cried wolf, this time describing the 11,000 British and Indian soldiers on the Persian frontier as a 'shield' that was fending off a Red Army thrust towards that country and Iraq. Armed with intelligence reports, he bombarded the cabinet with dire warnings about an upsurge of Russian intrigues in Afghanistan and the possibility of a Soviet alliance with the Kurds. After one of his tirades, Arthur Balfour remarked, 'I admired the exaggerated way you told the truth.'

Against the phantoms invoked by Churchill were the concrete and dispiriting realities of Britain's financial crisis. The government was desperately trying to balance the budget in order to live within its diminishing means and military expenses were soaring. It was costing £2.75 million to keep the Reds out of Persia with a garrison that was too small to handle either an invasion or a popular uprising. It was replaced with a paper guarantee, the Anglo-Persian treaty of 1921, in which Britain promised troops to resist a Soviet invasion. Four years later, Britain would engineer the installation of Cossack officer Reza Pahlevi as Shah. He was a reliable strong man who kept his kingdom within Britain's orbit and the oil continued to flow from Abadan.

Among the last telegrams from the British agency at Meshed was one which concluded that on the whole Persians had been and were unmoved by Bolshevik propaganda.[7] This contradicted much that had gone before and must have been galling reading for Churchill. He had exhausted his powers of hyperbole to push Britain into a war that had been waged half-heartedly against the better judgement of the public and many of his colleagues. Yet if he had ignored even the wildest claims of the Soviet leadership and their propagandists, he would have been accused of having been cavalier with the security of the Empire. As it was, Moscow had enough on its hands defeating the White generals and restoring Russia's imperial hegemony in Central Asia.

The Weight of the British Arm:
Policing the Empire, 1919–1922

Even without the distraction of the Soviet bogey, a revolution in Ireland and protracted popular agitation in India, Egypt and the Middle East added up to an unprecedented imperial crisis. The Empire was suffering from a sequence of hard knocks delivered by its own subjects and pessimists in the Tory press and on the Tory backbenches wondered whether their weight and persistence might prove fatal. Churchill's reaction was to hit back hard and in November 1920 he issued a characteristically bullish, public ultimatum:

Having beaten the most powerful empire in the world, and having emerged triumphantly from the fearful ordeal of Armageddon, we will not allow ourselves to be pulled down and have our Empire disrupted by a malevolent and subversive force, the rascals and rapscallions of mankind which are now on the move against us.

His audience cheered wildly. He then named the chief villains: the 'Irish murder gang', 'the Egyptian vengeance society', 'the seditious extremists in India' and their home-grown, left-wing sympathisers, 'the arch traitors at home'. Churchill promised that each would feel 'the weight of the British arm'.[1]

All proved stubborn and resilient adversaries. Nevertheless, by the beginning of 1921, Britain had gained the upper hand in India, Iraq and Egypt, but not yet in Ireland, where the IRA [Irish Republican Army] was outwitting the police and army. Belligerence was paying off, but Churchill the pragmatist knew that coercion on the scale required could not be sustained for ever because of the Treasury's curbs on the military budget. Public opinion applied a further constraint on how the big stick was wielded. The cabinet was facing press and Parliamentary criticism of the severity and, in some instances, the sheer brutality of the astringents being adopted. The shooting of approximately four hundred unarmed demonstrators by Brigadier-General Rex Dyer at Amritsar in April 1919 had provoked a major political scandal and, in the following year, there was a torrent of protests in the Commons and in the press against the policy of punitive reprisals in Ireland.

Public disgust was summed up by Lieutenant-Commander Joseph Kenworthy, an earl's son and the Labour MP for Central Hull, who predicted that if the atrocities in Ireland continued, then 'the Prussian spirit will have entered us'.[2] Clementine Churchill was also shocked by the counter-terror in Ireland and what she feared was her husband's conviction that 'the rough, iron-fisted "Hunnish" way will prevail'.[3] The cabinet seemed unable to rein in its subordinates or shake their faith in a whiff of grapeshot as the only antidote for every form of unrest.

Churchill was trapped between his instinctive urge to hammer the enemies of the Empire into submission and the need to uphold its moral character, which, he was convinced, rested on humane values, a uniform system of justice and the consent of its subjects. He wanted order, but he recoiled from the notion of an Empire upheld by intimidation alone.

Resolution in war excluded barbarity, which he found abhorrent and he had said so many times, most recently in his wartime denunciations of 'Prussian' brutality. Nevertheless, as Churchill knew from his own experience, lofty moral abstractions tended to evaporate during lengthy campaigns of pacification against dogged and ruthless adversaries. Humanity and patience were qualities unevenly distributed among officers and officials and, even when they were present, they were never inexhaustible. As a minister, Churchill had to accept that sometimes extenuating circumstances and political expediency prevented governments from taking morally proper decisions.

Novel forms of resistance were creating new moral dilemmas. How far could proconsuls and generals go to control unruly but unarmed crowds of Indians who rampaged through towns and cities, or run to earth elusive IRA guerrillas who were indistinguishable from civilians and waged war by sabotage and assassination? Both kinds of resistance jeopardised 'order' and 'stability', those talismanic objectives of imperial governance, and, therefore, the rioters and terrorists had to be brought to heel.

Achieving an equipoise between firmness and humanity was harder than it had been, for the war had created a new moral universe. It troubled Churchill, who found it alien and frightening. Reviewing events during and after the war, Churchill identified a pervasive moral decay. Its symptoms included the disappearance of formerly revered principles and those human bonds upon which the 'structure and ultimate existence of civilised society depends'. This deliquescence was marked by an erosion of those late-Victorian moral certainties which had served as the lodestar for his generation and the mainspring of its now abandoned optimism. The result was the malaise of 'civilised society', which Churchill feared was 'relapsing in hideous succession into bankruptcy, barbarism or anarchy'.[4] Maybe the heartlessness being displayed by a handful of the Empire's servants was further evidence of this wider fall from grace. Four years of industrialised warfare and mass slaughter must have bred a brutalising familiarity with violence and a hard indifference to its consequences.

Churchill had to cope with the practical as well as the ethical problems of imperial policing. In May 1920 he proudly asserted that 'British troops were the backbone of the British Empire', but they were now too expensive and too thinly spread to cope effectively with multiple and extended emergencies. Furthermore, he was under pressure to conform to the coalition's programme of retrenchment. His solution was to replace manpower with technology. 'Machines save lives' had been Churchill's mantra as Minister of Munitions; he applied the same prescription in 1918 and strongly urged its extension to the small wars of Empire.

Armoured cars, aircraft, bombs and gas were cheap and could deliver quick, knockout blows against adversaries who lacked the means to strike back. Churchill's infatuation with the modern technology of war led him to be blasé about the injuries and suffering it inflicted and impatient with anyone who questioned its application to imperial campaigns. Glory had finally departed from the imperial battlefield, although adventure remained and the exploits of W. E.

Johns's heroic pilot Biggles gave some glamour to aerial policing on the frontiers between the wars.

In May 1919 Churchill proposed using mustard gas against Afghan troops and Pashtun tribesmen, but was rebuffed by the Viceroy, Viscount Chelmsford, who argued that at the moment there was no military need for such a severe measure. Peeved by this response, Churchill riposted that gas was 'more merciful than explosive shell, [and] compels an enemy to accept a decision with less loss of life than any other agency of war'. Remembering his service on the North-West Frontier, he revealingly exempted the Afghan and the Pashtun from any pity, since they mutilated the wounded. All that they would suffer was a 'sneeze', which was a staggering understatement of the clinical effects of mustard gas on the human respiratory system.[5] Chelmsford remained unconvinced. Churchill stuck to his faith in gas: although then Chancellor of the Exchequer, he urged the use of gas against the forces of Chinese warlords who were endangering Hong Kong in 1927. Not to do so was to surrender to 'false logic and false sentiment and false humanity', and he was prepared to have used gas if the Germans had invaded in 1940.[6]

Churchill won his case for air power as an economic and effective addition to the armoury of imperial intimidation, although some of his fellow ministers were unhappy about its morality. Trial applications yielded encouraging results: after a series of aerial attacks on the defiant Gajaak Nuer tribesmen of the southern Sudan during 1919 and 1920, the RAF reported that 'the moral[e] effect was tremendous'.[7] The reactions of these primitive nomadic tribesmen to aeroplanes and the bombs that fell from them must have been similar to those of the people of south-eastern England to the Martian war machines in H. G. Wells's *War of the Worlds*.

Bombing raids on Kabul in May 1919 (targets hit included the gasworks and the Amir's harem), Dakka and Jalalabad were thought to have tipped the balance during the Third Afghan War. They also prompted the Amir Amanullah waspishly to compare the attacks on his capital with the wartime German air raids in London, which the British had vilified as a typical example of Prussian 'frightfulness'.[8] A year later, RAF bombers evicted the Mad Mullah of Somaliland from his remote desert strongholds and ended his twenty-two-year struggle against the Empire. This triumph was deeply satisfying for Churchill, who had suggested the use of airships against the Mad Mullah in 1914.

Aircraft were also deployed against rioters in Gurjanwala in April 1919 by the Lieutenant-Governor of the Punjab Sir Michael ('Micky') O'Dwyer, who was well pleased by the speed with which mobs scattered when strafed and bombed. The demonstrators had been taking part in a *hartal* at the orders of Gandhi, the new leader of the Indian National Congress, who hoped that this combination of a general strike and popular demonstrations would prove the invincibility of what he called *satyagraha* or 'soul force'. Together *satyagraha* and the *hartal* would convince the British of the unity of all the races and creeds of the people of India and their determination to take control of their country's future.

Gandhi was in the process of remoulding the movement for Indian self-government. He wished to infuse what had previously been a force pursuing purely political goals with the essence of his personal religiosity. Under Gandhi's leadership, this spiritual dimension would dominate the public arena with the result that the inner lives of Indians would be recast in preparation for the struggle to secure self-government. Resistance would be obstructive but passive and draw an invincible strength from that inner spiritual harmony which Gandhi had achieved. All Indians would become like him and so qualify themselves to appeal to the conscience of the British nation. If its people were true to what Gandhi imagined was their ingrained sense of what was right, they would respond by making concessions to India as a moral obligation, rather than that mixture of political pragmatism and convenience which had hitherto been the motivation for extending self-government.

The collective soul of India was being mobilised to accelerate the progress of a national movement that had been making headway at a snail's pace. Statutes passed at Westminster in 1909 and 1919 established the principle that India would proceed towards eventual self-government and dominion status. The 1919 India Act set up provincial and national representational government, but restricted the areas over which the new assemblies could legislate. A step forward was accompanied by a setback; the Anarchical and Revolutionary

Crimes Act of 1919 was introduced by the Indian government, which gave the authorities wide powers of arrest and internment. They were denounced by the Indian National Congress as a humiliating device to smother all forms of political protest, peaceful or otherwise.

What followed was a trial of strength between the Raj and the Indian National Congress which was simultaneously a test of the spiritual mettle of Gandhi's followers. The *hartal* during the first week of April went horribly awry and triggered widespread riots, attacks on the police, looting and arson. The government was all but paralysed, but not in the way intended by Gandhi. 'Dear me,' remarked Chelmsford, 'what a nuisance these saintly fanatics are!' Gandhi was genuinely amazed by the entirely unlooked for lack of spiritual stamina and self-discipline among his followers, and he endeavoured to call off the *hartal*. Then and afterwards his awareness of the common temper of his countrymen was, to say the least, often extremely naive.

The disorders and sabotage of the railways and telegraph lines were worst in the Punjab. They were met head on by a counter-terror overseen by Micky O'Dwyer, who prided himself on his iron will and his iron fist which had enabled him to get the better of Punjabi revolutionaries and terrorists during the war. The governor's response was swift and lethal and his ferocity animated his subordinates. All shared a common fear that, if unchecked, the disturbances would spark off a second Indian Mutiny. O'Dwyer's melodramatic telegrams to the Viceroy (some were sent en clair and were intercepted by Russian intelligence) made the flesh creep and strongly suggested that he was in the grip of hysteria.[9] Nevertheless, Chelmsford approved O'Dwyer's diagnosis and, with some misgivings, the medicine he prescribed. It was, the Viceroy told London, 'only suitable for the Punjab' where, unlike the rest of India, fear seems to have been the prime ingredient of respect.[10]

O'Dwyer's terror spread across the Punjab with martial law, aerial attacks on rioters, mass floggings and troops firing on crowds in what was, in his fevered mind, a total war to regain control over the province. The heaviest blow was struck at Amritsar on 13 April, when a small detachment of Baluchi and Gurkha infantrymen, backed by armoured cars and commanded by Brigadier Dyer, opened a systematic fire on a crowd of about five thousand which had gathered in the Jallianwala Bagh, an enclosed space. There were at least fifteen hundred casualties, including about four hundred dead, and there would have been many more if, as he had wished, Dyer had been able to deploy his armoured cars with their machine-guns. At his orders, the wounded were refused medical assistance. Also at his orders, Indians were compelled to crawl at bayonet point along a street on which a woman medical missionary had been assaulted by rioters and from where she had been rescued by other Indians. Further humiliations were inflicted on Indians in Amritsar and elsewhere in the Punjab.

The literature of the Amritsar massacre is extensive and exhaustive.[11] What is important from the standpoint of Churchill's subsequent involvement was that O'Dwyer, Dyer and their apologists insisted that the drastic measures taken throughout the Punjab had narrowly averted a second Indian Mutiny. This, the Dyer camp alleged, had been the secret objective of Indian nationalists and the *hartal* had been a cover for a mass insurrection. This was conjecture, but it struck a chord with those nervous souls who imagined that British rule in India was fragile. The 1857 Mutiny still cast a baleful shadow; young officers who arrived in India in 1918 were given lectures on the uprising as a lesson in the need for constant vigilance.

Before he entered Amritsar, Dyer had heard rumours that the crowds were confident that Indian troops would never fire on them. After the massacre, O'Dwyer warned Chelmsford that Indian troops had been on the verge of mutiny and that the rebellion would spill over into the neighbouring United Provinces [Uttar Pradesh].[12] Paradoxically, his alarmism led Soviet propagandists to treat the reign of terror in the Punjab as a catalyst for revolutionary unity in India with allegations that Gurkhas had mutinied and Sikh troops had refused to fire on Muslims.[13]

Emergency press censorship prevented a precise picture of the events in the Punjab from becoming public knowledge for some months and, when it did, the details reached Britain in fragments and slowly. Chelmsford's first reaction had been to admit ruefully that 'Amritsar had been a very severe lesson', but, by August, he was painfully aware that the official terror in the Punjab had generated 'racial bitterness' across the sub-continent.[14] In the meantime and under pressure from Montagu, the Secretary for India, a commission under Scottish judge

Lord Hunter was instructed to uncover exactly what had occurred in the Punjab during the uprisings there. The commission's revelations, in particular Dyer's efforts to exonerate himself, were the prelude to a serious imperial crisis.

At the War Office, Churchill found himself bedevilled by the fallout from the crackdown in the Punjab. His immediate problem was how to handle the practical difficulties created by the exacerbated political, religious and racial tensions throughout India. By the autumn of 1919 Indian dismay and fury had become fused into a bond which briefly united Muslims and the largely Hindu Indian National Congress. It joined forces with the Pan-Islamic *Khalifat* movement which was protesting against Britain's plan to abolish the caliphate and dismember Turkey.

The emergent anti-British front coincided with Gandhi's new campaign of non-cooperation and an economic boycott of British manufacturers which threatened internal security and raised doubts about the future reliability of the Indian army. Like every other embattled proconsul, Chelmsford demanded more white soldiers. Churchill too was jittery: early in 1920, he conceded that 'the state of public opinion in India' demanded the retention in the country of as many Indian soldiers as possible. Worse still, 'the possibility of solidarity between Hindus and Muslims' suggested to Churchill that their loyalty could no longer be taken for granted. Reinforcements were needed to police the volatile Middle East and he decided that they would have to be found in East and Central Africa.[15]

This brief exercise in improvising a black army was placed in the hands of officers of the King's African Rifles and their efforts provided Churchill (and us) with a fascinating insight into contemporary racial attitudes and the nightmares which then disturbed soldiers and officials. An appraisal of the soldierly potential of East Africans revealed that they ranged from 'brave, reliable and very intelligent – but delicate' Abyssinians to the 'foolish' Lubwa and the 'useless' Meru. Colonial Office bureaucrats opposed to Churchill's scheme conjured up 'bogies' in the shape of 'large numbers of trained bloodthirsty blacks' who had absorbed 'Muslim fanaticism' during their service in the Middle East.[16] His expedient was revived in 1949, when objectors were again anxious about the black soldier having his head turned by subversive ideas.[17] Churchillian anxieties turned out to be groundless: Indian troops stayed loyal. Yet, when faced with a shortfall of sepoys during the Iraq rebellion in the summer of 1920, the government had to lure recently demobilised Sikhs back to the colours with 100 rupee [£10] bonuses.[18] Like the British army, the Indian seemed overstretched and close to breaking point.

Dyer was a further headache for Churchill. He read grisly forensic details of the Hunter Report which convinced him that the brigadier was a brute who had forfeited the right to command and deserved summary dismissal. This was the view of the cabinet and it was delivered by Churchill to the Army Council in May 1920. The generals growled and prevaricated. Sir Henry Wilson blamed the 'frocks' (i.e. politicians) for getting India into a 'mess' and his colleagues argued that, if Dyer was disciplined, it would create a dangerous precedent. Every officer who found himself in a situation akin to that in Amritsar would be handicapped by the fear that his superiors would throw him to the wolves if his judgement proved mistaken. Field Marshal Lord Rawlinson ominously warned that there were bound to be many similar cases in India and Ireland.[19] Churchill was adamant and the brass hats grudgingly agreed, in Wilson's words, to 'throw out' Dyer.

Dyer had been recalled to England and he and his supporters, led by O'Dwyer, were demanding a legal inquiry in which he could acquit himself, although he had had an ample opportunity when he had given his evidence to the Hunter Commission. Dyer's adherents had a mouthpiece in the *Morning Post*. It contrasted the stout-hearted brigadier, who had grasped the nettle and given the Empire's enemies the pounding they deserved and understood, with pussyfooting ministers who preferred to appease them. Such opinions were widely held by Conservative backbenchers and they were given the chance to air them in the Commons in a seven-hour debate on the Dyer case on 8 July.

It was a nasty, bad-tempered occasion. Tory venom was directed towards Montagu, a Jew, who, according to one listener, had 'thoroughly roused the latent passions of the stodgy Tories'.[20] His opening speech galled the ultras, who were enraged by his suggestion that the issue under scrutiny was 'the doctrine of terrorism' and whether it should be applied against everyone in India who criticised its government. Members faced a choice between 'terrorism' as used by Dyer and the 'modern ideas of what an Empire means' which embraced the 'principle of partnership for India in the British Commonwealth'. Montagu accused Dyer's champions of imagining that once an Indian had joined the 'educated classes' and had absorbed ideas about 'individual liberty' he somehow became an 'agitator'. This was too much for Tory blood pressure and there was a barrage of taunts against what one heckler called 'an incendiary speech'. Anti-Semitic gibes were heard over the braying.

That rock of Ulster Unionism Sir Edward Carson was Dyer's champion and he began by exalting his unblemished military career and reproaching the 'armchair politicians' who had discarded him. Dyer had been right, for India had been 'seething with rebellion and anarchy', which were the consequence of a vast underground conspiracy to destroy the Raj and, Carson added, to evict Britain from Egypt and 'destroy our seapower and drive us out of Asia'. Dyer's methodical fusillades had saved not only India but the entire Empire and, it went without saying, had frustrated the intrigues of its Bolshevik foes.

Churchill answered Carson's paranoiac rant with one of his most brilliant speeches. He outlined his own, liberal principles and accused Dyer of having violated them. He then dissected the brigadier's actions which had aroused unprecedented racial antipathy in India. Dyer had taken what Churchill admitted was always a 'painful' decision for any officer: firing on the 'citizens of our common Empire'. He had been wrong: were his targets violent, aggressive or armed, or, in Dyer's own words, 'a revolutionary army'? They were plainly not and their deaths were a gross example of 'frightfulness', which Churchill defined as 'slaughter or massacre' with 'the intention of terrorising not merely the rest of the crowd, but the whole district or the whole country'. 'Frightfulness is not a remedy known to the British pharmacopoeia,' he insisted, although its instrument 'terrorism' was a common remedy of the Bolsheviks. Members were reminded that the Jallianwala Bagh was smaller than Trafalgar Square, the crowd had been fired at for nearly ten minutes and many bullets passed through several bodies. British rule in India did not rest on brute force, but on moral foundations. Churchill concluded with a return to his original theme: Dyer had 'united' Indians against Britain and it was now the task of the government to restore harmony and regain Indian loyalty and respect. This cogent, tightly argued appeal to the conscience of the Commons swung the debate against Dyer and towards the government, which won by 247 to 37 votes.[21]

Subsequent speeches did, however, reveal the mental chasm that now separated liberal imperialists like Churchill from those Tories who thought that the Empire had to be preserved by coercion and plenty of it. This was the opinion of that preposterous authoritarian Sir William Joynson-Hicks ('Jix') who had just returned from India. He reiterated the legend that Dyer had been the country's saviour, noted that he was universally supported by Europeans who lived there and predicted worse troubles to come.* 'After they have read your speech!' interrupted the Labour MP Colonel Josiah Wedgwood. He took up Churchill's points, emphasising the need to cooperate with Indians and regain their confidence in British justice.

Wedgwood's remarks were a reminder of the continuing repercussions of the Amritsar affair. Indians discovered from their newspapers that there existed in Britain a considerable body of opinion which held their lives to be of little or no value. This impression of racial contempt was reinforced in the weeks after the debate, when just over £26,000 [the equivalent of £1 million today] was raised for Dyer by the *Morning Post* to fund a nest egg for his retirement. The most prominent donor was Rudyard Kipling. O'Dwyer continued to campaign for Dyer and in the early 1930s he joined forces with Churchill in the extra-parliamentary opposition to Indian self-government. He was shot dead in London in 1940 by an Indian who had been an eyewitness to the Amritsar massacre.

---

* Joynson-Hicks's pet hates were Jews, aliens and alcohol; his defeat of Churchill in the 1909 Manchester election launched a political career dedicated to negation. A brief and brilliant biography can be found in Ronald Blythe's *The Age of Illusion*.

Reign of Terror:

Churchill and Ireland, 1919–1923

Political assassination was the weapon of choice for the IRA. It was the military arm of Sinn Féin, the Irish republican party, which had won 73 of the 105 Irish seats in the general election of December 1918. Thirty-three Sinn Féin MPs gathered in Dublin (the rest were locked up in British gaols), from where they issued a declaration of independence and announced that their assembly, the Dáil Éireann, now represented the sovereign will of the Irish people. This made it the legitimate government of all Ireland, although this claim was violently contested in the six counties of Ulster where the Protestant majority favoured continued attachment to Britain. During the next two years, the Dáil constructed a parallel legal and fiscal administration which operated alongside its now brittle and beleaguered British counterpart in Dublin Castle.

The IRA had one strategic objective: to prove that the Dáil and not Dublin Castle was both the de facto and de jure government of Ireland. To do this, IRA units had to make Ireland ungovernable by kicking away the main props of the British administration, its police force, intelligence services and those Irishmen and women who collaborated with them. Through assassinations, kidnapping, personal threats and sabotage, the IRA placed the government and its servants in a state of siege. Operations were overseen by Michael Collins, who was director of intelligence for the IRA as well as finance minister.

To win, the IRA had to accumulate weapons and explosives. It was always under-equipped for a protracted campaign of terrorist attrition and was constantly distracted by the need to replenish its arsenal. At no stage in the conflict could the IRA's leadership contemplate a stand-up fight against the British army, which it was certain to lose for lack of numbers and firepower. During 1920 and the first half of 1921 more and more British soldiers were drafted to southern Ireland, backed by a 12,000-strong gendarmerie (the Auxis and the Black and Tans), aircraft, martial law and detention without trial.

The guiding spirit of the IRA's war had been Sinn Féin's philosophy, which was rooted in the nineteenth-century Continental tradition of romantic nationalism. Churchill understood this and, during the Anglo-Irish negotiations of December 1921, he asked Collins why he had not fought an open war of the kind waged by Garibaldi in Italy. This was unthinkable, given the strength of the British army. Yet, Sinn Féin's philosophy demanded that national liberation could only be secured through an armed struggle in which dedicated and heroic individuals showed themselves willing to place their country before their lives. The blood of martyrs was the cement of nationhood, for it elevated and hallowed the national cause. Sinn Féin's ideology of self-help and self-sacrifice ruled out any suggestion that independence might be gained through negotiation, or, even more shamefully, by accepting British concessions handed down from a position of superior strength. The future integrity and self-esteem of a nation created by the bravery and altruism of its people would be compromised if liberation was the outcome of bartering. It was, therefore, imperative for the IRA to break British power in Ireland by the only means available, terrorism.

Churchill's first reaction to Sinn Féin's coup had been secret satisfaction that a party which would have aligned itself with Labour in the Commons had gone into permanent exile in Dublin.[1] He quickly joined and sometimes led the chorus of his colleagues who denounced the IRA as a 'murder gang' who were to be treated as criminals rather than soldiers. Defending the minatory and brutal tactics of the Auxis and the Black and Tans, Churchill later wrote that they had deserved to be allowed 'the same freedom as the Chicago or New York police permit themselves in dealing with armed gangs'.[2] Churchill was both bewildered and angry that a 'humane' imperial government was the victim of an 'open rebellion' which took the form of systematic murder by partisans who rarely dared to engage the forces of the Crown.[3] Sinn Féin knew his feelings and identified Churchill alongside Sir Henry Wilson as 'chiefly responsible' for the 'reign of terror' in Ireland.[4]

Certainly Churchill equalled Lloyd George in intransigence and vocal contempt for the IRA. In October 1920, when the prison hunger strike of Terence MacSwiney was running its fatal course, he dismissed his protest as a squalid trick to get him out of gaol, adding that fasting required far less courage than enduring bombardment in the trenches.[5] In the Commons, Commander Kenworthy riposted that Churchill could not go without a drink for a day.[6] MacSwiney died soon after and Churchill regretted his callous gibe. While sitting for the Irish portraitist John Lavery, he told the artist that MacSwiney 'was a brave man! They are fine people, we cannot afford to lose them.' He added with what he must have known was unfounded optimism, 'We shall be shaking hands in three months.'[7]

The 'we' referred to the British Empire. The cabinet had treated the establishment of the Dáil as a declaration of war on the Empire. Lloyd George told Churchill that Éamonn de Valera, Sinn Féin's exiled leader, 'has practically challenged the British Empire and unless he is put down the Empire would look very silly'. This was a breathtaking understatement. Events in Ireland were being followed by Indian and Egyptian nationalists who were on the lookout for evidence of a weakening of the imperial will. The Bolsheviks were angling in these troubled waters and deciphered Soviet signals revealed their plans to implant 'germ cells' inside Sinn Féin.[8] In November 1920 Hamar Greenwood, Secretary for Ireland, warned the Commons that the nation was now confronted with 'a great conspiracy based on Ireland to smash the British Empire'.[9] Six months later, an overwrought Sir Henry Wilson predicted to Curzon that 'unless we crushed the murder-gang this summer we should lose Ireland and the Empire'. His vehemence 'frightened' the Foreign Secretary, who favoured a negotiated peace.[10]

This shrill alarmism was a reaction to two interlocked problems: Ireland's future relations with Britain and whether they should be dictated at gunpoint by Sinn Féin. It demanded an Irish republic, undivided and separate from the Empire. Churchill and the cabinet conceded the principle of Irish self-government, which had been laid down by the 1912 Home Rule Act, but insisted that Ulster should be excluded from the new Irish state, which had to remain within the imperial orbit as a self-governing dominion under the

Crown. Britain also required, and Churchill was emphatic on this point, naval bases on the south-west coast of Ireland. Furthermore, and this was central to government policy, the IRA had to be defeated. If it was not and Britain caved in, then it would be seen as a signal failure of imperial resolve that would have disastrous repercussions wherever and whenever Britain's authority was challenged.

This explains why Churchill believed that it was his duty to propose and support the toughest measures. It was easy for him to get his way, for his colleagues tended to share his fury at every new outrage committed by the IRA. As a consequence, the war escalated between the summer of 1920 and that of 1921. An increasingly desperate cabinet tightened the screws on the IRA: martial law was introduced in seven counties, as was internment (4,500 IRA suspects were locked up by July 1921) and, most controversial of all, the Black and Tans were permitted to transform the policy of calculated reprisals into one of random vengeance. Churchill praised them as 'gallant officers'.[11] His humanitarian instincts fell into abeyance and his mind was clouded by wild and vengeful passions; the man who had denounced Dyer for his heartlessness thought there was 'little harm' in police death squads shooting Sinn Féin supporters.[12]

True to character, Churchill took an intense interest in the conduct of operations and sent unasked for advice to commanders in the field. Exasperation with what he thought was a lack of progress made him eager to use aircraft for crowd control, a suggestion that was rejected by the cabinet at the end of 1920.[13] Churchill changed tack and pressed for aircraft to be used for reconnaissance and protecting motorised columns. The machines overhead would, he argued, be 'a great deterrent to illegal drilling and rebel gatherings', which would have been true if they had been equipped with the necessary wireless sets to summon up ground support.[14]

As Churchill warned the cabinet in July 1920, the IRA would only be defeated if war was waged at 'full blast'. It was during the next year, when 100,000 troops and gendarmerie were concentrated in disaffected areas. Even so, Sir Henry Wilson thought that twice that number would be required for outright victory, which would mean drastic reductions in the Indian and Middle Eastern garrisons and pruning the reserve troops held in mainland Britain to deal with industrial unrest. To some extent, the shortfall in manpower was compensated for by new tactics which relied on motorised patrols protected by armoured cars traversing the countryside in large-scale cordon and search operations. Mobility and a capacity to strike unexpectedly ceased to be the prerogatives of the IRA.

If the IRA no longer had things its own way, neither were they turning out to Churchill's satisfaction. At the close of 1920, Sinn Féin's London representative told Collins that Churchill was 'peeved and annoyed and doubtful' over the growing indiscipline within the army and the grimly obvious truth that the Black and Tans had become a Frankenstein's monster.[15] This news was of small comfort to Collins, for, like the security forces, the IRA was coming to realise that a conventional victory was now beyond its grasp.

Mutual exhaustion drove both sides towards a negotiated political settlement. As early as July 1920, an Irish judge, two senior civil servants and General Sir Nevil Macready, the commander-in-chief in Ireland, had presented a case to the cabinet which concluded that repression would fail and that the only way out of the impasse was to offer Ireland dominion status immediately. Both Churchill and Lloyd George were impressed, but the Ulster Unionists would have no truck with this solution.[16] They got their way, for the Government of Ireland Act, passed the following December, gave the six counties of Ulster autonomy within the United Kingdom.

Elections held across Ireland in May 1921 confirmed the split between the north and the south: in the latter the Unionists were dominant and in the former Sinn Féin was returned unopposed in 124 seats. Ireland had partitioned itself and, in the process, Ulster began to slither into anarchy as Protestants took steps to consolidate their ascendancy. During July and August over 8,000 Catholics were bullied out of their jobs in Belfast shipyards after they had refused to forswear their attachment to Sinn Féin, and there were sectarian riots in which thirty were murdered and over two hundred wounded. The Belfast government responded with the creation of a 20,000-strong Protestant gendarmerie of reserve policemen, the B Specials. Many were former UVF men and they were used to overawe the Catholic population in those counties that bordered on nationalist Ireland and which Sinn Féin claimed for Éire.

As the conflict began to spread northwards, Sinn Féin agreed to an armistice on 11 July. Churchill, who a few months before had been clamouring for more and more condign measures, backed the truce and with it a negotiated settlement. The protests of his wife may have helped swing him against continuing a distasteful campaign with no end in sight. Public support for the war was at best half-hearted because winning it offered no political or material advantages to Britain beyond preserving an increasingly threadbare national prestige.

Five months before, Churchill had been transferred from the War to the Colonial Office and his attention was diverted from Ireland to the Middle East. At Lloyd George's suggestion, he was invited to join the ministerial team for negotiations with Sinn Féin's representatives in October. The presence at the conference table of a minister with a reputation for urging stern measures in Ireland was a sop to those Tories who feared that the coalition might appease Sinn Féin. Churchill had been disappointed by the military outcome of the Irish campaign, for he had hoped that, like the Boers, Sinn Féin would be defeated and then gratefully accept a generous compromise from the hands of the victors.[17]

Up to a point Churchill behaved according to the expectations of his admirers and critics. 'Inclined to be bombastic' was Collins's appraisal of his demeanour during the negotiations. He was full of 'ex-officer jingo', but had a perceptive eye for detail, was always driven by 'political gain' and was not to be trusted.[18] Collins had every reason to be wary. In the weeks before the truce, the IRA had been fought to a standstill and its leaders feared that, if hostilities were resumed, then the military balance would decisively swing against it. Sinn Féin was seeking terms from a position of military weakness, as Collins acknowledged when he later admitted that 'in a contest between a great Empire and a small nation, this was as far as the small nation could get'. Arthur Griffiths, the head of the Irish delegation, agreed: 'the most we could do was to hold, and to barely hold the position we were in.'[19]

Sinn Féin was vulnerable to threats that Britain was eager to continue a now winnable war. During the exchanges, Churchill promised 'real war' and not mere 'bushwhacking' and, on 5 December, Lloyd George offered the Irish a final choice between signing the treaty and the renewal of war. He also considered a political offensive through a direct appeal to the war-weary population of southern Ireland. This was bluster and bluff, for, as Churchill privately assured one Irish delegate, 'England would not embark on further military operations in Ireland.'[20] In private, Lloyd George was of the same mind.[21] He and Churchill won this game of political poker and the Irish signed within twenty-four hours of the Prime Minister's ultimatum.

Under terms of the Anglo-Irish Treaty, Sinn Féin conceded partition and became a self-governing dominion under the Crown, without, at Churchill's insistence, the right to possess a navy.[22] Britain retained the right to occupy naval bases on Ireland's south-west coast in an emergency. This state born of a political accommodation with hints of blackmail was not the free, united Ireland of Sinn Féin's dreams. Yet, as Collins rightly boasted, the Treaty was the only deal available and it had got rid of the British army of occupation after nearly eight hundred years.

Nevertheless, purists were bitterly disappointed: nationalist ideals had been compromised or thrown to the wind. In January 1922 the Dáil approved the Treaty by a narrow majority and within weeks the radical republicans led by de Valera began a civil war to overturn it and the Irish Free State.

The British government supported the armed forces of the new dominion. Churchill pledged that Britain would intervene directly if the republicans gained the upper hand and General Macready supplied Collins with heavy artillery to shell the republicans who had seized Dublin's Four Courts. Collins also requested aircraft to bomb this stronghold and Churchill agreed, but Air Marshal Sir Hugh Trenchard, the Chief of Air Staff, indignantly refused to have his aeroplanes painted with the green, white and orange colours of Sinn Féin.[23] In the end, the machines were not needed for the defenders of Four Courts were shelled into surrender. In August, Collins was shot dead in an ambush. The civil war dragged on for a further year and ended with a victory for the Free Staters. George V's head disappeared from Ireland's postage stamps and was replaced by Gaelic images and a map of the new nation which included Ulster. Members of the Dáil and every official in the dominion were obliged to swear allegiance to the King. 'God Save the King' remained the official national anthem, although it was sung without any enthusiasm.

There was bitter dismay among Conservative imperialists. The *Spectator* feared that the 'Nemesis of the Irish Settlement' would have taught Indians, Egyptians and Palestinians that a faint-hearted Empire would buckle under the pressure of force if it was applied relentlessly. Further to the right, the *National Review* raved against those Conservative MPs who had connived at the 'disgrace and humiliation' inflicted on the Empire by the Anglo-Irish Treaty.[24] It was a phantom success for Churchill. Britain had salvaged an unwilling and intractable dominion from a war which it failed to win. In 1937 the Irish Free State officially became Éire and successfully negotiated the abandonment of the British naval bases, much to Churchill's fury. Two years later Prime Minister de Valera insisted that his state, although still nominally within the British Commonwealth, would be neutral in the war against Germany.

The Possibility of Disaster:

The Near and Middle East, 1919–1922

The scramble for the Ottoman Empire had taken a new turn during the final year of the war. Trotsky repudiated Czarist plans for depredations on Turkish territories and declared Russia to be the friend of emergent nationalist movements throughout the Near and Middle East. Britain and France stuck to their wartime arrangements and, in December 1918, Lloyd George persuaded Clemenceau to forgo French claims to Mosul (and its oil reserves) in return for assistance in the occupation of the Lebanon and Syria, which were now under British administration. Two new competitors entered the race; armed with wartime assurances, Greece and Italy demanded a slice of Anatolia, Thrace and the Dodecanese Islands.

The questions as to who took what and under what terms were now complicated by popular expectations of future freedom and the imminent birth of new, independent states, which is what Britain and France had promised during the war. Expectant nationalists were urged to be patient and wait while British, French, Italian and Greek statesmen haggled over who should get what, drew lines on maps and prepared the mandates that would be rubber-stamped by the League of Nations. Quite rightly, those whose futures had passed into the hands of foreigners feared the worst and, during 1919, they snatched the initiative. Arabs, Kurds and Turks attacked the armies that occupied their lands and took tentative steps towards creating their own, free polities.

As Minister of War, Churchill was primarily concerned with imposing stability on those areas occupied by British troops and governed by improvised military administrations, which endeavoured to reduce the banditry that was a natural consequence of wartime disruption, hold the lid down on political unrest and, where possible, collect taxes. The British army was responsible for the governance of Palestine, Iraq (areas already earmarked for British mandates),

Constantinople and neutral zones on either side of the Straits. Appeals to the dominions for reinforcements to keep the garrisons up to strength were twice rejected.[1]

Britain had found itself in a cleft stick. After brooding over the events that were unfolding in regions where British forces were thinly spread, Churchill concluded in December 1919 that it was pointless and dangerous to remain. Complete disengagement from Turkey and the Middle East was the only solution to problems that could only worsen. He explained why to his colleagues, arguing that the decision to dismember the Ottoman Empire had been a calamitous mistake, which, if uncorrected, would jeopardise Britain's position 'as the greatest Mohammedan power'. Indian Muslims now regarded Britain as either indifferent or inimical to their faith. Moreover, he argued, it was impossible to reconcile wartime promises made to the Zionist movement about Jewish colonisation in Palestine with pledges made to the Arabs, which, if repudiated, would be 'a crime against freedom'. Britain could not afford to stand by while the Arabs were bullied into acceptance of French paramountcy in Syria. Nor should it exacerbate ethnic and religious tensions by giving its blessing to the annexation of large areas of western Turkey by Italy and Greece.

Churchill offered a means of extricating Britain from this imbroglio: Turkey and its former provinces should be placed under the guardianship of the League of Nations with the United States responsible for internal security. Thus, the integrity of the Empire would be preserved and Britain could rid itself of a troublesome incubus. Far better, he suggested, that Britain invest its limited spare capital in its tranquil and potentially profitable African colonies.[2] Churchill continued to nag the cabinet about the value to the Empire of unproductive tracts of wasteland populated by unruly ingrates. In December 1920, he was urging disengagement from Iraq and there were moments when he contemplated withdrawal from Palestine, which, like Iraq, showed all the symptoms of being ungovernable. He continued to cherish the fancy that the United States could be persuaded to lend a hand in the Middle East. This was absurdly unrealistic: in November 1919, Americans had overwhelmingly plumped for an isolationist administration under President Warren G. Harding and the Senate had vetoed American participation in the

League. The richest nation in the world refused to be encumbered by the problems of the post-war world, which were a matter of indifference to most Americans who spent the next decade making and spending money.

Departure from the Near and Middle East was never an option for Britain. Much to his chagrin, Churchill was a slave to strategic geography and the heir to wartime expediencies that had entangled Britain in a web of contradictory agreements. The realities of imperial geo-strategy dictated that Britain had to safeguard an old lifeline, the Suez Canal, and two new ones. These were the planned pipeline which would run overland from the Persian oilfields to the terminal at Haifa on the Palestinian coast, and the projected 'red' imperial air routes between Britain, India, Singapore and Australia via Cairo and Baghdad. Blueprints for this and another air lane from Cairo to Kenya and Cape Town were being prepared by the Air Ministry during 1919 and 1920 with the passionate backing of Churchill.[3] This idea of a web of aerial connections caught his imagination, for it would both accelerate communications and tighten imperial bonds. By the 1930s and with official subsidies, Imperial Airways was running regular flights to India, Singapore, Hong Kong and Australia. All passed across the Middle East and used Egyptian and Iraqi aerodromes as staging posts.

Although he dismissed Iraq as an unprofitable land, Churchill appreciated the future value of the Mosul oil deposits. Iraq was a nuisance, but it was imperative that it remained a British nuisance and so he upheld Britain's monopoly of exploration and extraction rights and banned French and American companies from the region.[4] Drilling at Mosul started in 1927, but output grew slowly, so it was over twenty years before oil revenues made a substantial contribution to Iraqi revenues. Frustrated American oil magnates turned to the more obliging Ibn Saud, the King of Saudi Arabia.

Disputes over commercial access to oilfields were a reminder that Britain had to contend with the territorial ambitions of its allies. After eighteen months of horse-trading, the San Remo Treaty of May 1920 gave mandate for Syria and Lebanon to France and that for Iraq and Palestine to Britain. In July the Treaty of Sèvres neutralised the Straits, severely cut the size of the Turkish army, navy and air force, and sliced off chunks of an emasculated nation, which were delivered to Italy and Greece.

These two countries had already jumped the gun and asserted what their governments proclaimed were the rewards for their wartime sacrifices. In May 1919, a Greek contingent had joined the Allied garrison in Constantinople with all the bombast of a conquering army: military bands played patriotic airs, local Greeks cheered and Turks watched sullenly.[5] A far larger Greek force landed at Smyrna, which immediately became a bridgehead for incursions into Anatolia. Latent ethnic and religious passions exploded: Orthodox Greek mobs slaughtered Muslims and torched mosques. Greeks caught wearing the traditional Turkish fez were also murdered.[6] Retributive killings of Turks by the Légion Arménienne marked the advance inland from Alexandretta by French forces during the winter of 1918 to 1919. Further along the coast, Italian units disembarked at Adana, where they assured its population that they came as allies of the United States, presumably to win their trust.[7] This lie masked blatant empire building, for the nationalist newspaper *Tribuna* warned the Turks and anyone else who objected that: 'To oppose Italy in the East is to oppose civilisation'.[8] Churchill was dismayed by these events which further destabilised the region, but he was powerless to stop them. Any attempt to restrain French, Italian and Greek predation would have hampered British efforts to conclude a political settlement in Europe, where it relied on the cooperation of these powers.

The carve-up of Asia Minor seemed unstoppable, but the participants soon got bloody noses. The Greek, French and Italian invasions were the catalyst for the Turkish national resurgence that would eventually be led by Kemal Atatürk, then a general in the army of the Sultan Mehmed VI who ruled in Constantinople as the stooge of Britain. Secularist modernisers of the old CUP united with Muslim traditionalists to form a patriotic front against the intruders. In April 1920 the new Turkish assembly at Ankara elected Atatürk as the nation's leader and proclaimed that: 'All we want is to save our Country from sharing the fate of India and Egypt.'[9] The solidarity and resolve of the Kemalist movement impressed Admiral Sir Somerset Calthorpe, High Commissioner in Constantinople, who, in June, warned his government that 'the movement is so natural and I feel is so universal, that it seems to me hopeless to endeavour to stop it'.[10]

Churchill too recognised the vigour and justice of the Turkish national revival and, in November, called on the cabinet to jettison the 'weak and fickle' Greeks in favour of Atatürk. A strong unified Turkey was, he reasoned, the surest way of forming a barrier against Bolshevik penetration of the Near East. Active friendship towards Turkey would also restore the goodwill of Indian Muslims who hailed the secularist Atatürk as a champion of their faith. Churchill was also fearful of a Turko-Arab alliance, which would have grave consequences in Egypt and Afghanistan as well as Palestine.[11] Representatives of the *Khalifat* movement had travelled from Afghanistan and India to the nationalist assembly in Ankara in May 1920. They included Mustafa Saghir from Peshawar, whom the Turks arrested, tried and hanged as a British agent. According the Pan-Islamist newspaper *Ittifah-i-Islam*, he confessed that Lord Curzon had ordered him to assassinate Atatürk.[12] The same journal also accused the European powers of using Greece to debilitate Turkey as part of their global war against Islam.[13]

This allegation made sense, for Lloyd George detested the Turks in the same way as Churchill detested the Bolsheviks. 'Has the Ottoman Turk done other than destroy what he has conquered,' the Prime Minister wrote in his memoirs of peacemaking. The Turk was unfit for the imperial responsibilities, since he had never 'shown himself able to develop what was won by war'. Lloyd George the child of the Welsh chapel vilified Constantinople as the 'hot bed of every Eastern vice'. When a Turkish mission visited London in January 1921, he confided to George V that its leader visited male brothels and that Atatürk was a homosexual.[14] The ascendancy of the 'decadent' and shifty Turk was over, he told a sceptical Sir Henry Wilson, and Greece was now the 'coming power in the Mediterranean'. Lloyd George's prejudices turned Turkey into an enemy and added immeasurably to Britain's difficulties in the Middle East.

The Turkish national renaissance coincided with those of the Kurds and the Syrian, Palestinian and Iraqi Arabs. When Arthur Balfour had made his famous declaration in November 1917 that vouchsafed future British sponsorship for a Jewish homeland in yet-to-be conquered Palestine, he had also spoken airily about the liberation of all peoples 'whose progress had been impeded by the Ottomans'.[15] This codicil has often been ignored or forgotten, but then and afterwards the former subjects of the Sultan imagined that its spirit would guide Britain's post-war policy towards them.

In particular, Britain had kindled the political ambitions of the Hashemite dynasty of Hejaz. Its ruler Sharif Hussain and his sons Faisal and Abdullah, who had commanded Arab forces attached to General Allenby's army during the last two years of the war, hoped to establish themselves as autonomous Arab rulers. Both princes were aware of Anglo-French plans for post-war spheres of influence in the Middle East, which, together with other files revealing Allied secret diplomacy, had been mischievously published by Trotsky in November 1917. Nevertheless, Faisal and Abdullah hoped that Britain would not renege on its obligations to their family. Furthermore, their nationalist credentials were impressive and won them widespread support from the Arabs of Syria and Iraq. During 1919 Abdullah had established himself as the ruler of the future Transjordan [modern Jordan] and Faisal was making friends with Syrian nationalists.

The Hashemite princes and their adherents were right to be optimistic since by November 1918 the Foreign Office had accepted that recent events in the Middle East had invalidated the Sykes–Picot arrangements. And so it seemed, for an Anglo-French declaration promised joint support for Arab autonomy, but offered no indications as to how and when this would be achieved. France had no intention of relinquishing its claims to Syria, and at Versailles Clemenceau reminded Faisal that his country's interests in the Levant stretched back to the Crusades. The prince asked who had won those wars. France would not be deflected by an apt riposte and was already pouring troops, including Algerians, into the Lebanon and Syria.

After eighteen months of Allied procrastination and duplicity, the Arab world erupted. In April 1920 racial tensions in Palestine reached boiling point and Arab mobs murdered and injured over two hundred Jews in Jerusalem. As in Turkey, religious and political passions coalesced; the rioters chanted 'Long live King Faisal!' and 'God is with us!' In Damascus a Syrian national assembly rejected the French mandate, issued a unilateral declaration of independence and elected Faisal as king in July. In the same month, there was a general insurrection throughout Iraq and most of the country soon passed into rebel hands. Iraqis had had enough of being pushed around and squeezed for taxes by Sir Percy ('Cokkus') Cox's rigid and oppressive Anglo-Indian administration. Its policies and methods were so hated that ancient blood feuds and the traditional Sunni–Shia antipathy were suspended during the revolt.

Churchill was, in his own words, 'at his wits end' to find sufficient troops to suppress the Iraqi uprising and he warned the cabinet that Britain was now facing the 'possibility of disaster'.[16] The situation became so desperate that in September detachments had to be rushed from Constantinople at the very moment when the authorities there were preparing to contain the popular backlash against the treaty of Sèvres.[17] The line just held in Iraq: 102,000 British and Indian troops eventually won a hard-fought campaign in which there were 2,000 Anglo-Indian casualties and four times that number of Iraqis. Operations against pockets of resistance continued well into the following year and the future peace of Iraq now rested on a garrison of 80,000 which was costing the British taxpayer £30 million a year.

Aircraft played a crucial role in the fighting and Sir Hugh Trenchard successfully asked Churchill for a new type of bomb which was to be filled with gas for use in Iraq. In August 1920, the distraught local commander General Sir Aylmer Haldane requested conventional gas-filled shells and, with Churchill's consent, they were transferred from stocks held in depots in Egypt. None reached the battlefield because of transport problems. Nevertheless anti-imperialist myth has long alleged that Churchill used gas against the Iraqis. This was untrue since there is no evidence whatsoever of the deployment of gas during the 1920 Iraq campaign nor in later operations against the Kurds. This lack of proof has not quashed the canard that Churchill 'gassed' Iraqi tribesmen which has become part of the anti-imperialist folklore of the left. The truth was that Churchill and local commanders were keen to use gas, but supplies were not to hand.[18]

Hitherto, Churchill's part in Far and Middle Eastern affairs had been confined to conjuring up soldiers for policing operations in areas which Britain neither needed nor could afford. As late as December 1920 he was arguing for a strategic withdrawal from northern and central Iraq to a defensive perimeter around Basra that would protect the Abadan oilfields. He was reminded that this retreat would nullify Britain's claims to the Mosul oil reserves.[19] Moreover, it remained axiomatic that as an imperial power it could not afford to create a vacuum that rivals might be tempted to fill. Britain's exit from northern Iraq would be a signal for France or Turkey or both to step in.

In February 1921, Lloyd George transferred Churchill from the War to the Colonial Office. The Prime Minister was confident that Churchill's experience as an administrator and conciliator uniquely qualified him as the man who could clear up the mess in the Middle East and find the means to consolidate British power there. Churchill took sole charge of regional policy and was free to overrule the Foreign, Indian and War Offices whose inter-departmental bickering had hitherto hindered policy making. He was backed by a Middle East Department staffed by specialists all of whom he had selected. Curzon vainly protested on behalf of the Foreign Office and, in a sulky mood, he predicted that Churchill would 'be under an irresistible temptation to proclaim himself King in Babylon'.[20]

Churchill was also expected to create the new empire on the cheap. Interest payments on wartime loans, a faltering economy, the burden of welfare payments to the growing number of unemployed, and the Treasury's insistent demands for cheeseparing combined to impose severe restrictions on Britain's imperial policies. Churchill sympathised with the men who held the purse strings and he had already called into question whether new imperial commitments in the Middle and Near East were a squandering of scarce resources. As a doctrinaire Victorian liberal he wholeheartedly endorsed the coalition's policies of deflation, fiscal discipline and balancing the books. He also had to take on board public opinion, which refused to tolerate an empire that rested solely on armed coercion.

Churchill's task was, therefore, to balance thrift with imperial security and create a Middle East where pro-British local rulers kept the peace in return for subsidies and protection by RAF squadrons, which were cheaper to maintain than garrisons. These arrangements required compromises with Arab nationalism and, perhaps trickiest of all, persuading the Arabs that their future interests and prosperity were compatible with Jewish immigration into Palestine, as promised in the Balfour Declaration.

Having for the past two years alleged that Britain had bitten off more than it could chew, let alone digest, Churchill had to acquiesce to the idea that Britain would somehow have to maintain a durable and dominant presence in the Middle East. He believed that its chances of success would be greatly improved by extending a friendly hand to Atatürk's national movement, but, much to his frustration, he had to live with Lloyd George's purblind faith in the capacity of a Greek army to beat a Turkish one and his refusal to accept Turkey as a national entity.

If they could be coaxed into believing that Britain was a sympathetic patron and friend, the Arabs were the natural partners for Churchill's new enterprise. When the Commons had debated Middle Eastern policy in June 1920, there were a number of interventions by young MPs with wartime experience in the region who argued that Britain was under a binding moral obligation to the Arabs who had fought alongside Britain and that their goodwill had to be regained. William Ormesby-Gore, formerly of the wartime Arab Bureau, invoked Britain's 'moral duty to an Arab civilisation and an Arab state'. He slated Cox's Anglo-Indian administration for its crassness towards the Iraqis which had lost their respect. He reminded members that: 'The British officer, in the old-fashioned phrase, treats the Arab as a gentleman, and the Arab sheikh treats him in the same way.' Aubrey Herbert, whose personal knowledge of the people of the region was extensive (he may have been the model for John Buchan's Sandy Clanroyden) warned that Britain had forfeited trust in the Middle East, but it could easily be restored by an Arab parliament in Baghdad.[21]

These criticisms became Churchill's guidelines and the most forceful critic of British regional policy, Colonel T. E. Lawrence, became the Colonial Secretary's mentor. His opinions had the authority of experience and, through his journalism, he had successfully projected himself as uniquely qualified to see the world through Arab eyes. A former intelligence officer, he had liaised with Faisal's forces between 1916 and 1918 and commanded Bedouin partisans in a number of daring operations against the Damascus-to-Medina railway. The revelations of his exploits coincided with his appearance at the Versailles Conference (he was Faisal's interpreter) in exotic Arab costume. Politicians and the public were entranced by this charismatic intellectual and heeded what he had to say about the Arabs and their aspirations. If these were ignored, Lawrence warned Sir Henry Wilson, then Britain would soon be 'kicked out' of Turkey, Iraq and Persia.

Lawrence's arguments blended imperial expediency with his passionate sense of moral justice. Their wartime sacrifices had qualified the Arabs for a place within the British Empire, but on their own terms. As he wrote in *The Times* in July 1920, the Arabs had fought not to become British or French subjects, 'but to win a show of their own'. Honour demanded this because of Britain's promises to the Hashemite princes Faisal and Abdullah and, if, as Lawrence proposed, they were made kings of Iraq and Transjordan, then the Empire would acquire two loyal dependencies. Iraq, Lawrence predicted, might even outpace India in the constitutional race to become Britain's first 'brown dominion'. Like Churchill, he saw the Empire as an evolving organism that was constantly mutating, but always in accordance with liberal principles.

The views of Lawrence and his allies prevailed. The first imperative was to bring the Hashemites onside and convince them that Britain would fulfil their dynastic dreams. They were potential irritants who enjoyed a widespread following among Arab nationalists of all complexions. Abdullah was asserting the regal equivalent of squatters' rights in the Transjordan where he was de facto ruler over 300,000 Arabs. The local commander-in-chief General Sir Walter ('Squibby') Congreve admitted that a lack of manpower made it impossible for Britain to intervene, even if the political will had been present. There were well-founded fears that, unbridled, Abdullah and Faisal would stir up further trouble in Syria that would drive a wedge between Britain and France. Opportunities also existed for Abdullah to exploit the tensions between Arabs and Jewish settlers in Palestine.

Barely pacified Iraq was Churchill's most pressing problem. It was, and some might allege, still is a geographical abstraction: it had no natural boundaries beyond those of the three former Ottoman *vilayets* [administrative districts] which it once comprised. Three-quarters of its population were Sunni Arabs, the rest Shia Arabs and Kurds, who had no love for the majority. At first, British occupation had been welcomed in many quarters. A Kurdish sheikh who, like the rest of his people, imagined that liberation would be followed by autonomy, declared in November 1918 that: 'The English are good men. We live on good terms with them, we give and take maidens with them.'[22] There had been no reciprocity of any kind and since the Kurds were concentrated on the northern, oil-bearing district, Sir Percy Cox had dragooned them into the projected Iraqi kingdom. To have detached the Kurds and their homeland would have stripped the country of its only hope for economic self-sufficiency.

At the end of December, the cabinet approved the establishment of an Iraqi kingdom under British tutelage and offered its throne to Faisal. In January 1921 he agreed in principle to be Britain's candidate for the throne. He also surrendered his claims to suzerainty over Palestine, which was a relief for the government, who feared that Faisal might have rallied the anti-Zionists there and across the Middle East. According to that expert judge in such niceties, Curzon, the future king 'behaved like a real gentleman and with a fine sense of humour and loyalty'. He had no choice in the matter, for, as Churchill bluntly put it, it was Faisal's last opportunity of acquiring a crown.[23] History appeared to be on Churchill's side, for he later overrode objections to the foreigner Faisal being foisted on Iraq by recalling that William I and George I had both been foreigners and became highly effective monarchs.[24]

With a compliant Faisal in his pocket, Churchill was free to proceed with hammering out the details of a settlement. To this end, he called a conference in which his own experts from the Middle East Department would join local administrators and senior officers to produce a coherent and durable regional policy. Baghdad was intended as the venue, but it was rejected in favour of the marginally safer Cairo, where Churchill and his wife arrived in the second week of March. As they were driven through the city Egyptians shouted 'À bas Churchill!'

During the preceding weeks Churchill had placed himself in the expert hands of a band of specialists whose experience and knowledge directed his thinking. The most influential was Lawrence, whom he had first met at Versailles and quickly came to respect; there was an empathy between two creative writers who admired each other's style and shared a common disregard for the mundane and conventional. A further, deeper bond was their sense of being men of destiny endowed with the power to understand and direct the forces of history. Several years later Lawrence summed up Churchill's virtues: 'The man's as brave as six, as good humoured, shrewd, self-confident and considerable as a statesman can be; and several times I've seen him chuck the statesmanlike course and do the honest thing instead.'[25] Another eccentric of the Middle East Department, Colonel Richard Meinertzhagen, watched the pair at work and, with characteristic scepticism, concluded that their rapport rested on Churchill's 'hero worship' and Lawrence's reciprocal 'cheap flattery'.[26]

Churchill was also advised by Gertrude Bell, a zealous supporter of Arab nationalism and an Iraqi state. She had travelled extensively in the country before the war and her bearing had caused one overawed sheikh to declare that if British women were like this, then their men were truly to be feared. Cox too was asked to attend the conference, although Churchill had no faith in him. Nevertheless, his intimate knowledge of the personalities and nuances of tribal and religious politics was essential for stage-managing Faisal's election and the transfer of power. Fabricating a cheap and effective military apparatus to safeguard British interests (and the rulers who upheld them) was the responsibility of two men whom Churchill liked and trusted: Sir Hugh Trenchard and Sir Walter Congreve.

What emerged from the Cairo Conference was a compound of old and new imperial artifices. Following tradition, Churchill negotiated mutually beneficial pacts with local potentates whose authority would be enhanced through British protection and subsidies. Such arrangements had been made with the princes of India and more recently with their counterparts in Northern Nigeria. As Lawrence observed of Abdullah, his eminence and lineage would command the obedience of the tribal sheikhs and a society accustomed to hierarchies of birth and power.[27] As agreed earlier, Faisal was nominated as a candidate for the Iraqi throne and it was left to Cox to pull the right strings to secure his election. In August he swept the poll, receiving 96 per cent of the votes cast, which was to be expected, given his popularity and Cox's deportation of his potential opponents.[28] At Faisal's insistence and against the better judgement of Churchill and Lawrence, the Kurds and the Mosul oilfields were forcibly incorporated into his kingdom.

Churchill decided to seal the Anglo-Hashemite alliance by negotiating with Abdullah in person in Jerusalem. This amiable and relaxed prince was persuaded to abandon his claims to Palestine, to cease meddling in Syria and to use his authority to stifle anti-Zionist agitation in Palestine. In return, Churchill gave him the throne of the Transjordan, an annual subsidy of £180,000, British officers and equipment for his army (the Arab Legion) and RAF support against his internal and external enemies. Churchill assured Abdullah that Jews would not be allowed to settle in his kingdom and that mass Jewish immigration into Palestine would never occur.[29] As Lawrence had predicted, Churchill and Abdullah got on well and Churchill was pleased by the King's 'commonsense and humour'.[30] Like Faisal, Abdullah was served by a coterie of British civilian and military advisers and each monarch submitted to Whitehall's control over their foreign policies.

The Cairo Conference also decided to pass regional security into the hands of the RAF, which was what Churchill had long intended. In December 1919 he had told the Commons that 'The first duty of the Royal Air Force is to garrison the British Empire' and he introduced measures designed to transform its officers into men fit to uphold the prestige and dignity of the Empire. In order to infuse the new service with the army's regimental spirit, he insisted on competitive examinations for officers, who he hoped would all be public school men.[31] A typical RAF officer would always be an 'officer and a gentleman' whose overseas duties were to enforce the policy of 'Air Control'. Churchill was convinced that it provided the only affordable and efficient means of upholding imperial prestige and chastising the lawless and recalcitrant. Nineteen of the RAF's twenty-five squadrons were deployed for imperial policing: eight in India, seven in Egypt, three in Iraq and one in Aden. In the Middle East, aircraft were supported by armoured-car units and locally raised levies under British officers.

Churchill had intended that bombing and strafing would always be instruments of last resort and, in June 1921, he forbade Cox to use aircraft to punish tribes who had defaulted on their taxes. His injunction followed a hideous incident in which bombers had machine-gunned fleeing villagers and stampeded their herds after they failed to show the subservience that Cox expected. 'To fire wilfully on women and children is a disgraceful act,' minuted an appalled Churchill, but Cox and Wing-Commander Amyas ('Biffy') Borton, the local RAF commander, had no qualms about mass murder, and they refused to hold anyone to account.[32] Churchill found himself squeezed into a corner: a public reprimand for this pair would add to the embarrassment of a government already tainted by the Amritsar and Black and Tan scandals. It was Natal all over again and Churchill had to ignore the prompting of his conscience.

Aerial coercion continued to be brutally applied. In 1923, 144 Iraqis were killed in the Samawa district for not paying their taxes. One RAF officer felt sorry for the victims of such raids who had resented having to fund the salaries of those they called 'tomato-eating *effendis* in Baghdad'.[33] Among these sybarites were the British advisory staff in Baghdad who, in the opinion of Meinertzhagen, were a 'gang of bounders', including Colonel Lord Gough who got drunk and insulted ladies in between commanding Iraqi levies. Service in Iraq seems not to have been a magnet for the best sort of sahib.[34]

Air Control did succeed as Churchill hoped it would in curbing unrest. RAF bombers suppressed several Kurdish insurrections between 1922 and 1924 and saved the Transjordan from an invasion by thousands of puritanical *Wahabi* fanatics from the Saudi Arabian interior in 1924. Aircraft and armoured cars based in Amman were summoned and their combined firepower shattered the masses of camelry and horsemen, killing at least five hundred. Churchill's promise to Abdullah that the RAF would keep him on his throne was amply fulfilled. Faisal too had reason to be grateful to Air Control. On returning from a visit to Iraq in 1925, Leo Amery observed that: 'If the writ of King Faisal runs effectively throughout his kingdom it is entirely due to British aeroplanes. If the aeroplanes were removed tomorrow, the whole structure would inevitably fall to pieces.'[35]

There was extensive criticism of Air Control. The army was jealous of the Johnny-come-lately service which had, with Churchill's connivance, usurped its customary role of imperial peacekeeping. During the Cairo Conference, Trenchard had been cold-shouldered by senior army officers, which turned out to be a blessing, for he was thrown into the more lively company of Lawrence and Gertrude Bell, both incidentally enthusiasts for Air Control. It and the political settlement agreed in Cairo infuriated Sir Henry Wilson, who dismissed the arrangements as 'hot air, aeroplanes and Arabs'. In a fit of the sulks, he delayed the transfer of armoured cars to the Middle East with the excuse that they were needed in Ireland.[36]

Churchill was triumphant; in March 1922 he brushed aside charges that the introduction of Air Control was a dangerous gamble. 'The British Empire', he declared to the Commons, 'has been built up by running risks.'[37] He had taken a chance and it paid off in Iraq, at least in terms of saving cash. By 1923, the annual charges for Iraq had fallen from £30 million to £7 million and for Palestine from £8 million to £2 million.

Money was saved, but many of the post mortem reports of Air Control in action made grim reading. With repulsive relish, 'Biffy' Borton reported that a village which had been a 'hot bed of malcontents' had been completely flattened by a hundred bombs.[38] Terrified Kurds called the aeroplanes 'the roaring lions of the air', but their victims sometimes fired back at them. Enough details of what is now euphemistically called 'collateral damage' of aerial operations in the Middle East and on the North-West Frontier filtered through to the public to cause consternation. After Churchill had left the Colonial Office, there were sporadic controversies over the morality of Air Control. It may have satisfied the penny pinchers at the Treasury, but did it win the respect and goodwill of the Empire's new subjects? At the Cairo Conference, General Sir Philip Chetwood had protested that Air Control was 'a form of terrorism which would involve the death by bombing of women and children', which of course it did.[39] In September 1932 *The Times* pertinently asked whether bombing raids generated 'bitterness' among tribesmen and, during a debate in the House of Lords, Field Marshal Lord Plumer wondered if Air Control was the most efficacious way of demonstrating 'the integrity, justice and humanity of British rule'.[40]

Concerns over the morality and efficacy of Air Control merged with the wider, inter-war debate over whether large-scale aerial bombardment would be decisive in a European war. One who was adamant that it would be was Arthur Harris, a Rhodesian-born RAF officer, whose experience of flying sorties against Pashtun villages convinced him that bombing had utterly demoralised the tribesmen. Relentlessly applied, aerial bombardment would do the same to Europeans. Harris subsequently rose to lead Bomber Command and applied the lessons of Air Control on a gigantic scale to the industrial towns and cities of Germany.

In fact, his case rested on a flawed premise; the Pashtun had quickly discovered how to fight back by contriving a system of what would be called Air-Raid Precautions, including warning alarms and shelters.[41] Nor had sustained bombing brought them to their knees. The British Minister in Kabul percipiently and, in the light of popular reaction to the Blitz, correctly observed that the bombing raids on frontier communities failed to disorientate and demoralise their victims. Rather, these impersonal and terrifying attacks generated an 'undying hatred and desire for revenge'.[42] This was exactly what Afghans felt about the application of modern versions of Air Control by Russia in the 1980s and America after 2003.

Early evidence of a future source of Middle Eastern strife confronted Churchill on his railway journey from Cairo to Jerusalem at the end of March 1921 after he had ordered his train to stop at Gaza to inspect the site of Lord Allenby's victory over the Turks four years before. His party was greeted by an angry crowd of Arabs chanting slogans. Taken aback, he asked Lawrence for an explanation. 'I say, Lawrence, are these people dangerous? They don't seem pleased to see us. What are they shouting?' Lawrence said that there was nothing to be worried about and translated the words as 'Down with the British and down with the Jewish policy!' He may have glossed, for another version of this episode had the Arabs shouting 'Down with the Jews! Cut their throats!'

The demonstrators were voicing Palestinian opposition to Zionism. It was an ideology that had emerged during the second half of the nineteenth century and its aim was the creation of a Jewish homeland, preferably within the Ottoman province of Palestine. The need for such a sanctuary had been dramatically and revoltingly demonstrated by the pogroms in Russia during the 1890s and early 1900s, which had been blessed by both the state and the Russian Orthodox Church. Even more terrifying, in that it occurred in France, one of the most enlightened states of Europe, was the outburst of anti-Semitism during the Dreyfus affair. The publication of Emile Zola's '*J'accuse*' article in 1898 was a signal for the ultra-nationalist and Catholic press to spew out a torrent of anti-Semitic abuse which drove mobs on to the streets, howling 'Death to the Jews!' The message was horrifyingly clear: the Jew remained a perpetual outsider, whether in reactionary Russia, or in liberal France.

Europe's Jews needed a safe refuge, even if they lived in outwardly tolerant nations. In terms of religion and history, Palestine seemed perfectly suited to play such a role and early Zionists had funded small agricultural settlements of immigrants with the permission of the Ottoman authorities. On the eve of Allenby's advance towards Jerusalem, the British government issued the Balfour Declaration of November 1917, which promised that Britain would make Palestine a Jewish homeland. A month later, the Turkish Grand Vizier told a German journalist that his government would continue to be friendly towards Jewish immigration, although it objected to Jewish settlers retaining their Russian citizenship.[43]

Churchill had taken no part in drawing up the declaration. He sympathised with the Zionist movement, having been converted by his contacts with Manchester's Jewish community during his pre-war electioneering in the city, and his attachment to Zionism remained strong throughout the rest of his life. It was idiosyncratic in that its components were an admiration of Jewish virtues, compassion for their historic predicament and pragmatic imperialism.

The genius and industry of the Jews, Churchill believed, would prove the redemption of Palestine. Here, they would 'exercise their capacities' and create a prosperous community that would prove a 'great strength' to the Empire.[44] He thought that such dynamism and vision were beyond the Arabs. In July 1921, he told Smuts that the Arab was 'a stagnant element in a backward country' who was blocking 'civilisation by his mulish rejection of Jewish brains, money and innovation'. Progress, he later told the Commons, had been impossible, thanks to the historic inertia of 'a handful of philosophical people in the wasted, sun-scorched plains' allowing 'the waters of the Jordan continue to flow unbridled and unharnessed into the Dead Sea'. In 1937, when he gave evidence to Viscount Peel's commission on the future of Palestine, Churchill repudiated the suggestion that the Arabs had been unjustly treated. 'The injustice', he argued, 'is when those who lived in the country leave it be a desert for thousands of years.[45]

This was the same case that had been made to justify European colonisation since the sixteenth century and, more recently, it had been used to validate the settlement of the white dominions and the westward expansion of the United States. This may go some way in helping to explain why American support for Israel became so strong during the later twentieth century; states founded by pioneer settlers in the teeth of indigenous opposition were bound to share a common outlook. In essence, Zionism was an offshoot of nineteenth-century imperialism in so far as it assumed that the ultimate right of territorial possession rested with the occupiers' ability to make the best use of what nature had provided.

By the same token, incomers who mastered nature and released its potential deserved praise and encouragement, which was why Churchill heaped both on the white settlers in Rhodesia, who, he told the Commons in July 1921, were 'men against the wilderness' struggling for their existence and livelihood. How sad it was, Churchill remarked, that only a pittance was available to help these pioneers, while millions were doled out to fund garrisons in deserts.[46] Jewish regeneration of a section of this wasteland would transform Palestine into a self-reliant and thriving imperial dependency. Interestingly, this was also the opinion of the Labour Party leader Ramsay MacDonald who, in 1922, described the typical Jewish immigrant in Palestine as 'an idealist and a worker' whose exertions would increase the country's wealth a hundredfold. Again, like Churchill, MacDonald was appalled by the lack of enterprise among the Arabs.[47]

There was also a powerful quasi-religious element of Zionism which meant nothing to Churchill, although it had a strong emotional appeal to those of his countrymen for whom the Old Testament revealed the mind of God. Despite moments of opacity and crustiness, Jehovah's overall intention was for His chosen people to inhabit Palestine which He had promised them. Divine Providence delivered its title deeds to the Jews and Zionists believed that they were still valid. The Bible also dictated the geography of Palestine. When the Zionist leader and Churchill's friend Chaim Weizmann asked for the area between the River Jordan and the Damascus-to-Medina railway, he based his claim on their occupation by the tribes Reuben, Gad and Mannaseh two-thousand years before. These lands were now home to the Arab subjects of Prince Abdullah, and Churchill wisely ignored the Old Testament version of history and decided to keep them that way rather than exacerbate Arab-Jewish tension.[48]

Churchill's attitude towards the Jews was not, however, wholly benevolent. During 1919, along with many other public figures, he had been perturbed by the number of Jews among the Bolshevik leadership in Russia, Germany and Hungary. This fact was grist to the mill of conspiracy theorists who had swallowed the contents of the bogus *Protocols of the Elders of Zion* which had just been published. It alleged that all Jews everywhere were engaged in a vast plot to subvert and dominate the world and that the Bolshevik revolution had been integral to this enterprise. A handful of imbeciles on the extreme right of British politics believed this nonsense, but soberer figures did acknowledge the existence of a universal and influential body of Jewish opinion which was called 'world Jewry'.

Gaining its goodwill had been one of the motives for the Balfour Declaration and, when Churchill defended it in the Commons in July 1921, he drew members' attention to the 'support which Jews could give us all over the world, particularly in the United States'. His belief in the power of the Jewish community remained strong; in 1937 he invoked what he called 'the legitimate international influence' of the Jews as a possible means of putting pressure on Nazi Germany.[49] On a quite different tack, he hoped Zionist schemes in Palestine might somehow lure Jews away from their imagined affinity towards Bolshevism.[50] Whether or not this worked, Churchill assured the Commons that 'Bolshevik riffraff' would be weeded out from the Jews who were flocking to Palestine to escape the White Russian pogroms.[51]

*

These refugees fled one form of hatred to stumble into another. Friction between Jewish immigrants and native Palestinians pre-dated the British occupation and grew in bitterness after the publication of the Balfour Declaration.[52] In 1918 the total population of Palestine was just over 750,000, of whom 600,000 or so were Arab peasant farmers and Bedouin nomads, 84,000 were Jews and 71,000 Christians of various nationalities and denominations. The numbers of Jewish immigrants soared during the Russian civil war, which fuelled Arab anxieties that they would soon be outnumbered and elbowed out of their country.

As the occupying and later mandatory power, Britain had to keep the peace and, crucially, had to reconcile the indigenous Arabs and the Zionists. If no accommodation could be reached, then British relations with the wider Arab world would be tainted. The Palestinians understood this and, in a petition presented to Churchill during his brief tour of their country in March 1921, he was warned that the Arabs were the 'key to the East' and that Britain needed their goodwill. There was also a note of menace: 'The Arab is noble and large hearted; he is also vengeful, and never forgets an ill-deed.' A denunciation of the Jews followed which echoed the slurs of European anti-Semites: 'The Jew is the Jew all the world over. He amasses the wealth of a country and then leads its people, whom he had already impoverished, where he chooses ...'[53] Accusations that the Jews were 'clannish and unneighbourly' may even have struck a chord with Churchill, who, in 1937, prepared an article analysing the roots of anti-Semitism. One was Jewish exclusiveness and detachment from the societies they inhabited, a point also raised by Lloyd George in a contemporary piece for the *Evening Standard*.[54] Both men begged the question, could a sense of apartness ever justify the persecution of Jews, who were in every way industrious and loyal members of society throughout western Europe?

During his stay in Palestine, Churchill paraded his Zionist sympathies and did nothing to calm the Arabs or dispel their fears. He expressed his wonderment at the Jewish settlements inhabited by 'splendid open air men [and] beautiful women' whose labours were making 'the desert bloom like a rose'. The Arabs were curtly reminded that two thousand British troops had died in the campaign for Palestine and that by right of conquest Britain had the legal authority to determine its future. Arab anxieties as to what this might be were swept aside by a Churchillian prediction that the flow of investment that was underwriting Jewish immigrants would generate a prosperity that would erode and finally eradicate present animosities. He was correct about the money; between 1919 and 1939 American Jews provided the settlements with $41 million, but wrong about the decline in Arab hostility.[55]

All that Churchill had offered the Palestinians was an exhortation to show forbearance while the Jewish immigrants gathered the ingredients for a feast that everyone would enjoy at some future date. According to local military intelligence, his insensitive handling of Arab grievances contributed to the riots which broke out in Jaffa in May.[56] There were fifty deaths, forty-two of them Jewish. Lawrence, who was then advising Abdullah, and the local commander-in-chief General Congreve feared the onset of a civil war. Sir Herbert Samuel, the Commissioner, took fright and immediately suspended Jewish immigration; recent arrivals were hurriedly shipped off to Alexandria. Afterwards, a pessimistic Congreve warned Churchill that public order could only be guaranteed if some curbs were applied to the Zionists.[57] Like many other British officers serving in Palestine, he found it easier to engage with the Arabs than with Russian and Eastern European Jews, a trait that the ultra-Zionist Meinertzhagen attributed to anti-Semitism. Churchill was displeased by Congreve's comments and contemplated transferring responsibility for Palestine to the RAF.

Squibby Congreve had been right. In August, Churchill was forced to admit to the cabinet that the situation in Palestine was still fraught as 'both Arabs and Jews are armed and arming, ready to spring at each other's throats'. To help keep order in what seemed an ungovernable province he recruited seven hundred redundant Black and Tans, who formed the nucleus of the Palestine Police Force. Policy remained unchanged, for Churchill was determined to stick by the Balfour Declaration. He said so to an Arab delegation which visited London at the end of the year, again recommending them to cooperate with the Jews. Paradoxically, this was also the platform of the Jewish Socialist Workers party, which he was then trying to ban.[58]

He rejected Arab demands for an elected government on the grounds that they were certain to secure a majority that would terminate Jewish immigration.[59] The status quo and Britain's continued commitment to a Jewish homeland in Palestine were embodied in an official White Paper in June 1922. Soon after its publication, Arab nationalists were rejoicing in the news of Atatürk's victories over the Greeks. Churchill too was glad to hear this news, but for different reasons.

For the past three years, Churchill had strenuously urged the cabinet to back the new regime in Turkey since it had a capacity to make trouble for Britain in Iraq and Palestine. Lloyd George too feared a resurgent and irredentist Turkey, but believed that the only way to neuter it was to support the Greeks in their war against the Turkish army in western Anatolia. He had backed a loser: the Greeks were trounced by Atatürk during the twelve-day battle of the Sakarya River in August 1922, a defeat that shattered the Prime Minister's hopes of winning this proxy war. Turkish forces converged on Smyrna, where, true to past form, they slaughtered Greeks and Armenians. Then, Atatürk shifted his attention northwards to Constantinople and the neutral zone surrounding the Straits, which was garrisoned by British and French forces under General Sir Charles Harington.

The Allies feared that a repetition of the Smyrna massacre in Constantinople (home to half a million Greeks and Armenians) would be an unbearable humiliation. Hitherto a zealous Turkophile, Churchill suddenly switched sides and stood shoulder to shoulder with Lloyd George. Another scrap was beckoning and Churchill was looking forward to it with unashamed excitement; walking through St James's Park, he confided to Hankey that he was keen for Atatürk to attack the British positions.[60] The explanation for Churchill's change of heart can be found in the wording of orders sent by the cabinet to Harington on 21 September. It was now 'a point of immense moral significance to the prestige of the Empire' that any advance by Atatürk's forces must be resisted. An attack on the units holding Chanak [Çanakkale] was to be treated as an attack on Britain, an assertion which must have shaken Harington, for he was heavily outnumbered there and in Constantinople. Nor could the Royal

Navy prevent Turkish forces from crossing the Straits to Thrace on the European side.

Britain was friendless. The dominions refused to be bamboozled into an imperial war against Turkey; Churchill's appeal for troops was met with a brusque refusal from Canada and tepid prevarication elsewhere. France and Italy opted out of a venture whose objective was the blatant assertion of British power in the Near East and their troops pulled out, leaving Harington to face Atatürk alone. The general prudently decided against delivering an ultimatum to the Turks and, instead, negotiated an armistice with their local commander. At the end of October a new treaty was agreed between the Allies and Turkey at Lausanne, which settled its frontiers, acknowledged its independence and declared the Straits a neutral waterway. Britain's bravado had failed to deter the Turks, its bluff had been called and the upshot was a peacetime humiliation on a scale that would not be seen again until the Suez debacle in 1956.

The Lloyd George coalition was the only casualty of the standoff at Chanak. 'Stop this War' had been the *Daily Mail*'s headline on 18 September and it reflected a widespread public anger at their government's sabre rattling. In a letter to *The Times*, Bonar Law suggested that playing the role of global policeman was not in Britain's best interests, and the public agreed. Nemesis followed quickly; the Conservatives defected from the coalition after a meeting of its MPs in the Carlton Club (the origins of the 1922 Committee of backbenchers) and Lloyd George resigned on 31 October.

On 15 November the Tories won a general election in which Churchill, suffering from appendicitis, lost Dundee to a slightly dotty Prohibitionist, Edwin Scrymgeour. The campaign on the hustings had been rough with 'Dardanelles' being a favourite catcall of Churchill's opponents. T. E. Lawrence, now a ranker in the RAF, commiserated: 'What bloody shits these Dundeans must be.' Churchill later gamely jested: 'In the turning of an eye, I found myself without office, without a seat, without a party, and even without an appendix.'

The long-term consequence of Churchill's Middle Eastern settlement are still with us. He had achieved an armistice in the war for the Ottoman succession, which has now evolved into smaller struggles between Kurds, Arabs, Jews and Sunni and Shi'ite Muslims into which the United States has been drawn as a force majeure. Churchill cannot be blamed for what followed in so far as money shortages had given him very limited freedom of manoeuvre, and he had proceeded on the premise that British regional paramountcy was the only way to secure the stability that was necessary for imperial security. Withdrawal would have saved money and tears, but it would have encouraged France and Turkey (which had its eyes on Kurdistan and Mosul) to fill the void. Instead, it was filled by subsidised conservative princes supported by the firepower of the RAF.

Nationalist aspirations remained, bubbling away under the surface of Pax Britannica: there were anti-Jewish riots in Palestine in 1929 and in 1936 a full-scale Arab uprising. The reins on Egypt were loosened in 1924 and in 1936 an Anglo-Egyptian treaty allowed autonomy, but the British garrisons remained guarding the Suez Canal and RAF bombers regularly flew over Cairo. Young Abdul Gamal Nasser shook his fist at them and he noted that his father had hung a portrait of Atatürk on the wall of their house: here was a leader who had defied Britain and then proceeded to build a secular and progressive state.

PART FOUR

1923–1939

The Will to Rule:

The Struggle to Keep India, 1923–1936

Churchill's career blossomed during the 1920s and withered during the 1930s. He rejoined the Conservatives and, between 1924 and the Labour general election victory in August 1929, he served as Chancellor of the Exchequer under Stanley Baldwin. In the next two years, he distanced himself from the Tories and became a backbencher. Many thought that his eclipse would prove permanent; the shooting star had at last burned itself out, and a good thing too thought many Conservatives who had never forgiven the turncoat for his attacks on their party twenty years before. Yet his stamina and vitality were as great as ever; as one civil servant percipiently remarked, Churchill was like camomile, for 'the more he is trodden on, the more he flourished'.

Churchill's imperialism was his undoing. From 1930 to 1935 he was a Cassandra, warning the country that the government's policy of allowing self-determination for India would be a catastrophe for Britain and mark the beginning of the end for her Empire. His language was stark and his imagery apocalyptic: India was facing a prolonged crisis which successive governments had failed to resolve. The fault lay with the feeble measures applied by weak men who had lost faith in their country's imperial mission. Their timidity contrasted with the vigour and resolve of the rulers of Italy and Japan, whose countries were emerging as aggressive rivals to Britain in the Middle and Far East.

The picture of Churchill during this period as a shunned figure wandering in the political wilderness is only partly right. He was still a political force to be reckoned with. His memoirs of the years between 1914 and 1922 and his biography of Marlborough (which absorbed much of his time and creative energy during this period) were bestsellers. Most important of all, in terms of his public stature, Churchill was a prolific journalist and, from 1932, a broadcaster whose opinions on current affairs were aired on the BBC and American networks. To judge from the flood of requests from newspaper editors in both countries, his thoughts on all kinds of subjects attracted enormous interest. Churchill had a fortnightly column in the *Evening Standard* and his articles appeared regularly in the *Daily Mail* and the *News of the World*.

Unknown to his millions of readers, Churchill was remarkably well informed, because he had access to secret intelligence material. 'Tell him what he wants to know, keep him informed' had been the new Prime Minister Ramsay MacDonald's instructions to the relevant authorities in 1929 and his successors Baldwin and Neville Chamberlain were similarly obliging.[1] After 1933, classified information came Churchill's way via his friend and confidant Major Desmond Morton of the SIS. His specialism was industrial espionage, but he passed on intelligence about national defence, foreign and imperial affairs; for example, he gave Churchill details of Nazi plans to sell artillery to Afghanistan, which was still, according to the CID, a 'minor danger' to Indian security.[2]

Before following Churchill into his battle to keep control over India, it is helpful to pause and consider the roots of his thinking. His critics imagined that they were dealing with a dangerously articulate adversary who, for all his invocation of History, had failed to appreciate the direction that it was now taking. Nor had he shaken off, or even reconsidered the imperial ideals of his youth. This emerged from conversations between Churchill and Leo Amery, formerly Baldwin's Colonial Secretary, during a transatlantic voyage in August 1929. Churchill mourned the absence from the political landscape of the titans of his youth such as Gladstone and Salisbury and lesser luminaries such as John Morley. Afterwards, as he prepared to go to bed in a long silk nightshirt with a woollen cummerbund against the ocean's chills, Amery quipped, 'Free Trade, mid-Victorian statesmanship and old-fashioned nightshirt, how appropriate a combination.' Churchill's opinions and nightclothes confirmed what Amery had long suspected: 'the key to Winston is to realise that he is Mid-Victorian, steeped in the politics of his father's period, and unable ever to get the modern point of view. It is only his verbal exuberance and bounding vitality that conceal this elementary fact about him.[3]

Baldwin placed Churchill in a slightly later generation. Once he had launched his campaign against Indian self-government, he commented that he was 'once again the subaltern of Hussars in 1896' and that the eternal cavalryman yearned to lead the Tories back to the pre-1914 world when the Empire had been governed with 'a strong hand'.[4] Baldwin's toady, Geoffrey Dawson the editor of *The Times,* echoed his confederate when he dismissed Churchill as 'the omniscient subaltern' who was mentally quarantined from the contemporary world.[5] Churchill's thinking had become ossified and obsolete.

Of course, the past mattered enormously to Churchill, but he was not shackled to it as Baldwin and Amery fancied. His Empire was never frozen in the 1890s; it was constantly evolving and adapting to new circumstances, including the growth of popular nationalism among its subjects. Churchill welcomed the devolution of power, so long as it did not weaken imperial ties with Britain. As he told Canadians in August 1929, 'I've put through Parliaments two of the most daring experiments self-government ever attempted in connection with the Transvaal and the Irish Free State.'[6] This achievement had been recently acknowledged by Baldwin when he had briefly contemplated the appointment of Churchill as Viceroy of India, solely on his merits as a mediator.[7] In principle at least, Churchill had not objected to Indians being given responsibilities for their own local government. The Indian counterpart of elected County Councils was allowable, but never in the foreseeable future did he envisage a full-blown sovereign parliament.

Applying liberal democratic principles to the Empire required extreme caution. As Churchill would constantly argue, one of its prime objectives was to protect its subjects from each other and preserve civil peace. Britain had become the guardian of minorities whose interests would be trampled on if authority was handed to majorities who were hosts to ancestral religious and political animosities. This duty was paramount and, in the summer of 1929, Churchill had been shocked by the way in which the newly elected Labour government had ignored it when dealing with a crisis in Egypt. After another confrontation with the *Wafd* [the main Egyptian nationalist party], accompanied as ever by riots and looting, MacDonald had sacked the tough-minded High Commissioner Lord Lloyd and agreed to the withdrawal of British troops from Cairo to the Canal Zone.

Churchill immediately execrated what he saw as a signal exhibition of weakness in the Commons and later he alleged that it had led directly to a wave of anti-Jewish disturbances in Palestine, where, he claimed, the Arabs had been quick to detect a softening of the imperial will to rule. The Jews suffered, as other minorities would whenever Britain faltered. As he told a Canadian audience, not only the Jews had been betrayed but Britain's wider 'mission in the East'.

Minorities would always need protection from overbearing majorities. Churchill repeatedly claimed that Britain's hegemony in Egypt prevented the exploitation of the rural peasantry by the rich *effendiya* class which, he imagined, was the backbone of the nationalist movement. This was a simplification: during the largest anti-British disorders in March 1919, there had been strikes by doctors and lawyers and riots by high-school students, but the protesters also included workers in railway workshops and labourers.[8] Over thirty years later, when musing on his early career, Churchill told his personal doctor Sir Charles Wilson (later Lord Moran) that, when he served under Lloyd George, 'I wanted to bring in radical reform in Egypt, to tax the Pashas [landowners] and make life right for the fellahin.'[9] In February 1945, Churchill lectured King Farouk on the need for a more democratic parliament in Egypt and urged him to do all in his power to reduce the inequality in the country.[10] President Roosevelt delivered a similar remonstrance, but, like Churchill's, it was ignored by that idle playboy prince. Churchill may have urged a form of *noblesse oblige* as the salvation of Egypt, but he did nothing to implement it during the period of British dominance in Egypt.

Material and social progress appeared to be the admirable goal of the French administration of Morocco, which Churchill visited in January 1936 and, after his return, he reported on what he had seen in the *Daily Mail*, praising the farsightedness of the French officials who were dedicated to the 'enrichment' of everyone in Morocco. Their zeal contrasted with the 'apologetic indifference' displayed by Britain towards its Asian and African colonies.[11] His words contrasted with his attitude towards state investment in the colonies, which was a mixture of lassitude and acquiescence to Treasury orthodoxy. Thus, in 1919 he had called for an annual budget of £50 million for funding colonial development, but, at the end of Churchill's chancellorship, the amount available was only £1 million. The gulf between rhetoric and performance dismayed Leo Amery, a fervent believer in large-scale official investment in the colonies. He suspected, with good reason, that, as an old-fashioned Free Trader, Churchill frowned on any form of government intervention in the market.[12] In many colonies, the consequence was the stagnation, poverty, poor diet and disease which Clementine witnessed during her visit to Barbados in 1935. At the end of her letter to Winston she wrote: 'And this is a sample of the British Empire upon which the Sun never sets.'[13]

Churchill's notions about race were all too evident throughout his campaign to scupper the India Bill. What Churchill had to say on this subject may repel readers, but it must always be remembered that his views were widely shared by men and women of all political complexions in Europe and the United States. In any case, Western assumptions of superiority have not vanished entirely; they permeate the sermons periodically preached to Third World nations on such subjects as human rights and are the basis of that disparaging modern concept of the 'failed state'.

Churchill believed in a worldwide racial hierarchy that had been predetermined by complex physical and historical circumstances, but it was not eternal. In 1907, he had predicted that with the benign guidance of the white man those 'light-hearted tractable ... *British* [my italics] children' the Kikuyu would eventually arise from 'their present degradation'.[14] He treated History as the narrative of human progress and concluded that certain races had advanced more rapidly than others. Britain had set the pace and he boasted that during the nineteenth century it had arrived 'at or around the summit of the civilised world'.[15] It was a broad plateau with abundant room for other races, and the British Empire offered the dynamic force to propel them upwards. Churchill insisted that material improvement should always come before political advancement: clean drinking water and railways took precedence over democracy. Mastery of the environment and scientific and technical ingenuity were significant yardsticks for measuring Churchillian civilisation. In 1921, when a delegation of Kenyan Indians reminded Churchill of what their people had done to build the colony's railways, he riposted that they could never have invented the railways.

Churchill had also told the Indians that he wholeheartedly endorsed Cecil Rhodes's dictum of 'equal rights for [all] civilised men'. This was all very well in theory, but in private Churchill described the Kenyan delegates as members of the 'vulgar class of coolies' and to allow them the same political rights as white men would inflame Europeans throughout East Africa.[16] This was the primordial Churchill speaking. Many years later, he confided to Lord Moran: 'When you think of a race as inferior beings, it is difficult to get rid of that way of thinking; when I was a subaltern the Indian did not seem to me equal to the white man.'[17] There was another impediment to the political advancement of Indians in Kenya: their connection with the Indian Congress Party. For the past few years branches of the nationalist Young Men's Indian associations had been springing up in Kenya's towns.[18]

It was indeed hard for Churchill to shed old prejudices or suppress them. They surfaced in splenetic outbursts that were recorded by Major Morton, Lord Moran and others, and have been sensibly and dispassionately discussed by Andrew Roberts.[19] The Bedouin was a 'cut-throat' whose diet was camel dung and who was as 'trustworthy as a King Cobra', and all Arabs were 'worthless'. It seems that while Churchill admired T. E. Lawrence's *The Seven Pillars of Wisdom* it had obviously failed to arouse in him any sympathy for its Arab protagonists. Negroes were 'niggers' and 'blackamoors', the Chinese were 'chinks' and 'pigtails', Indians were 'baboos' [a derisory term for native clerks], the Germans were 'Huns', the Italians were 'organ-grinders', and so on.

Racial insults peppered Churchill's private conversation, usually when he was in a choleric mood, relaxing with whisky or brandy, or when he was being mischievously provocative. Churchill's lapses on this score should not be allowed to obliterate his sincere concern for the welfare of the people he sometimes derided. He was a creature of his age: racial jokes and caricatures were part of the bedrock of contemporary British humour and were regular features of *Punch* during the inter-war years and after. Furthermore, Churchill's view of the global racial dispensation was endorsed by the country's political elite. In December 1935, Major Morton told him that official circles dreaded the repercussions for European prestige of an Italian defeat at the hands of the Abyssinians who were 'far from being either Christian or civilised'.[20]

Since before the war, British governments had been tormented by the question as to what to do about the future political development of India. Churchill's view was simple: Britain was sowing the seeds of material and moral improvement in the sub-continent, but it would take a long time for them to germinate and reach maturity. In the meantime, India needed firm and just administration. Baldwin agreed, up to a point, and, when he introduced the Government of India Bill he described the country as having been 'impregnated ... with Western ideas' and that Britain was now 'reaping the fruits of our good works'.

Churchill believed this harvest was dangerously premature. He had explained why in an article for the *Daily Mail* in November 1929. The British Raj, he explained, had been responsible for 'The rescue of India from ages of barbarism, tyranny and internecine war' and was now guiding the country's progress towards 'civilisation'. Justice and the 'streams of health, life and tranquillity' were already in place, but beneficial changes had been hampered by what he called a 'forbearance towards religious custom and dogma'. He had in mind the stigma and degradation which the Hindu faith imposed on sixty million Untouchables (*Dalits*) whose hereditary misfortunes would be perpetuated if the Hindu majority took power, as they were bound to when India became a dominion. The very fact that the British government was prepared even to consider dominion status indicated that the will to rule was unsteady and the pusillanimity displayed by Westminster and Whitehall had already demoralised the otherwise stout-hearted officials in India.[21]

This article was the opening movement of what became a vast and complex symphony of rage and despair. Motifs had been introduced that would be played again with variations and always fortissimo. One theme predominated and that was Churchill's insistence that the Empire's rulers had lost confidence and resolve. Baldwin was a prosaic 'businessman' who had fallen under the illusion that 'the time had passed for any robust assertion of British Imperial greatness'. His instinct was to find and pursue the line of the least resistance, aided and abetted by the equally timorous Labour and Liberal parties.[22] Tergiversation and compromise were the guidelines for the imperial policies of the National Government which replaced the Labour administration in the autumn of 1931.

Churchill had already identified the Labour Party as inimical to the Empire. Since its genesis in the early 1900s he had always loathed a party that thrived on class hatred and which, he was certain, lacked a patriotic heart. During the November 1924 General Election he had told his Epping constituents that, after a year of Labour in office, 'this great country, so powerful and so splendid but a few years before' was now 'almost ready to apologise for our existence, ready to lay down our burden in one of the great Oriental countries [India] if a stick be shaken at us by any irresponsible chatterbox'. Labour, particularly its middle-class intellectual wing, was the natural soulmate of those 'chatterboxes' who were making nuisances of themselves in India and Egypt; in other words, educated individuals who had studied John Stuart Mill, or, worse still, Karl Marx. As for the dominions 'who sent their brave men to fight and die by scores of thousands', Labour treated them with a 'frigid repulsion' which contrasted with its 'fawning veneration of the Soviet Union'. The party had provided Churchill with further proof of its hostility to the Empire in 1929 when Ramsay MacDonald flinched in the face of unrest in Egypt.

The Conservatives had hardly done better. They too had made concessions in India in the face of persistent and often violent pressure from Gandhi and the Congress Party. One palliative had been the Simon Commission, sent to the sub-continent to sound out local opinion in 1927. The commissioners returned home and recommended the adoption of elected provincial assemblies with an eye to a federal constitution being established in the future. Ominously, the Commission's report noted that: 'There are inflammable elements in the population and jealousy and ill-feeling between communities which from time to time cause riot and disturbance.'[23]

Civil disorders were proliferating. During the Commission's visit 150 Indians were murdered and over 700 were wounded and, between

1930 and 1932, troops had to be called out to suppress riots, most of which had been triggered by clashes between Hindus and Muslims over public religious rituals and processions. Over a thousand had been killed in sectarian riots in Cawnpore in March 1931, which led Churchill to conclude that 'the struggle for power is now beginning between the Hindus and Muslims', a point he reiterated in the Commons.[24] He had always feared that civil order would dissolve once Indians sensed that their rulers were losing their nerve. In January 1930 he had urged the Viceroy Lord Irwin [from 1934 Viscount Halifax] to grasp the nettle and destroy the 'evil elements' and so demonstrate that Britain would never tremble in the face of Congress-generated lawlessness. For the next four years, Churchill insisted that stability and British prestige could only be restored by a formidable reassertion of the 'will to rule'. Condign measures would be required: 'Gandhi-ism and all it stands for, sooner or later has to be grappled with and forcefully crushed.'[25] Paradoxically, the man who had so passionately abjured the use of 'terror' as an instrument of imperial government after the Amritsar massacre was now demanding its application in India.

Belligerence was alien to the natures of Irwin, MacDonald and Baldwin. Unlike Churchill, they were essentially pacific men who imagined that limited concessions would satisfy Congress. Appeasement had always played a part in the governance of India, for in the eighteenth and nineteenth centuries Britain had cut deals with its aristocratic elite, the native princes. Now she would broker bargains with representatives of a new, home-grown and largely middle-class political elite and, in so doing, would acquire a new cadre of collaborators. Once the Congress moderates were enticed onside and given a taste of power, then order would be restored and the extremists would be isolated. Concede, divide and rule were henceforward the objectives of all three parties, although the stiffer elements among the Tories favoured tougher, Churchillian policies.

The process of wooing the Congress Party had been started by Irwin in October 1929, when he announced that India would follow the path taken by Australia and Canada and become a self-governing dominion. As a token of goodwill, those convicted of politically motivated crimes would be released from gaol and representatives of all races, religions and classes were invited to a Round Table conference held in London in the autumn of 1930. Churchill likened this policy to feeding cat's meat to a tiger, a metaphor which outraged Irwin, who found gladiatorial politics distasteful.

Save for a common passion for fox-hunting, Irwin was the aristocratic antithesis of Churchill. He was reticent, aloof, disdainful of popular feeling and a pious Anglo-Catholic who was moved by Gandhi's mysticism. Irwin's faith required him to do good in the world, and, as Viceroy, he recoiled from the use of force to maintain order, for it would have been the admission of personal moral failure. His declaration to the Indian people, which had been approved beforehand by Baldwin, was as much a moral as a political gesture which, he hoped, would convince Indians that Britain did not wish to keep them 'in perpetual subordination to a white Empire'.[26] In many ways, Irwin was a high-minded, other-worldly public school headmaster determined to discover virtue in even his more perverse and obdurate pupils.

Gandhi was one of them. Like Churchill he had a combative spirit and his first response to Irwin's declaration was intransigence. Freedom and independence would be won by 'our own strength' and not accepted as a gift from Britain, which Gandhi rightly guessed would have strings attached. He demanded complete self-government and dominion status within a year, refused to attend the Round Table conference and approved a fresh campaign of disobedience. Jawaharlal Nehru (Harrow and Trinity College, Cambridge), the current President of Congress, took charge of the protests, which included a boycott of British textiles. Not that this would have much impact, for Japanese imports were gradually edging out British cottonware.

There followed two years of intermittent disorder with riots, arrests and mass imprisonment. Gandhi ended up in gaol, but was released to make a personal compact with Irwin by which he promised to call off his campaign and attend a second Round Table in London in return for amnesty for the thousands of Indians imprisoned for political offences. Churchill was 'appalled', writing in the *Daily Mail* in February 1931 that: 'The more Lord Irwin, Viceroy of India, does obeisance before Gandhi, the more impudent become Gandhi's demands.'

Both Round Table conferences turned out to be futile. Congress boycotted the first and the second (attended by Gandhi) ended in an impasse in December 1931. The sticking point was the concoction of a voting system that would protect minorities who might otherwise remain permanently at the mercy of the Hindu majority. Gandhi was obstinate about this measure, which he suspected was a variation of the divide-and-rule principle. It was left to the predominantly Tory National Government to proceed with legislation that would create elected provincial administrations in India as the first step towards dominion status.

Churchill had used the two years of negotiations as an opportunity to warn the public of the consequences of Indian constitutional changes. Labour, he had alleged, wished to surrender power and now, to his dismay, the Tories were content to collaborate. A new and highly significant element had recently intruded itself into the debate on India's future. At the close of 1931 the Statute of Westminster had legally defined relations between the existing dominions and Britain. Their independence, conspicuously asserted when they had refused to send troops to fight the Bolsheviks and Atatürk's Turks, now had the foundation of law. Furthermore, each dominion now had the legal right to detach itself from any association with Britain.

This prospect alarmed Churchill, who predicted that the projected dominion of India could break all ties with Britain.[27] In geo-strategic terms such a defection would be disastrous: Britain would lose the Indian army which was the foundation of its power in the Middle East and Asia. This was no longer secure, as Churchill reminded listeners in a BBC broadcast in January 1935. He contrasted an enervated Britain, which was letting its Empire slip through its fingers, with a virile Japan, which was extending its territories in Manchuria and China.[28] In the following year the CID identified Japan as a 'pistol' pointing towards India, although intelligence analysts correctly concluded that Burma and Australia were Japan's preferred objectives.[29] There was, however, worrying evidence of Japanese subversion in Burma.[30]

Churchill's broadcast, made while the India Bill was in its final stage in the Commons, ended a campaign that had begun five years before with the foundation of the India Empire Society. It contained many retired Indian officials, including a clutch of provincial governors (Micky O'Dwyer of the Punjab was one) and its aims were backed by the mass circulation and nominally Conservative *Daily Mail* and the *Daily Express*. Its proprietor Lord Beaverbrook told Churchill that 'it is obvious that the Government must shoot up or shut up Gandhi'.[31] The India Empire Society held rallies, where Churchill was a frequent speaker, issued pamphlets and made some headway in the local branches of the Conservative Party. This grass-roots support worried ministers and party managers, who knew that the rank and file were easily swayed by Churchillian oratory.[32] In the Commons, the Whips kept a tight ship and in the regular divisions over Indian policy, Churchill's allies seldom mustered more than fifty. In the country at large, political debate revolved around knife-and-fork issues such as unemployment and, after 1933, pacifism, collective security and rearmament. All aroused far greater passion than the future of India.

At every phase of its campaign, the India Empire Society emphasised the damage that independence would inflict on the mass of Indians. Churchill repeatedly declared that Britain's overriding duty was to 'advance the material condition of the masses'. The rash political advancement of Indians would interrupt and possibly terminate their march to prosperity. The even-handed British Raj would be replaced by the venal 'Gandhi Raj' of Congress. 'Highly educated Hindus' would drag India 'into the deepest depths of Oriental tyranny and despotism, equal only to the anarchy now prevailing in China'. Administrative, judicial, medical and transport systems would fall apart, public works and irrigation schemes would vanish and nepotism and graft would be installed as 'the handmaidens of Brahmin domination'.

'Denied by the Hindu religion even the semblance of human rights', sixty million Untouchables would languish without hope of any amelioration of their lot.[33] Ninety-seven per cent of Congress members were Hindu, which was why Churchill repeatedly emphasised the possibility that self-government would mean Hindu paramountcy. He ignored Gandhi's claims that the new Indian state would not be sectarian and that Muslims had nothing to fear. They were never wholly convinced. Churchill also slyly suggested that the Indian industrialists who were bankrolling Congress were keen to have British labour legislation repealed, the better to sweat their workers. Gandhi attracted Churchill's most venomous polemic: he was 'a fanatic and an ascetic of the type well known in the East', 'a half-naked fakir' and 'a malevolent fanatic'. Churchill's attitude towards Gandhi softened after he began his campaign to secure humane treatment for the Untouchables.

Lurking behind Churchill's rhetoric was the suspicion that the Hindus were temperamentally unfit to rule fairly. After his service in India he had expressed the hope that education would gradually erode Hinduism, which he considered an impediment to progress. There is reason to think that his animus against Hinduism, natural enough in an atheist, had been strengthened by his reading of *Mother India* written by Katherine Mayo and published in 1927. It was a quirky book that ought to have been treated as nonsense, since its principal contention was that Hindu men were degenerate. Among the proofs she offered was their custom of child marriage, an inclination towards sodomy and heterosexual excesses that reduced most males to impotence by the age of thirty.[34] *Mother India* reinforced Churchill's existing prejudices, which was why he said he had been impressed by its contents.

By early 1935, Churchill had sensed that he was losing the battle and was turning his attention to the baleful consequences of the India Bill becoming law. This 'unsure, irrational compromise' would bring nothing but misery for the Indian masses who would soon endure a 'cruel new burden of taxation'. 'The faithful, trustworthy Indian police' who were 'the mainstay of peace and order' would be tormented by divided loyalties.[35] On this subject at least, Churchill was not overstating his case; between 1937 and 1939, when the new machinery of provincial government was being installed, a police intelligence report revealed that Hindu police officers were protecting their posts by subscribing to Congress. Their Muslim counterparts feared selective persecution by the predominantly Hindu anti-corruption department. Resources were being stretched by 'the creation of a mass of subordinate jobs in mushroom social services for Congress adherents'.[36]

The India Bill was passed in June 1935. In what was a grand finale to his long symphony of opposition, Churchill denounced it as 'a monstrous sham erected by pygmies'. The cheers of the triumphant Tories were, he predicted, the 'knell of the British Empire in the East'. His passions quickly ebbed away and, like the camomile, he was soon springing back.

Churchill accepted defeat with good grace. In August, he warmly welcomed the Indian industrialist Ghanshyam Birla, who visited him at Chartwell, where he was busy laying a brick wall. Their luncheon conversation was animated and cordial and revealed to Birla Churchill's haziness about conditions in modern India. A magnanimous loser, he advised the new provincial governments to do all in their power to bring about universal prosperity – 'I do not mind about education, but give the masses more butter. I stand for butter.' Churchill offered Gandhi his goodwill: 'Tell Mr Gandhi to use the powers that are offered and make the thing a success.' He added that 'if India could look after herself', then Britain would be released from the expensive strategic burdens of the Singapore base and the upkeep of forces in the Middle East. His thoughts and energies were already turning towards a new threat to the Empire.

18

An Unnecessary War,

Part I: The Japanese Challenge, 1931–1939

Like its predecessor, the Second World War was an imperial conflict. Germany, Italy and Japan went to war to gain land and resources. Japan was the first competitor to enter what turned out to be the final lap in the global race for empire. Its position was ambivalent, for, while acquiring Formosa and Korea, it had represented itself as sympathetic towards Asian people then under European rule. At the Versailles Conference Japan had declared itself the 'champion of the Asiatic races'.[1] At that time, it was taking tentative steps towards assisting Indian nationalists, who since its defeat of Russia in 1905 had looked to Japan as the nation that gave the lie to European notions of intrinsic Asian inferiority.[2] Japan reciprocated: it offered sanctuary to Indian nationalist émigrés and its secret service put out feelers towards nationalist and terrorist groups in Bengal. The Japanese press vilified the British Raj; after riots in Calcutta in September 1918, one newspaper described the 'severe repression' of Indians who were treated as 'slaves', while the educated class was united in their 'hatred of England'.[3]

Then and afterwards Japanese Pan-Asian sympathies were a fig leaf for self-interest and aggrandisement. At the same time as Japan was welcoming Indian dissidents, its army was crushing a nationalist rebellion in Korea. Conquest and colonisation were Japan's regional objectives, which Churchill identified in 1927 when he predicted that Japan's long-term goal was the extinction of all British, American and European influence throughout what he disparagingly described as the 'yellow world'.

Pre-war Japanese imperial ambitions received light coverage in Churchill's memoir of the decade before the outbreak of the war, *The Gathering Storm*. Its focus is Europe, Britain's response to events there and his efforts to jolt a complacent and fearful nation into action, which, when it came, was too late. In October 1943, when its outcome was certain, Churchill spoke of Britain being engaged in an 'unnecessary war', a phrase which he repeated in the introduction to *The Gathering Storm*.[4] Churchill's version of the coming of war gives few indications that the Empire was in jeopardy, or that he had understood this at the time, which is extraordinary, given his earlier obsession with the Bolshevik threat to the Empire. One explanation for this omission may be that *The Gathering Storm* was written during 1946 and 1947 and was setting the scene for a narrative of a war, which, in its later phases, was perceived as a conflict that would radically reform or even sweep away the old empires and the ideas that had justified their existence. Dwelling on pre-war anxieties about the survival of the British Empire would have been against the grain in a history of causes of a war that ended with millions of participants and onlookers believing that the age of empires was at last over. This was the feeling of President Roosevelt when, in 1942, he told a journalist that: 'It seems that the Japs were a necessary evil in order to break down the old colonial system.'[5]

Churchill shrewdly underplayed the imperial dimension of the origins of war. Yet his papers reveal that he had been acutely aware of and often alarmed by the threats that Japanese and Italian expansionism posed to the British Empire. As will be seen, Germany's ambitions were confined to the Continent and Russia, although from 1938 onwards it was ready to make trouble in the Middle East and Afghanistan to divert Britain's attention (and armed forces) from Europe.

Japan was prepared to go further in stirring up trouble and, during and immediately after the First World War, had given a forewarning of its desire to patronise anti-colonial movements in India and the Dutch East Indies. At this time, Japan was still allied with Britain, but, under pressure from the United States and Australia, which had always been uneasy about the arrangement, the cabinet agreed not to renegotiate this alliance in 1922. Churchill was ready to forfeit the security of Japan's friendship rather than jeopardise the goodwill of the United States, which, he hoped, might one day be drawn into a close *entente* with Britain. Henceforward, the security of Australia,

New Zealand and Britain's Far Eastern and Pacific colonies no longer depended on Japan's friendship, which was replaced by the Singapore strategy.

The Singapore strategy rested on two premises. The first was that at some future date the Japanese would launch the NanShinRon, an all-out amphibious offensive against the Dutch East Indies and Australia. This had been the surmise of Admiral Lord Beatty, who had toured the area in 1919 and, in essence, he was correct. The second premise was that a massive naval base at Singapore would block the NanShinRon. The island fortress would contain a huge complex of dockyards, repair workshops, and naval stores that would transform it into the Gibraltar of the Indian and Pacific Oceans, commanding the sea lanes that ran to China and Australia. Supporters of the Singapore strategy were confident that at least 50,000 men would be needed to besiege it and that it could hold out for at least four to five months, Churchill believed six.[6] During this time, the Royal Navy would assemble an armada that would steam through the Suez Canal, cross the Indian Ocean, relieve Singapore, refit and then engage the Japanese battlefleet. American strategists devised a similar war plan with its fortified bases in the Philippines serving as a tripwire that would delay the Japanese and allow time for the concentration of a fleet large enough to win a decisive battle for mastery of the Pacific.

The Singapore strategy was very expensive. As Chancellor of the Exchequer in 1925 Churchill challenged its spiralling costs with the question: 'Why should there be a war with Japan?' His opinion was that there was only 'the slightest chance in our lifetime'. He added that Japan 'cannot menace our security' since it was 5,000 miles away from Australia, a fact of strategic geography that he later repeated.[7] Treasury objections to the Singapore budget continued to be raised, but the funds were slowly forthcoming and the complex was completed in 1936.

From the start there had been too many 'ifs' about the Singapore strategy. It took for granted that the fortress would withstand a protracted siege that was bound to include aerial bombardment and, if it did, Britain would find enough ships to match the Imperial Japanese Navy. Furthermore, it was imagined that a great fleet action between battleships would prove decisive, as it had been at Trafalgar and ought to have been at Jutland in 1916, where, Churchill privately believed, Jellicoe had thrown away an outright victory.[8]

This prognosis overlooked the latest advances in naval air power; in 1918 British aircraft had sunk the German cruiser *Breslau* and, in 1925, the American aircraft designer Billy Mitchell had demonstrated how a battleship could be sunk by bombs. The battleship was about to be supplanted by the aircraft-carrier, but Churchill clung to the idea that capital ships remained the masters of the oceans and were, therefore, the yardstick of global power as they had been when he was a young man. In 1930 he regretted the cull of Britain's battlefleet by Labour ministers 'anxious to prove their pacifism' and he warned that their folly would diminish Britain's international status.[9] The stark truth was that the era of British maritime omnipotence was over: Britannia could no longer afford to rule the waves. This had been admitted by the 1922 Washington Naval Treaty which laid down the ratio of capital ships as five each for the Royal and United States Navies and three for the Japanese. Churchill approved this arrangement for the same reason he had approved cuts in the military budget in the Middle East, it saved money.

Since 1922, Churchill imagined that imperial security in the Far East and the Pacific could only be achieved by an understanding with the United States, which, to say the least, was unlikely because of American isolationism. It was deeply ingrained, negative and summed up by the novelist John Dos Passos who observed that: 'Rejection of Europe is what America is all about.' Thomas Jefferson had cautioned his countrymen against 'entangling alliances' and the United States's experience during and after the First World War had proved him right. Europe had quickly reverted to its bad old ways and disdainful Americans wanted no part in its quarrels and rivalries. Nevertheless, and in the teeth of isolationist indifference, Churchill stuck to his faith in an Anglo-American partnership throughout the inter-war years. During the negotiations for the 1922 naval treaty, he warned the cabinet that it would be 'a ghastly state of affairs' if Britain and America squabbled over the relative sizes of their fleets. Naval parity accorded with the Churchillian vision of a future in which the two powers united to provide universal peace and prosperity.

A sullen Japan had settled for dominance in the Western Pacific, but in 1934 it tore up the Washington treaty and began to lay down more carriers, battleships and cruisers. Within five years, the Imperial Japanese Navy had seven carriers, while the Royal Navy had seven with a further six on the stocks and due for completion the following year. Only one, HMS *Eagle*, was stationed in the Far East. In London Chancellor of the Exchequer Neville Chamberlain and many others hoped that Japan could be persuaded to follow its expansionist policies without impinging on local British interests.[10]

Churchill had shared this assumption that Britain and Japan could co-exist. He showed a sanguine tolerance towards Japanese aspirations and he urged the cabinet to adopt policies towards them which were tantamount to appeasement. In 1924, he had asked Baldwin to withdraw the flotilla of submarines from Hong Kong which he considered to be provocative since they were there to attack Japanese shipping in the China Sea in the event of war. The same desire not to antagonise Japan was behind Churchill's opposition to reinforcing the Shanghai garrison in 1927.[11] He sympathised with Japan's imperial ambitions because it was on 'the side of civilisation against barbarism and brutality'.[12]

The Japanese agreed. After her programme of accelerated industrialisation and modernisation at the end of the nineteenth century, Japan had cultivated an image of herself as an advanced and civilised nation. Japanese imperialists had adopted social Darwinism to justify expansionism: it was Japan's mission to improve and elevate the backward races of Asia through example and instruction.[13] During the 1930s, Japanese imperial ideology mutated: the notion of providing regeneration was overlaid with the mystical concept of the Japanese as a divine race.

This assumption was at the heart of the gospel of the *Kominka* movement which gained favour with the young, fiercely nationalist officers who were the coming men in the government during the late 1930s and many of their superiors. The chief tenet of the *Kominka* creed was *kokutai* ['national essence'], a distillation that distinguished the Japanese from lesser peoples and gave them the right to impose their culture, values and blind loyalty to the divine Emperor Hirohito on all their future Asian subjects. Europe's empires had become degenerate and infirm and their subjects could be duped by the slogan

'Asia for the Asiatics'. In fact, and in accordance with the *Kominka* ideology, one racial elite would supplant another; the 1942 Japanese Army memo on behaviour towards newly conquered peoples insisted that the Japanese were *shujin minzoku*, that is 'master peoples'.[14] Like the Germans and Italians, the Japanese saw the world in terms of superior and inferior races and believed that the former had a genetic and moral mandate to lord it over the latter.

The Eastern master race had started its bid for a new Asian empire in 1931. Japan's economy had always been dependent on imported foodstuffs and it had been hobbled by the Wall Street Crash of 1929. Exports fell by 13 per cent in the next three years and Japan's predominantly military ruling elite concluded that collapse could only be staved off by commandeering raw materials and acquiring captive markets. China, riven by civil war, was Japan's first target for a sequence of swift offensives. Manchuria was overrun between 1931 and 1934 and settled by 250,000 Japanese farmer immigrants who grew rice for the homeland. In 1932 Japanese forces occupied the Chinese quarter of Shanghai; penetration of northern China began in 1935 and was the prelude to a full-scale invasion of the central and eastern provinces in July 1937. Terror was integral to Japanese strategy: the victims of the massacres in and around Nanking in December outnumbered the casualties from the nuclear attacks on Hiroshima and Nagasaki in August 1945. In 1936 Japan joined Germany and Italy in the Anti-Comintern Pact and, at the end of 1938, the Prime Minister Prince Fuminato Konoye declared that a 'New Order in Asia' was imminent, but he gave no indication as to how or when it would be installed or its final extent.

Churchill was a nervous onlooker at the violent birth of a new empire. His earlier benevolence towards Japan gave way to anxiety and fear once Japan's policies revealed the scope of her ambitions and her will to secure them. After the subjugation of Manchuria in 1934, he wrote of 'the tremendous thrust for conquest and empire by trade and the sword that the Japanese people are making and are going to make'.[15] The implications for the Empire were unnerving, and a few months later Churchill was contemplating the 'formidable problems' that lay ahead for Britain and other nations with possessions and interests in Asia.[16] In January 1936, he contrasted the 'two predatory military dictatorships' of Germany and Japan with 'the helpless Baldwin and his valets' who were temperamentally incapable of understanding the inner forces which drove these two powers.[17] Churchill did, and in November he alerted readers of the *Evening Standard* to the presence in the Far East of a 'martial race of more than sixty millions' in thrall to 'military minds' which were intoxicated by 'dreams of war and conquest'.[18] As yet there was no direct threat to Australia, New Zealand and Malaya since, as he later reminded the 1922 Committee, Singapore was impregnable.[19]

Japan had abandoned the customary rules and customs of diplomacy. Puzzled outsiders considered her decisions foolhardy, eccentric and potentially self-defeating. Churchill thought that Japan was striding towards disaster, for, as he wrote in January 1938, it 'cannot possibly compete with the productive energies of either branch of the English-speaking peoples'.[20] This assumed that Japan was bent on a future war with Britain and the United States, although both powers were being conspicuously supine when confronting Japanese aggression. Nonetheless, the Japanese government was uncomfortably aware that Britain and America could have imposed debilitating economic sanctions if they had the will.[21]

Certainly Japan was indifferent to high-minded international opinion, which pacifists in Britain vainly imagined would make all warmongers think again. At the first sign of objections to its policies, Japan strutted out of the League of Nations in 1932 and set the precedent which Germany followed in October 1933. Defending its puppet state in Manchuria (renamed Manchukuo), Japanese propagandists tartly observed that their country was following policies of intervention and coercion currently adopted by Britain towards Egypt and America towards Panama and Cuba.[22]

Japan could afford to behave as it wished because it thought that its rivals were losing their resolve. The Foreign Office, which collated such incidents, noticed that since 1931 the Japanese had shown ostentatious contempt and insolence towards British subjects in China.[23] During the summer of 1939 the Japanese inflicted a calculated humiliation on the British concession at Tientsin, confident that Britain's European preoccupations would rule out any retaliation.

Americans, in particular missionaries, also suffered brutal treatment.

This provocation was a reflection of the feeling that historical forces now favoured Japan: the European empires in the East were in terminal decline and would soon be toppled by a dynamic and thrusting rival. The war of empires was gathering momentum in South-East Asia and British intelligence detected covert preparations for offensives against Malaya, Burma and the Dutch East Indies. Japan's secret service was running a knot of agents in Singapore, including White Russian exiles, and Colonel Hiroshi Tamura, the former military attaché in Bangkok, spent the summer of 1938 snooping on bases and airfields in Malaya.[24]

Japanese espionage and subversion were most intensive in Burma, which was strategically vital for Japan's war against the forces of General Chiang Kai-Shek, leader of the Kuomintang nationalist movement. Completed at the end of 1938, the Burma Road conveyed arms and equipment northwards into southern China, where Chiang's army was concentrated. By allowing this flow of war matériel northwards, Britain was waging a proxy war, for, if more and more Japanese resources were drawn into the Chinese quagmire, there would, in theory, be less available for operations against British possessions. For this reason, Chamberlain's government refused Japanese demands to sever China's lifeline and its obstinacy won Churchill's approval. In June 1939 he told an audience at the Carlton Club that Japan's strength was 'ebbing away' on the battlefields of China.[25]

The Burma Road gave an added incentive to covert Japanese activities in the colony, which suggested that an invasion was being planned. From 1936 onwards, vessels from the Japanese shell-fishing fleet operating in the Bay of Bengal were surveying the Burmese coastline. Japan was also was recruiting a fifth column in Burma, which included a local film star, and it ran a network of agents, many of whom were photographers. During 1938 these spies with cameras and potential collaborators were disseminating rumours in country districts that the Japanese would invade Burma and were smuggling weapons from Thailand to arm Burmese nationalists.[26] The Japanese were also funding anti-British newspapers and one report revealed that a Japanese businessmen had boasted that his country would invade Burma and Malaya from bases in Thailand, which was already in his country's pocket, and that Singapore would be attacked from the air and the sea.[27]

Japan's campaign of sedition in India was revived. During 1938 agents were putting out feelers towards non-Gandhian nationalist groups and paying newspapers for editorials that stressed the Pan-Asian and anti-European elements in modern Japanese thought. Twenty thousand rupees [£20,000] had been allocated for espionage and propaganda in Afghanistan and Soviet Central Asia. A spy cell was established in Bombay which would send reports of British shipping to Italy and Germany during 1940 and 1941.[28]

As well as winning the hearts and minds of fellow Asians, Japan was collecting military intelligence. In March 1939 a Japanese consular official was caught taking photographs in a prohibited area in Hong Kong, and later in the year there were several reports of Japanese passengers photographing the defences of Hong Kong, Singapore and Aden as their ships entered these ports.[29] It was obvious where Japan intended to go, but a British government beset by difficulties in Europe could offer little practical help beyond advising the local authorities to maintain a close surveillance of all Japanese residents in Malaya and Burma, which were now considered highly susceptible to subversion.[30]

By 1939 everyone was on edge about the scope and scale of secret Japanese penetration to the point where the proliferation of Japanese dentists in Malaya and India caused serious alarms. Whitehall tended to be sceptical and, after 1945, allegations of pre-war Japanese subversion and espionage were advanced in order to excuse the slackness and incompetence of the civilian and military authorities who had failed so disastrously to resist the Japanese invasions during the winter and spring of 1941–2.[31]

The limits of British power in South-East Asia were becoming increasingly and painfully obvious. After the consul-general in Batavia [Jakarta] relayed Dutch intelligence fears of an impending Japanese *coup de main* against eastern islands of the Dutch East Indies, the Chiefs of Staff confessed in January 1938 that Britain could not retaliate. Not even an alliance with the Netherlands would induce Britain to hazard a war against Japan to save Dutch colonies and their oilfields.[32] Nor could it, even if it had wished to, for the Chiefs of Staff also admitted that Britain lacked the men and ships to uphold its own Far Eastern interests. This was understood in Tokyo and explains why Japanese officers in China felt free to tweak the lion's tail with impunity.[33]

Sudden, untoward events during the summer of 1939 put a brake on Japan's long-term plans. In May, hawkish and headstrong Japanese officers of the Kwantung Army launched a series of cross-border attacks against the Mongolian People's Republic, a Soviet satellite. Fighting dragged on until the last week of August, when the Japanese suffered a signal defeat by Marshal Konstantinovich Zhukov. Two days later, the Nazi-Soviet Pact was signed, which, seen from a Japanese perspective, allowed Stalin to reinforce Russian's eastern frontier. The war there lapsed, but plans for offensives against Europe's South-East Asian colonies had to be suspended until the Russian threat had been removed. The timing of the *NanShinRon* would depend on developments in Europe.

An Unnecessary War,

Part II: Appeasement, 1935–1939

One chilling truth dominated the minds of British ministers and civil servants between the Italian invasion of Abyssinia in October 1936 and the outbreak of war in September 1939: the British Empire would lose a war against Germany, Italy and Japan. Almost too terrible to contemplate, this calamity could be averted through the diplomacy of appeasement, whose chief objective was to forestall an alliance between these three powers. As Anthony Eden the Foreign Secretary told the dominion prime ministers in May 1937, Britain's 'patience' in the face of German and Italian provocation would have a steadying influence over their rulers.[1] The opposite occurred: Hitler and Mussolini treated every attempt to assuage or sidetrack them as cowardice and proof that a now feeble British Empire was tottering towards collapse.

Defenders of appeasement have argued that it gave Britain a vital breathing space in which it could implement its hurried rearmament policies, in particular the creation of an integrated and, as it turned out, very effective system of aerial defence. The acceleration of measures to defend Britain's skies was Churchill's political hobby horse during this period, although like everyone else, including RAF Intelligence, he overestimated the strength of the Luftwaffe.[2] He believed that the beneficiaries of appeasement were Hitler, since it smoothed his path to dominance in Europe, and Mussolini, who found himself free to go empire building in Africa. On the left, there was the suspicion that appeasement was part of a plot to preserve Western capitalism by pushing Hitler into a war against the Soviet Union. This conspiracy theory was popularised by the 1940 bestseller *Guilty Men* (whose co-authors included the future Labour leader Michael Foot) and widely believed at the time. Official and private papers released subsequently have shown that its conclusions were fiction, although many Conservatives hoped that Germany and Russia might fight a war of mutual destruction.

The debate over the motives and effectiveness of appeasement is by the way. What mattered and dictated the course of events was the character of Hitler and his vision of Germany's future. One can never underestimate or brush aside his manic will for war which had its roots in his megalomania, his twisted interpretation of Germany's historic destiny and his venomous racial fantasies. All contributed in various ways to his ultimate aim of making Germany the master of Europe and conquering an empire in western Russia.

Churchill always took the Führer at his word and he sensed the terrifying nature of the inner demons that drove him. For him, Hitler embodied the post-1918 world with its deracinated masses, its scornful rejection of the ideals and social structures of the past, its worship of violence, its crazy hatreds and its yearning for saviours and systems that would bring happiness and prosperity. Fascism and Nazism superficially satisfied these crude desires, but at an immense cost, for both creeds replaced the reasoned debate of liberal politics with wild passion and substituted action for thought.

Above all, there was Hitler's urge to restore and enhance Germany's greatness. Churchill was quick to appreciate this and in July 1935 he told the Commons that the 'great fear of Europe' was 'the power and might of the rearmed strength of Germany'. History supported Churchill's case and he warned that Hitler was a reincarnation of those power-hungry autocrats who had hoped to subdue the Continent by intimidation and war: Phillip II of Spain, Louis XIV, Napoleon and Wilhelm II. In a broadcast to the American people delivered in August 1939, Churchill concisely and correctly insisted that: 'If Herr Hitler does not make war, there will be no war.'[3]

Hitler's views on the British Empire were ambivalent and coloured by his racial theories. The British were Aryans, that is to say they possessed that semi-mystical genetic strain which gave them the moral authority to govern lesser breeds and, by this token, Hitler warmly approved of the British Empire. He knew virtually nothing about its inner workings or its ideals beyond those portrayed in the Hollywood film *Lives of the Bengal Lancers*, which he watched often and with pleasure. No doubt he interpreted the scenario of gallant soldiers defending civilisation on the North-West Frontier as an example of what, in 1930, he called the struggle of the 'lower Indian race against the English Nordic race'. This race had the 'right to rule the world' and, on their first meeting, he advised the former Viceroy Lord Halifax on how Nordic supermen should exercise their birthright in India. 'Shoot Gandhi,' he suggested, and if this did not do the trick, then shoot a dozen Congress leaders, and, if this failed, shoot a further two hundred, and so on until India was pacified. Indians, the Führer believed, were genetically susceptible to Communism, and Göring alleged that Gandhi was an 'anti-British Bolshevik'. Indians who visited Berlin quickly became aware of their degraded status in the Nazi scheme of things.[4]

The Japanese shared the racial disabilities of the Indians and, like them, were beneath the Aryan race. When the bien pensant historian Arnold Toynbee went to see Hitler in February 1936 to chat to him about peace, he was told that Singapore was the 'eastern frontier of Europe' and that Germany would gladly lend Britain soldiers to help defend it against the Japanese.[5] On another occasion, the Führer offered troops to stiffen the Indian garrison and, after the fall of Singapore in February 1942, he was furious that the 'yellow men' had trounced Aryans.[6] Nonetheless, the courtesy due to an ally demanded that the Japanese were officially invested with the merits of Aryan blood.

Bland public statements of respect for the British Empire and a publicly expressed willingness to share in its defence (a hint here, surely, that it could not do so on its own) may have disarmed ingenuous visitors and some British politicians, but Hitler distrusted Britain. In the months after the Munich agreement, Goebbels's propagandists execrated Britain for blocking Germany's legitimate quest for wealth and supremacy in Europe. Early in 1939, Hitler brooded over 'the British question', which, he told the commander-in-chief of his navy, Admiral Raeder, would only be resolved by an enlarged German fleet combining with those of Italy and Japan and challenging Britain on the oceans. Once its maritime arteries had been severed, the British Empire would fall apart, but not for some time since Hitler's crash programme of naval rearmament (Z Plan) was scheduled for completion at the end of 1944.[7]

*

In the meantime, Italy was in a position to inflict immediate and serious injuries on the Empire since it held the key to the Mediterranean. If the Singapore strategy was to work, Britain had to maintain supremacy in those waters where its fleet would gather and begin its voyage eastwards to relieve the base and defend Australia and New Zealand. It was, therefore, vital that Italy was a benevolent neutral or, better still, was actively friendly towards Britain. Italy's potential to sabotage the Singapore strategy, as much as the fear of a German aerial offensive against Britain, was a source of constant disquiet. In 1936, official fears were summed up by the First Sea Lord, Admiral Lord Chatfield, who observed that the Empire was '... disjointed, disconnected and highly vulnerable. It is even open to debate whether it is in reality strategically defensible.'[8]

When he snatched power in 1922, Mussolini offered Italy stability, purpose and a chance to secure the territorial prizes, which, he alleged, had been denied by Britain and France at Versailles. Under the Duce a regenerated Italy would fulfil its imperial mission, which, he fancied, had been inherited from Rome. Fascism would create a 'new man' who was a virile warrior and colonist with the courage and stamina of a Roman legionary. As Italian troops entered Abyssinia in 1935, Mussolini declared that Italians had ceased to be 'mandolin players' and were now 'grenade throwers'.[9]

Led by the Duce, a rejuvenated Italy would spread its power across the Mediterranean, into the Balkans and Africa, and, in the process, expel Britain from Gibraltar, Cyprus and Egypt and the French from Corsica and Tunisia. This would allow Italians *spazio vitale*, that is strategic security, and conquered regions such as Libya and Abyssinia would provide land for Italian colonists. Ethnic origins predetermined an individual's place in the hierarchy of the greater Italy: Italians occupied the apex, below came other Latin races, Slavs and Greeks and at the bottom of the pile were Turks, Arabs and Egyptians.[10]

Terror was freely applied to anyone who resisted Mussolini's new order. It was in Abyssinia and, between 1941 and 1943, in Yugoslavia, where the Italians permitted the Croatian Ustase death squads of their puppets General Ante Pavelič and Cardinal Stepinač to massacre Jews, Muslims and Orthodox Christians.[11] The scale of mass murder within the Italian empire was far less than that in the German and

Japanese, but the racial theories and expediencies which justified it were similar.

Churchill had characterised Mussolini as a 'swine' in 1923, a judgement that cannot be bettered. When she met him a few years later, Clementine was bowled over by the Duce, like other upper-class English ladies who seem to have been peculiarly susceptible to his macho swagger, bristly chin and head-waiter charm.[12] In October 1935, her husband ranked the Duce as 'a common tom cat' in comparison with Hitler who was a 'Bengal tiger' and he wrote off Italy as a 'poor sort of first-class power'.[13] This was true at that date, but Italy was rearming rapidly in a bid for naval supremacy in Mediterranean. By 1939 it had three battleships and four nearing completion, nineteen cruisers with fourteen on the stocks, fifty-nine destroyers and eighty-five submarines. A large proportion of these warships had been laid down over the past fifteen years.

Mussolini's invasion of Abyssinia in October 1935 was the occasion for his first regional trial of strength with Britain and ironically it was undertaken when the balance of maritime power was tilted against Italy. Marshal Badoglio warned Mussolini that a war against Britain would be suicidal because of deficiencies in the navy and air force; at best the Italian fleet could just manage to fight a 'guerrilla war' at sea.[14] Mussolini was willing to gamble and Britain was not.

Churchill's sympathies were with the Abyssinians, whom he described as 'fighting as well as they can in their primitive way to defend their hearths and homes, their rights and freedoms' against 'all the resources of science'.[15] He hoped, as did Baldwin's government, that this unequal contest could be ended by sanctions imposed by the League of Nations, sickness among Italian troops and a partisan war waged by the Abyssinians. Everything hung on international sanctions, which, to be effective required an oil embargo and the closure of the Suez Canal to Italian shipping. Only the Royal Navy could enforce this blockade (nearly two-thirds of Italy's imports passed through the Straits of Gibraltar) and it could have easily escalated into a war.

Public opinion was against a war to save Abyssinia and the dominions wanted no part in it. There were secret misgivings as to whether the navy was fit for such a contest, for it had been starved of cash and many of its ships were obsolescent; in 1932 Neville Chamberlain as Chancellor of the Exchequer had refused funds to modernise the Fleet Air Arm. The naval big stick was brittle and worm-eaten and sanctions were therefore risky. Rashness was not a vice of Baldwin's so, true to character, he contrived an escape route; in December the Foreign Secretary Sir Samuel Hoare and his French counterpart Pierre Laval agreed a deal which effectively delivered Abyssinia to Mussolini. Churchill denounced the arrangement as 'a fiasco, ludicrous if it was not so tragical'.

Yet, while he despised the cynical Hoare–Laval pact, Churchill shared the government's misgivings about the outcome of a naval war against Italy. Defeat would be unthinkable and unlikely, but the inevitable wastage of warships would have weakened Britain's hand in the Far East. The Singapore strategy continued to prevail over all other considerations for Churchill, who reminded the Commons in March 1936 that it was Britain's 'sacred duty' to protect Australia and New Zealand. In the same year, the government began a naval rearmament programme, laying down five battleships, four aircraft-carriers and fourteen cruisers, all scheduled for completion during 1940.

It was galling for Churchill, a child of the age of Britain's maritime supremacy and global reach, to come to terms with the new practical limitations on British power. He yearned for those bare-knuckle Palmerstonian responses that had once frightened anyone who flouted Britain's will. In the early days of the Abyssinian crisis, Churchill had been 'out for blood' and he was confident that the Italians would cave in at the first hint of British determination because they were 'no good at fighting'.[16] Perhaps so, but they had enough men in the right places to hurt the Empire where it was vulnerable. As Churchill knew, there were 50,000 Italian troops in Libya (ten times the number of the British garrison in Egypt) and 370,000 in East Africa.[17] Looking around for a whip with which to bring Mussolini to heel, he considered long-range bombing raids on Italian cities, but this needed French collusion which would not then have been forthcoming.[18]

Angry at the harm that had been done to British prestige by the Abyssinian debacle, Churchill vented his frustration on a ministry whose recent capitulation to Indian nationalists had inspired Mussolini's aggression in Africa. He predicted that the vigorous

'Roman' empire was poised to supplant its craven counterpart.[19] The perils were obvious, but Churchill was uncertain as to how they could be countered without pushing Italy permanently into the orbit of Germany. This was why he favoured a rapprochement with Italy, which, between January 1937 and February 1938 agreed to accept a status quo in the Mediterranean. This gave Mussolini time in which to strengthen his navy for a confrontation that was inevitable, given his long-term ambitions. 'England is our gaoler,' he declared early in 1939, 'it wants to hold us shackled in the Mediterranean.'

Churchill remained convinced that the Mediterranean would be 'our decisive battleground at sea' and he foresaw that the struggle to control it would include an invasion of Egypt from Libya, where Mussolini was stiffening his garrison with armoured units.[20] It all boiled down to the Duce's nerve and, in April 1939, Churchill told the Commons that he thought Italy had not yet decided to enter a 'mortal struggle' with Britain for the Mediterranean.[21]

Mussolini did, however, have the stomach for an underground war against Britain. It was waged by the transmitters of Radio Bari, which poured out anti-British propaganda, and Italian secret agents with full purses and instructions to woo Britain's enemies throughout the Middle East. This war of words and subterfuge was well timed, for Churchill's 1922 settlement was beginning to unravel. It might have lasted, but for one drawback: British policy towards Palestine. The masses (and their rulers) needed reassurances about the future of Palestine: would it stay an Arab country, or would it over time become a Jewish one? By the mid-1930s, the resolution of this question became crucial for the survival of British influence and prestige in the region. Unwavering in his Zionism, Churchill was nagged by fears that the Palestinian imbroglio was poisoning Anglo-Arab relations at a time when Britain desperately needed Arab sympathy. His apprehension was shared by the man-on-the-spot who had to placate and reassure local opinion, Sir Miles Lampson the ambassador to Egypt, who thought that Britain's Palestine policy question would alienate not only the Arab but the wider Muslim world.[22]

In 1936 there were 840,000 Arabs living in Palestine and 180,000 Jewish settlers. The demographic equilibrium was beginning to shift, for over the past four years the annual total of immigrants had risen threefold to 35,000. It was obviously going to continue to increase in direct response to Nazi persecution and, to a lesser degree, the recrudescence of officially tolerated anti-Semitism in Poland and Romania. In the light of these baleful developments, the Zionist movement pressed for the doubling of the annual quota to at least 60,000. The Palestinians took fright and, at the close of 1935, the Arab High Committee demanded a halt to immigration, a ban on further land sales to Jews and an elected assembly in which the Arabs would be a permanent majority. The cabinet refused to countenance what was effectively a repudiation of all its past promises to the Jews. In April 1936 the Arabs rebelled and attacked Jewish settlements.

Between April 1936 and September 1939 the army and navy were engaged in subduing a determined uprising that had far-reaching international repercussions. The leader of the Palestine National Movement, Hajj Muhammad el-Hussein the Grand Mufti of Jerusalem, was a wily and resourceful fox who realised that the best hope of Arabs was to find allies who could twist Britain's arm. First, he tried to enlist Britain's princely clients Kings Ibn Saud of Arabia, Ghazi of Iraq and Abdullah of Transjordan. All were unhappy about the influx of Jews, but what Lampson called their residual 'warmness' towards Britain made them hesitant about voicing their objections. The Mufti then turned to Italy and Germany, which, he rightly guessed, would be glad of a chance to drive a wedge between Britain and the Arab world. In October 1937 he left Palestine to begin a peripatetic exile during which he canvassed Mussolini and later Hitler.

Mussolini welcomed the Mufti, for he wanted to exploit Pan Arabism for his own ends. During a tour of Libya in March 1937 he had proclaimed himself the 'Protector of Islam', which led British intelligence analysts to believe that he was aspiring to 'the leadership of the African and Asian peoples'.[23] Given his suppression of Libyan nationalists and the recent conquest of Abyssinia, this was, to say the least, rather far-fetched, but the evidence of Italian subversion was beyond doubt and disturbing.

In May, Eden told the dominion prime ministers that there were signs that Ibn Saud might swing towards Italy, whose occupation of Abyssinia had made it a Red Sea power capable of confronting

Britain. A year later the Foreign Secretary was disturbed by the unease created among Egyptians by what they saw as the emergence of 'a vigorous, expansive non-Muslim state' [i.e. a Jewish-dominated Palestine] on their border. Always resentful of Britain's grip on their country, Egyptians were infuriated by events in Palestine and there were threats of a new wave of anti-British agitation.[24] It coincided with the emergence of the 'Blue Shirt' movement, the youth wing of the Wafdist party, which caused Lampson some consternation, although he was assured that the Blue Shirts were nothing more than an athletics club.[25]

All over the Middle East there was a growing and credulous audience to Italian radio propaganda and Britain found itself facing a resurgence of a popular Pan-Arabist movement that Churchill had hoped to stifle in 1922.

Italian agents were active in the Yemen and at the end of 1936 there were rumours in Cairo that the Italians were poised to annex the country.[26] In fact its ruler, the Imam Idrissi, was robustly pro-British and in December 1936 he assured Lampson that he kept a close eye on Italian intrigues and advised him to treat the Egyptians with the utmost firmness. Mussolini financed anti-British and French newspapers in the Lebanon, where he also bankrolled pseudo-Fascist, nationalist parties.[27] The principal weapon of subversion remained Radio Bari's Arabic channel, which, with the help of the Mufti, pumped out propaganda that harped on alleged atrocities committed by British forces during counter-insurgency operations in Palestine. In July 1937 Churchill invoked this offensive over the airwaves as a pressing reason for reinforcing the army in Palestine and the Mediterranean fleet. He may also have got wind of intelligence reports of Italian agents stirring up tribes on the Sudanese frontier, for in February 1939 he was fearful that Mussolini might launch a pre-emptive 'raid' on Khartoum. The Duce's clandestine war, like Lenin's twenty years before, was making everyone fearful. Discrediting Britain was a prelude to Italy's grand imperial gambit in the Mediterranean and the Middle East.

Mussolini's secret service was stirring up trouble for Britain further afield. In 1938, the Italian consul general in Calcutta was disseminating anti-British propaganda and, more alarmingly, Italian agents were attempting to approach Mirza Ali Khan the Faqir of Ipi, who was then waging a *jihad* against Britain on the North-West Frontier. The Faqir was promised guns, money and wireless sets to help his guerrilla campaign, which was tying down between 40,000 and 50,000 British and Indian troops and several squadrons of aircraft.[28] He was a pest whose nuisance value was inflated because it diverted troops that were desperately needed in the Middle East, which explains why the Italians were keen to secure his cooperation. Mussolini was also cultivating Amanullah the deposed Amir of Afghanistan who was living in Rome with an Italian mistress and showed an interest in regaining his throne.[29]

By this date, Hitler had joined in the secret war against the Empire. Germany sent arms to the Palestinian partisans, which were smuggled in with the connivance of the Iraqi and Saudi regimes and, in the following year, German broadcasters added their voice to Radio Bari with tales of an Anglo-Jewish plot to steal Arab lands.[30] In April 1939 Goebbels, accompanied by eleven Nazi propagandists, made a brief visit to Cairo. Here and elsewhere in the Middle East there was an audience, chiefly young, urban and educated, which was keen to hear what Nazism and Fascism had to offer. Each ideology projected itself as dynamic and modern; the future belonged to Italy and Germany, while Britain and France were flyblown has-beens clinging to outdated capitalist and liberal doctrines. During May 1939, German wireless propaganda appealed to Arabs to form a united block against the Jews in Palestine, noted that the British were urging the Emir of Kuwait to block political reform, and referred to increasing dissatisfaction with British rule in Gibraltar, Malta and Cyprus.[31]

Britain was suffering a sustained attack by midges whose multiple stings, while not fatal, caused irritation and distress. Italian and German propaganda made it clear that both countries were sympathetic to nationalists and Pan-Arabists who wished to dismantle the post-war Middle Eastern settlement. Hitler and Mussolini not only found potential friends among the disaffected, they were forcing Britain to concentrate forces in strategically vital areas of the Empire. As a result, Britain's room for manoeuvre in Europe was cramped.

Debilitating imperial sideshows impinged on the Czech crisis in the late summer and autumn of 1938. While Hitler was preparing to absorb the Sudetenland into the Reich, Chamberlain's government was struggling to find the manpower to cope with campaigns in Palestine and the North-West Frontier. In August, the military authorities in Palestine urgently begged for reinforcements and were promised troops from India, where the army was still contending with the tenacious Faqir of Ipi. The War Office was in a quandary since reserves had to be kept in readiness for deployment in France in the event of a war with Germany. The Chiefs of Staff warned the cabinet that failure to secure Palestine would imperil the Suez Canal and the entire network of imperial communications between Europe and Asia. The Empire came first and so eight days before Chamberlain made his first flight to meet Hitler, his government decided to send additional forces to Palestine in spite of the European crisis. Behind this decision was the fear that the Singapore strategy might have to be activated suddenly since Japan might choose the outbreak of a Continental war as the perfect moment to begin an offensive in South-East Asia.[32] In the last resort, Malaya, Australia and New Zealand were infinitely more valuable to Britain than what Neville Chamberlain called 'a faraway country of which we know nothing'.

Other factors contributed to the Prime Minister's willingness to accommodate Hitler at Munich. Canada had no desire or reason to fight to preserve the Czech state and the other dominions were at best lukewarm about engaging in a war that served none of their interests. Australia's Prime Minister applauded the Munich agreement and pestered Chamberlain to do all in his power to appease Mussolini. British air defences were unready for a contest in which, thanks to RAF Intelligence miscalculations of German strength, the odds appeared stacked against Britain. Churchill condemned the Munich agreement as a defeat and posterity has tended to sympathise with his judgement, but the alternative was to risk a war in which defeat was a distinct possibility.

The worst-case scenario was rather melodramatically outlined by Leo Amery at the height of the Munich crisis in a letter to the Australian Prime Minister Billy Hughes:

Here we are on the run at a rate that should bring our cabinet to Australia next week with Hitler close on their tail demanding the cession of the hock-yielding districts of South Australia, with Victoria and New South Wales thrown in to 'round off' the territory, while Japan, with his blessing, takes the rest.[33]

This cocktail of pessimism and hysteria revealed that an otherwise level-headed imperial statesman could imagine that a war against Germany in 1938 might end with the overthrow of the Empire. For Amery's countrymen and women, the Munich agreement lifted the immediate and terrifying prospect of massive air raids and tens of thousands of dead, even though many rightly wondered whether that war had just been postponed rather than prevented, as Chamberlain had claimed.

Immediately after Munich, additional troops were drafted to Palestine and within a year peace had been restored. A political solution contrived to calm the Arabs there and beyond was offered by a White Paper issued in May 1939. It proposed a five-year ban on Jewish immigration and an elected assembly in which the Arabs were certain to have a permanent majority. Churchill faced a dilemma. On one hand, he was uncomfortably aware that the survival of Britain's power in the Middle East required the goodwill of the Arab world, and, on the other, he feared that this imperative would force the government to renege on the Balfour Declaration. At a Zionist dinner party held at the house of Clement Attlee the Labour leader in June 1937 and, after too much whisky and brandy, Churchill lambasted the 'lily-livered' Chamberlain for failing to stand up to the Arabs.[34] Churchill was similarly infuriated by the White Paper, which he condemned as the 'appeasement' of the Arabs, adding that Britain: 'is on the run again. This is another Munich.'[35]

The long retreat was now over. In March 1939 Hitler ratted on his Munich pledge and seized what was left of Czechoslovakia, which prompted Britain and France to promise to fight to defend the territorial integrity of Poland. Taking his cue from Hitler, Mussolini reminded the world that Italy was still greedy for land. In April he invaded and annexed Albania, the opening gambit of his planned extension of Italian influence across the Balkans. At the end of May, Mussolini formally hitched himself to Hitler's bandwagon by signing the Pact of Steel. It was an alloy with inbuilt flaws, since Italy's armed

Churchill in the full-dress uniform of 4th Queen's Own Hussars, 1895.

...urchill in tropical field kit, ...galore, 1897.

Churchill and Kaiser Wilhelm II at the German army manoeuvres, 1906. The uniforms were nineteenth century, but the weaponry was modern; here Churchill first sensed that he had th capacity of a master strategist.

The first Lord takes to the air: Churchill in the cockpit of a RNAS aircraft after a flying lessor May 1914.

o Constantinople! HMS *Goliath* shells Turkish positions in the first phase of the Gallipoli
paign, 1915.

dy for the Reds: British troops heading for the Russo-Persian frontier, 1920.

Counter terror: British troops and armoured car on patrol, Kenmare, Co. Kerry, 1921.

King-in-waiting: Churchill introduces his wife Clementine to the Emir Abdullah of the Transjordan during the 1921 Cairo conference.

Air control: RAF Wapiti bombers flying over Fort Busaiyah, Iraq, 1929.

Fear and Loathing in Palestine: one of many clashes between the police and Arab anti-Zionist demonstrators, Jaffa, 1933.

For Allah and the New Rome: Mussolini brandishes the 'Sword of Islam' in Tripoli, Libya, 1937. The weapon had been presented to the Duce by Arab sympathisers.

perate measures: French sailors abandon ship during the bombardment
Mers-el-Kébir, July 1940.

asy allies: Churchill and de Gaulle, Marrakech, 1944. The General never
ndoned his fears that the British coveted the French Empire.

3rd officer Daphne Jones and Chief Petty Officers Moina Imam, Joan Campbell and Betty Khan of the naval wing of the Indian Women's Auxiliary Corps, 1944.

Trinidad Royal Navy reserve policemen, 1944.

Australian gunners shelling Japanese positions, Borneo, July 1945.

ighting trim: the battleship HMS *Malaya* steams out of New York harbour after a
t in an American yard, July 1941.

de in the USA: Kittyhawk fighters, Tunisia, 1943. These machines had been shipped
he Gold Coast, re-assembled and then flown across the Sahara to bases in Egypt.

An Indian sepoy guards the Abadan oil refinery, 1941.

Jordanian Arab Legionnaires and obsolescent biplanes keep watch over the oil pipeline to Haifa, 1941.

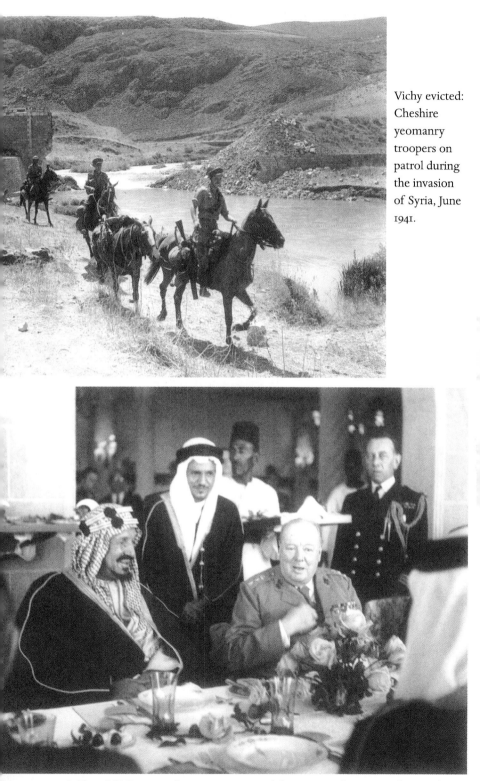

Vichy evicted: Cheshire yeomanry troopers on patrol during the invasion of Syria, June 1941.

:ain resurgent? Churchill discusses the postwar regional disposition of power with King Ibn d, February 1945. The Arab monarch wondered whether the future might lie with America.

No laughing matter: Gandhi and Sir Staffo[rd] Cripps enjoy a joke during discussions on India's future, March [1942]. They proved fruitless, much to Churchill's s[atisfaction].

A Hard Knock for Nippon: an Aussie biffs a Japanese officer while a Churchillian bulldog bites his rump. Australian poster, c. 1942. At the time, Australian politicians felt that they had been left in the lurch by Churchill.

TOGETHER FOR VICTORY

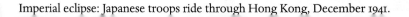

Imperial eclipse: Japanese troops ride through Hong Kong, December 1941.

ving Britain's Empire: US marines come ashore at the beginning of the reconquest of
e Solomon Islands, 1943.

The Empire restored: the Union Jack hoisted over Tarawa, the capital of the Solomons, 1943. Many American politicians and commentators were appalled that their servicemen had died in a campaign to reinstate colonial rule.

Waiting for Roosevelt: Churchill watches as USS *Augusta* enters Placentia Bay, Newfoundland, August 1941

Sharing out the cake: Roosevelt and Stalin attending Churchill's sixty-ninth birthday party at the British legation, Tehran, November 1943.

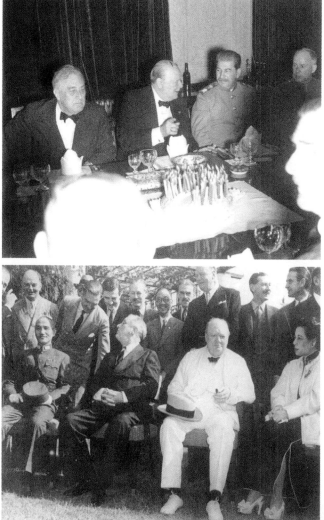

Cold shoulder? A peeved Churchill sits next to Madame Chiang Kai-Shek during a meeting in which her husband [seated far left] and Roosevelt discuss a postwar Asia, United States embassy, Cairo, November 1943.

...nese surrender, Singapore, September 1945.

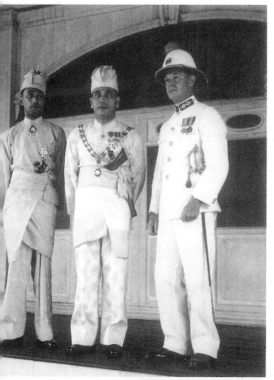

The old order returns: HH the Sultan of Kelantan and his British adviser, 1947.

Cold War in the jungle: British patrol hunting Communist guerrillas, Malaya, 1954.

British forces arrest a Mau Mau suspect, Kenya 1954. Churchill was distressed by the harsh measures employed to restore order in the colony, but failed to intervene.

A great power withou empire: British hydrog bomb test, Christmas Island, 1957. Churchill endorsed Attlee's deci to develop an Atomic bomb and approved th development of its mc destructive successor.

forces were encumbered by outdated weaponry, technical deficiencies and shortages of tanks and aircraft, the weapons which won modern battles. The parlous state of the Italian war machine was understood by the CID, which concluded in September 1938 that the 'position of Italy vis à vis the British Empire ... is inherently weak'.[36] Mussolini could not be bought off and in April secret preparations were in hand for a British sponsored, anti-Italian 'insurrection' in Libya and another in Abyssinia if war broke out.[37]

Mussolini's soldiers landed in Albania on Good Friday, which mortified the devout Halifax. Churchill boiled over with justifiable rage against the government which, although forewarned of the Duce's intentions, had failed to assemble the scattered units of the Mediterranean fleet. It could have intervened and prevented what he called 'the rape of Albania'. This outrage did, however, provide the chance for the BBC's Arab service to remind its listeners that Mussolini, the self-appointed champion of Islam, had shown his true colours by invading a Muslim nation, Albania.

A minor propaganda success could not hide Britain's strategic predicament in the summer of 1939. There was a helter-skelter rush to collect allies: Russia was the prize, but efforts were also made to corral Greece, Romania and Turkey. Churchill concurred and pinned his hopes on Turkey as a powerful regional counterweight to Italy. 'Italy is a prey,' he told the American journalist Walter Lippmann, 'Turkey is a falcon.' He had already advised Chamberlain to focus his attentions on the Mediterranean on the twin assumptions that Mussolini would honour the Pact of Steel and that 'swift and striking victories' there would be crucial in the war against Germany. Dominance of the Mediterranean would also isolate Mussolini's African colonies, for Churchill imagined that Libya would become a springboard for an offensive against the Canal by Italian troops under German command. He had correctly guessed the course of what turned out to be the next phase of Italy's bid for empire.

With Italy in a bullish temper, the Singapore strategy was now in limbo. Since 1936 the question uppermost in everyone's mind was no longer how it would be implemented but whether it could be. The CID doubted that it was any longer viable and felt that Australia would be better off if it made approaches to the United States.[38] Certainly the Australian government was very jumpy and kept badgering Britain for additional assurances, and it got them at the May 1937 dominion conference, where the question of Italy was discreetly ignored. New Zealand seems to have been more composed over this issue.[39] Italy of course was the crux of the problem and no one in the Admiralty knew for certain whether any ships could be spared for the Far East if Mussolini declared war. If he did, Australia was expected to play its part in the defence of the Middle East and so, in March 1939, Britain reaffirmed its pledge that the Singapore strategy would be activated come what may.[40]

Recent developments had drained these promises of credibility. Anxious about an Italian invasion of Tunisia from Libya, France was becoming very edgy about the possible reduction of Britain's Mediterranean Fleet. Lord Stanhope, the First Sea Lord, was worried about the harmful effect which the withdrawal of many big ships would have on Britain's standing with its potential allies Greece and Turkey, and in the Arab world.[41]

Indian security also depended ultimately on the Mediterranean. Fifteen years of pruning the military budget had left India's defences in a parlous condition and in 1936 the CID concluded that its garrison could not withstand invasion by a 'major power', by which they meant Russia rather than Japan.[42] Japan was, however, considered a danger and one which needed to be countered.

A hasty rearmament and modernisation programme was in hand, but India's safety would as ever require reinforcements from Britain which, like those earmarked for the Far East, had to pass through the Suez Canal.

By 1939 Japan and Italy were ready to start a War of the British and French Succession in which the two powers would gobble up the possessions of both powers in the Far East, Pacific, the Mediterranean, the Near East and Africa, while Hitler consolidated and extended Germany's grip in Central and Eastern Europe and, later, Russia. Yet, by an amazing stroke of good luck, Britain did not have to face the nightmare of a simultaneous war against Italy and Japan for just over two years. With a prudence born of an awareness of the deficiencies of his air force and army, and a dread of having to contend with both

Britain and France in the Mediterranean, Mussolini left Hitler in the lurch in September 1939. He sat on the fence until the outcome of Germany's war against Britain and France was clear and then he played his hand. Japan too had no choice but be circumspect, for the Hitler–Stalin pact meant that the USSR continued to constitute a major threat to Manchuria, which ruled out any immediate adventures in South-East Asia and the Pacific.

With Russia neutralised, Hitler was free to begin the next phase of his grand imperial project with the invasion of Poland on 1 September. Within a month it had been partitioned between Germany and the Soviet Union.

In the six months before the invasion of Poland, Churchill's reputation soared. For the past three years he had been an isolated figure, although with a small coterie of like-minded allies in the Commons, including Anthony Eden, who had parted company from the government early in 1938. Like many others, he recognised that Churchill had been right persistently to cry wolf over Hitler, for he had understood the nature of the beast and its diet from the start. This creature would only be deterred by the massive rearmament advocated by Churchill, which was why both the pacifist Left and the disciples of Baldwin and Chamberlain branded him a warmonger. Churchill's siren voice grated on a public which yearned for peace, was haunted by the nightmares of the last conflict and which feared that another would be so destructive that civilisation would be destroyed for ever.[43] Churchill shared this dread; in February 1935 he told Clemmie that another war would led to 'the end of the world'.[44]

Gradually the country fell into step with Churchill. German and Italian backing for General Franco's Nationalists in the Spanish Civil War confronted the Left with the need to decide between pacifism and militancy in the face of the pan-European ambitions of Fascism. Socialists of all complexions reluctantly concluded that a war was preferable to the extinction of their creeds at the hands of Nazism and Fascism. The consequences of Munich justified Churchill's denunciation of the agreement and added to his popularity as a clear-headed statesman whose judgement had been well-informed, sound and, as events turned out, far-sighted. In fairness, however, the government had undertaken an effective rearmament programme, which, whilst tardy, did result in the country being far more ready for war in September 1939 than it had been a year before. Moreover, Churchill's demands in 1937 and 1938 for medium-range bombers and enlargement of the army turned out to be mistaken.[45] Revealingly, Hitler imagined that Churchill's intransigence could be discounted because he had estranged himself from the British establishment.

That establishment was beginning to wobble during the spring and summer of 1939. The *Daily Mirror*, *Daily Telegraph* and *Manchester Guardian* all called for Churchill's immediate entry into the cabinet and he was finding increasing support from the Liberal and Labour parties and among those Tories who were not enslaved to the Whips and were sick of continual abasement to a pair of brutish bullies. The mass of their colleagues stuck to Chamberlain, who with that stubbornness characteristic of the purblind, refused to admit Churchill into his cabinet until the actual outbreak of war. On 3 September 1939 Churchill returned to the Admiralty to fight a war in defence of an Empire that was soon fighting for its life.

PART FIVE

1939–1945

A War of Peoples and Causes:
Churchill as War Leader and Strategist

Six weeks before the outbreak of war, General Sir Edmund Ironside visited Churchill at Chartwell and found him animated by 'patriotism and ideas for saving the British Empire', although he confessed to sleepless nights spent agonising over its future.[1] On 3 September 1939 he entered the cabinet as First Lord of the Admiralty and on 10 May 1940 he became Prime Minister after Chamberlain had resigned, piqued by the defection of forty-one of his supporters, mostly Tories, in a vote of confidence. Churchill formed a coalition government with Liberal and Labour support, but for a time he was encumbered by the deadwood of Chamberlainite ministers and the sour mistrust from a swathe of Tory backbenchers and from King George VI and Queen Elizabeth, who had felt comfortable with Chamberlain.

In his *Finest Hour*, Churchill later wrote of his 'profound sense of relief' that the moment had at last come for him to fulfil his destiny as the nation's saviour. In fact his mood was bleak: when his bodyguard, Detective Inspector W. H. Thompson spoke to him of the 'enormous task' he now faced, Churchill remarked with tears in his eyes, 'God alone knows how great it is. I hope it is not too late, I am very much afraid it is. We can only do our best.' Three days later, when passers-by cheered him on the street with cries of 'Good luck, Winnie, God bless you', he observed forlornly: 'Poor people, poor people. They trust me, and I can give them nothing but disaster for quite a long time.'[2]

His diffidence was uncharacteristic and misplaced, for in May 1940 the only alternative was Halifax, who had hardly any fight in him, was addicted to temporising and, by his own admission, lacked the charisma to lead the country in a war. Churchill had this quality, first-hand experience of war and an understanding of tactical and strategic principles, although his competence in this field was contested by some of the generals, admirals and air marshals who advised him or whose egos had been scalded by his invective. Their modern champions have kept alive old grievances.[3]

One of Churchill's first and most far-sighted decisions was to make himself Minister of Defence and, in effect, commander-in-chief of all imperial forces on all fronts. One general called Churchill a 'super Commander-in-Chief' and was horrified by the prospect.[4] For the next five years, Churchill controlled and directed the imperial war effort. This was a masterstroke since it eliminated the backstairs intrigue and the cancerous bickering between commanders and ministers that had blighted the management of Britain's war effort during the First World War. As Churchill knew, the brass hats had lost none of their appetite for conspiracies. During the winter of 1939–40 a cabal of senior officers with the connivance of George VI had waged an underhand and successful campaign to unseat Leslie Hore-Belisha, the Secretary of War.[5] The venomous spirit behind the plot was embodied in Lieutenant-General Sir Henry Pownall's description of Hore-Belisha as 'an obscure, shallow-brained, charlatan, politico Jewboy'.[6]

'The man's mad' was Pownall's judgement of Churchill after he had been in office for a fortnight. A backbiter, the general ought to have been grateful for a prime minister with a grasp of the essentials of imperial strategy since for the past seven years he had been grappling with ministers whom he had found to be utterly ignorant of the subject.[7] What grated with Pownall and senior officers in other services was Churchill's frequent and acerbic exposure of their timidity, short-sightedness and administrative blunders. All were invoked by him in July 1940 during discussions at Chequers over a proposed assault on the Italian Red Sea port of Massawa. He was delighted by the III Corps's motto 'Hitting not Sitting', exploded with rage when he heard that its weaponry had not been delivered and commanded Field Marshal Sir John Dill the Chief of Imperial General Staff to take immediate remedial action. As to the attack on Massawa, Churchill grew impatient with objections and angrily declared, 'You soldiers are all alike; you have no imagination.'[8] His experience of the last war had made him painfully aware of the catastrophes that had been the direct outcome of letting the brass hats get their own way.

Churchill purged timeservers and mistrusted officers who had been promoted merely for not earning any black marks, once telling Dill that: 'It isn't the good boys who help win wars. It is the sneaks and stinkers as well.' When faced with a succession of crises in North Africa during 1941 and 1942, he issued a sequence of warnings whose tone and import were summed up by a secret directive sent after Rommel's first advance to the Egyptian frontier:

It is to be impressed on all ranks especially the highest that the life and honour of Britain depends upon the successful defence of Egypt. It is not expected that the British forces of the land, sea and air in the Mediterranean would wish to survive so vast and shameful a defeat.

'Anyone', he added, 'who can kill a Hun or even an Italian has rendered good service.'⁹ Courts martial and firing squads were threatened for generals who threw in the towel after Rommel's capture of Tobruk in June 1942.¹⁰

Churchill's open and flexible mind quickly grasped the immense importance of the successes of the codebreakers and analysts at the Government Code and Cipher School at Bletchley Park. By May 1940, they had made great progress deciphering German naval, military and air force communications, and, for the rest of the war, Churchill treasured the decrypts which were delivered to him each day. His enthusiasm for this source of information was not always shared by the generals and admirals who benefited from it.¹¹ Churchill's old zeal for novel gadgetry was as vibrant as ever. In September 1940, he stared in wonderment at a high-definition enlargement of an aerial photograph recently taken of German fortifications on the French coast, picked out a car passing along a road, put his finger on it and declared, 'Look, there is a horrible Hun. Why don't we bomb him?'¹²

Churchill's volatility, his passionate and occasionally cranky enthusiasms, his impatience with duller minds and his faith in his own talents as a strategist created tensions between him and his subordinates. Senior officers and bureaucrats were exasperated by the wilder flights of Churchill's imagination, which tended to soar in the early hours of the morning and were usually triggered by a sturdy intake of brandy or whisky. Alexander Cadogan, Permanent Secretary at the Foreign Office, called these brainwaves 'midnight follies', and Hugh Dalton the Minister for Economic Affairs observed that the Chiefs of Staff were 'in constant terror of what he may do, or decide, without consulting them'.[13] Nonetheless, Churchill eventually won the admiration and affection of Brooke, Cadogan and many others who were willing to forgive the late hours, the crustiness and the outbursts of fury. They and humbler members of his staff warmly recalled a life force swilling champagne, brandy and whisky in what seemed frightening amounts, puffing his cigar and dictating memos in a richly embroidered red dressing gown, or, on at least one occasion, naked and vigorously applying his back scratcher.

The Prime Minister took a keen interest in every aspect of waging war; nothing was too obscure or trivial for his attention. During November 1941 he issued memos on U-boat losses, the wastage of aircraft, allowing married internees to have shared accommodation in prison, assistance to partisans in Yugoslavia and the treatment of Polish officers stationed in West Africa.

Administrative lassitude and procrastination were ticked off with reprimands or curt requests for more adequate or lucid information. The flavour of Churchillian interventions was reflected in some of his instructions issued that month: 'I must beg you to have the matter more searchingly examined', 'Let us hurry up the arrangements', 'When was this decision to abandon operations for manoeuvres taken and by whom?'[14]

The Prime Minister did not have things his own way, for official mechanisms of restraint existed and they were applied. Staff officers and civil servants dissected Churchill's nocturnal conceits and assessed their practicability. Rows and tantrums followed, as the diaries of Brooke, Cadogan and Colville reveal, but Churchill was always susceptible to reasoned arguments and gave way to them, not always graciously.

Two decisions taken by Churchill during his first three months as Prime Minister turned out to be war winners. The first, of which more later, was to do all in his power to enlist the support of the United States for Britain's war effort, since he realised that the British Empire's resources were insufficient to defeat Germany and (after 10

June 1940) Italy. Only what turned out to be substantial American assistance could tip the balance. The second decision is less well known, but equally crucial: the refusal to negotiate with Germany at the end of May 1940.

Between 24 and 27 May 1940, a number of senior cabinet ministers succumbed to a bout of quivering during which they urged Churchill and their colleagues to seek terms from Germany. The chief victims were Halifax, Chamberlain and R. A. Butler, the Under-Secretary at the Foreign Office, who regarded Churchill as 'the greatest adventurer of modern political history' and a 'disaster' for the nation, a view that still prevailed among the many Tory partisans of Chamberlain.[15]

The background to this infectious failure of nerve was the German armoured advance through Belgium and the Ardennes, the collapse of the British Expeditionary Force and the pell-mell retreat of the French army. Some of its fugitive units joined with British forces and converged on Dunkirk, closely harassed by German dive bombers. Between 27 May and 1 June nearly a third of a million British, French and Belgian servicemen were evacuated across the Channel, but masses of weapons, ammunition and equipment had to be left behind. It had been a close-run thing and Churchill insisted that details of the debacle were withheld from the dominions.[16]

Watching the disintegration of Allied resistance, Ironside told Eden (then Halifax's deputy at the Foreign Office) that 'This is the end of the British Empire'. A contemporary opinion poll indicated that his pessimism was shared in the country, but was stronger in the middle class than in the working class. Inside the cabinet old appeasers trembled and pressed for making peace terms before it was too late, with Halifax and Chamberlain making the running. The latter proposed that 'we could get out of this jam by giving up Malta and Gibraltar and some African colonies'. In other words, the price of peace would be the delivery of Britain's African subjects into the hands of the SS. Halifax repeated his old, threadbare mantra that Hitler was 'sincere', again mistaking that quality for honesty. Butler suggested that Mussolini could be approached to act as a mediator, which implies either gross naivety or negligence, for since 19 May intelligence reports had been revealing that Italy had begun mobilisation and analysts suggested that it would soon declare war.[17]

Churchill was adamantine, accusing Halifax of dallying with treason, for which he later apologised, and vehemently declared that Britain would fight on, come what may. He engaged the waverers forcefully and ended one peroration with a typical flourish: 'If this long island story of ours is to end at last, let it end only when each one of us lies choking in our blood upon the ground.' His arguments against a peace were realistic and unanswerable. It would have involved national humiliation, a possible collaborationist regime under the Fascist leader Sir Oswald Mosley (who was locked up in gaol for his own and the nation's safety), the surrender of warships, the loss of vital strategic bases and the virtual end of an Empire whose subjects would have lost faith in Britain. Even if Hitler proffered generous terms, his past record showed that he could and would break them if he saw it to be in his interests.

The cabinet swung behind Churchill with strong support from its Labour and Liberal members: Britain would continue fighting despite the odds mounting against her. As predicted, Italy declared war on 10 June, which did not prevent Butler from putting out feelers to Mussolini a few days after; his chronic misjudgements did not impair a career which ended with self-satisfied retirement as the head of a Cambridge college.[18] Chamberlain died from cancer a few months later. Halifax was despatched to Washington as ambassador in December.

The history of these crucial five days of cabinet debate has only recently been fully revealed and has been brilliantly reconstructed by J. Lukas. He touches on the question as to whether Hitler would have been willing to horse-trade with Britain after he had just subdued Norway, Denmark, the Netherlands, Luxembourg and Belgium and was on the verge of defeating France. Lukas cites remarks made by Hitler after the event in which he spoke of how, at Dunkirk, he had deliberately allowed the British army to escape to rescue the British Empire, which he had never wished to 'inherit'. This was either humbug or delirium. Hitler ordered the German air force to do all in its power to obliterate the troops at Dunkirk and, when things were going well for him during 1941 and 1942, he was keen to kick down the props of British imperial power in the Middle East.

We Felt We Were British:
The Imperial War Effort

'Don't worry; Barbados is with you.' This buoyant telegram from a tiny colony arrived at the Colonial Office within hours of the self-pitying broadcast on 3 September 1939 in which Chamberlain announced Britain's declaration of war. Within weeks, BBC listeners were heartened by Vera Lynn singing 'There'll Always Be an England' with its comforting chorus line, 'The Empire too, we can depend on you'. This was so; yet India and the colonies had no choice but to join the imperial war effort. The dominion parliaments made up their own minds and, with the exception of Éire, threw themselves behind Britain. Churchill was profoundly moved by this solidarity, which he called 'one of the finest things that the world had ever seen', but he admitted that any attempt by Britain to browbeat the dominions would have provoked resistance.[1]

Without the Empire, Britain could never have sustained its six-year war effort. The dominions and colonies supplied Britain with food, raw materials and, as the war progressed, aircraft, warships, tanks, guns and ammunition were produced by rapidly expanded local industries. The bulk of the weaponry was made in Canada, the only industrialised dominion. Its factories reached peak production in 1942 and during the last quarter of 1944 they manufactured 2,600 warplanes (some of them American models such as Catalinas), 3,100 tanks and nearly 14,000 trucks and jeeps. The Empire also provided just under half of Britain's armed forces; the total for India, Australia, New Zealand, Canada and South Africa was about 3.5 million servicemen and women, and Britain's African colonies supplied 375,000 askaris and 46,000 pioneers. Nearly all were volunteers, although Canada introduced conscription in 1944, sending the draftees to garrison the West Indies, a non-combat zone. In Kenya the authorities resorted to forced labour to raise the crops that helped feed Britain and her forces in North Africa and Asia.

*

The war was the ultimate test of that contract between rulers and ruled that gave the Empire its legitimacy. In theory, its subjects submitted to alien governance in return for peace, progress and prosperity, words often used by Churchill when he listed the merits of the Empire. These gifts had created a powerful sense of moral reciprocity which persuaded many of the Empire's subjects to volunteer. Aziz Brimah, the son of a Gold Coast [Ghana] chief and cola-nut trader, felt himself under an obligation when he enlisted in the army:

... we felt we were British, that we were safe under British administration. That is why, when they requested help for the British in Abyssinia, in Burma, we surrendered ourselves and went ... the British helped to quench our tribal wars [and] if they had trouble elsewhere we went.[2]

In January 1942, when Japanese troops were advancing down the Malay peninsula, the Sultan of Johore broadcast to his subjects a reminder of their debt to the Empire: '... for many generations we have lived in harmony, in peace and prosperity under the guidance and protection of our closest friends, the British.'[3] This debt was acknowledged by many blacks in Northern Rhodesia [Zambia], but in some quarters there was a feeling that Britain had neglected its side of the bargain. Some asked:

You want our help now that you are in trouble. But what have you done for us? What are you going to do for us? You say German rule will be bad. How do we know? Yours is not so good, anyway.[4]

Such cynicism was strongest in the Copper Belt, where black miners were aggrieved by a colour bar that reserved the highest paid jobs for white workers.

Similar reproaches were aired in the Gold Coast, where a 'vociferous minority' demanded to know what Africans could expect in return for fighting Britain's wars.[5] Members of the colony's educated elite foresaw a peacetime dividend in the form of greater political freedom and, in 1941, some were talking about 'the promise of a New Africa'.[6] Its appearance seemed close in the summer of 1945, when East African askaris serving in Burma looked forward to a better future and their letters home were full of hopes for new schools and hospitals. Some wished to improve themselves through vocational training. Nigerian soldiers were reading local nationalist newspapers and were angered by their suppression by the colonial authorities.[7]

The expectations of African soldiers were part of a wider phenomenon that emerged during the final two years of the war among British servicemen: an ardent desire for a post-war world from which past social and economic iniquities had been banished. The blueprint for Britain's new age was the 1942 Beveridge Report which promised extensive welfare and educational reforms. Its colonial counterpart was the Atlantic Charter, which Churchill and Roosevelt agreed on their first meeting in Newfoundland in August 1941.

The Charter's third and, for Churchill, highly contentious clause promised 'to respect the rights of all peoples to choose the form of government under which they will live; and they wish to see sovereign rights and self-government restored to those who have been forcefully deprived of them'. Roosevelt and most of his countrymen took this to mean that peace would be followed by the disappearance of all colonial empires, including Britain's. Churchill rejected this interpretation of the Charter, which, he insisted, applied only to the conquered states of Europe. As he explained to the Commons, the Charter's pledges did not embrace the 'progressive evolution of self-governing institutions in the regions and peoples which owe allegiance to the British crown'. The route and pace of the colonies' journey towards self-determination would be decided in Whitehall.

Clement Attlee, the Deputy Prime Minister, disagreed. Not long after the Charter had been published, he told a meeting of West African students in London that it would be extended to their countries. His audience was delighted and their spokesman told him: 'West Africans were proud of the Empire and were pleased to march shoulder to shoulder with the British to fight this war.'[8] Churchill's view prevailed in the cabinet, but for the rest of the war, he and his ministers had the awkward task of explaining to sceptical Americans that the British Empire deserved exemption from the terms of the Charter.

Many of the volunteers from the colonies were uninterested in

politics. They felt strong emotional ties with Britain, like Connie
Macdonald, a member of the Jamaican middle class and the
descendant of slaves, who enlisted in the ATS. 'We were British,'
she remembered. 'We were proud to be British ... England was our
mother country. We were brought up to respect the Royal Family.
I used to collect pictures of [Princesses] Margaret and Elizabeth,
you know. I adored them.'[9] 'England was a special country to me,'
recalled Charles Adams, a Cape Coloured who joined up and drove
supply trucks in North Africa. This identification with Britain and a
sense of belonging were reinforced by King George VI's Christmas
broadcasts of 1941, 1942 and 1943 in which he emphasised the concept
of the Empire as a vast, extended family.

In colonies where British authorities governed in harness with
native rulers, the latter were encouraged to use all their influence
to entice recruits into the army. In February 1942 the recruitment
drive of the Fijian chiefs foundered in the face of impassive young
men who said that they had no quarrel with the Japanese. Persistence
succeeded and within six months 'a healthy, truculent spirit' had been
engendered among the Fijians and the volunteers poured in; the old
warrior spirit was still alive and the chiefs demanded that the recruits
should be drafted to the front in North Africa as quickly as possible.[10]

Patriotism was often blended with self-interest. Paul Gobine of
the Seychelles came forward 'To serve the country and to serve the
King; and at the same time to leave poverty behind'.[11] This was a
motive that Churchill appreciated and wished to foster. In 1940 he
gave his blessing to the formation of a Caribbean regiment that, he
hoped, would reduce the high levels of local unemployment.[12] This
unit's genesis had begun as a spontaneous outburst of patriotism in
Trinidad, where a public meeting voted to raise 25,000 men. Official
wet blankets were quickly applied to the scheme, with the governor of
British Honduras arguing that, after the war, the black soldiers would
return home as stroppy political activists, just as their predecessors
had done in 1919.[13]

The war was indeed exposing volunteers from the colonies to novel
and sometimes strange surroundings which, together with their
often bewildering experiences, altered their perspective on the world
and their place in it. Old hierarchies tumbled. Askaris accustomed

to call an Indian 'bwana' [master] in Kenya found themselves being addressed as 'sahib' by Indians in Burma. A Jamaican undergoing officer training for the RAF called his batman 'sir' and was corrected: 'No, sir, it is me who calls you "sir".'[14] These and other colonial servicemen watched newsreels, listened to wireless programmes and read those service newspapers which circulated on every front and which were laced with propaganda contrived to stimulate exertion and boost confidence. Yet, in what Churchill had characterised as a war of ideals, propagandists encouraged all participants to look beyond victory to a regenerated and fairer world, both in Britain and its Empire.

Colonial public opinion mattered and it was carefully monitored. So too were the views of Indian and colonial servicemen, whose letters were scanned by military censors under orders to keep their eyes open for statements of exemplary patriotism and murmurs of discontent. This surveillance was complemented by an intensive propaganda offensive throughout the colonies which explained why Britain was fighting and warned that the defeat of the British Empire would inflict unimaginable sufferings on all its peoples.

Nazi racial theories were an incalculable bonus for British propagandists who repeatedly reminded Britain's negro subjects of Hitler's contempt and loathing for them. This and their likely fate under German rule was widely understood, although a handful of better educated blacks in the Gold Coast wondered whether Hitler was as bad as he was painted.[15] Their counterparts of the 'clerk and teacher class' in Northern Rhodesia accepted that they would face a hideous future if the Germans won and were, therefore, 'conscious of their stake in the Allied victory'.[16] They were right to be fearful; following the fall of Tobruk in 1942, over two hundred black and coloured pioneers from the South Africa Labour Corps were murdered after they had been taken prisoner by Rommel's Afrika Korps.[17] The Field Marshal was not, as some historians have depicted him, the 'decent' face of the Wehrmacht.

German and Italian anti-imperial propaganda virtually ignored Britain's black subjects and concentrated on Cyprus and Palestine. Early in 1940, Greek Cypriots were told that they were the 'muleteers and slaves' of England and were urged to seek inspiration from

Ireland's long struggle to win independence.[18] Nazi broadcasts to the rest of the Middle East continued to spew out pre-war anti-Semitic harangues and appeals to the Arabs to combine and expel the Jews from Palestine.[19] During December 1941, Radio Berlin called on Arabs to welcome Japan's entry into the war and to treat her victories as blows struck for 'the Arab cause against British tyranny and aggression'. Roosevelt was a 'stooge' to the Jews and Churchill was his 'servant' and both were agents of the Jewish conspiracy to dominate the world. The recent British occupation of Syria and Iraq proved that the Allied championship of the 'oppressed and weak nations' was a fraud and that Japan's entry into the war had thwarted Britain's planned invasion of Afghanistan.[20]

Imperial counter-propaganda reproduced the Churchillian ideal of the Empire as an engine for progress. Colonial cooperation could not be taken for granted and so various official organisations were hastily created, including a film unit, whose job it was to advertise the blessings of imperial government. In the first year of the war, press releases for colonial newspapers included stories about building aerodromes in Nigeria, investment in sponge gathering in the Bahamas and a telephone system in Swaziland. There were also congratulatory pieces about malaria eradication and falling infant mortality in India.[21] This all sounded very impressive, but it should be remembered that the inter-war years had been marked by a dearth of capital for colonial projects. Nonetheless, propaganda was given a belated credibility by the 1940 Colonial Development and Welfare Act which injected £5 million a year into colonial economies with a further £1.5 million for development.

Propagandists working for the Colonial Office and the Ministry of Information soon found themselves having to contend with one shortcoming of colonial government: widespread illiteracy. In Nigeria only one in six hundred of the population went to school and most Mauritians spoke either Hindi or an indigenous French patois.[22] The islanders did, however, show a reassuring patriotism, with framed portraits of King George VI displayed in many homes. Problems of communication were overcome by cinema and radio, often communal sets. There were forty-six cinemas in Mauritius that, by 1941, were showing officially supplied shorts; footage of aircraft and warships were very popular, but audiences were understandably bored by scenes of Britain's factories in full wartime production. In Nigeria, the wireless was the chief propaganda medium, with programmes in Hausa, Ibo, Yoruba and 'simple English'. Either on film or through recordings of his speeches, Churchill became a familiar figure in the colonies.

The mood in the dominions had been sober and resigned when war was declared. There was none of the manic flag-waving and appeals for imperial unity that had occurred in August 1914, although New Zealand MPs sang the National Anthem after approving their country's declaration of war. The same patriotic spirit was expressed in a petrol-rationing policy that virtually abolished motoring for pleasure.[23] Elsewhere, memories of the mass slaughter in France ran deep and prompted fears that it would be repeated. The *St John's Daily News* welcomed Newfoundland's joining the 'struggle for the survival of human liberty', but, recalling the terrible losses suffered by the Newfoundland regiment in the last war, urged young patriots to disperse themselves by enlisting in the Canadian forces.[24]

In Ottawa, Prime Minister Mackenzie King was glad that Canada was fighting for those liberal values he had always cherished, but he too was mindful of the lives that had been squandered on the Western Front and, therefore, he did not wish Canadian troops to be deployed in France. They were sent to help the defence of England in 1940 and to man some of the fifty obsolescent destroyers that were requested from the United States. Plans were then in hand to evacuate the Royal Navy's training facilities to Canada in the event of their destruction by aerial bombardment.[25] Beyond the reach of aerial attacks, the dominions offered perfect sites for pilot training and flying schools were established in Canada, Australia, South Africa and Southern Rhodesia. In all, 170,000 airmen graduated from these courses, over two-thirds of them Canadians.

South Africa's entry into the war was not a foregone conclusion. The atmosphere in the country was equivocal and Prime Minister Smuts needed all his political dexterity to secure 80 votes for a declaration of war against 67 for neutrality. Opposition came from the white supremacists of the Afrikaner Nationalist Party, who were receptive to Nazi racial theories, in particular the concept of the *Volk*. In March 1942, when a German victory was still a possibility, one Nationalist MP hoped that the Nazis would treat South Africa as a friend because of his party's resistance to the war effort that included minor sabotage and assistance to German POWs on the run.[26] Objections to petrol rationing were so strong that Smuts dared not impose it.[27] British newsreels, keen to stress imperial unity, ignored Boer resentment and, in 1940, cinema audiences were comforted by footage of South African volunteers with a commentary that declared that 'Afrikaners and Britons stand together'.[28] Out of a white population of 2.1 million, 186,000 men and women joined up and 123,000 volunteered for various labour and transport corps from the black and coloured population of 8 million.

Japan rather than Germany was Australia's bogey and had been for twenty anxious years. Australia entered the war full of misgivings about what Japan would do next. All that stood between the dominion and a Japanese seaborne invasion was Singapore and a hypothetical armada of warships that Britain had pledged to send eastwards. Robert Menzies the Australian Prime Minister feared that the plan might never be implemented once the Royal Navy became engaged in a struggle with Italy for the control of the Mediterranean.

Menzies was in his early forties and was an intelligent, cocksure and ambitious egotist yearning for a larger stage on which to display his talents for statecraft and strategy. Before the war, he had urged appeasement and in May 1940 Stanley Bruce, the Australian High Commissioner in London, added the dominion's voice to calls for negotiations with Germany. Menzies and Bruce believed that Churchill was a rash warmonger whose intransigence would jeopardise the agreement of a peace that alone would preserve the Empire.[29] It certainly would have saved Australia, for once Britain had disengaged from the European conflict, it would be free to send ships, aircraft and men to deter the Japanese.

Menzies continued to be at loggerheads with Churchill, although in public he felt obliged to praise his leadership. In private, Menzies distrusted the Prime Minister, regarding him as a capricious autocrat who had deliberately surrounded himself with yes-men who were overawed by his willpower and bad temper. Churchill had to be pinioned and Menzies believed that the best constraint was dominion representation in the cabinet. It was an idea he first mooted early in 1941 when he visited London after a morale-raising tour of Australian forces in Egypt. He picked up some allies, including a jealous Lloyd George, who harboured the notion that Churchill's misfortunes might somehow facilitate his own political resurrection.

Matters came to a head in August 1941 when Menzies returned to London for a meeting of dominion Prime Ministers, attended by Mackenzie King and New Zealand's Peter Fraser, Smuts having thought it prudent to keep an eye on things in Pretoria. Mackenzie King and Fraser rejected Menzies's scheme for a permanent dominion presence in the cabinet and the former suspected that he was angling for the job to satisfy his vanity.[30] Churchill concurred and observed that Menzies 'loathes his own people. He wants to be in England.'[31] Never the most patient of men, George VI found Menzies and his countrymen tiresome, confiding to Mackenzie King 'how different Australians seemed to be to any of the other Dominions; that Canada, New Zealand and South Africa seemed to work in close harmony, but that in Australia, they were always being critical'.[32]

Churchill trumped the idea of dominion representation with a cast-iron legal objection. A dominion prime minister or his nominee was constitutionally disqualified from cabinet office since they could not answer through Parliament to the British people. Menzies's kite-flying gave Churchill the opportunity to set down his own forthright views of the essentially subordinate nature of wartime relations between Britain and the dominions. Britain, he explained, was the 'flagship' of the Empire and it would be foolhardy for the 'captains' (i.e. the dominion prime ministers) to be summoned on board during severe and persistent storms.[33] The inference of the metaphor was clear: Churchill was the admiral who commanded the fleet and the dominion prime ministers were the captains who obeyed his orders and stuck to their own quarterdecks. This arrangement fitted with his remarks during a BBC broadcast in which he likened Britain to a lion and the dominions as its cubs, an analogy that had been used on a First World War poster.[34]

Checkmated, Menzies flew back to Australia where his coalition had been ousted and a new Prime Minister, Arthur Fadden, had formed a government. The importance of this episode lay in Churchill's exposition of the role of the dominions: they pursued their own war efforts and submitted to him as the supreme arbiter of strategy.

India's entry into the war was a fraught and messy affair. Lord Linlithgow issued the declaration, which was fully within his constitutional powers as Viceroy. All the Congress provincial ministries resigned as a protest against an act that seemed to symbolise India's continued subjection. The Muslim-dominated governments of Bengal and the Punjab stayed put and agreed to support the war effort. Dr Muhammad Jinnah, leader of the Muslim League, realised that political capital could be earned by collaboration. It was, however, conditional; in March 1940 Jinnah publicly named his price, which was partition and the creation of an independent Muslim polity after the end of the war. It would be called Pakistan.

The division of India was an anathema to Gandhi. He treated the war as irrelevant to India's progress towards independence; his appreciation of the issues at stake was shallow and at times he appeared unhinged. If he was aware of Hitler's racial disdain for Indians, he preferred not to mention it. Gandhi's overview of the European conflict was subjective and permeated by the assumption that the continent's problems could only be resolved by the application of his private spirituality. The upshot was a self-indulgent scattering of platitudes: Gandhi advised German Jews and Czechs to follow his doctrines of non-resistance and, in 1940, he urged Britain to submit to German occupation. The Mahatma even admired Hitler, whom he judged to be a 'patriot' and 'not a bad man'.[35]

Congress realists were not so blinkered or blasé. Nehru was repelled by Nazism and Fascism and inclined towards socialism as the model for post-independence India, while Subhas Chandra Bose, the party's other leading grandee, was swinging towards Fascism. No clear party line emerged and, for the first two and a half years of the war, Congress oscillated between the extremes of non-cooperation and limited assistance to the war effort. Many of the rank and file believed that collaboration would win concessions from Britain and eventual independence. Contrary to official expectations, there was a steady flow of volunteers into the services, many from districts that were traditionally loyal to Congress. Two-thirds of the Indian officers serving in Malaya in 1941 felt that their exertions would quicken the pace of progress towards independence.[36] At the close of the war, a sepoy stationed in Burma told his family: 'I have joined the army to serve my country .... This is a people's war.' Reward was now close at hand and Indian soldiers were cheered by the news of Labour's victory in July 1945, for the party was pledged to remove all the hurdles to Indian self-government as quickly as possible.[37]

Churchill would have been distressed by the idea of the Indian soldier wearing khaki to emancipate his country, rather than out of a sense of allegiance to his King Emperor. His views of India remained blinkered and anachronistic. In April 1941, he was heartened by a report of the performance of Indian troops in Eritrea, which prompted memories of his own service on the North-West Frontier. He rejoiced as 'one who had had the honour to serve in the field with Indian soldiers from all parts of Hindustan'.[38] 'Hindustan' had a distinctly Victorian timbre to it and there were echoes of Churchill's paternalism the following August when he promised that the Anglo-Russian occupation of Persia 'will keep the war away from the Indian people we have under our care'.[39] His India was still a land of gallant sepoys true to their salt and grateful peasants tilling their fields under an even-handed and benevolent Raj.

Once he became Prime Minister, Churchill restarted his old campaign against Indian independence by blocking attempts to reach an accord with Congress that would exchange political trade-offs for wholehearted backing for the war effort. He lectured the cabinet about Britain's duty towards the 'poor masses' of the sub-continent and, in July 1940, he warned the Secretary of State for India Leo Amery that 'he would sooner give up political life at once, or rather go out into the wilderness and fight than admit to a revolution that meant the end of the imperial crown in India'.[40] For the rest of the war, Churchill remained unyielding on India, sweeping aside the possibility of a bargain with Congress in the most vitriolic language.

Nominally independent Egypt was bludgeoned into entering the war, as it was legally bound to do as Britain's ally under the terms of the 1936 Anglo-Egyptian treaty. The cudgel was wielded by the British ambassador Sir Miles Lampson, whose grouse shooting with

King George VI at Balmoral had been interrupted by the 'utterly damnable' Hitler at the end of August 1939. He flew back to Cairo, where his assertiveness jolted the Egyptian Prime Minister Ali Meher into persuading his cabinet to declare war. Lampson noted in his diary that Meher was a careworn, bedraggled figure who had been 'rather frightened' by the ambassador's trenchancy. The cabinet majority for war was narrow and Lampson detected defeatism among Egyptian politicians and King Farouk's courtiers, but the Abdin Palace was a short drive from the British barracks and 5,000 Indian reinforcements soon arrived to remind Egyptians that they had best knuckle under.[41] This arm-twisting had been necessary, for Egypt was about to become the fulcrum upon which the defence of the Empire would depend for the next four years.

For Churchill the dedication and scale of the imperial war effort vindicated all that he had ever said about the Empire. Here, surely, was unequivocal proof of these ties of kinship, affection and gratitude which, he believed, were the bedrock of the Empire and its guiding spirit. The experience of war had immeasurably strengthened an Empire which remained the foundation of Britain's claim to world power. In his victory broadcast on 13 May 1945, he boasted that 'the British Commonwealth and Empire stands more united and more effectively powerful than at any time in its long, romantic history'. Churchill would have been delighted by a home letter from a British soldier in Burma who described his Gurkha and Sikh brothers-in-arms as 'the finest set of fellows that any Empire can have to fight for them'. He would, however, have been mortified by the conclusion of a gunner whose contact with Indian soldiers had made him 'all in favour of giving India its independence'.[42]

A Disaster of the First Magnitude:

Holding the Middle East, 1939–1941

On 21 September 1940 Churchill read the Ultra decrypt of Hitler's order to postpone Operation Sea Lion; the Battle of Britain had been won and there would be no cross-Channel invasion in the foreseeable future. One imperial front had been successfully held and Churchill was now free to divert forces to another, equally vital theatre of war. He ordered the concentration of warships, troops, tanks and aeroplanes in the Middle East to defend a barrier that stretched from Gibraltar through Malta to Egypt and overland to the oilfields of Iraq and Persia. For the next three years, a greater part of the resources and manpower of the Empire were assembled in this area to pursue what was an essentially imperial objective: the preservation of British maritime and political power.

With Hitler paramount in Europe and Mussolini bent on overturning British power in the Middle East, Churchill had no choice as to where he could wage war. On 9 May 1940 he had told Menzies that 'any alternative' to holding Egypt 'cannot be contemplated'.[1] Egypt with its vast and constantly expanding complex of encampments, training grounds, airfields, oil depots, workshops and storage facilities became both a citadel and the powerhouse of Britain's regional war effort. Churchill warned local commanders in April 1941 that expulsion from Egypt would be a 'disaster of the first magnitude' second only to the invasion and conquest of Britain.[2]

Egypt took precedence over the Far East. It had to, for the Empire lacked the wherewithal to defend the Middle East from a real threat at the same time as protecting Malaya and Australasia from a hypothetical one. It materialised in December 1941 when Japan declared war and Churchill was compelled to justify his earlier priority. He defiantly declared: 'If the Malay Peninsula has been starved for the sake of Libya and Russia no one is more responsible than I, and I would do exactly the same again.'[3] Churchill elaborated on this decision in his memoirs when he described the Mediterranean and Middle Eastern theatres as the 'hinge of fate on which our ultimate victory turned'.

It was also the region that Mussolini coveted as the heartland of his renascent Roman Empire. Within a few weeks of declaring war, his diplomats presented Hitler with an invoice for his yet-to-be-undertaken services on the battlefield. His chief demands were a slice of south-eastern France, Corsica and Tunisia, all of which would be extracted from a defeated France, and, given that Britain seemed to be on its last legs, he later threw in Aden, Malta, Egypt, the Sudan and bases in Syria, Jordan and Palestine.[4]

Mussolini's war of imperial conquest got under way during the late summer and autumn. Libyan garrisons were beefed up for the invasion of Egypt, Italian forces overran British Somaliland, Aden was bombed and small detachments edged into the southern Sudan. There were not enough troops to save Somaliland, but Churchill was angered by a reverse that damaged imperial prestige. At the end of August, when Eden was sent to Egypt as Churchill's representative, the Prime Minister warned him, 'If you lose Khartoum, your name will live in History', a chilling admonition for which he later apologised.[5]

His fears of an Italian onslaught were reasonable, given Mussolini's ambitions and the sheer numbers of the troops, tanks and aircraft he had at his disposal in Libya and East Africa. Yet, within the next six months it became obvious that the Duce's appetite for conquest far outstretched his powers of ingestion. One ignominious reverse followed another in quick succession. In October his army got a bloody nose in Greece, the advance into the Sudan petered out, the invasion into Egypt was repelled and, by January 1941, British, Commonwealth and Indian forces were sweeping into Libya.

A debacle was only forestalled by the arrival of German reinforcements in the spring, when Rommel's Afrika Korps rescued the last remnant of Mussolini's African empire. The quality of its men and armour tilted the balance of power against Britain and for most of 1941 and 1942 Egypt was in a state of virtual siege.

Elsewhere, Mussolini's African empire had collapsed swiftly. Less than a year after Italy had entered the war, Somalia and Eritrea had been occupied and Abyssinia had been liberated. Britain's former hegemony in East Africa was restored, convoys were able to pass through the Red Sea unmolested and nearly a quarter of a million British, Commonwealth, Indian and African troops were released for deployment in North Africa. Looking back on these events at the close of 1941, Churchill characterised the Empire's enemies as 'the Hitler tyranny, the Japanese frenzy and the Mussolini flop'.[6] Schoolgirls playing hopscotch on the pavement chanted:

> *Hippetty, hippetty, hippetty hop;*
> *Musso, Musso, he's a wop;*
> *The bigger, the bigger, the bigger the flop.*[7]

As the struggle for the Middle East unfolded, Churchill found himself confronted with a new contest for mastery of the Atlantic. The war against the U-boats assumed an equal importance to that in the Middle East; in May 1941 he assured Roosevelt that if Hitler lost the Battle of the Atlantic, he would ultimately lose the war.[8] Oil was a common and crucial factor in both campaigns; it was the lubricant of modern war and it was beyond question that whichever side secured wells and reserves would ultimately prevail.

The Empire had a head start in the competition for oil. Before the war, Iraq, Persia, Trinidad and the Dutch colonies of Curaçao and Aruba had been Britain's chief suppliers of oil products. The former two were in Britain's grasp and the security of the Dutch oilfields presented no difficulties. Immediately after the defeat of the Netherlands in May 1940, a destroyer was sent from Trinidad with orders to land a detachment of infantry on Curaçao and occupy its oil wells and those of Aruba. The Dutch government-in-exile warmly endorsed this coup and the islands were subsequently garrisoned by Canadian and American forces.[9] The wells continued production and in 1944 supplied Britain with 16.8 million tons of oil products.

Total oil imports during 1940 had been just over 50 million tons, of which about a fifth came from Persia and Iraq. Two million were pumped through the pipeline that ran to the Haifa terminal, a vital asset that made it possible to supply oil to forces in North Africa relatively safely. By 1944 Iraqi and Persian output had risen to 16.8 million tons, of which 500,000 tons of aviation fuel were sent overland to the USSR.

Control over regional sources of oil gave Britain what turned out to be a decisive advantage in the Middle Eastern theatre: fuel could be delivered directly to British forces, whereas Italian and German aircraft and tanks depended on fuel that had to be shipped across the Mediterranean in tankers that were vulnerable to air and submarine attack. Nonetheless, in the early phases of the war huge amounts of fuel and munitions did get through; between June and December 1940 690,000 tons of shipping passed between Italy and Libya.

The ease with which the Axis powers fuelled, fed and equipped their forces in North Africa by sea was stark proof that the Royal Navy had forfeited its supremacy in the Mediterranean. Italy's declaration of war had transformed the sea into a battle zone, through which convoys passed at their peril. Malta came under a protracted aerial siege and Italian submariners and pilots preyed on British shipping to the point where cumulative losses outweighed any advantages that might have been gained from taking the shortest route to Egypt. By August 1940, the Admiralty conceded that it was safer for convoys to take the long haul southwards to Cape Town and then northwards through the Indian Ocean and Red Sea to Egypt. Time was lost – the voyage took forty-two days for 15-knot convoys and sixty for 10-knot – but cargoes and troops reached their destination with only marginal losses.

Churchill was incensed by what was a retreat from an area where the Royal Navy had been historically paramount. He locked horns with the Admiralty over one convoy carrying desperately needed tanks to Egypt, but backed down; the ships arrived. A few fast convoys which were given the operational code initials 'WS' did make the dash through the western Mediterranean, but the bulk of reinforcements and supplies were shipped via the Cape until the end of 1942. Recalling the perils of the Mediterranean passage in December 1944, Churchill proposed the permanent British occupation of the island of Pantelleria, a key Italian air base sixty miles south of Sicily.[10] The future security of imperial communications through what was once again a British lake nullified all his public statements about Britain not seeking any post-war annexations.

The partial closure of the Mediterranean forced a revolution in imperial logistics. The upshot was a new pattern of communications that exploited the geography of Britain's African colonies and the loyalty of South Africa. Both allowed the Royal Navy to dominate the Atlantic and Indian Oceans so that Britain could transport troops from Australia, New Zealand, South Africa and India to Egypt and feed and equip them. Merchantmen carried grain from Australia, and coal from Bengal and South Africa, while Egyptian phosphates were exported to raise yields on Australian, New Zealand and South African farms.

These lifelines needed limited protection, for the South Atlantic and Indian Oceans lay far beyond the operating range of the U-boats. Patrols of Sunderland flying-boats and Hudson bombers flown from bases in the Gambia and Sierra Leone covered West African waters and cut the depredations made by the tiny number of U-boats that had begun hunting in this area at the end of 1940. Their presence and the likelihood of their reinforcement dictated exigency plans for an amphibious attack on the Azores in the event of German attempts to establish a U-boat refuelling base and airfield there. Efforts were to be made to persuade the Portuguese government that a British occupation of the islands was a temporary, wartime measure.[11] It was also a last resort, for the government hoped that the United States would take responsibility for the security of the mid-Atlantic.

Air power decided battles, a truth that was acknowledged by the local commander-in-chief, General Sir Archibald Wavell, in April 1941 when he told Churchill that the 'whole position in the Middle East' was dependent on aerial superiority.[12] It was achieved thanks to a hastily improvised transit system contrived in the autumn of 1940 to bypass the Mediterranean. Either crated or transported on aircraft-carriers, the warplanes were shipped to Takoradi on the Gold Coast, reassembled when necessary, and then flown via Lagos, Kano and el Obeid to Khartoum. From here they flew north to front-line bases in the Nile Delta.

Swathes of desert acquired fifty or so years before were the salvation of Britain's war effort in the Middle East. At the end of February 1941 the RAF began to receive desperately needed consignments ·of American-manufactured Baltimore bombers and Kittyhawk and Tomahawk fighters that had been shipped to Takoradi and then flown across the Sahara. The initial order was for 875 machines and, by June, about 200 a month were arriving and others, together with bombs, were being shipped directly from the United States by way of the Pacific, the Indian Ocean and the Red Sea.[13] Many of these aircraft were delivered to Australian, New Zealand and South African squadrons stationed in Egypt. An astonishing piece of logistical improvisation provided Britain with the means to keep abreast of the Axis air forces. During 1942 the flow of American machines increased and British and dominion air forces gained the superiority that saved Egypt and secured the decisive victory at El Alamein.

23

Supreme Effort:
Distractions, Chiefly French

Churchill's Middle Eastern strategy had been severely handicapped by the surrender of France on 23 June 1940. A vital prop was knocked away, since before the war France had pledged reinforcements for the defence of the Suez Canal and had earmarked its substantial North African army for diversionary sorties into Libya. The allies had also agreed to use Tunisian airfields for a joint bombing offensive against Sicily and southern Italy, in return for which the RAF was committed to transfer fighter squadrons from Egypt for the defence of France.[1] As in 1914, the safeguarding of the British Empire required considerable French help, which explains why Churchill went to such extraordinary lengths to urge France to stay in the war during the last fortnight of May and the first of June.

The Franco-German armistice transformed a former ally into a malevolent neutral, the Vichy regime. It walked in step with Hitler and controlled southern and western France and, most alarming of all, ruled nearly every French colony in the Middle East, Africa, the Far East and the Caribbean. Churchill was prepared for this emergency; on 17 May he had asked a cabinet committee to draw up exigency plans to be implemented the moment that France was defeated. It concluded that Britain's best bet was to sponsor a government-in-exile with its headquarters either in Algeria or Morocco, which of course would strengthen British power in the Mediterranean.[2] Dakar in Senegal was a tempting alternative because it offered Britain 'another base in the East Atlantic'.[3]

These suggestions turned out be wishful thinking because most French colonial bureaucrats and soldiers accepted Vichy as the legitimate successor to the Third Republic, which was to be expected, given their strong conservative and nationalist sympathies. Presided over by the now decrepit saviour of Verdun, Marshal Philippe Pétain, the new regime buried the liberal ideals of the Republic and exhumed the reactionary France of the priest and peasant. Piety and quietism were exalted and anti-Semitism and Anglophobia were officially promoted.

Above all, Pétain had to do everything in his limited power to protect the integrity of the French Empire. This proved a tricky task, for a defeated and humiliated nation was now at the mercy of two voracious predators, Italy and Japan. Many Frenchmen believed that Britain too would profit from their country's defeat and make a bid for some of its colonies. In a war of empires it seemed very likely that the French was on the verge of partition; immediately after the armistice and with Hitler's blessing Italian advisers were installed in Tunisia, Algeria and Syria and, with the consent of local officials, Indo-China became a Japanese satellite. Further losses could, however, be averted if Vichy kept on the right side of Germany, which was winning the war and continued to do so until late 1942. Hitler had no desire to possess French colonies since Vichy had obligingly delivered Germany a surrogate empire. It was bound by the terms of the armistice to export colonial raw materials to the Reich. France's West African colonies supplied industrial diamonds, Madagascar provided graphite and Indo-China rubber. These commodities were shipped to Vladivostok and, in accordance with the Nazi-Soviet pact, were sent by train across Russia to Germany.[4] The French Empire was also a potential repository for unwanted people; for a short time in 1940, those German planners in charge of racial policy discussed projects for the mass deportation of Jews to Madagascar and France's West Indian colonies.[5]

France's surrender had swung the global balance of naval power against Britain. Churchill's cabinet committee had already discussed this eventuality and the First Sea Lord, Admiral Sir Dudley Pound, had proposed that unless the French fleet was somehow neutralised it would have to be sunk.[6] The future of the scattered French navy lay in the hands of its commander-in-chief Admiral François Darlan, a chauvinist and an Anglophobe, who was inordinately proud of an ancestor who had been killed at Trafalgar. In the last week of June he convinced himself that Britain would shortly be defeated.

The terms of the Franco-German ceasefire required Darlan to

surrender the French fleet to Germany and Italy, but he toyed with the idea of sending all the warships in French ports to the United States or one of France's Caribbean islands. This arrangement would have satisfied Britain since President Roosevelt would have automatically invoked the Monroe Doctrine to exclude the navies of the Axis powers from the West Indies. Darlan prevaricated, sending out a stream of contradictory signals to his commanders of ships, including those that had taken refuge in Portsmouth and Alexandria.

For Britain the immediate danger was a formidable French squadron of four modern battleships that was anchored at Mers-el-Kébir near Oran. If these joined the Italian fleet, then the Royal Navy would be outgunned in any big ship action in the Mediterranean and, since Britain was under threat of invasion, no extra capital ships could be spared. Churchill acted swiftly and resolutely. On 3 July he ordered Admiral Sir James Cunningham to deliver a six-hour ultimatum to the commander at Mers-el-Kébir who was offered three choices: internment in America, the scuttling of his ships, or their destruction. No reply was received and, after a three-minute bombardment, three battleships were sunk or crippled and nearly 1,300 French sailors were killed. Just before Cunningham's ships opened fire, Darlan revealed his true colours by sending a signal ordering the squadron to engage the blockading force, and promising air and submarine support.[7]

What for Churchill had been a distasteful decision had been vindicated. He trumpeted the Mers-el-Kébir incident as signal proof of Britain's determination to fight on. Moreover, by 'striking ruthlessly' against her former ally, the nation was 'securing for a while ... the undisputed command of the sea'. This was confirmed in November by what he hailed as the 'glorious victory' at Taranto, in which carrier-based Swordfish biplanes sank or disabled a trio of Italian battleships as they lay at anchor. The aeroplane now dominated the war at sea as it did the war on land. The lesson of Taranto was repeated off Crete the following May, when Axis bombers damaged three battleships and an aircraft-carrier and sank three cruisers.

Mers-el-Kébir had removed one threat, but Vichy and its empire retained a capacity to hurt Britain. Pierre ('Pretty Boy') Laval, the

Prime Minister, and Darlan, now Minister for War, pressed for active collaboration with Germany since only Hitler could protect French colonies from further Italian encroachments. In return, France would place ports in West Africa and the Caribbean at the disposal of the *Kriegsmarine* for refuelling and watering U-boats patrolling at the furthest limit of their operational range. No formal agreement was made, but in the spring of 1942 the Admiralty received intelligence of U-boats receiving covert assistance in French Guiana, Martinique and Guadeloupe.[8]

Churchill loathed the Vichy regime, which he accused of 'fawning' on the Germans.[9] Yet he had to proceed circumspectly towards a hostile state which controlled the 70,000 strong Armée du Levant and over 100,000 mainly Arab and black troops in North and West Africa where they outnumbered local British garrisons. If, for whatever reason, Vichy threw its whole weight behind the Axis, its colonial garrisons could inflict considerable injuries on the British Empire.

The best solution to the Vichy problem was political and took the form of British sponsorship and funding of a government-in-exile headed by General Charles de Gaulle. He was the only hope that Churchill had of challenging the legitimacy of Vichy and, most important of all, of enticing France's colonies into Britain's orbit. On 30 July 1940 de Gaulle broadcast from London with an appeal to rally behind him and fight alongside Britain as part of '*La France Libre*'.

De Gaulle's bombast, vanity, testiness and incessant rows with Britain and the United States have been very well covered by the biographies of François Kersaudy and Jonathan Fenby. The General had persuaded himself that he was France's man of destiny, a saviour in the mould of his heroine, Joan of Arc. Churchill admired de Gaulle (and needed him) but he soon became exasperated by his egotism and his tendency to forget that Britain equipped and paid for Free French forces.

There was one massive and insurmountable obstacle to harmony between the British government and de Gaulle: the sour and unfinished history of Anglo-French colonial rivalry. De Gaulle shared with his

Vichy rivals a nagging intestinal fear that Britain was conspiring to deprive France of its colonies, using wartime necessity as both cover and justification. *La Perfide Albion* was up to its old tricks and new Fashodas were in the offing. French colonial administrators in West Africa suspected Britain's motives when they were approached on behalf of de Gaulle and refused to be moved by bribes and promises to pay their salaries and pensions.[10] In December 1940 Radio Dakar warned the natives of Senegal that 'Britannia is attempting to obtain our Empire's soldiers and make them fight for her'.[11]

Churchill repudiated these allegations and so did everyone else engaged in persuading Vichy colonial officials to defect. Australian negotiators charged with enticing officials in Tahiti and New Caledonia into the Free French camp stressed that Britain would not annex the islands after the war.[12] Such undertakings never dispelled the misgivings either of the Vichy regime or de Gaulle.

Apprehension about Britain's expansionist ambitions intensified after the descent on Dakar in September 1940. The capture of the port was a project that particularly appealed to Churchill, who retained his old fondness for imaginative and audacious masterstrokes, which, if they succeeded, could change the course of history. The Dakar coup was one of those plans which would have been hailed as genius if it had succeeded and been condemned as madness if it had failed. Preparations for the expedition drawn up in August listed among the prizes on offer a naval base with a well-equipped dockyard and an opportunity to inject some spirit into the Free French movement, which was languishing.[13] The response to de Gaulle's radio appeal had been disappointing: Félix Eboué, the black, Martinique-born administrator of Chad had plumped for the Free French and de Gaulle had won over the Cameroons and the French Congo, where he established his 'capital' at Brazzaville. Elsewhere he had been cold-shouldered, but there were optimistic intelligence reports of strong support for him among the black population of French West Africa and local Muslim leaders.[14]

The Dakar coup initially rested on the premise that the loyalty of the garrison and administration was shallow and that de Gaulle would easily coax the governor into surrendering Senegal. He was to be accompanied by a mixed squadron of French warships with

Free French crews and Royal Navy vessels flying French colours. An essentially soft approach was replaced by coercion on a grand scale in the shape of a powerful armada, including battleships and an aircraft-carrier, that would prepare the way for an amphibious landing. It miscarried, thanks to stiff resistance by local land and air forces, and afterwards Churchill was slated in the press and the Commons for recklessness. Memories of Gallipoli were disinterred, while in private Churchill blamed the expedition's commanders for pussyfooting and a lack of offensive spirit.[15]

Dakar remained a plum worth picking. A second attack, including air raids from neighbouring Gambia, was being considered early in 1941 and, in May, the United States Navy drew up plans for a huge seaborne assault that would have involved 100,000 soldiers and 500 aircraft.[16] Britain and America were only concerned with acquiring the naval facilities, but Frenchmen of all persuasions wondered whether the two powers were thinking in terms of a long-term, possibly permanent occupation of French soil.

Vichy's power to hamper Britain's war effort was greatest in the Middle East, where Syria and the Lebanon were well placed to make trouble in Palestine and Iraq. Their potential for mischief was recognised by Hitler's secret services which, during the early part of 1941, masterminded a campaign of subversion designed to generate panic, divert British forces from the Libyan front and to secure airfields in Syria for air raids against Iraq, the oil installations at Haifa and the bases in the Nile Delta.

Hitherto, Hitler had confined his war against the British Empire to wireless propaganda. Arabs heard Britain defamed as an arrogant and grasping overlord working hand in glove with the Jews to steal Arab lands for a post-war Jewish state in Palestine. Hitler proclaimed himself the future liberator of the Arab world and the Grand Mufti declared a *jihad* against Britain, a service that earned him the status of an honorary Aryan. These claims must have been very puzzling for the Arabs, for, while Hitler promised them emancipation, Mussolini sought to engross their lands and make them subjects of the Italian empire.[17]

Mussolini's ambitions were fully understood in Syria, where both

Vichy administrators and the local population had interpreted the recent Italian political penetration of their country as a prelude to annexation.[18] Germany was the only power that could bridle the Italians and, at the same time, protect Syria from the British. With the approval of Darlan, General Henri Dentz the Vichy Commissioner was happy to go along with German plans, despite the likelihood that his compliance might provoke the British invasion he feared.

In April 1941 Hitler's policy towards the Arabs shifted from vocal support to active intervention. The change had been made on the advice of his Foreign Minister, Joachim von Ribbentrop, whose agents had been fomenting an anti-British insurrection in Iraq. Its chances of success would be infinitely improved by the intervention of the Luftwaffe, whose planes would attack local British forces and boost the morale of the insurgents while arms were smuggled to the rebels through Syria. Germany's Iraqi gambit was an offshoot of the major offensive in the Balkans during April and early May that had added Yugoslavia and Greece to Hitler's empire. In the process the German air force acquired a base at Thessalonika from which sorties could be flown against Iraq, although the planes had to be refuelled at Syrian aerodromes made available by Dentz.

The catalyst for the Iraqi revolt was Britain's demand to install a garrison in Basra to protect RAF workshops in which aircraft shipped from America were to be reassembled.[19] Rashid Ali el-Kilani, the Iraqi Prime Minister, refused permission for Indian troops to come ashore on 31 April and his forces besieged the RAF base at Habbaniya, confident that German aircraft would soon arrive to help them. Baghdad Radio told Iraqis that the uprising was national and democratic.

Rashid Ali was a nationalist and a Pan-Arabist who had been embittered by Britain's pre-war Jewish policy and his discontent had been nurtured by German diplomats and the Grand Mufti, who recently had been spirited into Baghdad. For the past two years, Rashid Ali had been surreptitiously rearming his 60,000-strong army with weaponry imported from Germany and Japan, including anti-aircraft batteries.

Churchill was quick to recognise the danger posed by Rashid Ali's defiance and he insisted upon rapid and overwhelming retaliation, the traditional and proven method of handling any internal challenge to imperial authority. Wavell's first response had been to seek talks with Rashid Ali, which Churchill saw as an admission of weakness that would reverberate across the Middle East and damage imperial prestige. On 8 May he informed Wavell that there was to be 'no question of negotiation' which would allow time for the Luftwaffe to consolidate its position in Syria. Intelligence sources were warning Churchill of 'a grievous danger' looming with the possibility that thousands of German parachutists would seize Syria – this was within a fortnight of the successful airborne attack on Crete. With this in mind, Wavell was ordered to 'fight hard' against the Iraqi insurgents.[20]

The commander-in-chief again fumbled. His army had just been beaten in Greece and Crete and he was hard pressed to scrape together enough men, aircraft and tanks to fend off Rommel's imminent offensive in Libya. On 11 May Wavell questioned Churchill's judgement, dismissing the Iraqi uprising as of 'minor importance' when compared to the defence of Egypt, although he was anxious about the security of the oilfields and feared that the unrest in Iraq might spread to Palestine, Aden, the Yemen and even Egypt.[21] Churchill was emphatic, Wavell gave way and ordered an offensive against the Iraqi rebels.

What followed was one of those small-scale, improvised operations of the kind that the British army was always very good at and which Churchill had witnessed as a young soldier. The rebels were stunned by a rapid sequence of hammer blows. A scratch force from the Transjordan Arab Legion (prudently stripped of untrustworthy units) and armoured cars relieved Habbaniya, where a makeshift air force, including obsolescent biplanes, had given the Luftwaffe a rough time.

Aerial supremacy was soon achieved and counter-attacks were made on the German landing strips in Syria. By the end of May, the revolt had crumpled and Rashid Ali fled to Persia along with the Mufti, whose family was taken and deported to, of all places, Southern Rhodesia. He made his way back to Berlin.

A pro-British ministry was established in Baghdad guarded by British, Indian and, later, American troops. At Churchill's orders, 'most energetic action' was taken to secure the Mosul oilfields.[22] Hitler had given Britain a nasty turn by adding to its woes in the Middle East, but this was small beer. His mind was now wholly concentrated on his great enterprise: the subjugation and colonisation of Russia. Operation Barbarossa began on the night of 21–22 June and Churchill celebrated the news by presenting Eden with a cigar.

The small-scale imperial punitive action in Iraq was the prelude to a larger campaign against Vichy France. The Syrian incubus remained: the Luftwaffe retained its bases in the country and there was every reason to believe that they would be reinforced with the connivance of Dentz. On 8 May Churchill issued an 'Action this Day' memo in which he demanded a 'supreme effort' to keep the Germans out of Syria. Wavell was ordered to get on with the job, stop cavilling and not to worry about any Vichy response.[23]

Churchill was taking a gamble when he ordered the attack on Syria. A localised war could further destabilise Palestine, where Arab–Jewish antipathy was simmering, and within Syria there was little love for the Free French in whose name the country was to be invaded.[24] There was also the inevitable sense of trepidation, strongest among French officials, that the British intended to take over their country. After a French officer had been killed in an air raid on a German landing strip, Dentz announced that loyal French servicemen were about to suffer the same merciless treatment that had been handed out to the sailors at Mers-el-Kébir.[25] When the fighting started, the Germans evacuated their airfields so as to give the impression that the British invasion was an act of imperial aggrandisement rather than a legitimate defensive measure.[26]

De Gaulle provided a further difficulty. On the eve of the invasion and under British pressure, he had proclaimed that the Free French would relinquish the Syrian and Lebanese mandates and grant independence to each country after the war. His declaration exonerated Britain of any imperial designs, and of course was an advance renunciation of French sovereignty over two of its most prized possessions The statement was welcomed by the Syrians and Lebanese.

British, dominion, Indian and Free French forces entered Syria on

8 June and, after a hard-fought, five-week war, Dentz capitulated. He had banked on assistance from France: four cruisers from Toulon carrying troops and supplies were expected and the Royal Navy and RAF were on standby to intercept and sink them once they had passed the Straits of Messina.[27] Towards the end of the campaign, Germany offered to airlift reinforcements from France via Thessalonika.[28] Dentz's army, which included Algerian and Moroccan contingents, fought stubbornly and confirmed intelligence reports of widespread hostility towards the Free French. Wavell warned the Foreign Office that they were 'almost universally unpopular', and that the Syrians and Lebanese were looking forward to complete independence.[29]

Aware of local passions, the commander-in-chief in Syria, General Sir Henry ('Jumbo') Maitland Wilson, a convivial, Falstaffian figure, tactfully agreed the repatriation of all Vichy POWs. De Gaulle was furious, for he had imagined that they would flock into his own army, but of the 38,000 who surrendered a mere 5,700 enlisted with the Free French. He believed that he had been double-crossed by the British who wanted to jockey France out of Syria and he went so far as to wonder whether there had been a secret deal between Britain and Germany to bring this about.[30]

Wavell thought that de Gaulle regarded the 'assertion of French sovereignty as far more important than taking measures to win the war' and that his mood was so truculent that if he did not get his way he would 'do a Samson act and threaten to bring down the Free French movement'.[31] Churchill instructed his special representative in Syria, General Sir Edward Spears, to be 'very stiff' with the Free French. 'They can not be allowed to mess up our Syrian position and spoil relations with the Arabs.' De Gaulle's imperial 'pretensions' were to be squashed and, if he remained obdurate, then threats of force were to be made to bring him to heel.[32] The General was also reminded that he and his forces relied on British cash and equipment. In a fit of pique, he retired to Brazzaville, where he told an American journalist that Britain was hustling France out of its empire.[33]

The solution of a strategic problem created a political one. What was to be done with the two French colonies that had fallen into Britain's hands and whose inhabitants had been led to believe that their conquerors were liberators? Syrian and Lebanese nationalists were full of hopes that independence was just over the horizon and their optimism increased after the announcement of the Atlantic Charter at the end of August.[34] Churchill could not afford to disabuse them, for he needed political credit in the Arab world and this was best obtained by proving that Britain was the friend of Arab nationalism. On 9 July, he had informed Eden that 'Arab independence [in Syria] is a first essential and nothing must conflict with this'.[35] The Syrians and Lebanese trusted Churchill and in May 1942 Spears reported to him that their faces lit up whenever they saw his photograph.[36]

Their reactions were understandable, given that he had effectively terminated the French mandate in Syria and Lebanon. It had been a casualty of Churchillian expediency, but once Axis forces had been expelled from the region, he wondered whether he had conjured up a genie that might create mischief for the British Empire. 'What people might learn to do against the French in the Levant might be turned against us later,' he confided to Spears in December 1943. 'We should discourage the throwing of stones since we have greenhouses of our own.'[37] In September 1944 Churchill castigated Spears for not keeping the lid down on anti-French agitation in Syria. It was too late; it and the Lebanon were now virtually self-governing and their independence had been recognised by the United States and the Soviet Union. Of the original European inheritors of the Ottoman Empire, only Britain now remained.

Winning the war was what mattered for Churchill and he embraced any expediency that could help defeat the Axis. After Hitler's invasion of his old bête noire the Soviet Union he had famously declared that he would make a pact with the devil if it would hasten victory. The course of the Russian war soon had repercussions in the Middle East. In August 1941 German forces were poised for the thrust southwards through the Caucasus towards Persia.

British and Soviet intelligence had found evidence (probably exaggerated by the Russians) that the Germans would be welcomed by Persia's ruling elite. Since the start of the war, Axis agents had undertaken a campaign of subversion that indicated that a Fifth Column might emerge to coincide with the German advance. No chances were to be taken: on 25 August British forces based at Basra occupied the Abadan oilfields, which were now as essential to the Russian as to the British war effort. Within a month Persia had fallen to Anglo-Soviet forces and Shah Reza Pahlevi was deposed and a biddable government was established in the name of his twelve-year-old son, Reza Muhammad, the Shah who would reign until his overthrow in 1980 by Muslim zealots.

As Churchill intended, Persia became a conduit for the delivery of arms, munitions (mostly manufactured in the United States) and fuel to Russia. All were vital for his new war aim, which was as pressing as the defence of the Middle East: keeping Russia in the fight by equipping its severely battered army and air force.

The Middle Eastern line had acquired a fresh importance for Britain. Churchill was also keen that it should serve as a launching pad for a counter-offensive that, he imagined, might be launched through the Balkans, which he later famously described as the 'soft underbelly' of Europe. He had tentatively probed it with the luckless offensive in Greece and its aftermath in Crete (where 11,000 British and dominion troops were captured) did not prevent him from arguing for similar enterprises which, he believed, might lure Turkey into the war. In the middle of the Syrian crisis there had been a suggestion that the Turks should be invited to join in the invasion and occupy Aleppo.[38]

The Turkish alliance was a Churchillian hare that was started, chased but never caught. It offered protection for that imperial flank which rested on Syria and Iraq and would have allowed the transfer of men and resources holding the line in Libya, where an outright victory had turned out to be elusive, much to Churchill's chagrin. Compensation was provided by the minor operations undertaken at his insistence in Iraq, Syria and Persia, which expelled Vichy from the Middle East, checkmated German intrigues and preserved the flow of oil.

These sideshows laid the foundations for the post-war perpetuation of British paramountcy in the region. Present strategy complemented long-term imperial objectives. Despite setbacks in Greece, Crete and Libya, Britain was doing remarkably well. Although on the defensive and under pressure, she still dominated the central land mass of the Middle East and retained the capacity to concentrate men and resources there. Almost a third of a million servicemen and women were stationed in the region at the end of 1941 and about half of them were from the dominions, India and the colonies. Most of their aircraft, trucks and jeeps had been manufactured in the United States.

Britain's Broke:

Anglo-American Exchanges, 1939–1941

From Roosevelt downwards, most Americans distrusted empires and believed that the world would become a happier place once they had disappeared. Yet, by the spring of 1941, the President and the vast majority of his countrymen had been persuaded to hand over a substantial part of their national wealth to help save the British Empire, although the President, aware that such a cause might not fire his countrymen, preferred to describe the transaction as one that would make the United States the 'Arsenal of Democracy'. Masses of American tanks and aircraft were already being deployed in defence of the British Empire and more were coming. In April, Roosevelt's aide Harry Hopkins told Lord Halifax the ambassador in Washington: 'You tell me what Wavell wants in the Middle East and I will arrange to get it to him.'[1]

All this had been Churchill's doing. For nearly a year he had coaxed and cajoled Roosevelt with arguments that relied heavily on the sentimental bonds between Britain and the United States. He prevailed and on 11 March 1941 Congress approved the Lend-Lease Act, which gave Britain the credit it needed to pay for its war effort and continue fighting. It was a loan and not a gift, but this did not stop Churchill from exalting it as a measure of pure altruism.

For Roosevelt, pumping dollars into the British Empire was an act of realpolitik, as a victory for the Axis powers would have been a catastrophe for the United States. Americans had not suddenly fallen in love with the British Empire, far from it. From the midsummer of 1940 onwards, the great majority of Americans had slowly come to terms with the fact that Britain's defeat would leave their nation strategically and economically exposed in a hostile world dominated by Germany, Italy and Japan. It was in America's interest to prop up the only nation still resisting the Axis powers.

Churchill's interpretation of American history was the narrative of a nation populated by the descendants of English, Scottish and Scots Irish immigrants who had perpetuated the values and institutions of their homeland. Of these, the most important was a reverence for individual freedom and government by consent, the principles which of course had led America to break away from the British Empire in 1776. Personal experience seemed to support Churchill's peculiar insight into the American character. He crossed the Atlantic in 1895, again in 1900, and several times between the wars. His travels were largely confined to the New England states, although he once ventured to the Pacific coast and stayed in Hollywood. The cosmopolitan, Anglophile Americans he met impressed him favourably and he found virtue in what repelled his more fastidious (and snobbish) countrymen:

Picture to yourself the American people as a great lusty youth – who treads on all your sensibilities, perpetrates every possible horror of ill manners – whom neither age or tradition inspire with reverence – but who moves about his affairs with a good hearted freshness which may well be the envy of older nations of the earth.[2]

Churchill was impressed by a tour of an American warship in 1895. A common ancestry counted, he concluded, for 'It is the monopoly of the Anglo-Saxon race to be good seamen'. For the rest of his life, Churchill's sense of historical continuity led him to emphasise the Anglo-American genetic inheritance, and he tended to overlook the vast influx of Irish, Italian, Slav and Jewish immigrants during the late nineteenth and early twentieth centuries. They were being gradually assimilated into a country whose political elite was predominantly Anglo-Saxon and would remain so for most of his lifetime. Bloodlines defined character, or so Churchill imagined.

Churchill linked kinship with a common destiny. Its future direction became plain to him when the United States entered the First World War. During a tour of the Western Front in July 1918, he was overcome by an 'emotion which words cannot describe' after witnessing 'the splendour of American manhood striding forward on all the roads of France and Flanders'. This sight represented the 'supreme reconciliation' of Britain and the United States and was a portent of a forthcoming golden age in which 'England and the United States acted permanently together'.[3]

Churchill was to be disappointed. A partnership with the British Empire had nothing to offer Americans, most of whom had been schooled in a version of history that portrayed their country's period of colonial rule as a time of injustice and oppression. The Declaration of Independence had defined Americans as a people who had spurned imperial government and the philosophy behind it. Henceforward, anti-imperialism, together with the rejection of monarchy and hereditary aristocracy, formed the bedrock of the American creed.

Churchill, therefore, faced an uphill struggle in his attempts to convince Americans of the virtues of the British Empire. They were, however, more susceptible to the notion of inherited Anglo-Saxon superiority since it validated their concept of Manifest Destiny. This idea had provided the impetus and justification for westwards expansion, conquest and settlement from the 1840s onwards. Divine providence directed the wagon trains westwards and they brought with them civilisation, progress and, of course, colonists whose inherent stamina and ingenuity would soon make them masters of their environment. In 1889 Theodore Roosevelt declared that: 'During the past three centuries the spread of the English-speaking peoples over the world's waste spaces has not only been the most striking feature in the world's history, but also the event of all others most far reaching in its effects and its importance.[4]

Yet most Americans closed their minds to any suggestion that the opening of the West had anything in common with contemporary European imperialism, which was all about the invasion of other people's countries and the stifling of liberty. The American historical consciousness never made a connection between say Custer's campaigns against the Sioux in 1876 and Chelmsford's invasion of Zululand three years later. Franklin Roosevelt shared this blind spot. In January 1945 he remarked to Oliver Stanley the Colonial Secretary, 'I do not want to be unkind or rude to the British, but in 1841, when you acquired Hong Kong, you did not acquire it by purchase.' Stanley's riposte was sharp and pertinent: 'Let me see, Mr President, that was about the time of the Mexican War, wasn't it?'[5] In 1846 the United

States had defeated Mexico and stripped it of California, Texas and New Mexico.

When Congress and the Senate debated aid to Britain, isolationists quickly focused on the iniquities of the British Empire. In 1940 Senator William E. Borah, a Democrat from Idaho, declared that Britain had 'not the slightest conception of democracy' and showed no inclination to give up India 'or any of her imperialistic rights'.[6] Another Idaho backwoodsman imagined that the British were fighting for 'gold, trade, commerce and the maintenance of their ruling classes'.[7] In essence, the Britain of 1940 was unchanged from that of 1776.

These prejudices were strongest in the Mid-West, the home of Sinclair Lewis's Babbitt and his cronies. They loved their country, worshipped the stern Protestant God who took care of it, knew next to nothing of the world beyond their state and were suspicious about what they did know. The Babbitts only read provincial newspapers and distrusted politicians who operated in Washington, particularly clever ones with cosmopolitan horizons. Churchill never visited this America until after the war when its inhabitants revered him as a hero, listened to his speeches and awarded him honorary degrees.

Middle America's suspicious ignorance mattered between 1939 and 1941. It caused consternation in Britain after censors of incoming mail from the United States discovered a widespread hostility towards the British Empire.[8] It did not go away when the United States entered the war, rather its tenor became more strident. Three months after Pearl Harbor, American newspapers and radio stations were denouncing the Empire and welcoming its imminent extinction.[9]

Nevertheless, Churchill stuck to his guns and continued to believe that Americans could somehow be persuaded to see the Empire through his eyes and accept that their nation shared with Britain a birthright that endowed them with a unique moral authority. Moreover, Churchill thought that a wartime alliance could be transformed into a permanent Anglo-American *entente* that would secure the peace of the post-war world. In January 1941 he spoke of how Britain and the United States now had the opportunity of 'setting the march of mankind clearly and surely along the highroads of human progress'.

Both nations were the future guides and protectors of mankind. 'The day will come', he predicted in a BBC broadcast in March, 'when the British Empire and the United States will share together the solemn but splendid duties which are the crown of victory.'[20]

President Roosevelt never wanted America to become a permanent partner with the British Empire, but supporting it in 1940 was a price worth paying to prevent Britain losing the war. From 1939 until the Japanese attack on Pearl Harbor, he did all he could to keep Britain fighting. How this might be achieved was the subject that dominated his increasingly intimate relationship with Churchill. In November 1939, Churchill had, with Chamberlain's blessing, opened an ostensibly private correspondence with Roosevelt. It had been intended for the two men to speak to each other via the trans-Atlantic 'phone line, but this so distorted Churchill's voice that he sounded like Donald Duck. Thereafter, the exchanges were conducted by cipher telegrams. Up to a point, Churchill was frank with the President. But when expediency demanded, he was elastic with the truth: he did not reveal the Ultra telegram in which Hitler postponed the invasion and, when Harry Hopkins visited England in January 1941, he reported back that the government was still bracing itself for an invasion which was confidently expected in May.[11] Disinformation was vital since Churchill had to convince the President that Britain remained in dire peril and aircraft, tanks, weapons and ships were urgently needed. Most, of course, went straight to the Middle East.

Strict neutrality had never been an option for the United States: an unchallenged Axis supremacy in Europe would have had fatal economic consequences. Germany, Italy and Japan were protectionist powers and so American businessmen found themselves facing a future in which their products would be squeezed out of territories under Axis rule. The supply of essential raw materials from European countries and their colonies would dry up: at the outbreak of the war 90 per cent of America's supplies of crude rubber and 75 per cent of her tin came from Malaya and the Dutch East Indies.

Furthermore, Britain's defeat would place its enormous industrial capacity in Hitler's hands and, if he gained part or all of the Royal Navy, Axis fleets would control the Atlantic and the Pacific. Roosevelt outlined this nightmare scenario on 29 December in his fireside chat with Americans. 'If Great Britain goes down,' he warned, 'the Axis powers will control the continents of Europe, Asia, Africa, Australasia, and the high seas – and they will be in a position to bring enormous resources against this hemisphere. It is no exaggeration to say that all of us, in all the Americas would be living at the point of a gun ...' Britain was now America's outlying bastion.

The President was also acutely aware that the ideals that defined America's nationhood were in jeopardy. As the Wehrmacht sliced through France, he described the Allies as fighting the 'battle for freedom' and predicted that, if they lost, then America would become 'a lone island in a world dominated by the philosophy of force'. Opinion polls indicated that four-fifths of Americans concurred and were behind the Allies in spirit, but there remained a strong reluctance to declare war.

Roosevelt had already begun a crash programme of enlarging America's Atlantic and Pacific fleets, but it would take four years to achieve comfortable superiority over the Axis navies. After discounting the Royal Navy, United States Navy [USN] staff planners presented Roosevelt with a statement of the current maritime balance of power in January 1941: It made unnerving reading:

	Combined Axis Fleets	United States Navy
Battleships	20	15
Cruisers	75	37
Destroyers	271	159
Submarines	284	105[12]

The United States Army Air Force [USAAF] feared that if the Nazis could extract West African bases from Vichy, then the Luftwaffe would be able to launch raids on South America. Pro-Axis subversion in this region, abetted by its large immigrant German and Italian communities, was already causing alarm in Washington, where strategists imagined that any Nazi attack on the United States would be launched from Latin America. For these reasons, Roosevelt was relieved to hear of the sinking of the French squadron at Mers-el-Kébir and the expedition to Dakar. Most reassuring of all was Churchill's guarantee that if Britain did succumb then the Royal Navy would seek sanctuary in

Canada, from where it would continue to fight. America's Atlantic frontier was already a war zone in 1940.

It was against this background that on 31 July Churchill asked Roosevelt for fifty obsolescent destroyers to replace vessels lost at Dunkirk and reinforce convoy escorts in the Western Approaches. In return, Britain would lease bases in Newfoundland and the Caribbean to the United States for ninety-nine years. This idea had first been mooted by the American Treasury a year before and its chief attraction was the provision of additional maritime security at little cost. On 27 August Roosevelt agreed to barter the destroyers for bases in Newfoundland, Bermuda, the Bahamas, Jamaica, St Lucia, British Guiana and Trinidad.

Trinidad was strategically the most important since it was soon designated as America's first line of defence against any hypothetical attack from South America or French West Africa. When completed, this stronghold contained dockyards for capital ships, airfields and a garrison of 3,000 troops.[13] In January 1941 USAAF aircraft were stationed in Curaçao and Aruba and GIs replaced the British units that were guarding the oilfields.

The effect of the bases for destroyers deal was the transformation of the British and Dutch West Indies into a de facto American protectorate, since the small print established American enclaves in British colonies and authorised American troops to suppress civil disturbances. In Jamaica, where there had been considerable economic unrest before the war, the governor was scandalised by the idea of American soldiers firing on rioters, but he was overruled.[14] British officers in Bermuda, Antigua, St Lucia and Trinidad were placed under American command.[15]

The Bermudan assembly grumbled about what its members saw as America's expropriation of their colony and Churchill was unhappy about having to bully them.[16] Tory backbenchers were restless and one complained that Churchill had given 'chunks of our colonial possessions away' without a debate in the Commons. The Prime Minister felt a pang of guilt about bartering colonies and during the Washington Conference at the end of December 1941, he pressed Roosevelt to declare that America had no intention of ever claiming sovereignty over the British West Indies.[17]

In the colonies, the arrival of American servicemen was welcomed, because construction of naval bases and airfields offered jobs in a region that had been suffering chronic unemployment. In April 1941, when the Stars and Stripes were first hoisted at the new base on Goat Island, the local paper *The Gleaner* claimed that Jamaicans had much to celebrate:

Any defence of the island by the United States of America will be to our imperial and insular advantage ... It is therefore not as a foreign nation, but as one aligned by blood and tradition, by speech and political aspirations to England that we Jamaicans look upon the United States of America.[18]

These were exactly Churchill's sentiments.

The 290,000 inhabitants of Newfoundland also welcomed the Americans, who revitalised their stagnant economy. In 1934 the island had forfeited its status as an independent dominion after the collapse in the world market for fish and a public debt crisis which forced its government to pass control of its financial affairs to a Whitehall commission. The American base at St John's provided 15,000 jobs and would inject $112 million US and Canadian dollars into the economy, transforming an annual revenue deficit into a bumper surplus within four years.[19]

When Harry Hopkins met Churchill in January 1941, he delighted the Prime Minister with his assertion that 'we're only interested in seeing that that goddam son-of-a-bitch, Hitler, gets licked'.[20] He had been sent by the President to report on conditions in Britain, particularly national morale and the popular standing of Churchill, and to advise him on how best to enlist the support of ordinary Americans for the Lend-Lease bill. The result was a speech in which the Prime Minister promised: 'Give us the tools, and we will finish the job.' He added: 'We do not need the gallant armies which are forming in the American Union. We do not need them this year, nor next year; nor any year that I can foresee.' Bankrolled by America, the British Empire could beat Hitler.

This was a highly tendentious claim, but it comforted Americans who feared that Lend-Lease was the beginning of a process that would conclude with the United States entering the war and millions of its young men being sent abroad to die. Roosevelt allayed their fears during his campaign for a third term in office. In a broadcast speech delivered in Boston at the end of October 1940, he affirmed, 'Your boys are not going to be sent into any foreign country.' It was a vote winner, but a few months earlier the President had been considering what the international situation might be at the close of year. He imagined that the British Empire would still be intact and the Royal and United States Navies would be cooperating in the Atlantic, the Red Sea and Persian Gulf. American sailors would be fighting in 'foreign' countries.[21]

Americans shrank from what was called 'active' belligerency, fearing that, as in 1917, it would cost lives and achieve nothing. On the other hand, they knew that the war was good for business, as it had been during the years of neutrality between 1914 and 1917. The good times began to roll again on 3 September 1939 when the Wall Street index of industrial stocks jumped the equivalent of a hundred points. Britain and France could not get enough of American weaponry and equipment and their demands triggered a rapid surge in industrial productivity and a fall in unemployment. It was just what was needed in a country where the post-recession recovery was running out of steam.

The war was creating jobs and filling up order books. Roosevelt exploited this economic resurgence during his presidential campaign: Seattle voters were reminded that Boeing was taking on more hands to produce aircraft for Britain and Boston shipyard workers were told new jobs were being created to satisfy British demands.

By November 1940 Britain was running out of dollars, or as the new ambassador Lord Lothian told American journalists: 'Well, boys, Britain's broke. It's your money we want.' The solution, which became known as Lend-Lease, was to create a huge overdraft facility that would give Britain the credit to acquire whatever it needed. By the end of the war, the total owed was $27,625 million.

Roosevelt justified this massive allocation of American revenues as vital for the nation's short-term security. 'The defence of the United States' was, he argued, 'the success of Great Britain defending itself'. He also justified Lend-Lease in moral terms by inventing the notion that

America was indirectly waging a war to extend the 'Four Freedoms' to the whole world. These were freedom of speech and worship and freedom from fear and want, and all were somewhat mawkishly portrayed in four paintings by the artist Norman Rockwell.

American taxes were going to a good cause, but many, particularly in the Treasury and business circles, wondered whether Britain had been withholding the truth about its finances. It was not on the verge of the bankruptcy and in fact had an abundance of assets still untapped. In January 1940 Britain's dollar reserve stood at $346 million and the United States Treasury calculated the total value of all imperial assets at $14,000 million, which was an overestimate.[22] The extreme isolationist *Chicago Tribune* suggested that Britain might sell off some colonies.

Britain did have to sell off assets as a precondition of Lend-Lease. Churchill was indignant, but he had no choice but to swallow his anger and submit to the gruelling terms imposed by Congress as the quid pro quo for Lend-Lease. Assets were hurriedly liquidised, not always at the best prices since the value of British investments had fallen over the past year. Among the securities sold were gold reserves worth $50 million stored at Cape Town (Roosevelt was very insistent about these) and Courtaulds (USA) which was purchased by Viscose for $54 million. Greater austerity at home was another price paid by Britons for Lend-Lease. Income tax and the duties on cigarettes and spirits were raised to prove that Britain was doing all it could to help itself.

Churchill also acquiesced to a covenant with the United States that would radically change the future economy of the British Empire. Britain agreed to promote multilateral trading agreements after the war, which in effect meant the eventual withering of imperial preference. J. M. Keynes went to Washington to negotiate the arrangements that were contained in the Mutual Aid Agreement of February 1942. One clause committed Britain to cut tariffs and abolish discrimination against non-imperial goods, although Roosevelt tried to persuade Churchill that this provision did not mean the complete abandonment of imperial preference. Perhaps so, but neither was it a green light for its continuance.

It is important to remember that the United States favoured

universal Free Trade and that throughout the war and after it would work for its implementation, which made sense for the nation with the world's largest industrial capacity. When Britain had been in same position a hundred years before, it too had tirelessly promoted global Free Trade. Closed markets restricted competitive capitalism and, therefore, were an anathema irrespective of the nation that imposed them. In July 1941 Adolf A. Berle Jr, Secretary of State at the Treasury, was fretting about advantageous secret trade deals being hatched between Britain and Yugoslavia and Syria.[23]

Churchill had stayed attached to the Free Trade orthodoxies of his youth and on this issue he was still at odds with the Conservative Party. Its members, most notably Amery and Beaverbrook, were aghast that the Prime Minister had been willing to concede imperial preference as part of the price of American aid. Churchill chose to gloss over this contentious issue, which he regarded as secondary to the great matter in hand, which was winning the war. In his war memoirs he was silent about the bickering that had accompanied the negotiations of the terms of Lend-Lease and the subsequent rows about reopening the Empire to Free Trade. The United States became in 1941 the paymaster of the British Empire in the same way that Britain was the paymaster of de Gaulle and the Free French. The public rhetoric of Churchill and Roosevelt deliberately and for propaganda reasons played down this fact of life, but it remained true, and would have tremendous repercussions for Britain and the Empire during and after the conflict.

There were 317 votes in favour of Lend-Lease in the House of Representatives and 71 against. Its opponents had been a ragbag of isolationists, chiefly from the Mid-West where any hypothetical threat to a distant maritime frontier meant little, and a handful of crypto Fascists and Nazis. More numerous were the rabid Red haters like Joseph Kennedy, the former ambassador to London and father of President Kennedy, who had been uttering shrill prophecies about Britain's imminent collapse since Dunkirk. A brother ambassador summed him up as 'a very foul specimen of a double crosser defeatist' and Roosevelt found him a 'pain in the neck'.[24] These objectors were not voices crying in the wilderness. An opinion poll taken in December 1939 revealed that 82 per cent of Americans were against lending money to the Allies, but 65 per cent were happy to advance it to Finland for its war against Russia.

British propaganda helped swing America towards the view that Britain was fighting on the side of humanity and liberal values against evil men and ideologies. The successful film *The Sea Hawk* (1940) with Errol Flynn as Sir Francis Drake was deliberately designed to compare Britain's stand against Hitler with its resistance to Philip I of Spain. The message was understood by the New York *Mirror*, which described the film as a tale of how 'back in the days of Good Queen Bess, the British island kingdom withstood a Spanish blitzkrieg as it is standing off the Nazis in this day of George VI'.[25] Just what the latter involved had become familiar to millions of Americans through the vivid and moving broadcasts of Ed Murrow which relayed the sounds and terror of the London blitz.

Churchill had got what he needed from the United States at a pivotal point in the war. Thanks to Lend-Lease, Britain could continue to fight. But, had he been hoodwinked by Roosevelt into agreeing a Faustian pact? Like Faustus he secured what he wanted, but, also like Faustus, he had preferred not to think too deeply about the frightening consequences of his bargain: Lend-Lease would have to be paid back. Moreover, repayment would have to be made by a nation that had, as a condition of its overdraft, depleted its collateral. German air raids were weakening its industrial base. By contrast, the Soviet Union had refused to reveal details of its economic circumstances when it sought American credit, and still got it.

A Shocking Tale:

The Singapore Debacle, 1941–1942

Italy's declaration of war effectively abrogated the Singapore strategy. Henceforward, responsibility for the defence of Australia, New Zealand and Britain's Far Eastern and Pacific colonies would pass to America. Churchill acknowledged this in June 1940, when he reminded Roosevelt that: 'I am looking to you to keep that Japanese dog quiet in the Pacific.'[1] He imagined that this beast was at heart a skulking cur which would cringe in the face of Anglo-American steadfastness. In January 1941 he told Harry Hopkins that Japan would never dare to provoke Britain and America together, an assumption he repeated when he met Roosevelt in August.[2] Japan would not be bullied into passivity, but neither would it declare war rashly.

Australia remained jumpy. In July 1940 its government had received details of Britain's Middle Eastern strategy and sent the bulk of its forces to Egypt to help carry it out. A month later, when Britain was bracing itself for invasion, Churchill promised that Britain would 'proceed to your aid, sacrificing every interest except only the defence and feeding of Britain'.[3] This was a comforting falsehood, which could be excused by Churchill's belief that Japan would never invade Australia. Menzies was less confident, fearing that a sequence of British reverses would encourage Japan to do just that.[4] Australia's best hope, therefore, was to secure American protection. In 1937 an official approach had been made to Roosevelt, who responded with the assurance that, 'If serious trouble arose in the Pacific, the United States would be prepared to make common cause with members of the Commonwealth.'[5] In April 1941 an American flotilla sailed across the southern Pacific on a goodwill cruise that, according to *The Times*, attested to the 'close friendship' between the United States and the Empire.[6]

*

Japan was not unnerved by these developments. The clique of expansionists who dominated the imperial cabinet wanted war, but realised that precise timing would be the key to success. The ministerial consensus that emerged during 1941 was that the odds would only favour Japan after Germany had defeated Russia, since it could never hope to fight Britain, the United States *and* Russia with any hope of victory. This was why German efforts to persuade Japan to attack Russia in Siberia were rebuffed. As British signals intelligence revealed, Japan was prepared to go to great lengths to keep on good terms with the Soviet Union, even after the German invasion.[7]

Everything hung on the outcome of battles fought in western Russia during the summer of 1941. In May, the Japanese Foreign Minister Yosuke Matsuoka had visited Berlin, where Ribbentrop told him that the Soviet Union would be overwhelmed within two months. Japan was now free to attack Malaya, which, of course was to Germany's advantage because Britain would be forced to divert forces from the Middle East to save its colony. Once the war in Russia was under way, Matsuoka concluded that early German successes indicated that a total victory would be achieved by the end of the year.[8]

The assertions of Anglo-American resolve on which Churchill had set great store did not intimidate Japan's leaders. They correctly forecast that Britain and America would fight to defend their interests in the Far East and the Pacific, but that their combined fleet could be beaten and that the capture of Singapore 'should not be difficult'.[9] By the autumn, when German forces had reached Moscow, the Japanese cabinet agreed that the circumstances were right for war and the opportunity could not be missed. Further delay would be fatal; a month before Pearl Harbor, General Hideki Tojo the ultra-hawkish Minister of War declared: 'I fear that we would be become a third-class power if we sat tight.'[10]

Japan was planning for a war that would end with Japan firmly established in Europe's former colonies and the Philippines, and impregnable in the Pacific and Indian oceans.[11] Britain and the United States would be fought to a standstill and forced to make peace on Japan's terms, which were the recognition of its new, enlarged empire that encompassed much of China, Indo-China, Thailand, Burma, Malaya, Borneo, Sarawak, the Dutch East Indies and all British, French and American islands in the southern and central Pacific. Some naval planners pressed for securing air bases in Australia to protect the Japanese empire's southern flank. The Japanese army, however, was uneasy about an enterprise that would be a drain on manpower and serve no useful purpose since Australia would already have been effectively isolated by Japan's conquests to the north and east.[12]

Japan's former political goals were sidelined; the war would not fulfil the pledge of 'Asia for the Asiatics'. The Japanese offensives in December 1941 were not intended as a campaign of colonial emancipation and the cabinet ordered commanders to avoid 'premature attempts to encourage independence movements'. Burma was an exception for purely strategic reasons, since by allowing it independence, Japan would provide a stimulus for nationalist unrest in India that was bound to reduce its value to Britain as a base for counter-offensives in South-East Asia.[13]

London and Washington understood the scope of Japan's imperial ambitions and knew that its government was closely following the course of the war in Russia in order to chose the right time to open hostilities. During the third quarter of 1941 intelligence reports from Tokyo indicated that Japan's moment of truth was approaching, but Churchill still clung to the assumption that war would be prevented by taking a tough line. At the end of August, Menzies suggested that battleships might do the trick and Churchill concurred, although the Admiralty insisted that there were not enough available to overawe the Japanese. Nevertheless, Churchill thought that an exercise in gunboat diplomacy would have a salutary effect, for, true to what he imagined to be the Oriental character, the Japanese would back down when threatened. Eden's permanent secretary Oliver Harvey summed up the mood in Whitehall when he noted in his diary for 16 October that one battleship alone might suffice because the 'Japs were so hysterical a people'.[14] Then and during the next few months, British and American policy makers applied similar crass and contemptuous racial generalisations to the Japanese. Arrogance skewed judgement and contributed to Allied blunders.[15]

On 20 October the modern battleship *Prince of Wales* was ordered to Singapore to join the older *Repulse* as the core of a squadron that would eventually be expanded and which, Churchill imagined, would 'serve as a deterrent on Japan'. This was a desperate and foolhardy gesture; he had grossly underestimated the moral stamina of the Japanese and overestimated the psychological impact of a single capital ship. The Imperial Japanese Navy had studied the action at Taranto and were confident that their torpedo bombers would sink battleships.

A more reliable guarantee of the future security of Britain's Far Eastern territories was received by Churchill on 4 December, when Roosevelt pledged that America would treat any Japanese attack on British or Dutch possessions as an act of war against itself.[16] Such protection was now redundant, for a week before a Japanese armada had begun its voyage towards Hawaii. On 7 December Pearl Harbor was attacked and the greater part of the battleships of the United States Pacific Fleet were sunk or crippled.

On the same day, Europe's Far Eastern colonies suffered the first of a series of sudden hammer blows. Japan had aerial and naval superiority on every front, which allowed armies to land wherever they chose. On 7 December Japanese troops invaded Malaya and Thailand, which threw in the sponge without even a flicker of resistance. Japanese aircraft based in Indo-China sank the *Repulse* and *Prince of Wales* on the 10th and four days later the port of Penang was abandoned to an enemy which had seized and would keep the initiative in Malaya. On 16 December Burma was invaded, Japanese landings occurred in Borneo and Sarawak, and Hong Kong came under siege on the 18th. It surrendered after a gallant defence on Christmas Day. By now, Japanese forces were overrunning the Dutch East Indies and had gained a strong foothold in the Philippines.

Churchill was dazed by these events. The Empire was slipping away and all he could do was to order its outnumbered and under-equipped defenders to 'resist stubbornly'.[17] His message to the garrison of Hong Kong was: 'We expect you to resist to the end. The honour of the Empire is in your hands.'[18] In a message to the high command in Singapore, Churchill warned that officers were expected to die at their posts rather than surrender.

Hentyesque rhetoric could not push back the limits of human

endurance and they were quickly reached in Malaya, where imperial forces were herded down the peninsula towards Singapore, a fortress constructed only to resist an attack from the sea. A retreat became a rout distinguished by extraordinary courage and appalling stupidity and cravenness. The latter were very much in evidence on Penang, where loyal Malay typists stayed at their posts while troops and then women and children withdrew in the face of what the governor Sir Shenton Thomas called 'a particularly cruel Asiatic foe'.[19]

Thomas was the wrong man in the wrong place at the wrong time; his judgement was flawed and he was neither a natural leader nor an organiser. He misread the temper of the Chinese community, who were fiercely loyal, accusing them of being a potential Fifth Column and he hid the deteriorating situation in Malaya from Australia, whose troops were assisting in its defence.[20] According to Duff Cooper, whom Churchill had sent to report on how Malaya was coping with the invasion, Thomas's subordinates were ham-fisted duffers who hindered operations. The secretary for Chinese affairs was 'tactless and rude' and, therefore, unloved by a community prepared to support the government. Stanley Jones, the colony's chief secretary, was a 'sinister figure' who was 'universally detested' and responsible for the utterly inadequate Air Raid Precaution measures in Singapore.[21] Shortly before his departure on 4 January 1942, the local naval commander-in-chief urged Cooper to persuade Churchill to sack Thomas and replace him with a resolute military man.[22] By then it was too late.

What was happening in Malaya was a prolonged and gruelling test of the imperial system, its rationale, its methods and personnel. The Malayan administration was wanting on all counts. Moreover, and this would later provoke the sharpest criticism, its officials had manifestly failed to ignite a patriotic unity and a sense of common purpose among Europeans, Malays and Chinese. Instead there was fragmentation and racial tension. Given that modern war was an assay of the spirit of a nation and the stamina and ingenuity of its people, colonial Malaya was woefully deficient.

Churchill sensed this and after poring over Cooper's messages, he minuted on 13 January that this was 'a shocking tale'.[23] Worse was to follow; the collapse of public morale was accompanied by an erosion of military discipline. Imperial forces retreating southwards became disheartened, which was understandable since they lacked air cover and were being outwitted by an audacious enemy who advanced swiftly through the jungle led on by able commanders. Many of their own officers were losing their nerve and Sir Roland Braddell, a Singapore lawyer, was shocked to find one hotel 'full of escaped officers'. Other eyewitnesses noticed how the fatalistic mood of whites transmitted itself to the Malays: volunteer units melted into the jungle and soon after the invasion had started labourers fled from the Singapore dockyards.[24]

Australian troops quickly discovered that the odds against them were mounting; on 9 January Thomas was astonished by the number of Australian officers applying for leave.[25] At the end of the month, an eyewitness encountered Australian units in Port Swettenham who were 'completely undisciplined'.[26] The rot spread as imperial forces converged on Singapore at the beginning of February and, once the city came under siege, the Australians became a rabble. 'The greater part of the Australian infantry were undisciplined,' observed Braddell, who saw swarms of deserters, many drunk, struggling to get on to the ships that would take them away.[27] Other eyewitnesses reported Australians bullying their way on to boats, looting and raping Malay and Chinese women.[28] These reports were read by Churchill and then withheld from public scrutiny for fifty years, no doubt to satisfy Australian sensibilities.

Australian fractiousness was contagious and infected Indian troops who traditionally looked to white soldiers as models of discipline. One exchange summed up their dismay and, incidentally, a stereotype of Australians as a species that was shared by many British officers. After seeing Australian airmen fleeing from the base at Kuantan, a Sikh asked his officer: 'How is this possible? They are all sahibs.' 'They are not sahibs,' the officer answered. 'They are Australians.'[29] General Gordon Bennett the Australian commander ignored his own men's misdeeds and shifted the blame for the rout in Malaya on the Indians. He was a conceited booby whose version of the campaign opened with the claim that 'Eastern races [were] less able to withstand the strain of war' – to which one staff officer had added in the margin 'Japs?'[30] The stress of battle proved too much for Bennett, who snatched the first chance to get a boat out of Singapore; Australian troops called their running plimsolls 'Gordon Bennetts' in memory of his flight.

There were still many brave men left in Singapore; Braddell was impressed by the staunchness of the Gurkhas and the Argyll and Sutherland Highlanders. Courage alone could not offset bad generalship or slipshod planning, and so British forces were corralled into a fortress with no landward defences. On 14 February Churchill gave permission to Wavell, now commander-in-chief in the Far East, to authorise the surrender of Singapore and its garrison of 85,000 British, Australian and Indian troops.

Churchill later described the fall of Singapore as the 'greatest disaster to British arms in history'; it was also the greatest single catastrophe ever suffered by the British Empire. Churchill could salvage no glory from a humiliating defeat, which was captured by Japanese cameramen who filmed Singapore's commander General Arthur Percival, a spindle-shanked figure in voluminous khaki shorts with a Union Jack on his shoulder and a tin hat on his head, walking to meet his victorious counterpart. It remains the most vivid image of what turned out to be the first act in the dissolution of the British Empire.

Churchill accepted responsibility for the debacle in so far as he had concentrated imperial resources in the Middle East and withheld them from the Far East. His calls for heroic, last-ditch resistance had gone unheeded, and he later confided to Lady Bonham Carter that he had a 'dreadful fear' that 'our soldiers are not as good fighters as their fathers were'.[31] He did not, however, agree to the restoration of the death penalty for cowardice and desertion, a proposal made by General Sir Claude Auchinleck, who had replaced Wavell in the Middle East.[32] Churchill's misgivings about the fighting spirit of British soldiers was shared by Sir Alan Brooke, who noted in his diary three days after the surrender: 'Cannot work out why troops are not fighting better. If the army cannot fight better than it is doing at present we shall deserve to lose our Empire!'[33]

The military, political and psychological reverberations of the capture of Singapore shook the Empire. A case can be made that it never wholly recovered from a blow that had brutally exposed its internal weaknesses as well as its inability to defend its subjects. The

New Zealand *Evening Post* regretted the 'immense loss of prestige' throughout Asia, while the Newfoundland *Daily News* referred to the defeat as 'a bad business', but reiterated its faith in Churchill's leadership.[34] The *East African Standard* spoke of 'a great imperial defeat', which one Indian reader later blamed on the way in which his people had been treated as 'intruders and gatecrashers' by the whites in Malaya whose aloofness had also alienated other races. Another correspondent replied: 'if we must be slaves, we cannot make a better choice of slave-owners in the world than the British.'[35] Those whom Gold Coast officials classified as 'educated blacks' were reported to have been 'somewhat shaken' by the fall of Singapore, although their minds were focused on the possibility of the war spreading southwards from North Africa.[36]

At home there was an eruption of political recrimination and finger pointing combined with a heart-searching appraisal of the imperial idea. Enough was known of what had just occurred in Malaya for *The Times* to castigate its civil service as a collection of torpid timeservers who were out of touch with the people they ruled.[37] The Left wheeled out its old Aunt Sally, Colonel Blimp, that porcine, walrus-moustached symbol of the reactionary old guard created by the New Zealand cartoonist David Low. Inflexible and bone-headed Blimps were running the Empire and making a mess of it.

Blimp was invoked in the vinegary Commons post mortem of the events in Malaya. The Liberal Frederick Pethick Lawrence saw 'blimpery' as losing the Empire, while a Labour MP denounced the 'rascals' employed by the rubber, tin and oil companies who were concerned only with squeezing profit from Malaya. When the Japanese occupied their country, Malayans had 'merely exchanged one set of vultures for another'. Lionel Gammans, a former colonial official, believed that the fault lay with hidebound bureaucrats who believed that conformity was a greater virtue than competence. A telling comparison was made between the apathy of the Malays and the resistance put up by the Filipinos whom the Americans had promised independence.[38]

The imperial malaise had other symptoms. Lady Brooke-Popham, the wife of the air officer commanding in Malaya, blamed the loss of Malaya on the complacency of its European community whose lives revolved around bridge, dinner parties and dances which deadened their senses to the impending crisis.[39] This was also the picture painted by Cecil Brown, a CBS journalist expelled by the Singapore authorities for his candour. He likened the sybaritic, sleep-walking European community in Singapore to Parisians before the fall of France.[40] American commentator Walter Lippmann went further and treated Singapore as the epitome of the entire British Empire. The 'white man's imperialism' was 'obsolete and obviously vulnerable' and a denial of the values recently proclaimed by the Atlantic Charter.[41]

Lippmann's opinion was seemingly confirmed by the fall of Burma during March, when the pattern of events in Malaya was repeated. Colonel Clark, a deputy commissioner in Mandalay, reported having seen British officers deserting and commandeering cars to escape the Japanese. The country dissolved into anarchy with the 'haves' protecting their property and the 'have nots' looting it. Fleeing troops were ambushed by Burmese nationalist partisans and civilian and military morale wilted.[42] An American reporter also witnessed this chaos, which, he argued, was the product of the 'tropical British colonial psychology linked to bogged-down, red-taped civil service tradition' and a 'snobbish' sense of racial superiority. The writer was also incensed by the discovery of 'millions of dollars worth of Lend-Lease material' on the dockside at Rangoon being bombed by the Japanese. The officer responsible had refused to remove it to safety since it would have interrupted his weekend recreation.[43]

Some Whitehall officials urged Churchill to reply to these criticisms by reminding Roosevelt of the errors made by his subordinates before Pearl Harbor and during operations in the Philippines. He refused to be drawn into an exchange of insulting recriminations. Yet, he was conscious of the faults that had been revealed in the imperial system and he asked for 'every assurance' to be given to the Malays that their former wrongs will be 'righted in final victory'.[44] There was some consolation elsewhere; in the Solomon Islands the natives showed 'amazing loyalty' when the Japanese invaded, refusing their new masters' demands for forced labour and giving every assistance when the Americans began their counter-attack. Moreover, they treated the Japanese as 'an inferior being for whom they could never have the slightest respect'.[45]

In the Solomons and elsewhere it was self-evident that loyalty did exist in the British Empire. After watching enthusiastic islanders cheering a departing Fijian battalion in 1943, an American officer remarked: 'I never dreamed there was so much patriotism in this place ... there is more to this Empire business than meets the eye.'[46] There was, but Americans tended to believe what they read in their newspapers and reports of events in Singapore and Burma validated their prejudices about empires in general and the British in particular.

Churchill had been jubilant at the news of Pearl Harbor and his elation swelled after the fortuitous declarations of war on the United States by Germany and Italy. He was in 'such a state of excitement that the wildest schemes seem reasonable'.[47] Bad news from Singapore did not dent his optimism; 'We must KBO,' he told one of his private secretaries, the letters standing for 'Keep Buggering On'.[48]

'Buggering on' involved an immediate trip to Washington (against the advice of Roosevelt and Eden) and a series of conferences that would set the targets and priorities of Allied strategy. Churchill made the crossing in HMS *Duke of York* the sister ship of the *Prince of Wales* and disembarked on 21 December. He remained in America for three weeks during which he, the President and their senior military advisers began to formulate a global strategy which, as Churchill had intended, placed the defeat of Germany as the Allies' primary objective. This was still a long way off; for most of 1942 Churchill was preoccupied with convincing Roosevelt that it was in America's interests to commit a large slice of its resources to the defence of a battered and embattled empire.

The Dark Valley:

Perils and Panic, 1942

The capitulation of Singapore was the first of a rapid succession of seismic shocks that left the Empire tottering. Within six months Japanese forces overran Borneo, Sarawak, the Solomon and Gilbert and Ellice islands and invaded Papua and New Guinea. The Royal Navy yielded its two-hundred-year-old supremacy in the Indian Ocean, the RAF lacked the aircraft to protect the eastern coast of India from Japanese bombers, and Australians were clamouring for American assistance to repel what they mistakenly thought was an impending Japanese invasion. Indians were both frightened that the Japanese would attack their country and, at the same time, some wondered whether their arrival might be the right moment to rise up and get rid of the British. In South Africa diehard Boer nationalists were shaken; one, his mind concentrated by a Japanese armada sailing at will in the Indian Ocean, declared that his people must now rally to save their 'Fatherland' but not, he added, the Empire.[1]

The future of the Empire looked precarious and obituaries were already being published. A Tokyo newspaper declared: 'These serious setbacks suffered by the British Navy and Air Force in the Indian Ocean are nothing but an elegy for the downfall of a once mighty Empire.'[2] *Time* magazine reached the same conclusion and cited defeats in Malaya and Borneo as evidence that the British Empire 'was going to pieces'.[3]

The Axis had reached the zenith of its power and was preparing to deliver further blows against an enemy that had lost the strategic initiative. During the spring German and Japanese staff officers were contriving synchronised offensives on all fronts in the Middle East, Asia and the Pacific that would destroy what was left of British power in these areas.

Hammer blows were planned to expel the Allies from Asia and the Middle East. The Japanese would drive all before them in southern

Asia and the Pacific and Indian Oceans, while German forces in southern Russia and North Africa intended to coordinate a massive pincer movement that would encircle Egypt, the Levant, Iraq and Persia. Rommel's Afrika Korps would advance into Egypt and beyond, and German armoured and motorised units in the Caucasus would simultaneously move southwards towards the Persian Gulf.

Recent German and Japanese victories strongly suggested that their forces had the energy, stamina and mobility to accomplish such an ambitious enterprise and eventually achieve a rendezvous somewhere on the shores of the Indian Ocean. Such an assignation was on Ribbentrop's mind when, in June, he told the Japanese ambassador: 'It would be of especial importance if we could shake hands somewhere in the Indian Ocean in the near future.'[4]

Churchill recognised the implications of the new Axis grand strategy and he was fearful that it might be implemented before the human and industrial resources of America could be brought to bear. He had persuaded Roosevelt that they were most desperately needed in the Middle East and North Africa and, despite the reservations of some of his military advisers, he had agreed to give the Middle Eastern front priority over the liberation of Europe. The presidential decision was crucial for the survival of the Empire, for while Churchill was in Washington in June, the news arrived that Rommel had captured Tobruk and was advancing on Cairo.

This debacle was further proof that the Axis was in the ascendant, choosing where and when it would fight. Churchill had to bide his time and wait on events against a background of press and Parliamentary censure. At times he gave way to spasms of pessimism and impatience. Auchinleck in Egypt was reminded that: 'Retreat would be fatal. This is a business not only of armour, but will power.' After the fall of Tobruk and in a boiling rage, he revived his old threat to have generals who ordered their men to surrender to be tried on capital charges.[5]

Even if abler generals had been in charge, the safety of the Middle East and its oilfields ultimately depended upon the outcome of Germany's summer offensive in southern Russia. If it succeeded, then British forces in North Africa would be outflanked even if they held on to Egypt. Churchill appreciated this, although to his regret, there was little that he could do to assist Stalin beyond stepping up bombing raids on Germany and keeping open supply routes through the Indian Ocean and Persian Gulf. If things went very badly, he was willing to transfer fifteen RAF fighter squadrons from the Middle East to southern Russia.[6]

The first blow of the Axis grand strategy was struck by the Imperial Japanese Navy against Allied lines of communication in the Indian Ocean. Few warships have created so much terror as those of Admiral Osami Nagano's armada which entered the Indian Ocean on 4 April. It took the Andaman Islands, sank a British carrier and two cruisers, and its aircraft flew sorties against Colombo and Trincomalee and towns on the Indian coast, causing a disproportionate panic. Nagano's objective was to transform the Indian Ocean into a Japanese lake and he was successful in so far as the Royal Navy's big ships pulled back to Kilindini near Mombasa.

While Nagano was creating havoc and blowing British prestige to pieces, Japan launched a submarine offensive aimed at the convoys on the last lap of their passage from the Cape to Egypt and the Persian Gulf. A hitherto secure lifeline would be disrupted and the Allies would be forced to fight the equivalent of the Battle of the Atlantic in the Indian Ocean. This was exactly what the Axis wanted and early in March there were intelligence reports that German and Japanese agents were making approaches to the sympathetic Vichy authorities in Madagascar to acquire Diego Suarez [Antsiranana] for a future submarine base.[7]

Churchill responded by approving an amphibious assault on the port, although the experience of Dakar made him nervous about its chances. In the event, the landing succeeded and Diego Suarez was taken on 24 April and the rest of the Vichy forces on Madagascar were mopped up within five months. The Japanese submarine attacks continued and during June and July 94,000 tons of shipping was lost, including four vessels torpedoed off Aden. This total would have been far higher if the Japanese had not been denied a base at Diego Suarez and, by the end of the year, the total of sinkings had begun to drop. What mattered was that aircraft and tanks (including the new and superior

American Grant) continued to flow, as did munitions for Russia.

All were now urgently needed. Hitler's offensives in southern Russia began in June, the same month as Rommel captured Tobruk, together with 33,000 of its defenders. The Afrika Korps was fighting a campaign of imperial conquest, for Hitler had ordered Rommel to establish a German administration in Cairo in which, contrary to former promises, the Italians would have no part. The Egyptians were to be gulled into thinking that the Germans had come to free them from British rule.[8] Some might have believed this, for in February, student rioters in Cairo had chanted 'Long Live Rommel!'[9]

Nazi imperialism was taking a new tack. Certain that the Soviet Union was within his grasp and beyond recovery, Hitler was entertaining grandiose notions of further enlarging the Nazi imperium. The forthcoming campaigns would deliver swathes of the Middle East and Asia into German hands and the Führer was contemplating the occupation of Egypt, Palestine and Syria and, using the Caucasus as a springboard, advances towards Afghanistan and even India.[10] Ribbentrop assured Chandra Subhas Bose, now a fugitive in Berlin, that once German troops captured Tbilisi, just over two hundred miles from the Persian frontier, the way to India would be open.[11] Ultra decrypts revealed that the German and Japanese air forces were planning to inaugurate a flight path between the two countries that would use Kabul as a staging post between Rhodes and Rangoon.[12]

Hitler's new imperial strategy would terminate Britain's hegemony in the Middle East and, of course, deprive it of the oil it needed to stay in the war. In another flight of fancy, he considered overturning what was left of British power in the Mediterranean by taking Malta and Gibraltar and by occupying West Africa, the Canaries and the Azores as bases for a long-range aerial war against the United States.[13] Hitler also believed that Britain might even make peace and join Germany in a war against the United States. This was madness, but the Führer's daydreams about expansion in Asia were not. He had been intoxicated by his victories in Russia, which had both embellished his self-image as a master strategist and vindicated his vision of the Nazi imperial order in Russia. He had been proved right before and he would be proved right again. A member of the German military mission in

Tokyo assured the Japanese that Hitler was a second Alexander the Great and, like him, he would extend his empire to India.[14]

Another factor that encouraged Hitler (and the Japanese) had been the recent events in Malaya and Burma, which seemed to prove that the Empire's subjects no longer feared or respected Britain. This was the message of various Indian and Arab nationalist exiles, including Bose and the Grand Mufti, who had flocked to Berlin to procure Nazi help. Hitler found them a lacklustre crew without drive or leadership qualities, although in February 1945 he regretted that he had not used them more effectively. A massive anti-British revolt in the Middle East was a missed opportunity, for which he blamed his own diplomats and the Italians.[15]

Hitler's attitude towards the British Empire had never been consistent: before the war he appeared to admire it, in 1940 he was willing to impose terms on Britain that would have seriously weakened it, and, in 1942, he was considering a strategy that would deprive it of its Middle Eastern and Asian heartlands. The Empire was losing the conventional war and contained potential accomplices, ready to help Hitler and the Japanese. British intelligence was aware that the pattern of disaffection that had been revealed in the Far East might be reproduced in Middle East. There were fears that the fall of Egypt would trigger a revival of Arab attacks on Jews and defections were expected from the Transjordan Frontier Force. There was even some evidence that there were covert Nazi sympathisers among the Palestine Police, some of whom were former Black and Tans.[16]

Britain's Pacific Empire lacked the means to defend itself. Singapore had been designated as its first line of defence, although sceptical and twitchy Australian politicians placed more faith in the American Pacific Fleet as their future protector. Churchill had no objection: he had consistently judged the Japanese threat to the Australian mainland to be hypothetical and, therefore, treated the reinforcement of Singapore as a waste of resources and manpower that were better employed fighting the Germans and Italians in North Africa. The Australian government had agreed in principle and so, in January 1942, 100,000 Australian servicemen were stationed overseas, most in the Middle East.[17]

Allegations about their performance in Greece and Crete in April 1941 provoked a bad-tempered row between Churchill and the Australian government, which stirred up bitter memories of Gallipoli. He accused the Australians of a lack of grit and was irritated by Menzies's interference in the arrangements for the evacuation of Crete. Australian politicians defended their soldiers' honour and challenged the strategic wisdom of sending their young men to Greece; one Labour MP accused Churchill of 'cold-blooded murder'.[18]

This ruckus was the prelude to a longer, more serious and infinitely more acrimonious quarrel between Churchill and the Australian government in the months after the fall of Singapore. At its heart was the Australian cabinet's belief that the conquest of Malaya was the first phase of the long-feared *NanShinRon* and that it would end with large-scale, amphibious landings on the Australian coast.

Events during the first three months of 1942 suggested that this might be the case: Japanese forces swept through the Dutch East Indies, Papua and New Guinea and the archipelagos of the western Pacific. On 19 February the harbour at Rabaul in New Britain was occupied and immediately Japanese engineers began to transform it into a fortified base that would dominate the home waters of Australia. The war was getting closer to Australia and on the same day that Rabaul fell Japanese bombers raided Darwin. A million gasmasks were hastily ordered from Britain, air-raid drills were held, the entire adult male population was mobilised and alarmist rumours circulated. One, which got into print, alleged that aircraft bearing German insignia had bombed an island near Darwin.[19]

In a message delivered on 19 January, Churchill had urged Australians to take a positive and stoical view of their predicament:

You must not be dismayed or get into recrimination, but remain united in true comradeship. Do not doubt my loyalty to Australia and New Zealand. I cannot offer any guarantees for the future and I am sure that great ordeals lie before us, but I feel hopeful as never before that we shall emerge safely and gloriously from the dark valley.[20]

Adopting a distinctly Churchillian tone, John Curtin the Australian Labour Prime Minister broadcast an appeal to the nation immediately after the Darwin air raid, during which 'the armed forces and civilians conducted themselves with the gallantry that was traditional in people of British stock'. Inspired by their example, it was time for all Australians to 'gird up our loins and steel our nerve'.[21]

In private, Curtin was distraught and casting about for a scapegoat. During January he despatched a series of telegrams to London in which he castigated Churchill for his neglect of the defences of Singapore and pleaded for warships and soldiers to defend Australia. Churchill found his messages tiresome, suspected that they did not reflect the temper of the Australian people, and wondered whether the root of the trouble was 'bad [i.e. convict] stock' of the Australians.[22] Early in March and against the advice of Churchill and Roosevelt, Curtin insisted that Australian troops detached from the Middle East for the defence of Rangoon were shipped home to meet the expected Japanese invasion.

In his private correspondence with Sir Stafford Cripps the Lord Privy Seal, Dr H. V. Evatt the Australian Minister for External Affairs poured out a stream of spiteful invective against Churchill. He had broken faith with Australia and left it to its fate by refusing to give it the means to defend itself. A new airing was given to Menzies's charge that Churchill was 'suffering from a dictatorship complex which approaches megalomania'. Furthermore, Churchill was guilty of playing partisan politics for he 'seems to have a deep hatred of Labour governments'.[23] When Evatt appeared in London in May to plead Australia's case, Sir Alan Brooke found him 'a thoroughly unpleasant type of individual' who viewed the war from a blinkered Antipodean perspective.[24]

This was excusable; what was not was the hectoring manner of both Curtin and Evatt. At every stage, Churchill had made it plain that he did not regard the situation in Australia as 'desperate' (this was Curtin's word) and that if a large-scale invasion occurred, then Britain would transfer forces from the Middle East to help repel it.[25] He had always been sceptical about the possibility of such an attack on Australia and intelligence reports of Japanese intentions supported his doubts. The Japanese naval attaché in Lisbon had told the Portuguese General Staff that landings were scheduled for 26–28 February. This was treated as disinformation by the War Office, which correctly predicted that the Japanese would move against Java, Sumatra and Burma.[26] Chinese sources suggested that an assault might occur in May and, on 30 June, Radio Tokyo announced that the invasion of Australia was imminent. The first was disinformation and the second was propaganda since Japan's recent defeat at Midway had severely curtailed its navy's capacity for amphibious operations.[27] What is now known about Japanese strategic planning supported Churchill's contention that Australia was safe.

In fact, the Japanese high command was split as to whether or not to invade Australia, and the issue was rigorously debated during February and early March. Naval staff favoured an attack to prevent Australia from becoming a base for an American counter-offensive against the Philippines, New Guinea and the islands of the western Pacific. The army disagreed, arguing that an invasion would stretch manpower and impose an enormous burden on Japan's already extended logistical systems. In the end, it was agreed to use the forces that were available for operations against New Caledonia, Fiji and Samoa. Once in Japanese hands, these islands would complete the strategic isolation of Australia.

All this was unknown to Curtin who, in May, was still warning his countrymen and women that an invasion remained a possibility.[28] During their earlier exchanges, Churchill had endeavoured to convince the Australian Prime Minister that the United States would take care of his country. This had been accepted by Curtin in December 1941, when he had announced on the radio that 'Australia looks to America free of any pangs as to our traditional links with the United Kingdom'.

This choice of words had angered Churchill, for they were a public admission that Britain could no longer defend its Empire, a truth that would soon be confirmed in Malaya, Burma and the Indian Ocean. Events forced him to acquiesce to reality and during the next three months he stressed Australian reliance on the United States. On 19 February there were 6,000 American servicemen stationed in Australia and a further 26,000 were expected within three weeks. By the end of April the total had risen to 60,000.[29]

What might be called 'the great Australian invasion scare' was an episode that rankled with Churchill. He published some of his acerbic exchanges with Curtin in *The Hinge of Fate,* in which he reiterated his arguments that the North African and Russian fronts deserved priority over and against what he believed was a phantom threat to Australia. Addressing the Commons in September 1942, Churchill praised the New Zealand government for not succumbing to invasion anxieties and keeping its forces in the Middle East, where they were needed. The same point was made in his memoirs when he contrasted Australian demands to bring home its forces from the Middle East with the level-headedness of the New Zealand government which fully understood the global strategic situation. Churchill would have liked to have been more forthright, but was persuaded to tone down or excise phrases that might have damaged present (1950) relations with Australia. Among those deleted was a reference to 'The usual stream of complaint and reproach from Mr Curtin'.[30]

A faltering and cornered Empire was saved by four battles. The first was fought between 3–8 May in the Coral Sea, south-west of the Solomon Islands. American and Australian warships defeated a Japanese force on its way to attack Port Moresby in Papua. On 4 June, a larger Japanese task force was decisively beaten by the United States Navy at the Battle of Midway. Losses, particularly of carriers, aircraft and air crew, compelled the Imperial Japanese Navy to rethink its Indian Ocean strategy. In July plans for an amphibious attack on Ceylon were suspended until such time as the Germans had achieved a breakthrough in the Caucasus. Although the Japanese submarine offensive in the Bay of Bengal and East African waters continued until October 1943, an American naval victory in the Pacific had restored British paramountcy in the Indian Ocean.

The possibility of a German advance from the Caucasus on which the Japanese were pinning their hopes had always been conditional on the capture of Stalingrad, which occupied a vital position on the eastern flank of the Wehrmacht's projected route to the south. On 7 July what developed into a see-saw contest for the city began; it ended with the surrender of 90,000 survivors of the German Fifth Army at the end of February 1943.

The disintegration of Hitler's German Empire was now a matter of time. British interests in Iraq and Persia were at last completely secure and Hitler would not repeat Alexander the Great's march to Afghanistan and India. It was one of many ironies of the Second World War that the Red Army had contributed to the resuscitation of British imperial influence in Asia. It was a fortuity that Churchill did not mention in his memoirs, although during the war he never missed a chance to praise the stamina and bravery of the Russians.

The fourth victory at El Alamein was won by British, dominion and Indian forces commanded by General (later Field Marshal) Sir Bernard Montgomery. The battle ended on 4 November and four days later, American forces came ashore at three points along the Algerian and Tunisian coasts (Operation Torch) to block passage of Axis forces fleeing westwards. Britain's predominance in the Middle East was now unassailable and its former influence in the Mediterranean was about to be re-established.

In just under six months, the Empire had undergone an astounding reversal of its fortunes and Churchill was soon taking steps to consolidate and strengthen its revived power, particularly in its former stamping ground, the Middle East.[31]

A State of Ordered Anarchy:

India, 1942–1943

For the first nine months of 1942 the affairs of India were dominated by a clash between two equally resolute men with closed
minds: Churchill and Gandhi. Both laid claim to a monopoly of
rectitude and each was convinced that he knew what was best
for India's future. Roosevelt endeavoured to mediate between the
antagonists, Churchill in particular, but neither was inclined to
compromise.

Churchill's intransigence rested on his immutable faith in the
benefits of imperial rule in India, his forebodings about the miseries
that would follow its departure, and the overriding imperative of
winning the war. He required all Indians to abstain from political
activity and shoulder their share of the imperial war effort without
complaint. Churchill also hoped that he could retard Indian
independence for as long as possible and he was prepared to bully
his colleagues to get his way. Ministerial arguments in favour of
negotiations with Congress infuriated the Prime Minister, who stuck
to his old assertion that it was not the true voice of India. As he told
the Commons in September:

The Indian National Congress does not represent all India. It does not
represent the majority of the people of India. It does not represent the
Hindu masses. It is a political organisation built around a party machine
and sustained by certain manufacturing and financial interests.

Churchill had long been spoiling for a fight with Congress
that would prove beyond question that British power in India was
supreme and impregnable. His chance came at the end of July, when
intelligence reports revealed that Congress was preparing for a trial
of strength. Barely suppressing his pleasure at this news, he predicted
that the outcome would 'soon demonstrate the very slender hold

which the Congress have both on the Indian masses and upon the dominant forces in Indian life and society'.[1] A wartime emergency provided the excuse to shed all political inhibitions and impose those condign measures, which, he had always believed, would snuff out sedition.

Gandhi too thought that the war would be advantageous to his cause, because Britain was distracted and its prestige was in tatters. He wanted the British out of India as quickly as possible and this objective overruled all other considerations, including the possibility that the Japanese would replace them. Their successes in Malaya and Burma during February and March had been an unexpected bonus for Congress: Britain could no longer fulfil its most basic function, the defence of its territories and their subjects. Now was the moment for a new mass campaign in favour of immediate independence.

There were huge risks involved for ordinary Indians who might end up as one of Japan's subject races. For Gandhi this was by far the lesser of two evils, although he was disturbed by what the Japanese might have in store for his country.[2] Nevertheless, the Mahatma fervently believed that India's new masters would somehow be overcome by the collective spiritual will of Indian men and women. Hitherto, his philosophy of passive resistance had worked against the British, but Gandhi was apprehensive about how the Japanese would react to mass civil disobedience. When a journalist asked him whether Indians could expect a 'tougher time' if non-violence was used against an Axis occupation, he answered: 'Quite possible ... This is the time to live by our faith.'[3]

The price in death and suffering could be enormous and Gandhi was prepared for others to pay it. 'The resisters', he wrote, 'may find that the Japanese are utterly heartless and that they do not care how many they kill. The non-violent resisters will have won the day as they will have preferred extermination to submission.'[4] Gandhi's personal search for truth had created an inflexible dogma, which, he believed, was the only salvation for India. Fighting the Japanese either alone or as part of the British Empire was out of the question. When another journalist enquired whether Gandhi would intervene to stop one man from strangling another, he replied that he could not. 'My self esteem will not allow me to help strangle the strangler.'[5] For a public figure who had gone to elaborate lengths to create an image of himself as a man of peace, Gandhi was cavalier with the lives of others.

Those whom Gandhi was about to set on the path towards martyrdom were losing faith in their rulers. Indian responses to British defeats during the first four months of 1942 were a mixture of bewilderment, trepidation and hope. 'With whom are we going to negotiate?' asked Nehru. 'With an Empire which is crumbling to dust?'[6] The front line was moving inexorably towards the border with Burma, a Japanese squadron controlled the Bay of Bengal and Japanese aircraft were bombing targets on India's eastern seaboard. It appeared that Indians had exaggerated the military strength of an empire which now seemed unable to protect the sub-continent.

Japanese and German radio propaganda added to Indian jitters with claims that Indian soldiers had mutinied, that Indian women were pleading with their husbands and sons not to enlist and that Britain and Australia were at loggerheads. The first allegation was certainly true, for thousands of disheartened and disorientated sepoys had defected to the Japanese before and after the surrender of Singapore and were now being organised into the Indian National Army [INA]. Its Japanese sponsors promised that it would become part of the army that would eventually liberate India. Worst of all were the rumours of two impending invasions: a German through the Afghan passes and a Japanese through Burma.[7]

Towards the end of April, the Congress Working Committee discussed these developments and concluded that Britain had forfeited any moral right to govern India. Events in Burma were cited as irrefutable evidence of this. Its administration had been paralysed, the army had melted away, local air-raid precautions were useless, and there had been a flight of panic stricken Europeans, together with displays of the same racial arrogance that had been seen in Malaya. Henceforward, Indians had no choice but to rely upon their own resources to save themselves and their country.[8] Delhi banned publication of this jeremiad because of its possible impact on American public opinion, which tended to believe the worst of the Raj.

India's security was now in part dependent on the United States and its troops and aircrew who began arriving early in 1942. By May

1944 120,000 were stationed there, a total which increased to half a million by the end of the war.[9] Their main duties were to help defend India, to bomb targets in Burma and to facilitate the massive air lift of war material to Chiang Kai-Shek's Nationalist Army in southern China. India had become a war zone to which United States forces were committed and, inevitably, their government found itself drawn into the domestic politics of the sub-continent.

Ideological reasons also contributed to this engagement. Looking ahead to a post-war world order, Roosevelt did not want his country to become identified with what he considered the expiring imperial ancien régimes in Asia. All had failed their subjects and, for that reason alone, did not deserve resuscitation. Moreover, if the Atlantic Charter was a blueprint for the future, and Roosevelt felt that it was, then India had to take its place among the free, self-governing nations of the world. He outlined his views in a draft telegram to Churchill written a week after the fall of Singapore. The former 'master and servant' relationship between Europeans and natives in Asia was now defunct and beyond revival among peoples who were aware that 'a world change' had 'taken deep root'. This was why, the President argued, Indians could not be expected to fight enthusiastically.[10] He had second thoughts about how his blunt words would be received and he deleted these remarks. Nevertheless, he remained convinced that it was his duty to coax Churchill into making generous concessions to Indian nationalists.

Roosevelt had been wise not to wire this message to London. According to Churchill's memoirs, Roosevelt had 'raised the Indian problem on the usual lines', when they had met in Washington in December 1941. 'I reacted so strongly and at such length that he never raised it again.'[11] This was untrue; there was never a taboo on discussions on India's political future and the subject continued to be raised by the President and his advisers. More Churchillian tantrums followed.

The American argument ran that once Britain had satisfied what for Washington were legitimate demands, then a free, contented and independent India would throw itself wholeheartedly into the war effort and become a secure base for operations in Asia. Often seething with rage, Churchill rejected this case, which he treated as a personal as well as a political challenge. One of his closest aides told Harry Hopkins that: 'India was the one subject on which the normal, broad-minded, good humoured, give-and-take attitude between the two statesmen was stopped cold.' Churchill 'would see the Empire in ruins and himself buried under them before he would concede the right of any American, however great and illustrious a friend, to make any suggestion as to what he should do about India'.[12] Hopkins soon experienced a typical eruption on this subject and he was astounded by 'the string of cuss words' that 'lasted for two hours in the middle of the night'.[13] Churchill excused his foul tongue to Amery, who endured it as Secretary of State for India, on the grounds of 'the relief that really bad language gives in anxious times'.[14]

Amery bore the brunt of Churchill's fury, for it was his task to convince him that conciliatory measures were politically and militarily necessary. The Prime Minister was 'dictatorial, eloquent and muddleheaded' and there were racial undertones in his outbursts. When the issue of the authority of Indian officers over white other ranks was raised, Churchill complained about the 'poor British soldier having to face the extra humiliation of being ordered about by a brown man'.[15] Even more intolerable was the prospect of Britain losing India altogether; during a cabinet debate on 8 October the Prime Minister 'opened with a terrific tirade, just shouting at us all about the monstrous business of our being kicked out of India'.[16]

One reason for the intensity of this passion was that at the beginning of February Churchill had been compelled to back-pedal on India. His reasons had been pragmatic, as Amery explained to King George VI over lunch on 4 March: 'Winston ... hated the idea of giving up all his most deeply ingrained prejudices merely to secure more American, Chinese and Left Wing support.' Amery likened him to 'a virtuous maiden selling herself for really handy ready money', which amused the King, who then told 'a story that would not be good for the Dictaphone or its user [his typist]'.[17]

The result of Churchill's reluctant change of heart was the Cripps mission, which arrived in India on 23 March with the cabinet's authority to negotiate a constitutional settlement with representatives of all Indian parties and races. Churchill briefly considered flying out to India, but Cripps was better qualified for a task that required reserves of tact and forbearance that the Prime Minister obviously lacked.[18] Cripps was high-minded, ascetic and a warm friend to Indian national aspirations. He was also *sympathique*: like Nehru he was a socialist and a chain-smoker and, like Gandhi, he was a vegetarian, a quirk that amused Churchill. Additional and for the Prime Minister undesirable mediation was offered by Roosevelt's representative Louis Johnson, a former corporate lawyer who was then in Delhi advising on the organisation of the Indian war economy.

Cripps's brief was to guarantee India post-war independence, dominion status and the right to leave the Commonwealth, pledges which Gandhi dismissed as 'a post-dated cheque on a bank which is obviously going bust'. In the short term, Indians were offered additional participation in the viceregal council, although strategy and its implementation remained under British direction. Muslims were assured that they would not be dragooned into the new state, for those provinces in which they were a majority would be free to detach themselves from India. Secession was also offered as an option for the princely states. Pakistan came a step closer and Gandhi was horrified by the prospect of a fragmented India. Deadlock followed and Cripps flew home on 11 April without an agreement.

Churchill was secretly pleased by this result. It proved to him, his critics and, he hoped, Roosevelt that Congress was a blinkered movement which placed selfish political advantage before winning the war. The Prime Minister also suspected that Gandhi was a potential Quisling ready to cut cards with the Japanese in the event of an invasion. He voiced his fears to Hopkins, claiming that a Congress government would allow the Japanese to advance across northern India in return for arms with which to impose the Hindu will on Muslims and Untouchables.[19] Churchill intended to repeat this insinuation in *The Hinge of Fate*, but was persuaded to remove it because of the outrage it would have provoked in India.[20] There was no evidence whatsoever to back this far-fetched allegation, although, interestingly, the Japanese had thought it worthwhile to infiltrate a spy into Gandhi's *ashram* in 1937. He was a Buddhist monk called Maruyama who was deported by the government in October 1940. Later, he deceitfully boasted to his masters that he had converted Gandhi and Nehru to the Japanese cause.[21]

Efforts to wring a compromise from this pair were made by Chiang Kai-Shek and a Kuomintang delegation that visited India during May at the suggestion of Roosevelt.[22] This suited current American policy, which was to act as Nationalist China's patron and obtain parity for her as an ally alongside Britain and the Soviet Union. The Sino-American *entente* was rooted in America's investment in China (including a recent $500 million loan to Chiang's regime) and widespread popular support for American Christian missions in the country.

Chiang's publicity machine in the United States won him support (including Henry Luce, the anti-imperialist owner of Time-Life publications). In the long term, the Generalissimo needed America as a partner in a struggle that would expel the Japanese from China and pave the way for its emergence as the predominant power in South-East Asia. Like Roosevelt, Chiang thought that European influence in Asia was in terminal decline.

Nationalist China posed as America's ideological ally. After a conference with Madame Chiang Kai-Shek in February 1943, Roosevelt praised China as 'one of the great democracies of the world'. She replied that for thousands of years China had always been 'a social democracy', an answer that would have astonished its former emperors and its recent warlords, of whom her husband was one.[23] Churchill had no faith in Nationalist China's war effort and Roosevelt's promotion of it as a potential world power, but was prepared to humour him on the matter.[24] In private he was contemptuous about China's forces, its ruler, his wife and her regal pretensions.[25] The suggestion that Chinese troops might participate in the reconquest of Burma was firmly rejected since it would inflate Chinese pretensions and injure British prestige.[26] In *The Hinge of Fate* he gave vent to his feelings when he wrote sneeringly of China as 'at that time regarded in the United States as the supreme champion of Asian freedom'.

Chiang's mission to India was fruitless, but this did not deter him from continuing to meddle in Indian affairs with Roosevelt's blessing. The Viceroy Lord Linlithgow discouraged the emergence of a clandestine *entente* between Chinese and Indian nationalists by blocking telegrams between Chiang and Gandhi and Nehru. For the moment, Americans were mesmerised by the potential of China as the coming power in a new world order. Some newspaper and wireless commentators predicted that the post-war world would be dominated by the United States, the Soviet Union and China. Britain was a spent force, its Empire was an anachronism and Germany and France would be relegated to walk-on parts on the world stage.[27]

Yet the British Empire was fighting back. On 24 August *Time* magazine placed a portrait of Nehru on its cover and inside condemned the 'mad and tough measures' being taken by Britain to crush a nationalist uprising in India. Seen from the perspective of the editor's desk, the British were desperately attempting to save an empire that had already 'gone to pieces' and, in the process, sweep back those forces of history which a large number of Americans thought were desirable and invincible.

In fact the 'Quit India' movement was foredoomed, although it caused a few nail-biting moments in Delhi and London. For the past few months and with Gandhi's encouragement Congress had been planning a nationwide campaign of civil disobedience, strikes and sabotage designed to paralyse the administration, communications and the war effort. Public statues of the British worthies who had created and served the Raj were singled out for destruction as 'symbols of slavery'.[28] Gandhi intended that India would be plunged into a 'state of ordered anarchy', although elements of order were impossible to detect in the general mayhem.

Private grievances mingled with public causes and crowds looted property and attacked money-lenders, revenue collectors and land-lords, which was exactly what had happened during the first stage of the 1857 Mutiny. Congress's political intentions and details of their programme of disruption had been uncovered by the intelligence agencies, which kept one jump ahead of the protestors throughout the disturbances. Forewarned, the government struck back vigorously. Gandhi, Nehru and the rest of the Congress leadership were arrested and interned and all available police and troops were mobilised.

There were just over a quarter of a million policemen in India and 35,000 British troops were allocated to support them. They were just enough to cope with the demonstrations, riots, the burning of public buildings and sabotage, which included cutting telephone and telegraph wires and derailing trains. Aircraft were use to strafe gangs of saboteurs in isolated areas, which upset some Labour MPs. There was cheering on the other side of the House when Amery gave details of the aerial attacks on insurgents.[29]

Interestingly in the light of Roosevelt's interventions in Indian affairs, there were rebels who believed that American troops were being deployed against them. There were also false reports of the mass shooting of mutinous Indian servicemen in North Africa, that Russia was on the verge of collapse and that the German army was approaching the Persian border.[30] Many who joined the protests believed that the Allies were about to lose the war and that the Raj would come crashing down. They were wrong; Britain possessed both the will and capacity to put down a series of large but localised disturbances, which Linlithgow claimed had been the most dangerous challenge to British power since the Mutiny.

The Quit India movement had been a messy, bloody affair that had fizzled out by the middle of September. Indian casualties were haphazardly recorded and estimates ranged from 4,000 to 10,000. Gandhi had miscalculated his followers' appetite for martyrdom and millions of Indians had stood aloof from the disturbances. Churchill was pleased that the 'martial races' had been loyal and Sikhs and Muslims had shunned the protests. In his memoirs Churchill noticed with satisfaction that Congress's agitation did not hamper recruitment, which rose to 900,000 during 1942.

Nevertheless, the Quit India upheavals had deepened Churchill's animus against Indians. 'I hate the Indians,' he told Amery in September. 'They are a beastly people with a beastly religion.'[31] In fact, matters could have been far worse. During the disturbances there had been rumours that units of the Indian National Army and former POWs were being sent by the Japanese to stiffen the insurgents.[32] This was what Japanese military intelligence officers had in mind, but events stole a march on them; the Quit India uprising occurred before the apparatus for subversion in India had been put in place. Potential fifth columnists recruited from the INA were placed in a training camp on Penang in September, where they learned the arts of political subversion, incitement to mutiny and sabotage. The task of Japan's equivalent to Britain's SOE (Special Operations Executive) was to prepare the ground for an invasion of India. The first parties were put ashore from Japanese submarines in December and more were landed throughout the following year. In April 1944 British intelligence estimated that over 2,500 were in India.[33]

At the same time a few hundred sepoys who had defected in North Africa were being trained as parachutists at a camp near Rome, presumably for eventual service in India.[34] At the end of May 1942 the former English Fascist William Joyce ('Lord Haw Haw') had broadcast from Berlin on Azad Hind (Free India) Radio that Indian paratroopers would soon be dropping from the skies to help liberate their country, which added to India's ever-growing stock of defeatist rumours.[35]

History is not just about what happened, but about what people imagined was happening and might happen. It is, therefore, important to remember that during 1942 a large number of Indians believed rumours which, in sum, convinced them that Britain was losing the war, that India was about to be invaded and that the Raj would collapse. Its mystique and Britain's reputation for invincibility had been dissolved by the surrenders at Singapore and Tobruk, defeat in Burma and the Japanese incursion into the Indian Ocean. Psychologically the moment appeared to be right for Congress to give that final shove which might bring down the whole edifice. Its leaders were wrong, there was plenty of fight left in the Raj.

Churchill felt vindicated by the suppression of the Quit India movement, which he hoped would clear the way for a formidable reassertion of imperial power. On hearing in February 1943, that several Indian members of the viceregal council were on the verge of stepping down, he was exultant. 'It did not matter if a few blackamoors resigned,' he told the cabinet, for at last, 'We could show the world that we were governing.'

The Wealth of India:

Subversion and Famine, 1943–1945

Churchill did not imagine that the defeat of Congress's Quit India campaign had been decisive; Congress had not been broken, agitation for independence continued and seemed unstoppable. He snatched at straws and partially convinced himself that British power could be resuscitated if the Raj reinvented itself, an idea that was consistent with his view of the Empire as an evolving organism.

Restoring the authority of the Raj was essential to the Churchillian vision of the post-war global order in which the Empire would remain intact and, as ever, substantiate Britain's claim to global power. This required a tractable and contented India under British control and supplying troops to uphold British power in the Middle East and Asia. He believed that he had a formula that would accomplish this and, simultaneously, pull the rug from under Congress. In August 1944, Churchill outlined his plans for a new and secure Raj to Amery. The remaking of British India would begin with a purge of officials who had lost the will to govern and had become 'more Indian than the Indians'. Their replacements would oversee the elimination of the economic power of the landlords and money-lenders. At the same time, the government would introduce a sweeping programme of land redistribution for the benefit of the peasants and the Untouchables. This would involve 'collectivisation' on 'Russian lines'. This sweeping social and economic revolution would enable Britain to forge an alliance with the impoverished masses.

A conventional Tory, Amery was shocked and he told Churchill that he 'didn't see much difference between his outlook and Hitler's', which displeased the Prime Minister.[1] There was of course nothing Nazi about these proposals; Amery must have had in mind Stalin and his enforced collectivisation in the late 1920s. Churchill repeated his radical proposals in March 1945, when he again advocated a revolution from above that would, he claimed, achieve 'what the Russians have done on an even larger scale at the expense of Indian landlords and money-lenders', who, he thought were the backbone of Congress.[2] Its support would, he predicted, wither as the grateful masses recognised Britain as their true and generous friend.

Churchill's astonishing blueprint for a populist Raj was probably unworkable and, whatever its merits, was a hostage to British politics. In 1943 the Labour Party had affirmed that it would immediately grant independence to India if it won the general election. Wartime by-election results indicated that the Tories were on the verge of a political eclipse, despite Churchill's personal popularity. Even if it had been re-elected, it is hard to imagine that the party of capitalism and property would ever have swallowed Churchill's scheme for wealth redistribution in India.

In the meantime, India had to be governed and, for Churchill, this meant keeping the lid down on Congress. The collapse of the Quit India agitation had shown that its bluff could be called and had justified Churchill's assertion that all that was needed to rule India was fortitude and firmness. He shared with Linlithgow the conviction that, apart from Congress activists, the mass of Indians were politically apathetic.

Gandhi remained, in Churchill's words, a 'nuisance' and a 'rascal' with an unlimited capacity to embarrass the British. It was dramatically displayed in February 1943 with his twenty-one-day fast, a form of moral blackmail intended to compel Britain to grant independence. It was a possibly fatal enterprise for a frail man in his seventies and the government was anxious to avoid the calumny that would follow the death in British custody of a globally revered holy man. Gandhi survived and Churchill, who had always considered his spiritual pretensions as humbug, was pleased that what he called an episode of 'bluff and sob-stuff' had ended without embarrassment.

Churchill was acquiring a fresh grudge against India because of the British debt to the country. In June 1945 it stood at £1.292 million, a sum that covered all the costs of India's defence at a time when a section of its population had shown disloyalty and endeavoured to disrupt the war effort. He regularly raised this subject in cabinet meetings, with asides on ingratitude, and returned to it in *The Hinge of Fate.* 'No great portion of the world's population was so effectively protected from the horrors and perils of the World War as were the peoples of Hindustan,' he wrote. 'They were carried through the struggle on the shoulders of our small Island.' He added there had been overcharging for goods and services and insinuated that the auditing of the accounts had been slapdash.[3]

An ungrateful nation was also an untrustworthy one. During 1943, Churchill suffered intermittent hallucinations about an imminent repetition of the 1857 Indian Mutiny. In May he remarked that Britain was 'creating a Frankenstein [i.e. Frankenstein's monster] by placing modern weapons in the hands of the sepoys', and a few weeks later he was claiming that Indian troops would 'shoot us in the back'. In October the cabinet endured 'an eloquent but irrelevant discourse on the worthlessness and probable disloyalty of India's large and well-equipped army'.[4]

There was no reason for these outbursts; intelligence reports suggested that the morale of India's fighting men was good, there were no hints of mass discontent nor any signs that the mass defection of Indian troops after the fall of Singapore would be repeated. Moreover, Churchill's neurosis about the allegiance of Indian forces was at odds with his repeated praise for their patriotism, reliability and bravery of Indian troops. Perhaps he had in the mind the INA, some units of which had been engaged in the Battle of Arakan on the Indo-Burmese frontier in April 1943. The likeliest explanation for Churchill's fears was that they were part of that nightmare which haunted him in the last two years of the war: the possibility that Britain would win the war, but lose India.

The INA was infinitely more useful as a propaganda asset than on the battlefield. Its value had been raised in May 1943, when Bose disembarked at Singapore after an epic voyage from Germany, first in a U-boat and then in a Japanese submarine. When he arrived in Singapore, his hosts provided him with a dapper uniform cut in what might be called the Mussolini style and installed him as the *Netaji* [leader] of an Indian government-in-waiting. One of its first acts was to issue postage stamps inscribed 'Azad Hind'.

From its inception, the Japanese Azad Hind project was riddled with contradictions which became more pronounced as the fortunes of war turned against Japan. The nationalist credentials of its protégé Bose were impressive and he was a charismatic orator. Before the war, this Cambridge-educated former Indian civil servant had been one of the young lions of Congress and he had joined in its denunciations of Japanese imperialism in China. Yet, in 1942, Bose had declared his support for Japan's pledge of 'Asia for the Asiatics' and promised Indians that a Japanese army would emancipate them. In fact, the Japanese high command had not yet decided whether to invade India, having acquired its primary economic goals, and, by early 1943 further expansion was impossible as overstretched and under-equipped Japanese forces struggled to retain their recent conquests.

The exact role of the INA was always ambiguous. Its recruits had been conditioned to think of themselves as liberators of their homeland, but their Japanese sponsors were engaged in a war of imperial conquest. If they had overrun even a part of India, it would have been out of character for Japan's rulers to deliver their gains to a free Indian government. Gandhi had once identified Bose as a potential Quisling and he was probably correct. The *Netaji* was a tragic figure whose sincere nationalism had been perverted by an ambition that finally drove him into the arms of two imperialist powers, Germany and Japan, whose rulers regarded Indians as an inferior species.

Nevertheless, the military authorities in India took Bose and the INA seriously. An intensive propaganda counter-offensive was launched to discredit Bose as a Japanese stooge; one image showed him holding a chained and demure female figure (Mother India) whom he was about to deliver to a blood-stained, bespectacled Japanese officer.[5] This lady was in fact safe for the foreseeable future; at the close of 1943 the Chiefs of Staff concluded that there would be no invasion of India.

In a broadcast made on 24 September 1943 Bose promised that he could arrange for the Japanese to ship 100,000 tons of grain to India to alleviate the famine that had overtaken much of Bengal.[6] It was a cynical but shrewd propaganda coup that simultaneously exposed the shortcomings of the British administration and the generosity of the Japanese towards their fellow Asians. Given the food shortages in Japanese occupied territories, it is unlikely that the supplies could have been found.[7]

Like Bose and the INA, the Bengal famine of 1943–4 is unmentioned in Churchill's war memoirs. It was a massive catastrophe; no one counted the dead and estimates vary from an official figure of 1.5 million to twice or even three times that number. The causes have been extensively analysed by historians and economists, but there is no agreement as to what was the decisive factor, or whether the deaths could have been prevented.[8]

First there was a natural disaster, the cyclone that flooded Bengal and Orissa in October 1942 and drowned the harvest. Human coefficients also contributed to the dearth. There was the negligence and torpor of officials in Bengal and its elected Muslim–Hindu coalition administration and the failure of market forces that were being deliberately skewed by wholesalers who hoarded stocks to jack up prices. Wavell, who replaced Linlithgow as Viceroy in October 1943, described this factor as 'graft and knavery'.[9]

An allegation has recently been made that Churchill hindered the government's efforts to implement a famine relief policy in Bengal out of spite.[10] This charge deserves serious examination, not least because it was so uncharacteristic of a humane statesman. Once the scale of the famine was understood, Churchill accepted in principle the need to do whatever was possible to feed the Bengalis. At no stage during the crisis did the British government decide to leave them to their fate, although in April 1944 Churchill's adviser on scientific and economic matters Lord Cherwell wondered that, if all else failed, it was vital for the army in India to have sufficient rations even if this created a 'civilian shortage'.[11]

The cabinet faced a moral dilemma. Famine relief had to be balanced against wider strategic considerations. Allied logistics were stretched to breaking point during 1943 and 1944. Cargo space had to be found to supply Anglo-American forces on new fronts in Italy and North-West Europe and maintain the flow of war matériel to Russia. Current strategic wisdom insisted that the Allies would only prevail if they maintained an overwhelming superiority of men and firepower. It was calculated that, for an offensive to have any chance of success, the attackers needed a two-to-one advantage in manpower, five-to-two in artillery, twenty-to-one in tanks and twenty-to-one in aircraft.[12] Achieving such a dominance on the battlefield demanded huge and intricate logistical systems.

It was against this background that ministers intermittently considered assignments of grain to Bengal and the wider crisis faced by India, whose economy was creaking under the pressure of wartime demands. The case for large-scale relief was presented in the cabinet by Amery with telegraphic support from Linlithgow, his successor Wavell and the commander-in-chief in India, General Auchinleck. In the first week of September 1943, he warned that the famine would have 'a serious if not disastrous effect on forthcoming operations'.[13] The cabinet was sceptical, in particular Lord Leathers the Minister for War Transport, who shared a general Whitehall view that the Indian government had exaggerated a crisis that owed much to its own mishandling of food distribution. Amery also suspected that Cherwell, who agreed with Churchill's extreme views on India, was playing down the need for relief. Yet, at the cabinet meeting on 4 August, the Prime Minister had been sympathetic and approved of the allocation of 100,000 tons of Iraqi barley and 50,000 tons of Australian wheat to Bengal.[14]

At the cabinet meeting held on 24 September, Churchill conceded that 'something should be done', but 'was very strong on the point that Indians are not the only people who are starving in this war'. He added, devilishly, that the 'starvation of anyhow underfed Bengalis is less serious than that of sturdy Greeks'. Nevertheless, Amery extracted a further 50,000 tons of grain to augment the 200,000 tons allocated for the next four months.[15]

A significant pattern had been set: Churchill agreed that famine relief was necessary and used discussions about how it should be implemented as a chance to denounce Indian iniquities. On 10 November he ranted about Indians 'breeding like rabbits' and getting paid a million pounds a day for 'doing nothing about the war'. This was untrue and Amery once told the Prime Minister that his views on India were 'Hitler-like'.[16] They were also irrelevant and irksome, although nowhere does Amery suggest that Churchill's generalised outbursts on India swayed his colleagues' judgements on how the famine might be tackled. They and the Prime Minister also had to take into account food shortages that threatened stability in newly liberated southern Italy and Greece.[17]

Supplies of grain were reaching India, although 40,000 tons were lost after an explosion and fire in the Bombay docks in February 1944, which set back the relief programme. The situation remained desperate throughout the spring and exasperated Wavell, who was thought to be on the verge of resignation in protest against the procrastination and indifference of Whitehall.

At the end of April, Churchill responded with an appeal to Roosevelt to make up the shortfall in shipping which was hindering relief measures. He was 'severely concerned' about the famine and reiterated Wavell's latest appeal for a million tons of grain to feed the army and the rural poor of Bengal. Half of this quota had been stockpiled in Australia, and South-East Asia Command [SEAC] was willing to cut 'military shipments' to provide cargo space.[18] With large-scale operations under way in the Pacific and D-Day less than two months away, the Americans had no ships available.

Supplies did arrive, thanks to the perseverance of Amery and Wavell, who, by the end of 1944, had secured over a million tons of grain. The Viceroy introduced rationing and placed distribution in the hands of the army with encouraging results. His measures were overdue and an important reminder that administrative sclerosis together with profiteering by wholesalers and inflation had made matters worse.

Throughout the crisis, Amery had found Churchill anxious to help, but his tangential fulminations against India gave the unfortunate impression of an inner and close-run contest between his prejudices and his humanity. In the end it was the harsh calculus of operational necessity that dictated the history of the relief of the Bengal famine. Cargo space was not infinite and the need for secure swift victories on every front meant that famine relief in Bengal was never given high priority. This reasoning may strike some people today as callous, but from the perspective of those making the big strategic decisions in 1943 and 1944, it was ethically defensible. Shortening the war would and did reduce suffering everywhere.

The Flag Is Not Let Down:
Churchill, Stalin and Roosevelt

The last two years of the war were a fraught time for Churchill. Total victory was in the bag, which was a personal triumph since it vindicated all that he had said and done since 1940. Yet he remained uneasy, since the decisive Allied victories in Europe, Africa and the Pacific had troublesome implications for Britain's future as an imperial and global power. The final act for empires seemed about to begin: the German, Italian and Japanese were cracking up and the prospects for the French looked shaky. The British Empire had survived and by August 1945 had retrieved all its lost colonies, but not its reputation. 'No one ever worshipped the setting sun,' a prescient Indian nationalist remarked. By contrast the Russian empire was triumphant on the battlefield and was pushing its boundaries into eastern and central Europe.

American servicemen were playing a crucial part in the recovery of British colonies, a distasteful fact for Churchill. During the Tehran Conference in November 1943, he vehemently demanded the exclusion of American and Chinese troops from operations to liberate Burma. Imperial forces alone would restore imperial prestige.[1] A significant segment of American opinion believed that the British Empire was not worth saving. In February 1945 the virulent anti-imperialist *Chicago Tribune* protested against American boys fighting to reimpose 'slavery' in former European colonies and, in April, it sourly noted the haste with which British administrators reasserted control over the Solomon Islands immediately after their reconquest by United States forces.[2] In fact the local American commander had been deeply impressed by the 'loyalty' of the Solomon Islanders to their former rulers.[3]

American opposition to the re-establishment of the pre-war status quo was a formidable impediment to the fulfilment of Churchill's dreams of a post-war Empire stronger and more united than ever.

Imperial solidarity and cohesion had never been so vital for Britain with its overstrained economy, massive wartime debt, and shrinking currency reserves. The Prime Minister, his cabinet and the Chiefs of Staff were convinced that wartime setbacks and humiliations could be forgotten and that the Empire could be reinvigorated. In February 1945 his mood was defiant and assertive: 'the flag is not let down while I am the wheel.' He intended to steer the imperial ship away from the shoals and towards deeper and perhaps uncharted waters. Yet the prospects for the voyage were darkened by Churchill's morbid anxieties about the impending loss of India. He mourned the collapse of 'confidence' in 'our mission', was afflicted by premonitions of 'ugly storms looming up there' and the misfortunes that would follow the end of British rule.[4]

The fulcrum of a revitalised Empire was the Middle East and Mediterranean. Almost immediately after the Germans and Italians had been expelled from North Africa, Churchill began to build on wartime victories in the region and create an impregnable block of British territory and influence in the area. He talked the Americans into becoming accessories to this enterprise on the grounds that it would substantially contribute to the defeat of Italy and Germany. Roosevelt, if not all his staff, was persuaded to fall in with plans for joint invasions, first of Sicily and then of Italy.

The accord reached between Churchill and Roosevelt at Casablanca in January 1943 committed British, American and imperial forces to what turned out to be the piecemeal conquest of Italy. It began in July 1943 and ended with the capture of Milan in April 1945. In the final stages of this campaign, the fighting was undertaken by predominantly imperial forces, since 40 per cent of American service personnel had been transferred to France and Germany. Their redeployment was a further reminder that Washington did not regard the Italian front as a war winner, unlike the advance on Berlin which of course also liberated France, Belgium and the Netherlands.

From the British standpoint, the Italian campaign offered tempting dividends. In the short term, Churchill hoped that the success in Italy would help nudge Turkey into the war. In the long term, a reconstructed, neutered Italy was essential for regional stability and could become a buttress for British power in the Mediterranean. Italian colonies were secretly earmarked for British bases; in December 1944 the Post Hostilities Planning Staff Committee proposed a permanent garrison in Cyrenaica [western Libya] and the retention of Massawa and Italian Somalia as part of a wider Middle Eastern defence network.[5] The Atlantic Charter did not inhibit British staff planners.

Post-war British ambitions also lay behind Churchill's proposals for the opening of a Balkan front in conjunction with Turkey, although it still remained doggedly neutral. Assisted by local partisans (the Yugoslavs were the most numerous and effective), Allied forces would advance across the mountains and valleys of the Balkans towards Vienna and then Berlin. Whether or not Churchill's Balkan offensive would bring Germany to its knees, and, on the whole the British and American Chiefs of Staff thought that it would not, the result was bound to enlarge British influence in south-eastern Europe. The Balkan strategy was rejected during the Anglo-American summit at Cairo in November 1943 after stiff objections from Eisenhower and General George C. Marshall, the United States Army Chief of Staff. Roosevelt agreed and Churchill had to overcome his fear that the Normandy landings would lead to another Gallipoli deadlock.

Far Eastern imperial priorities carried little weight in Washington. Neither did Churchill's emphatic and repeated demands for Allied resources to be allocated to the reconquest of Burma and Singapore by unaided imperial forces. 'We believe in striking Japan at home, not at Singapore,' insisted Roosevelt's peripatetic Asian envoy Patrick Hurley, and a majority of Americans agreed, including the men behind desks in the Pentagon.[6] Their opinions counted, for they controlled the allotment of the landing craft that were crucial for Churchill's Burmese and Malayan offensives. But the vessels were not forthcoming since the Americans needed them for the Pacific and European fronts. Churchill was indignant and in June 1944 he complained about: 'The American method of trying to force particular policies by the withholding or giving of ... airplanes or LSTs [Landing Ship Tanks] in theatres where the command belongs by right of overwhelming numbers to us, must be objected to ... and strongly protested against.'[7] The Pentagon did not see the hoisting of the Union Jack over Rangoon and Singapore as vital for the defeat of Germany and Japan and so the landing craft went to Normandy, the Philippines and the Ryukyu Islands. Washington's priorities also dictated the timetable for the recovery of Britain's South-East Asian colonies. The offensive in Burma did not begin until April 1945 and, after several delays, the Malayan campaign was scheduled for the following August.

Churchill did get his way over the participation of a Royal Navy armada in the Pacific where American forces were edging their way northwards towards Japan. This commitment had been strongly urged by New Zealand and Australia, whose forces were already engaged on this front.[8] The local American commanders, Admiral Chester W. Nimitz and General Douglas MacArthur suspected that Churchill's offer masked a piece of imperial legerdemain and, in June 1944, they warned Roosevelt that Britain had its greedy eyes on the Dutch East Indies and would divert warships earmarked for Singapore to an amphibious attack on Sumatra.[9] A large fleet was sent to the Pacific theatre early in 1945, where it fought alongside the Americans, taking part in operations against the outer ring of Japanese islands.

American diplomats and commanders believed that there was no limit to British chicanery when it came to decisions that touched, however remotely, on the recovery of British colonies. It is worth pausing to consider why this was so and what it reveals about the nature of Anglo-American cooperation. The extent to which each country did or did not accept constraints on its purely national interests has become a matter of contention for historians in both countries. Neither Britain nor the United States suspended the pursuit of national interests during the war and neither was blind to the future political and economic repercussions of wartime strategic decisions. Like all alliances, the Anglo-American was a pragmatic arrangement in which the achievement of a common, agreed goal did not oblige its members automatically to forgo any of their long-term national objectives.

This was why Churchill made such a fuss about British forces alone liberating its former colonies and why he demanded a strong Royal Navy presence in the last phase of the war against Japan. When the fighting stopped, Churchill wanted the world to witness the new ascendancy of Britannia, now stronger than ever and ready to fulfil her old place in the world. Before the war, he had brooded over the decline of British power, but the war had provided opportunities for its restoration. His ambitions were recognised by Americans from Roosevelt downwards and many were unhappy about American blood and resources being spent to uphold the pretensions of imperial Britain.

Alliances did not and could not entirely dispel residual suspicions about the ulterior motives of the powers involved. Some national interests passed into a temporary limbo; the Treasury Secretary Morgenthau was keen to postpone discussions over Anglo-American financial arrangements until after the war, for fear of creating friction between Churchill and Roosevelt.[10] Other national interests like those of Britain in South-East Asia had to be compromised by military expediency.

Divergences of national interests permeated the debates between Churchill and Roosevelt and the diplomats, economists and staff officers who advised them and negotiated strategic priorities and their implementation. Suspicions about the true motives of each ally were reinforced by perceived national stereotypes. American prejudices were summed up by Roosevelt, who once remarked: 'It is always the same with the British, they are always foxy and you have to be the same with them.' Cunning was mingled with selfishness and greed. After the war, General Wedemayer, a staff officer who had had extensive experience in these matters recalled: 'There was no give and take between British and American planners. It was all take on their part.'[11] The British reciprocated with their catalogue of perceived flaws in the American national character, most notably a propensity for hysteria. Halifax complained that they were 'up and down all the time' and another diplomat regretted their tendency to 'emotionalism and exaggeration'.[12]

Personal antipathies regularly intruded into the Anglo-American partnership. Stilwell thought Wavell was 'an old fart' and Senator Henry Cabot Lodge found Montgomery unbearable, as did Eisenhower.[13] Nevertheless the two commanders suppressed their private animosity and achieved a working relationship. After his first meeting with John Foster Dulles of the State Department, Sir Alexander Cadogan wrote him off as the 'woolliest type of pontificating American – Heaven help us!'[14] Churchill told Eden of his dislike for Madame Chiang Kai-Shek, but asked the Foreign Secretary to keep the matter to himself. None of this should surprise us. Public servants dedicated to winning the war did not automatically shed their *amour propre* and professional rectitude the moment they entered a conference room. Individual temperament intruded into debates in which frustrated protagonists sometimes resorted to personal abuse. A maestro in this field, 'Vinegar Joe' Stilwell noted that during a senior staff meeting at Cairo on 23 November 1943, the peppery Admiral Ernest J. King, commander-in-chief of the United States Navy, nearly came to blows with the normally imperturbable Sir Alan Brooke. Stilwell was sorry that King had not 'socked' the general. The squall passed and King 'was as nice as could be' when he dined with Brooke that evening.[15]

The maintenance of morale in both countries meant that such theatrical incidents and the wider disagreements that lay beneath the surface were kept hidden from the British and American public. One lasting result of the suppression of the details of Allied differences was the emergence of a romantic and essentially heroic picture of the Anglo-American partnership. At its heart was the warm, open-handed and mutually admiring personal relationship between Churchill and Roosevelt. Churchill called it an 'intimate comradeship' and he hoped it would be continued by Harry Truman, who became president after Roosevelt's death in April 1945.

The personal chemistry and the benefits of this comradeship were extensively explored (and praised) in Churchill's wartime memoirs. He portrayed himself as a canny pragmatist whose willingness to resort to realpolitik was an essential counterweight to Roosevelt's idealism and other-worldliness. Seeds sown by him in wartime grew into a sturdy plant, the Anglo-American 'special relationship'.

Churchill had no equivalent rapport with Stalin. Each was watchful of the other, although there were moments of conviviality and even humour. At Churchill's birthday party in Tehran, he proposed a toast to the 'Proletarian masses' and Stalin responded with one to the 'Conservative Party'. The Generalissimo admired Churchill's resolve as a war leader, but he doubted his honesty.[16] 'Churchill', he once quipped, 'is the kind of man who, if you don't watch him, will slip a kopeck from your pocket.' Roosevelt was a more ambitious pickpocket who 'dips his hands in for bigger coins'.[17] Churchill found Stalin (or 'Starleen' as he called him) 'ill-mannered and stubborn' and, as early as August 1943, he was uneasy about Russia's long-term international ambitions. He confided his anxieties to Mackenzie King during the Quebec Conference. Soviet Communism exerted 'influence in all parts of the world' and Churchill believed that Russia was 'powerful enough to more than control the world'.[18] Two months later, the Post Hostilitics Staff Committee concluded that the Soviet Union was poised to become the 'greatest world military power'.[19] The last phase of the war was also the genesis of what soon became known as the Cold War; seen from a purely British historical perspective, this new contest was an extension of the Anglo-Russian rivalry of Churchill's youth.

Paradoxically, this conflict began when Churchill was straining to preserve the integrity of the British Empire and Stalin was looking for ways in which to extend and consolidate its Russian counterpart. The circumstances were right for such an enterprise, for, at the beginning of 1945, the Soviet Union was at the zenith of its power. Her armed forces were within striking distance of Berlin and were in the process of occupying Poland, Czechoslovakia, Hungary, Romania, Bulgaria and eastern Austria. Stalin had redefined Soviet foreign policy with a shift from ideological to strategic and territorial objectives. International Communism had been sidelined (the Comintern was dissolved in 1943) and replaced by a programme compounded of zenophobia, nationalism and, above all, expansionism.

The new Russian policy was implemented at the Yalta and Potsdam (July 1945) summits, where, through diplomacy, Stalin was able to secure British and American acquiescence to a new dispensation of land and power in Europe. It rested on the victories of the Red Army and created a buffer zone of subservient states that would soon be called 'peoples democracies'. Their legitimacy rested not on the popular will, but on Russian garrisons and a legion of collaborators, chiefly spies, and policemen. While working within the Grand Alliance, Stalin also made tentative tests of Anglo-American solidarity by laying claims to Tripolitania (eastern Libya), former mandates in the western Pacific and territory in the Russo-Chinese frontier.[20]

Russia was playing its old imperial game. In January 1945 British intelligence analysts predicted that, having gained military supremacy in Europe, Russia would soon turn its attention towards the Indian Ocean and might sponsor a 'Persian Soviet Republic'.[21] A memo compiled on future imperial security in April identified the Middle, Far East and India as areas where Russia would confront Britain. Using its predominance of land forces in Europe, it was feared it might even invade Britain.[22]

Churchill had watched the advance of the Red Army into Europe with dread. In May 1944 he told the Commonwealth prime ministers that 'he did not want the polar bear coming from the steppes of Russia to the white cliffs of Dover'.[23] Whatever its eventual destination, this beast endangered the stability and balance of power in Europe. It could not be stopped, as Churchill realised at Yalta, where he fought a quixotic rearguard action to preserve Polish independence. Roosevelt was less passionate over this issue, although there was nothing, short of war, that either leader could have done to dislodge the Red Army from Poland. By May 1945 there were 11.3 million Russian servicemen and women in Eastern and Central Europe, although nearly four-fifths of them would be demobilised during the next two years.[24] Churchill warned Truman to be prepared to square up to the 'Russian peril'.[25]

Churchill's paranoia was reciprocated. While he was concerned about enlarged Russian power on the Continent and the reappearance of Russian threats to imperial security, Stalin feared that he might be cozened by his allies. 'Russia wins wars,' he once told Foreign Minister Vyacheslav Molotov, 'but doesn't know how to take advantage of her victories' with the result that Russians 'are badly treated, get very little'.[26] He was determined that this would never happen again.

Yet there was a meeting of minds between the two statesmen based on their shared appreciation of realpolitik and the fact that each was the leader of an imperial nation with historic geo-political interests. At their meeting in Moscow in October 1944, Churchill on the spur of the moment suggested the partition of the Balkans into closely defined spheres of influence of the kind that would have been understood and approved by nineteenth-century statesmen. Britain was assigned 90 per cent of Greece, the Soviet Union was given the same proportion in Romania and Hungary, Yugoslavia was split evenly and Russia took

75 per cent of Bulgaria. Aware of the dismay this arrangement would provoke in America, Churchill called it his 'naughty' protocol.[27]

Stalin took the deal seriously in so far as he gave no aid to the Greek Communists in December, when British forces had intervened on behalf of the monarchists. Churchill had got what he wanted, for a friendly Greece was essential to the reconstruction of imperial power in the Mediterranean. The advances of the Red Army soon removed any chance of Britain asserting its paper interests in the rest of the Balkans.

At Potsdam, Churchill acknowledged the historic ambitions of imperial Russia when he accepted as legitimate Russia's claim ('as a Great Power and in particular as a Naval Power') to free passage for its warships through the Straits. They included Russia's share of the surrendered Italian fleet, which Churchill had been glad to hand over to Stalin. He did, however, reject demands for a Soviet naval base in the Dardanelles and, for the time being, Stalin let the matter rest.[28] Churchill was, however, sympathetic towards a request for a naval base at Port Arthur, a warm sea port that would have allowed Russia to resume its historic role as a naval power in the Pacific and the Far East.[29] For his part, Stalin revealed a brief sympathy for the British Empire at Yalta during a row between Churchill and the Americans over the latter's proposal that British colonies should be placed in the hands of trustees appointed by the United Nations. The Prime Minister furiously rejected this suggestion, and Eden noted that Stalin applauded his tirade; whether or not his pleasure reflected approval for the Empire or satisfaction at witnessing a public row between Britain and America is not known. It was probably the former, although he would have thought any external supervision of Soviet dependencies intolerable.

In handling Stalin, Churchill was adopting the traditional imperial policy towards Russia: a blend of concessions, denials and a willingness to treat her as a world power. This formula had to be adjusted according to the circumstances of 1945, which gave Russia military supremacy in Europe and a frontier that stretched from the mouth of the Elbe to the Danube basin. Nevertheless, Churchill acted on the assumption that Stalin was happy to engage in old-style great power horse-trading. Its flavour was reflected in discussions over the future of Italy's former African colonies. Stalin asked: 'Who has found them?' Churchill replied: 'The British army through heavy losses and indisputable victories had conquered them.' Stalin slyly riposted: 'Berlin had also been taken by the Red Army.'[30] What is fascinating about this exchange is that it could have occurred at the Congress of Vienna in 1815 or the Versailles Conference in 1919. On both occasions the leaders of the great powers took for granted the fact that victorious nations deserved rewards and that they alone had the right to determine their extent and distribution. Conspicuously and deliberately absent was any reference to the spirit of the Atlantic Charter. For the moment, Somalis and Berliners had no choice as to who ruled over them.

Churchill did, however, exonerate himself from charges of acquisitive opportunism by declaring in June 1945 that: 'It was not Britain's intention to steal the property of anybody in this war.'[31] Yet, he had already demanded the retention of Pantelleria between North Africa and Sicily, and his staff planners were bent on maintaining a military presence in former Italian colonies as part of an imperial defence network in the Middle East.

As ever, imperial security required a stable and tranquil Europe, which rested on an equitable balance of power. In May 1944, Churchill had revealed his vision of a 'united states of Europe' to the Commonwealth prime ministers, which, he naively hoped, might include Russia. Its cooperation was withheld and a year later Churchill found himself confronting a Europe dominated by Russian military power. It was a fearsome prospect, that he had attempted to avert at Tehran and Yalta by his insistence that France should be treated as a major European power, despite its wartime misadventures. Remembering France's collapse in 1940, Stalin dismissed its ruling class as 'rotten to the core' (Roosevelt agreed) and wrote off de Gaulle as a nonentity. In the end, Churchill prevailed and France was allowed a zone of occupation in Germany, as well as a seat on the security council of the new United Nations.

France's reinstatement made little difference to the distribution of power inside Europe. Germany was physically and politically fractured and partly under Russian occupation, while France and

Italy were debilitated and facing large-scale subversion by indigenous, pro-Moscow Communist parties. Britain was bankrupt, Lend-Lease was terminated within weeks of VE Day and she faced a protracted military commitment to Greek anti-Communists, Jewish terrorism in Palestine, unrest in India and Burma and the problems of restoring imperial rule in Malaya. France, too, was bedevilled by colonial disturbances in Algeria, Syria and Indo-China.

Britain alone could no longer hold the pass. As Churchill appreciated, the only way to correct the disequilibrium in Europe was the continuance of the Anglo-American partnership. Over the past four years, the United States had become a global superpower: it possessed the world's largest air force (15,000 machines) and navy (1,200 warships). Its preponderance was consummated by the detonation of a prototype Atomic bomb in the New Mexican desert on 16 July 1945. Churchill was not informed of the test, but he quickly appreciated that the United States now held an irresistible weapon with which it could coerce the Soviet Union. If he had not lost the general election ten days afterwards, he said that he would have urged Truman to use the threat of the Atom bomb as a cudgel with which to restrain the Soviet Union. This would not have been a hard task, for there was a substantial body of opinion in Washington, particularly in military and intelligence circles, which shared his mistrust of Russian ambitions.

Fraternal Association:
America and the Future of the British Empire

President Roosevelt liked flying kites. Circumspection and ambiguity were among his favourite political devices; they kept friends and enemies guessing and masked his tendency to postpone decisions until the last moment. Yet he was direct and candid in his 1943 Christmas broadcast. He told Americans that victory would mean 'the restoration of stolen property to its rightful owners and the recognition of the rights of millions in the Far East to build up their forms of self-government without molestation'. A year before, Churchill had announced that 'We shall hold our own' after the war, and that he had not become 'the King's first minister in order to preside over the liquidation of the British Empire'.

At this stage in the war, when victory now seemed assured, there was a widening divergence between British and American visions of the post-war world. Churchill wanted to recover the pre-war status quo as far as the Empire was concerned, but Roosevelt had set his sights on a global New Deal that would dispense with empires and lay the foundations of universal peace, democracy, liberty and free market capitalism.

America's Four Freedoms were about to be exported to the rest of the world. Leaflets dropped before the Torch landings in North Africa announced the imminent arrival of 'American Holy Warriors' who would 'fight the great Jihad of freedom'.[1] 'Freedom is coming soon' was the aerial message for the people of Java in 1943.[2] These pledges begged important questions. Tunisians, Moroccans and Algerians must have wondered whether the GIs would both drive out the Germans *and* the French, while the Javanese might reasonably assume that their Japanese masters would go and that their Dutch predecessors would never reappear. This was certainly what nationalists believed would happen after the Japanese surrender in August 1945.

America's self-appointed and self-proclaimed role as the global liberator was part of a far-reaching revolution in its relations with the rest of world. After 1941, the United States turned its back for ever on isolationism, which Churchill had wrongly feared might return once Germany and Japan had surrendered. The Roosevelt and Truman administrations did not shed the massive responsibilities imposed on the United States by the war. Rather, they were determined to maintain their country's new status as a superpower with extensive international obligations.

America was abundantly qualified for the task. It had immense reserves of capital, including three-quarters of the world's gold, and an unequalled industrial capacity that had made it the mainstay of its allies' war efforts. Within five years, American industry had given the country military dominance, a tiny arsenal of Atomic bombs and the technical knowledge to produce more. A superfluity of power generated self-confidence and positive, evangelical attitudes. In 1943 a British engineer officer building roads in Persia enviously noted: 'The Americans would rather move hills and fill in valleys than go round corners, and they have the resources to do it.'[3]

The global situation in 1945 was summed up by the future Secretary of State Dean Acheson, who likened the United States to 'the locomotive at the head of mankind' and 'the rest of the world is the caboose'.[4] There was, he believed, no one else either qualified or available to fulfil this duty. Years later, he recalled a moment of truth during that year when 'I looked at the map and saw that red on the thing, and, by God, that was the British Empire, the French Senegalese troops in East Asia and in Germany – all of this was gone to hell'.[5] Britain and France, he concluded, were of no greater importance than Brazil. This was an exaggeration that ignored the Anglo-French capacity for resuscitation, but Acheson and other Washington policy makers were conscious that their misfortunes had created a global power vacuum. It had to be filled, if only to prevent the Soviet Union from edging in.

Ideological imperatives and national self-esteem gave a moral dimension to America's plans for world leadership. The history of Europe, in particular that of the past twenty-five years, had reinforced America's sense of its own moral superiority. Since 1919 Germany and Italy had been infected with mass lunacy and a lust for conquest, France lacked the stamina and willpower to match its airs, appeasement had exposed British power as a façade, and its colossal war effort had left it all but penniless. Europe had also endured extended spasms of economic distress that had eroded democracy and smoothed the path for dictators. By contrast, and thanks to its dedication to equality, individualism, free-market capitalism and, above all, its democratic system of government, America had weathered the storms of the inter-war years and flourished. Roosevelt's New Deal was a shining example of Americans getting things right, although Republican diehards had condemned its principles as socialist and some still do. Nonetheless, in 1945 self-evident American achievements made it the most successful nation on earth and, therefore, qualified to act as torchbearer for the rest of humanity.

Roosevelt believed in the American mission with the same intensity as Churchill believed in the British Empire. In 1943 the President told the Prime Minister that he hoped that Persia would soon evolve into a capitalist state 'with an American pattern of government'. The President also volunteered a blueprint for Britain's West Indian colonies that included federation, compulsory education and universal suffrage under joint Anglo-American supervision.[6] His staff suggested further reforms, including a radio station whose educational programmes would include 'civics as portrayed in New York schools'.[7] Barbados and Antigua would be remade in America's image.

Churchill appreciated the generous soul of America and admired its civic virtues. He had also, throughout the war, dreamed of comprehensive and high-minded schemes for an international renaissance, which were close to those being contrived in Washington. There was, however, one significant difference. While the Americans insisted that the dissolution of the old empires was a prerequisite for the building of a new world, Churchill, with equal vigour, believed that the British Empire and Commonwealth were destined to be its vital components.

He clung to this assumption in full knowledge of the animus towards the imperial idea that was embedded in the American mind and was expressed, often bluntly, by Roosevelt and senior members of his administration. While Churchill dreamed of the British Empire rising like a Phoenix after the war, a substantial number of Americans looked forward to a post-war bonfire of empires. Early in 1945, a Gallup Poll revealed that 56 per cent of Americans regarded empires as essentially oppressive.[8]

American anti-imperialism did not shake Churchill's faith in the Empire, which had been reinforced by the wartime loyalty and self-sacrifice of the dominions and colonies. Listening to him during the meeting of Commonwealth prime ministers in May 1944, Mackenzie King was struck by his sense of imperial 'mission'. It was 'a vision of Empire that appeals to his religious and romantic instinct'.[9] Churchill's wartime certitudes would be perpetuated. 'You will find in the British Empire and Commonwealth good comrades,' Churchill told a Harvard audience in September 1943, adding revealingly that they were joined to America by 'ties of blood and history'.[10] Consanguinity still counted and so did the racial axioms of Churchill's youth. In April 1944, he cabled Roosevelt his approval of a scheme to promote 'Basic English' as an international language with the observation that it would be 'a powerful support to the influence of the Anglo-Saxon nations in world affairs'.[11]

In the meantime, Churchill had been proclaiming his vision of Britain's new imperial destiny. In November 1943 he predicted that 'the happiness of future generations depends on the fraternal association of Great Britain and the United States', who together now had the chance 'to secure the peace and freedom of mankind'.[12] Churchill returned to this theme the following April when he told the Commons how he looked forward to a 'more closely knitted Commonwealth and Empire' becoming 'more closely associated with the United States'.[13]

Yet most Americans would have defined 'happiness' as a condition where people ruled themselves, rather than submitted to outsiders, even those with the best of intentions. Their opinions would prove decisive, for, as Churchill the realist was well aware, the two brothers were not equal, nor ever would be. In his Harvard speech, he had conceded that the United States was 'in many ways the leading community in the civilised world', a plaudit that he would have once awarded to the British Empire.[14] It was no longer cock of the walk, as he admitted in March 1946, when he told an American audience that: 'The United States stands at the highest point of majesty and power ever attained by any community since the fall of the Roman Empire.'[15]

*

The new Rome mistrusted the old and was impatient for its extinction. American anti-imperialism was a barrier to any lasting *entente* between the two powers and the British government hoped to demolish it through an intensive propaganda campaign. During 1942 a stream of senior Foreign and Colonial Office officials crossed the Atlantic to sweep away American misconceptions about the Empire and prove that its spirit was liberal and progressive. The colonies were being shepherded along the 'road of social and economic development' towards 'the highest possible living standards' and 'the greatest measure of self government' that was possible 'for the communities to which they belong'.[16] This was a Churchillian view of the Empire, but, significantly, it said nothing about any timetable for self-determination.

This mission to sell the Empire foundered. There was no meeting of minds, rather a collision of preconceptions. At all levels Americans remained sceptical about the purpose and morality of the Empire and preferred their own prejudices. 'Fierce dogmatism and blind ignorance' characterised the views on the Empire expressed by senior officials in Washington.[17] Beneath these reactions lay a stratum of suspicion about British sincerity; Americans considered the British a wily people who always followed their own interests whilst professing altruism. This scepticism was reflected in what Sir Richard Law, parliamentary under-secretary at the Foreign Office, called a tendency to be 'touchy, truculent and difficult' and hiding 'an inner lack of confidence with a cloak of unnatural assertiveness'.[18] Behind these reactions was a sense that the British were incurably devious. General Brehon B. Somervell, who ran the United States's Army Service Forces, considered Churchill 'domineering and bamboozling', an impression then shared by other military men who suspected that the Prime Minister was keener on saving the Empire than beating Hitler and Hirohito.[19]

In some quarters there were misgivings about how Britain was surreptitiously exploiting Lend-Lease to further its imperial objectives. In 1944, Patrick Hurley accused Britain of 'using American lend lease and American troops not for the purpose of creating a brave new world based on the Atlantic Charters and the four free freedoms, but for

British conquest, British imperial rule and British trade monopoly'.[20] Rumours that Britain was distributing Lend-Lease supplies in the Middle East to solicit local goodwill persuaded Washington to stamp the packing cases with the Stars and Stripes and the message 'Gift of the USA'.[21]

While Churchill was set on retaining or regaining political control over the Empire, Americans were bracing themselves to assert what Law called 'economic imperialism'. 'Business interests', he predicted, would supplant the 'military caste' in Washington and they were bent on the 'industrialisation of the world'.[22] This involved the reorganisation of world trade in ways that would favour American manufacturers and bankers. Their aim, in the words of one State Department official, was the 'removal of discriminations which exist in the British Empire in various forms against American trade and finance'.[23] Big business had also set its sights on the French Empire. This anti-imperial enterprise had Roosevelt's blessing, for he once told Morgenthau that he wanted 'all those colonies ... open to all the world'.[24]

This was a subject about which Churchill knew next to nothing. At Quebec in August 1943, Mackenzie King had warned him that: 'private companies were the most powerful interests in the United States and that their lobbyists were the most powerful'.[25] They dominated the press and through it the government. As President Coolidge had observed nearly twenty years before, 'The business of America is business', and it remained so during the war. Churchill was stupefied and suggested that one of his junior staff investigated this matter. It was certainly unwelcome information, for it cut at the roots of his faith in the United States as a paradigm of selflessness and, therefore, it was best swept under the carpet.

Evidence collected by Whitehall indicated that America was already undertaking what was tantamount to an all-out economic offensive against the British Empire. American business needed open access to colonial markets, minerals, oil and rubber and its friends inside the administration were happy to lend a hand. One of the tacit conditions of Lend-Lease had been Britain's acceptance in principle of the gradual abandonment of imperial preference. The United States government wanted to accelerate this process and saw the war as a golden opportunity to do so. In the long term, universal free trade would be vital for the American economy: the momentum of wartime growth would be sustained, living standards would continue to rise and the government would receive the taxation needed to underwrite its new, global primacy.

India was a prime target for American economic penetration. It was well advanced by February 1943, when the Viceroy Lord Linlithgow complained to Whitehall about the underhand machinations of the OSS (Office of Strategic Services) branch in Delhi. Its agents were endeavouring 'to dig into the country with a view to the postwar period' with the backing of 'commercial interests' in Washington.[26] The openings were certainly there. British exports into India had dropped from 38 per cent of the national total in 1938 to 20 per cent in 1944–5 and the Japanese share of 17 per cent had disappeared altogether. Over the same period the American share of the Indian market rose from 6 per cent to 21 per cent.

It was also obvious that the British would soon leave India, whatever Churchill said to the contrary. Labour's victory in July 1945 made it clear that India, Burma and Ceylon would soon attain independence and so the OSS stepped up its clandestine political activities in these countries. It was a matter of urgency that the United States acquired sympathetic and cooperative allies among the nationalist leaders who were about to take over power. OSS agents cultivated figures such as Nehru and, in December, intelligence officers in Delhi and Colombo were instructed to commence 'long term' political activities.[27]

In South-East Asia, the OSS implemented policies contrived to hinder the reinstatement of the British and the French and assist America's client, Chiang Kai-Shek. Colonel George F. Taylor, the Far Eastern director of the OSS, tried to 'squeeze' British interests out of Thailand and Indo-China, areas where the Generalissimo was hoping for gains. Taylor's field officers also hampered British plans to raise an army of 30,000 partisans in Kwangsi [Guangxi] and Kwantung [Guangdon] to the east and north of Hong Kong that would facilitate the restoration of imperial rule.[28] Again, Chiang Kai-Shek was the intended beneficiary, for he had been pestering the United States for the return of Hong Kong.

Official America was doing all within its power to further the interests of business in other parts of the Empire. United States airlines, in particular the influential PanAm, were eager to extend their services worldwide with free competition on all routes. This was why USAAF negotiators insisted that American commercial carriers were assigned peacetime landing rights on the string of airfields being constructed to deliver aircraft to the Middle East. These included Ascension Island and the bases that stretched from the Gold Coast to Khartoum and Cairo. These concessions led to bickering, but, in May 1943, Churchill conceded control of all trans-African flights to the Americans.[29] At Potsdam he agreed that Britain would share 'common rights' with the United States on all Middle Eastern and African military airfields that had been financed by Lend-Lease.[30]

Corporate America was proceeding on the assumption that after the war the old European empires would either cease to exist, or, if they did survive, their impoverished rulers would be unable to resist pressure to relinquish trade monopolies. The Reynolds Metal Corporation demanded unrestricted access to Jamaican bauxite, but was initially opposed by the British government. It finally gave way in 1949 when a bauxite concession was exchanged for dollars desperately needed to pay off debts to the United States.[31] Coca Cola, Kodak and Westinghouse secured favourable trade deals with the Egyptian government and Wall Street provided the capital for a chemical plant at Assuan.

American anxieties over satisfying the spiralling demand for oil from its armed forces, coupled with the loss of the wells in South-East Asia early in 1942 led to a series of approaches to King Ibn Saud of Saudi Arabia. He was Britain's client whose annual subsidy was raised in 1942 from £400,000 to £3.8 million; nearly all of which was frittered away by the King and his extended family. At the time, the State Department was keen to make inroads into Britain's sphere of influence in the region and push the interests of ARAMCO. In June 1943, Secretary for the Interior Harold Ickes urged Roosevelt 'to counteract certain activities of a foreign power which presently are jeopardising American interest in Arabian oil reserves'.[32] Ickes was the cat's-paw of the oil companies and the anonymous 'foreign power' was Britain. Cordell Hull, the Secretary of State, was also keen to block 'the expansion of British facilities' that were being used to 'build up their postwar position in the Middle East' and keep out the Americans.[33]

The State Department began to lure Ibn Saud out of Britain's orbit, although one official was repelled by the idea of bankrolling 'a backward, corrupt and non-democratic society'.[34] The Foreign Office temporised, hoping that the two countries could share the oil, and Churchill assured Roosevelt that Britain had 'no thought of trying to horn in' on American interests in Saudi Arabia. Reassured, Roosevelt stopped off in Egypt on his return from Yalta in February 1945 to court Ibn Saud. The King was bowled over by his straightforward talking, which contrasted with what he thought was the deviousness of the British. 'What am I to believe', he asked, 'when the British tell me that the future is with them, and not the Americans?'[35]

Both nations were pleading for him to reach an accommodation over Jewish immigration and Roosevelt offered him dollars to fund irrigation and agriculture projects as a reward for compliance. Ibn Saud spurned the offer, for his people 'would rather stay poor than risk our children a heritage of Jewish infiltration'.[36] The President made the King a gift of a Dakota; one of its first flights was a pleasure trip for members of his harem. Soon after, Churchill met Ibn Saud at an hotel in the desert and presented him with a Rolls-Royce. It and the Prime Minister's assurances of future British friendship and protection did not allay royal fears about more Jewish settlements in Palestine.

Roosevelt had secured what he called an 'open door' from Ibn Saud, and so for the time being Britain's sphere of influence in the Middle East remained intact. To judge from his remarks, the King sensed a coming change in the regional balance of power and with it the opportunity to play off one power against the other. Churchill's position on this issue, as on American encroachments on the imperial status quo, had been tolerant. Matters such as the allocation of Saudi oil or landing rights at Khartoum airport were trivial when set beside the greater goal of perpetuating the wartime alliance.

A further and now little-known source of friction between Britain and the United States was conflicting attitudes towards race. The subject surfaced during a presidential press conference held for the

Negro Newspaper Publishers Association in February 1944. A black journalist recently returned from the Gambia expressed his horror of what he had seen: 'The natives are five thousand years behind us ... disease is rampant' and 'for every dollar the British put in [they] take out ten'. The President said that this was an issue he had raised with Churchill, and that after the war the United Nations would send inspection committees into such places. He added that the Prime Minister resented this suggestion and promised that he would send one of these committees 'to your own south in America'.[37]

Allegations about the subjection and mistreatment of American blacks were common knowledge in the West African colonies during 1942. The Colonial Office leapt to the defence of the moral reputation of Britain's ally and organised a propaganda campaign to refute the commonest charges. Statistics were cited to prove that life was not too bad for black men in America: 880,000 owned their own farms, 750,000 owned their own homes and 70,000 (under 1 per cent) owned their own businesses. Revealingly, it was claimed that Southern women had repudiated the notion that lynching was vital for their safety and that whites were sometimes lynched.[38]

West Africans also heard that segregation was disappearing, which would have surprised West Indian soldiers passing through Newport, Virginia en route to the Italian front in 1944.[39] They were warned by their officers not to travel on buses reserved for whites and to steer clear of white women. Moreover, and in retrospect this is staggering, during 1942 and 1943 the United States military authorities were demanding the extension of Southern segregationist codes for off-duty American servicemen in Britain. There was considerable resistance from the Colonial Office and a number of isolated protests by British people who were outraged by the brutality of the American military police towards black soldiers. Churchill was indifferent; after hearing that American officers had protested about the presence of a black Colonial Office official in a London restaurant, he quipped, 'That's all right; if he takes a banjo with him they'll think he's one of the band!'[40]

Throughout the war, Churchill had consistently and sometimes blithely brushed aside any issue that might have generated contention between Britain and America. His faith in the compatibility of purpose and common values of the two countries at times exasperated his more hard-nosed colleagues. Eden, for one, was a sceptical realist and he voiced the anxieties of others when he warned the Prime Minister in November 1942 that:

... no matter how satisfactory are the relations between yourself and the President, between the United States and the British Governments, or the two sets of Chiefs of Staff, I believe that the ideas held by a big proportion of the American people towards the British are false and dangerous – particularly in respect of the close relationship between the two peoples for the post-war period.[41]

Your Lofty Principles:

Gains and Losses, 1945

During the first six months of 1945, a noticeably flagging Churchill grappled with the problems that had been thrown up by the war and which would outlast it. It was 1918 all over again, but with one crucial difference: then the British Empire had come out on top, whereas in 1945 it was in third place, behind the two superpowers (a word invented two years before), the United States and Russia. This had prompted unkind whisperings at Yalta, where the 'Big Three' were spitefully likened to the Triumvirs with Roosevelt and Stalin as Mark Anthony and Octavian, and Churchill as the nonentity, Lepidus.

Churchill swung between a sullen acceptance of this truth and evading its implications. In public he boasted that the Empire was still a force to be reckoned with, declaring in his victory broadcast of 13 May that: 'the British Commonwealth and Empire stands more united and more effectively powerful than at any time in its long romantic history.' He was less triumphant in private.

History was no longer on Churchill's side, as he was beginning to realise. His moods of morbid melancholia (which he called 'black dog') became more frequent as he contemplated with foreboding the knowledge that Russia was supreme in Europe and that India was about to be lost. The Communist bogey of 1918 had returned, infinitely stronger and as malevolent as ever. In May 1944 he had lectured the dominion prime ministers about a possible Communist offensive against the British and French empires.[1] Once again, Churchill was a Cassandra, but this time his premonitions were aimed at an American audience. He told Eisenhower that Communism was 'Christianity with a tomahawk'.[2]

Physically and mentally, the Prime Minister was no longer up to tasks ahead. 'I am on old weary man, I feel exhausted,' he confided to Macmillan.[3] His wartime exertions had been heroic: he was seventy-one, and in the past five years he had shown an astonishing stamina of mind and body. His resilience was remarkable, for he had endured cardiac disorders, including a minor stroke, sundry colds, and gruelling, long-distance flights in often freezing aircraft to conferences in North Africa, America, Persia and Russia. During 1944 he had also flown to Egypt, Greece, Italy and France to get a first-hand impression of what was happening and to keep his subordinates on their toes.

He drank heavily, and draughts of champagne, whisky and brandy often stimulated his rages, but there is no reason to believe that alcohol ever seriously impaired his judgement on a major issue. At times its effects were conspicuous; he was 'rather sozzled' and 'bellicose and repetitive' at one late-night meeting with Foreign Office officials in December 1944.[4] By this date, he was frequently rambling and tangential during cabinet debates, but not so on 12 March 1945, when the rather tidy-minded Amery noted that the Prime Minister's laryngitis speeded up business.[5]

The fate of the Empire fuelled his bouts of despair. In the middle of the war he had confessed to Eden his deep fear that winning the war would be accompanied by the loss of India. As we have seen, during 1943 and 1944, it was a subject that provoked vituperative monologues during cabinet meetings. Black dog and brandy combined to produce an after-dinner outburst at Chequers late in February 1945, in which Churchill asked Air Marshal Harris for some spare bombers to obliterate the Hindus. Afterwards, he played a record of Gilbert and Sullivan's *Mikado*, which, he told his guests, embodied the spirit of an 'Antonine Age' that had sadly passed for ever.[6]

This reverie bore out Roosevelt's gibe at Yalta that Churchill was at heart a 'Victorian'. Amery agreed, but was more precise, when, at the very end of the war, he described the man who had saved Britain and its Empire as 'a retrospective Whig of the period 1750–1850'.[7] Then, as Churchill knew, Britain had trounced all its enemies, extracted territory from them, and so emerged richer and stronger. This was not the case in 1945, as he was forced to concede whenever he spoke of America's ascendancy and Britain's need to maintain its friendship in order to survive as a world power.

Churchillian pessimism was premature. Historians primed with hindsight have assumed that her wartime exertions had turned Britain into an incurably arthritic nation about to slide helplessly into decline. This was not how things seemed at the time. Churchill, his successor Attlee, and their ministers did not regard Britain and its Empire as on the brink of terminal decay, rather the opposite. Seen from the perspective of the victory celebrations in May and August 1945, Britain had every reason to feel assured that its economy would revive and flourish and that it would continue to command respect in the world.

Britain's war record had been astonishing. It was an achievement that has been disregarded in that historical narrative which treats the moment of victory as the starting post for a downhill canter towards economic decay and international impotence. Britain's war effort had been dynamic and effective, which was hardly to be expected from a nation on the threshold of desuetude.

Britain's wartime performance was a subject about which Churchill was very touchy. In January 1944 he instructed Halifax to remind the Americans that 'this small island [Britain] puts up four-fifths of the whole war effort of the British Empire and Commonwealth'.[8] Early in the following year, he requested an analysis of Commonwealth casualties to reveal the human cost of the war effort. The result showed that New Zealand forces suffered 1 in 180 casualties, the British 1 in 236, the South Africans 1 in 350 and the Australians and Canadians 1 in 380.[9] At this time, just under half of British aircrew were from India and the dominions, and Canada possessed the third largest navy in the world.[10]

The mobilisation of Britain and its Empire has recently been re-evaluated and the result is an impressive history of flexibility, inventiveness and imagination at every level.[11] Our scientific and technical ingenuity, industrial organisation, food distribution, transport systems, and the deployment of man and womanpower were far superior to those of the Axis powers. The Empire played a crucial part in all this: it provided food, including mutton and lamb from New Zealand (Britain's meat imports rose during the war years) and Canadian wheat saved Greece during the famine of 1943 to 1944. Dominion and colonial comestibles fed the imperial armies that held the Middle East and, as we have seen, Iraqi and Iranian petrol powered their tanks, trucks and aircraft.

All this was paid for by promissory notes in sterling issued by the British government and retained in London. By 1945, this pile of IOUs totalled over £3,800 million and was known as the sterling balances; India's share was by far the largest (£1,292 million) while the dominions were owed £481 million and Egypt £400 million. In effect, Britain had shouldered a huge part of the costs of defending the Empire, for in theory, the holders of sterling balances could withdraw sums whenever they chose. Yet this hidden debt boosted the status of sterling as an international currency and simultaneously reduced Britain's dependence on borrowed dollars. This did not stop Churchill from carping about Indian ingratitude.

Ingratitude, this time American, characterised the exploitation of British scientific and technical genius. Two of the greatest wartime inventions, the harnessing of atomic power and the invention of penicillin, had been the fruits of British research. At Churchill's wish, both were developed in the United States, although he thought that America's mean-spirited decision to permit Britain a mere 10 per cent of penicillin production was 'very disappointing'.[12] In 1946 Congress compounded this lack of generosity by passing the Mahon Act which excluded Britain from future participation in American nuclear research.

Imperial cohesion had been impressive, apart from the brief Anglo-Australian ruckus during 1942. There were deep wells of often heartfelt loyalty, like that of an unknown West African truck driver who composed his own imperial creed: 'I shall say of Britain, she is my refuge and fortress, my Empire, in her will I trust. God has set his love upon Britain.'[13] Churchill sometimes tended to take such sentiments and imperial support for granted. After watching Roy Boulting's *Desert Victory*, he upbraided the director for concentrating on the faces of British and imperial servicemen, rather than showing a grand victory parade, which he thought would please American filmgoers. Captain Boulting squared up to his critic and gave an unanswerable reply; his message was that ordinary men from across the Empire – 'Sikhs, Aussies, Anzacs [and] territorials from Tower Hamlets' – were the heroes of the battle and deserved to be honoured. Churchill demurred, as he usually did when faced with reasonable arguments expressed with determination, and *Desert Victory* went to cinemas unchanged, and won an Oscar.[14]

At the very beginning of 1945, Malaya, Borneo, Sarawak, much of Burma, and parts of Papua and New Guinea remained in Japanese hands, although plans for their reconquest were in hand. It was unclear under what conditions they would be returned to Britain. Roosevelt still cherished the hope that multinational agencies would take control of Europe's colonies, particularly in the Far East. Churchill scoffed at idea of these 'half-baked international regimes'.[15] As ever, he was determined to avoid a cleavage with America and so he procrastinated, arguing for the postponement of any decision on colonial problems until after Germany and Japan had been defeated. Churchill's stonewalling worked, for, in January 1944, Roosevelt appeared to have had a change of heart, for he told Halifax that Britain and the Netherlands 'had done a good job', while the French had been 'hopeless' as colonists.[16]

This was encouraging, but not for the French. Roosevelt had consistently singled them out for condemnation. In December 1943, in the presence of Halifax, he had informed the Chinese and Turkish ambassadors and the Egyptian minister that he intended to prevent France from ever reoccupying Indo-China, where her rule had been selfish and sterile.[17] On other occasions, he added Senegal and the French Pacific islands to the list of territories to be administered by the United Nations. Redistributing French colonies was a presidential project in which idealism mingled with prejudice. Roosevelt treated France as a nation that had forfeited its status as a world power because of the decadence and corruption that had been revealed by its precipitate collapse in 1940.

Churchill stood by France. 'As long as there is a kick left in my carcass', he told Lord Moran in July 1945, 'I shall support France's efforts to re-establish herself.'[18] He was also upholding a vital British interest, in so far as the post-war balance of European power required a vigorous France underpinned by its empire. Moreover, any concession to Roosevelt on this issue was bound to have dangerous implications for the British Empire; a principle applied to one empire could be applied to another.

This was why Churchill had demanded the restoration of French authority in its Pacific colonies, and he warned Roosevelt that the loss of other territories would enrage French public opinion. This and France's future standing in the world compelled Churchill to make hurried and radical readjustments to his policy towards the Lebanon and Syria, to which, in 1941, he had allowed virtual independence. By October 1944, he had convinced himself that the Syrians could never govern themselves without French 'supervision'. A few months later, the government accepted reality and warned France against opening a war to restore its control over Syria and the Lebanon, even going so far as to threaten to intercept convoys of French troops.

Paradoxically, it was Japan that settled the colonial question. On 9 March 1945 the Japanese overthrew the puppet Vichy regime in Saigon, locked up as many French officials and soldiers as they could catch, and placed Indo-China under direct military government. Indo-China was now a theoretic if frail ally, since tiny French units were harrying the Japanese, together with Ho Chi Minh's Communist Vietminh partisans. The appearance of a new front provided a welcome chance for de Gaulle (now President and head of France's provisional government) to ask America to reverse its policy towards Indo-China. If the United States did not assist France to recover its colony, then, in all likelihood, it might slip into Communist hands. At the same time, the French partisans in Indo-China appealed to SEAC [South East Asia Command] for arms and these were airlifted in from southern China.[19] In Washington Roosevelt wavered, for Churchill's argument that future regional stability rested on the re-establishment of French rule was now being repeated by his own Chiefs of Staff. The President died on 12 April, and, a week later, the Secretary of State Edward Stettinius assured de Gaulle that the United States no longer opposed the restoration of French rule in Indo-China.[20] In August, Truman told Madame Chiang Kai-Shek that the United States now regarded the policy of international trusteeship in Indo-China as moribund.[21]

It was formally interred at Potsdam, where Truman agreed that an interim Sino-British administration should be installed prior to the arrival of substantial French forces. On 13 September an Anglo-Indian contingent landed at Saigon to restore order; thousands of Japanese POWs were recruited for police duties (some offered their services to Ho Chi Minh), demonstrations were banned, and looters were shot.[22] A French army soon appeared and by February 1946 had secured most of Indo-China's cities and larger towns, but not the countryside.

America's moral objections to imperialism were being blown away by anxieties about the spread of Communism and new strategic imperatives. America's response to the crisis in Indo-China anticipated, at least in its intentions, the 1947 Truman doctrine of containment, that is to say active resistance to Communist infiltration wherever it appeared. To succeed, this policy needed the cooperation of the British and French imperial authorities, who, it was rightly assumed, would crush Communist insurrections in their colonies.

Moreover, as the United States came to terms with its new global responsibilities, it was becoming clear to its military planners that it would require naval and air force bases in every corner of the world. Empires that had appeared outdated and due for demolition in 1942 were now strategic assets. The new mood was apparent during negotiations held in London in February 1946, when America laid claim to sovereignty over a scattering of twenty-five Pacific islands under British and New Zealand administration.

Their value was purely military, although the American delegates also coveted the islands for commercial airports. Many of them were unpopulated, but one, Funafuti, had a thousand inhabitants, all subjects of George VI. Any feelings that they might have had about their transfer from British to American rule were considered irrelevant by the American representatives, although Colonial Office officials were unhappy.[23] The Atlantic Charter had discreetly and cynically been abandoned by the United States.

In Malaya there was a local resistance movement that called itself the Malayan Peoples Anti-Japanese Army. Little was known about it in Whitehall, save that its strength was estimated at about 10,000, mostly Chinese, and that it included Communists and Chinese nationalists who looked to Chiang Kai-Shek.[24] On 11 May 1945 the cabinet agreed to cooperate with this underground force, even though its members had no love for Britain. Making friends with the local nationalists was part of the preparations for amphibious landings that were scheduled for August.

Just over four years of Japanese rule had exacerbated racial tensions within the colony; the occupiers had favoured the Malays, who had formed the majority of collaborators. There had been food shortages, inflation and, in 1943, four sultanates (Kedah, Perlis, Trengannu and Kelantan) had been handed over to Thailand as payment for its cooperation.

The everyday experience of life under Japanese occupation in Malaya and other colonies had been as vile as that experienced by inhabitants of Europe and Russia under the Nazis and their local allies. The capture of Hong Kong was marked by the mass rape of at least 10,000 Chinese and European women (including nurses) and massacres of the kind that had occurred in Nanking three years before.[25] Extremes of wanton brutality and sadism were common on the Gilbert and Ellice Islands with the murder of Europeans, sexual assaults, beatings, forced labour and the massacre of 100 labourers and 150 lepers. This was unsurprising since, like the German empire, the Japanese rested on an ideology that denied the humanity of many of their subject races.[26]

In the sense that it marked a return to forms of government that respected human life and dignity, the restoration of British rule in South-East Asia and the Pacific was welcome and desirable. SEAC planners imagined that there was a strong residual loyalty to Britain in Malaya which would have been fortified by the cruelties of the Japanese.[27] The recovery of confidence in a British administration would, therefore, be easy. Reforms were instigated; as Churchill had promised after the fall of Singapore, a determined effort was to be made to assimilate the Chinese community and draw its members into public life. Yet, no chances were to be taken, for the blueprint for the governance of Malaya insisted that 'teachers refrain from reference to politics'.[28]

Political activity had increased under the Japanese occupation, particularly among the Chinese, for whom resistance to their new overlords was part of China's wider struggle against Japan. Almost immediately after Anglo-Indian troops had disembarked at Singapore early in September 1945, the Malayan Peoples Anti-Japanese Army told everyone that it alone had liberated the country.[29] Its large Communist element soon made its presence known and felt: the first year of the military administration was marked by a crime wave, and strikes and demonstrations against inflation and low wages. These disturbances were the first phase of a classic Communist stratagem: in the next three years Malaya was to be destabilised and its economy paralysed to create the ideal conditions for a popular revolution.[30]

Burmese nationalists had also used the war to widen their support and credibility. Before the war, they had been receptive to Japanese propaganda; one of their leaders, Aung San, had defected to Japan, and in 1942 nationalist guerrillas of his Burma Freedom Army had ambushed retreating British forces.[31] When they returned, at the beginning of 1945, they were struck by the chilliness of the newly emancipated Burmese: 'It wasn't a greeting such as [that] extended to troops in European towns.'[32] Many Burmese saw them not as liberators but as the advance guard of a restored ancien régime.

They were wrong; the British would soon leave Burma. Since late 1944 Amery, Lord Mountbatten (supreme commander of SEAC) and officials in London and Delhi had been drawing up plans for Burmese independence and a substantial grant for economic reconstruction. Churchill was displeased and growled about taking 'steps in miniature in Burma which will afterwards bring the destruction of our Indian Empire', but he caved in, grudgingly.[33] The alternative was a political row within the coalition (Labour was already committed to Burmese independence) and another with the men on the spot, Wavell and Mountbatten. Furthermore, any attempt to restore imperial government would have triggered an uprising by the well-armed and experienced Burma Freedom Army, which was estimated to be 10,000 strong.[34] An accord was reached with that consummate weathercock 'General' Aung San, whose guerrillas had switched sides and were now fighting the Japanese.* During the next two years, an interim military administration prepared the ground for self-government.

*

* His daughter Aun Sang Suu Kyi has become Burma's Joan of Arc.

Churchill would brook no compromise in the Middle East. Britain was now the outright winner in the twenty-seven-year-old contest for the Ottoman Empire, having seen off Italian intruders, pro-German insurgents in Iraq, squashed anti-British movements in Egypt, and bundled the French out of Syria and the Lebanon. Churchill was determined to build on wartime successes by the consolidation of British hegemony and the transformation of the region into the new hub of imperial military and political power. Oil supplies would be secure and, while the Middle East could not replace India, under British control it would provide a bulwark against any Soviet incursions southwards.[35] None was planned in 1945, but Stalin considered an offensive against Turkey and Persia in the following year. Russia would not passively stand by and let Britain do what it liked in its backyard.

Since late 1944, Churchill had been the mainspring behind policies contrived to reinforce Britain's Middle-Eastern imperium. The omens were discouraging. He hoped to negotiate a series of political accommodations that would satisfy Arab nationalists and keep their states within Britain's orbit. At the same time, Churchill the ardent Zionist wanted to create a Jewish polity inside the boundaries of Palestine. Post-war imperial strategy demanded that the new nation should be attached to the Empire, for it might have to host an emergency military base in the event of Britain losing control of Suez.

The Arabs had long made it clear that they wanted none of this, but, once the Axis threat to Egypt had been removed, their objections could be discounted. 'The Arabs', Churchill observed during discussions in Cairo in October 1944, 'have done nothing for us except to revolt against us in Iraq.' Nonetheless, they would require sensitive handling 'because of the Zionist pill which they'll have to swallow in Palestine'.[36] But could Britain force it down their throats without losing their already diminished goodwill?

The answer was plainly 'no' to judge from the protests of their rulers during the spring of 1945. Ibn Saud was adamant on the matter, so was the Regent of Iraq, who addressed Churchill as 'the noble person who represents the ideals of humanity' and the principles of the Atlantic Charter. 'Palestine', he insisted, 'is Arab as Devonshire is English, or

Virginia is American.'[37] In the same vein, Imam Yahia of the Yemen told Churchill that: 'I have no doubt that your lofty principles will preserve our hopes from destruction at the hands of some of the Jews of Europe.'[38]

King Abdullah of the Transjordan warned Churchill that the Arabs knew that Zionism now enjoyed the 'full sympathy' of America and that 'their future' rested in the hands of 'a great country other than Great Britain'.[39] He had clearly heard that a majority of Democrat and Republican candidates had endorsed the Zionist programme before the November 1944 Congressional election.[40] Roosevelt remained aloof, reluctant to become entangled in the Palestinian imbroglio for fear of adding to regional turbulence. Truman had no such inhibitions and soon declared himself pro-Zionist.

Among the concerns of the Regent of Iraq had been the spread of Jewish terrorist cells and clandestine paramilitary units. Their largely Eastern European membership adopted the violent political traditions of their homelands and, during 1944, they began a war of assassinations and sabotage. In the short term, their goal was the overthrow of the British authorities and in the long term they wanted an independent Jewish state in which the Arabs were subordinate. Some of the terrorists hoped to expel all Arabs and a few dreamed of a Jewish empire in the Middle East.

On 5 November 1944 two Stern Gang terrorists murdered Viscount Moyne, Churchill's friend and the Minister Resident in Cairo, and his chauffeur, Corporal Fuller. Moyne was sympathetic to Zionism, his driver's views are unknown. Churchill was profoundly shocked by a murder committed by what he later called 'a set of gangsters worthy of Nazi Germany', and he urged the authorities in Cairo to expedite the hanging of the assassins.[41] One had claimed before his execution that he [had] hoped to kill Churchill, a frequent visitor to Cairo.[42]

Like the IRA, which they so closely resembled in grit and ruthlessness, the Stern Gang attempted to extend their operations to Britain; in 1947 letter bombs were sent to Churchill, Attlee and Eden and an attempt was made to dynamite the Colonial Office in Whitehall.[43] It is one the grotesque ironies of history that two Stern Gang commanders, Menachim Begin and Yitzhak Rabin, became prime ministers of Israel, a nation that found itself waging war against the sort of terrorism they had advocated as the only path to nationhood.

Churchill's immediate reaction to the Moyne murder was to order a vigorous clampdown in Palestine, but without reducing the forces currently fighting the Communists in Greece. Hitherto, his dedication to the Zionist project had been as strong as ever; in 1941 he expressed the hope that a state 'inhabited by millions of Jews' would be a product of a post-war peace conference.[44] It would co-exist with an Arab union led by Ibn Saud and have American backing. A day before Moyne's death, Churchill had been discussing the future flow of Jewish immigration with Weizmann, who hoped that it would total a million and a half during the next ten years.[45] Most if not all would be men and women who had survived the Holocaust, whose scope was now known to the Arabs.

After Moyne's assassination, Churchill's enthusiasm for Zionism withered and his dealings with Weizmann became cold and formal. The terrorist offensive gathered momentum during 1945 and, during the second half of the year, there were attacks on Jews in Cairo, the Transjordan and Libya. The Zionist project which Churchill had sympathetically guided during its early years was unravelling and with it his hopes for an enduring Anglo-Arab accord in the Middle East.

Churchill had tried very hard, but he had always underestimated the depth of Arab passion and he had failed to understand that his zealous, public attachment to Zionism made him suspect in their eyes. Moreover, in the early days of Jewish colonisation in Palestine, he had advocated it as useful to British imperial interests, which, of course, did not win Arab hearts. Throwing money at princes did not convert them or their subjects, although it did secure their temporary passivity. In a sense, Churchill had failed, but then, no other statesman has yet succeeded in achieving harmony between the Arabs and the Jews, or an end to the intermittent and bloody war that began when Lord Moyne and his driver were killed.

PART SIX

1945–1955

Abiding Power:

The Empire and the Cold War, 1946–1951

Between 1945 and 1951, Churchill strenuously endeavoured to advance two causes close to his heart. The first was the British Empire, which he believed was falling victim to a crisis of confidence among his countrymen who seemed incapable of summoning up the will to rule. He chided them for their neglect of a precious asset and resurrected pre-war arguments in an attempt to delay Indian independence. Churchill also cast himself as a knight errant for what was now being called the Free World; he delivered uplifting and cautionary speeches to European and American audiences, which praised its humane virtues, and alerted listeners to the dangers of Soviet aggrandisement and Communist subversion. Although out of office, he used his reputation to assume the role of a world statesman and with it the right to communicate freely with foreign heads of state, in particular Truman.[1]

Churchill was also taking care of his reputation, writing, with the assistance of a team of historians, the six volumes of his war memoirs. He also led the Conservative opposition, which was not an entirely congenial task. As Macmillan observed, he 'rode magnificently in the saddle of the state but uneasily in that of the party'.[2] Churchill the social reformer and free trader was never wholly comfortable in a party with little sympathy for either cause, and which still contained crusty backbenchers who had never completely forgiven his past apostasies and the unseating of Chamberlain. Nevertheless, the diehards responded well to Churchill's contemptuous distaste for the 'Socialists', as he called the Labour Party.

Churchill's judgement on the first year of the Labour government was caustic and bleak: 'We are all under the harrow and our position in the East is clattering down in full conformity with our financial situation at home.' Major Attlee was dismantling the Empire at breakneck speed, starting with its keystone, India. Burma and Ceylon were on the eve of independence, and Churchill denounced the Foreign Office's efforts to reach an agreement with Egypt as a 'scuttle' that would deprive Britain of a base 'from which to pursue our imperial aims'. Meanwhile, Keynes was in Washington endeavouring to extract a loan to tide over a nation that was tottering towards insolvency. At home, bread was rationed and, in 1947, potatoes.

These misfortunes were the consequence of what Churchill saw as a supine acceptance that national decline was an irreversible. He could never fathom how Britain, having won the war, could allow its power to perish.[3] The old, high-minded and selfless ideals that had been the mainspring of the Empire were being shed by Labour, a party, which, he believed, had never cared much for them.

While Churchill deplored Labour's betrayal of the Empire, its ministers were cutting deals with Indian and Burmese politicians and contriving constitutions, which, it was hoped, would somehow protect the rights of ethnic and religious minorities. In December 1946 he condemned the helter-skelter rush to independence for Burma that denied those Burmese 'who appreciate the blessings of British rule' the chance to express their views. In India, an 'evil process' was now in motion that would end in yet another 'scuttle'.[4] The tragedy he had long foretold was approaching its hideous denouement. During 1946 and the first half of 1947, vast areas of the sub-continent were convulsed by 'strife and bloodshed, and the promise of worse' as Hindus and Muslims murdered each other in a grisly rehearsal for the large-scale massacres that accompanied the demarcation of the boundaries between India and Pakistan in August and September.[5]

Partition, Churchill thought, had some merit in so far that it would spare Muslims what he called 'Hindu caste rule'. It also served imperial interests, since the rejection of Muslim demands for an independent state would have added to anti-British grievances among the Arabs. Yet, ironically, Indian independence severely reduced Britain's military power and scope for manoeuvre in the Middle East. As Churchill reminded the Commons in July 1951, the nation could no longer deploy 'the well-placed and formidable resources of the imperial armies in India' to control the region.[6] The burden of policing the Empire was now being shouldered by eighteen-year-old national servicemen, for the loss of India had compelled the government to extend wartime conscription indefinitely.

Churchill's arguments rested on the hitherto unassailable logic of imperial security that had guided governments throughout his lifetime: the Indian Army was the linchpin of British power in Asia. The Chiefs of Staff agreed and, during 1948, they contemplated hiring Pakistani troops for service in the Middle East.[7] None were available because Pakistan needed all the men it could muster as it had become embroiled in what turned out to be a protracted armed confrontation with India over who owned Kashmir. Indo-Pakistani tensions gave substance to Churchill's old fears that a divided sub-continent would fall prey to Russia. In his mind at least, the Great Game was still being played.

Burma quickly left the Commonwealth, but India, Pakistan and Ceylon became dominions and republics. They did not automatically align themselves with Britain and the old Commonwealth in the Cold War. They pursued neutrality and India promoted itself as the leader in the United Nations of the growing block of uncommitted nations. It also used that forum to challenge the system of apartheid [racial separation] which, together with white supremacy, were the avowed policies of the Afrikaner nationalists who were elected into power in South Africa in 1948. When, in October 1948, a meeting of representatives of the dominion intelligence agencies was convened in London to coordinate intelligence responses to Communist subversion, it was thought prudent to exclude India, Pakistan and Ceylon.[8] Their anti-Communist credentials were dubious and so they could not be trusted with sensitive information.

Pre-war and wartime differences had clearly demonstrated that the old dominions were loyal in spirit, but independent in mind. Their governments were conscious that the war had reduced Britain's standing in the world and, by May 1944, they had doubts about her 'capacity' to remain one of the three great powers.[9] Events of the next six years did nothing to change their outlook and when the dominion prime ministers assembled in London in June 1951, their prevailing mood was deeply pessimistic. According to Macmillan, the general feeling was that 'England was finished' and that 'the sun had set'.[10]

The war against Japan had taught Australia and New Zealand to look to the United States for their future security. In August 1945,

Australia's Labour government was thinking in terms of their nation's future international role was as 'a principal Pacific power'. Dr Evatt predicted that Australia would assume the leadership 'of small and medium nations' within the United Nations.[11] Thereafter, Australia's attentions were drawn towards what Menzies (re-elected in December 1949) revealingly described as his nation's 'near north', that is the Far East.[12] New Zealand felt the same way and, in 1949, it sent troops to reinforce the Hong Kong garrison after the Communist victory in China. New Zealand, Australia, Canada and South Africa sent contingents to the United Nations forces during the Korean War (1950–3). The old, if not the new Commonwealth was playing its part in the Cold War.

Despite his belief that the Empire was continually evolving, Churchill never came to terms with the loss of India. His public appeals founded on his own faith in his country's imperial destiny had gone unheeded and, as he was aware, had made him unpopular with the electorate.[13] Between 1945 and 1947, voters were overwhelmingly concerned with keeping warm, having enough food to eat, and heeding official exhortations to work hard and rebuild the economy. Churchill's lamentations struck no chords with his countrymen and women, and their indifference seemed to him proof of the decay of those imperial certainties that had prevailed when he entered politics and which had survived the First World War. They had been nourished and applied because of the will of men like himself and their faith in Britain's mission. The Attlee government would have denied this; the Empire rested on the consent of its subjects and this had all but been withdrawn in India by 1946, if not earlier. Moreover, within the Foreign and Colonial Office plans were being drawn up to balance the loss of India by forming what was in effect a 'new' Empire whose foundations would be Britain's African colonies and Malaya. All was not lost.

As to Churchill's many references to national will, were they mere rhetoric, or were they capable of being translated into action? One of the most intriguing unknowns about Churchill was whether, had he won the election in 1945, he would have clung on to India. Would he have postponed independence by the application on a far larger scale of the tough measures that had broken the Quit India movement three years before? It was a subject on which Attlee once briefly speculated during a Commons debate in 1951, but drew no response from Churchill.[14]

Churchill seemed to provide an answer when, as Prime Minister, he attended the Bermuda three-power summit in December 1953. The two other delegates, President Eisenhower and French Prime Minister Joseph Laniel heard him praise what he called France's 'valiant effort to preserve her empire and the cause of freedom in Indo-China'. He then contrasted French resolve with Britain's loss of nerve in India, where she had 'cast away her duties' and precipitated a 'colossal disaster'.[15]

This was a staggering revelation, not least because France was in the eighth year of a grinding war against the Viet Minh partisans, during which yearly losses had averaged about 30,000 and annual campaign expenses were $1,000 million.[16] Churchill was well aware of this, which suggests that he would have been ready to dispense blood and treasure on such a scale to retain India.

The odds in such a war would have been stacked against Britain. From late 1945, India had passed into a limbo: rulers and ruled agreed that self-government was inevitable and everyone was waiting for the transfer of power. The old machinery of control and coercion had ground to a halt by early 1946, with the result that riots and massacres went largely unchecked. Millions of Indians, including ex-servicemen, had expectations of independence that would not have been dispelled by its postponement and the suspension of political life.

The loyalty of Indian forces could no longer be taken for granted (there were mutinies in the Indian navy and air force during 1946) and there were indications that British servicemen might not have had much stomach for a war to save the Raj. Servicemen in India wanted to be demobbed as soon as possible; newly conscripted eighteen-year-olds ordered to oversee the restoration of imperial government in Malaya were sullen; and there were fifteen mutinies by RAF personnel between October 1945 and April 1946, all Communist inspired.[17]

It was inconceivable that the British people, long conditioned to think that their Empire was benevolent in spirit and, therefore, well loved by its subjects would have tolerated a war to deny India its freedom. Truman's administration, which from 1946 was underwriting Britain's military budget, would also have been horrified and would certainly have intervened. In 1948, Washington threatened to cut off Marshall Aid to the Netherlands if it did not end its war against Indonesian nationalists. The Dutch withdrew, Indonesia became an independent republic and joined the non-aligned bloc of nations that was emerging under India's leadership.

America was facing a dilemma. It was ready to give wholehearted backing to any colonial war in which the insurgents were Communist and, for this reason, encouraged Britain to suppress the uprising in Malaya that began in June 1948. Yet it was desperately anxious not to be seen as the patron and ally of an imperialism that suppressed movements which sought independence and democracy. America had to show the world that the Free World was really on the side of freedom, and so, if a war of independence had occurred in India like that being waged in Indonesia (or in America after 1775), then the United States would have been morally shamed by its closest ally. Such conflicts, real or potential, would have been a godsend for Soviet propaganda. Political and economic realities meant that Churchill's call for old-style imperial resolve in India was foolhardy tub-thumping.

Henceforward, the Cold War would dictate imperial policy. It became, next to the Empire, Churchill's chief obsession. Speaking at Strasbourg in 1946, he predicted that Russia, abetted by 'Communist parties' in France, Italy and South-East Asia was now a threat to 'civilisation'.[18] His own Chiefs of Staff had concurred and, in June 1945, added the Middle East and Persia to the list of Soviet objectives.[19]

Churchill was game for another trial of strength with Britain's old imperial antagonist and he threw himself into the task of rallying the forces of the Free World. He was uniquely qualified to do so: the war had made him a heroic figure whose leadership, foresight and tenacity of purpose were universally admired. Of the three architects of victory, Roosevelt was dead and Stalin chose to stay put in Moscow, for he had a phobia about crossing Russia's borders and, with the exception of the Tehran Conference, insisted that foreign leaders met him on home ground. By contrast, Churchill was happy to go wherever he was asked to make speeches. He was now an oracle whose accumulated wisdom and experience gave authority to whatever he said.

Sibylline declarations were accompanied by advice as to how the capitalist democracies could best counter Russian aggression and subversion. He urged the speedy reconstruction of the non-Communist states of Europe and their integration into an economic and political union. In a speech made in Brussels in November 1945 he forecast that the 'United States of Europe' would bring a unity to the continent that had not been seen since the Roman era.[20] Yet Britain would remain aloof from this new entity, acting as 'the manager rather than a player in the European team'.[21]

Churchill had found a new world role for the Empire and Commonwealth as crucial as those it had played during two world wars. This was the gist of his famous address delivered at Fulton (Missouri) in March 1946. It is remembered for his image of the 'Iron Curtain' that now split Europe, but, as the Russians gleefully pointed out, the expression had been first coined by Goebbels towards the end of the war.[22] Churchill's principal message was one of hope, designed to stiffen the sinews of Americans. They were assured that there were eighty million 'Britons' of the Commonwealth and Empire standing shoulder to shoulder with them, allies of the spirit who were 'united in the defence of our traditions, our way of life and the world causes which you and we espouse'. Bonded by common ideals 'the English-speaking Commonwealth' and America would prove irresistible and ultimately triumphant.

Ninety-three Labour MPs protested that the Fulton speech had been provocative. Six years later, Churchill reminded the Commons that the anti-Communist front he had proposed was now Labour's own foreign policy.[23] There were the expected explosions in Moscow, where *Pravda* accused Churchill of cynically furthering British interests. 'The British Empire,' it alleged, 'although a junior partner, is continuing its policy of imperialist expansion.'[24]

This expression 'junior partner' had been used in one of the many Foreign and War Office evaluations of Britain's future in the post-war world compiled between 1944 and 1947. Their tone was surprisingly upbeat, with one report arguing that 'we must exert ourselves to the full to retain our prestige and authority without living beyond our

means'. Britain, the Commonwealth and Empire still remained a
great power, but one that was now the 'junior partner' of the United
States. British diplomats flattered themselves that their subordination
was balanced by an ample stock of 'worldly wisdom' with which to
guide the Americans, who did not always defer to this sophistication
which was often accompanied by condescension.[25]

Stalin suspected the Anglo-American ties were brittle and, early in
1946, he contrived a test to expose their true strength. In January, the
Pentagon received intimations that he was making tentative moves to
reassert Russian interests in two regions where it had always thrown
its weight around, the Near East and Persia. Both lay within Britain's
imperial sphere of influence and Stalin was eager to find out whether
the United States would come to the rescue if it was challenged. As
the Soviet ambassador in Washington later explained, 'the current
relations between England and the United States, despite temporary
attainment of agreement on very important questions, are currently
plagued with great internal contradictions and cannot be lasting.'[26]

Russia moved in a characteristically crab-like manner. Stalin
resurrected his request made at Potsdam for a naval base on the
shores of the Dardanelles and free passage for Soviet warships to and
from the Black Sea. In Russian eyes, this was a legitimate demand,
for, as Molotov explained to Ernie Bevin, the Foreign Secretary,
Britain had accepted similar demands during the First World War.[27]
Russia then beat the war drum; over half a million soldiers were
concentrated in Bulgaria to frighten the Turks. Britain's Chiefs of Staff
rightly suspected a bluff, but their American counterparts thought
otherwise.[28] Persia too was bullied to extract oil concessions: Russian
agents fomented subversion on its northern frontier and an armoured
column was ordered to Tehran to scare the Shah's ministers.

Truman dug in his heels. Hitherto he had been feeling his way
cautiously towards a firm policy towards Russia and he had been
taken aback by Churchill's uncompromising phrases at Fulton. A
few months later he felt the moment had come to get tough on the
grounds that: 'We might as well find out whether the Russians were
bent on world conquest now as in five years time.'[29] An American
armada anchored in the Sea of Marmora as a token of the President's
intention to protect Turkish integrity and his country's willingness

to uphold Britain's regional hegemony. Churchill was delighted and sent Truman a telegram of congratulations.³⁰ He later endorsed the President's subsequent warning that America would never flinch from using its growing arsenal of Atomic bombs in defence of the Free World.

Stalin backed off. America would risk war to preserve British paramountcy in the Near and Middle East. He had never intended to fight, nor was he in a position to do so if things had got out of hand. Russia was currently demobilising its wartime forces (Churchill was worried by the slowness of this process), pruning its military budget and reconstructing its industries. Justifying his withdrawal from Persia empty-handed, Stalin served notice that his sights were now set on the European empires in Asia and Africa. The Soviet Union was poised to 'unleash the liberation movement in the colonies', but first it was necessary to remove the Russian army of occupation from northern Persia. Not to do so, he argued, would have compromised 'our liberationist policy'.³¹

For the next forty years, Soviet propagandists undertook a titanic exercise in hypocrisy by their insistence that imperialism (its alternative label was 'colonialism') was one of the defining vices of all the enemies of Communism. As in 1918, Russia proclaimed itself the patron and helpmate of all colonial nationalist movements, which were now more widespread and more impatient than they had been then. America was compelled to tread warily, since it could never afford to be identified with colonialism for risk of driving Asian and African nationalists towards the Soviet Union, or, after 1949, Communist China. Paradoxically, Russia, the cynical champion of the oppressed of Africa and Asia, openly retained its old expansionist ambitions. As Molotov once remarked, 'I saw my task as foreign minister as that of expanding the bounds of our fatherland as far as possible.'³²

It is worth pausing for a moment to consider that Stalin, like Churchill, was a child of the age of empires described in chapter three and he had inherited many of its assumptions and preoccupations. Each leader saw the world in terms of power blocks jockeying for strategic and economic advantage and, where possible, settling their disagreements by a mixture of threats and give-and-take diplomacy. Both accepted in varying degrees a belief that national self-interest was paramount, although in Stalin's case it was disguised by ideological considerations, and neither had any qualms about the principle of one nation occupying and ruling over others. Of course there were divergences of opinion as to the rules by which subject polities were governed: the Soviet administration of Latvia, say, was infinitely harsher and more restrictive than its British counterpart in the Gold Coast. In essence, Stalin and Churchill treated the Cold War as a revival of the pre-1914 power politics.

Superficially, the Near and Middle East appeared to be in safe and strong hands. Since 1943, Churchill had been busy reanimating and adjusting the mechanisms of unofficial empire by which Britain had exercised its control over Persia, Iraq, Jordan (formerly Transjordan), Palestine, Egypt and the Yemen. Despite misgivings about Palestine, their hereditary princes were Britain's accomplices and, by birth and inclination, all hated Communism.

Yet, Britain's grip was slackening. It was being gradually prised open by indigenous nationalisms which thrived in universities, schools, officers' messes and on the streets, and their offshoot, Pan-Arabism. These movements were fissile and often divided by rows over methods, ideologies and aims, but they were united by Anglophobia; Britain remained an incorrigible and malevolent power bent on using all its strength to frustrate Arab aspirations. Before and during the war these had been focused on Palestine, where Britain had repeatedly ignored Arab protests about Jewish immigration and had brushed aside fears that it was willing to play fairy godmother to a future Jewish state.

Arab apprehension and a sense of collective impotence were ignited in September 1947 when Britain, wearied by its two-year-old war against Jewish terrorists, surrendered its mandate to govern Palestine to the United Nations. With the backing of Truman and American Zionists, the insurgents declared Israel an independent state. A civil war followed between Palestinians and Jews in which hundreds of Arabs were massacred and three-quarters of a million were herded into refugee camps in the Lebanon, Jordan and Gaza. Egypt and neighbouring Arab states invaded Israel and were repelled during 1948. This debacle proved a turning point in Britain's relations with the Arab world: its forces had failed to overcome Jewish terrorism, it had cut and run, and, as in India, the transition of power was chaotic and bloody. The stage was set for future conflict. Churchill had opposed the repudiation of the mandate, although he had not pressed for the severe measures which alone might have preserved it. He called for Britain to recognise Israel, although he regretted the recent metamorphosis of his idealistic Zionism into a pugnacious, acquisitive and racial nationalism.

What happened in Palestine during 1947 and 1948 was a bitter reminder that the Arabs were a people to whom things happened, rather than a people who made them happen. The immediate result was an eruption of fury across the Middle East which reached even the remotest areas. News of the events in Palestine sparked off anti-Jewish riots in Aden in December 1947, where the authorities were horrified to find the levies recruited in the backward tribal hinterland joined in the looting and murders. 'Stern repressive measures' restored order and there were a hundred casualties, most of them Jewish.[33]

The British soldiers who suppressed the Aden disturbances had been airlifted from Egypt. It was the unwilling host to 70,000 British servicemen who guarded and maintained a sprawling complex of airfields, storehouses, barracks and depots that covered 3,600 square miles alongside the Suez Canal. This base was the citadel of British military power in the region and an outlying Cold War bastion which guarded the oilfields and refineries of Persia, Iraq and their developing counterparts in Saudi Arabia, Bahrain and Qatar. All were crucial for the security of the West, for, as a CIA analysis of 1947 explained, 'Access to the oil of the Persian Gulf area and the denial of control over the Mediterranean to a major hostile, expansionist power [i.e. Russia] are deemed essential to the security of the United States.' Britain's local preponderance of power was necessary for political stability. A State Department regional assessment of 1952 warned that if the independent Arab states were ever tempted into Russia's orbit, then 'the immediate as well as the ultimate cost to the United States would be incalculable'.[34]

In the event of a war with Russia, Egyptian airfields were earmarked for America's aerial offensive against industrial targets, oil wells, refineries and communications in an area bounded by the Urals, the Caspian and the Black Sea. These attacks would be made by B29 bombers flown from the United States to Egypt and were to be complemented by raids from American airfields in eastern England against targets in northern Russia.[35] Atomic bombs were to be used (the United States Army Air Force had 80 in 1948 and 300 by 1950), but Washington kept the British government in the dark as to how many were to be dropped and where.[36] British strategists were also planning conventional sorties against Russia from Egypt. The highly secret British Atomic bomb programme, which had been approved by Attlee and a tiny cabal of ministers early in 1946, incorporated plans for the weapons' eventual use against Soviet and Romanian oil refineries.[37]

As Churchill had foreseen at Fulton, the Commonwealth and Empire had become deeply engaged in the Cold War. During 1948 and 1949, the Labour government opened talks with the dominions about the despatch of contingents to the Middle East in the event of war. The response was cool: Canada's commitment as a member of NATO was to assist keeping the Atlantic open, Australia and New Zealand were preoccupied with the security of the Far East and the Pacific, and South Africa had to be bribed with promises of modern jet fighters.[38] During 1949, the British government considered plans to enlist a 400,000-strong African equivalent of the Indian army for garrison duties in the Middle East, but these came to nothing. Among the objections were those of sceptical army officers who questioned whether Africans possessed the same martial qualities as the warrior races of India.[39] Commonwealth forces were also expected to take their share of the defence of the Mediterranean and southern Europe. In 1951 the Mediterranean Fleet based on Gibraltar and Malta included three aircraft-carriers, seven cruisers and sixty-nine destroyers and frigates, some of which were allocated to operations in Italy and Yugoslavia in the event of a Russian thrust southwards.[40]

These concentrations of ships, aircraft and men amply fulfilled Churchill's pledge that the 'abiding power' of the British Empire would play its part in the Cold War. American staff planners were uneasy as to whether Britain was up to the job. In 1947 William Clayton, a level-headed Texan and an assistant secretary at the State Department, minuted: 'The reins of world power leadership are now slipping fast from Britain's competent but weak hands.[41] This was woefully self-evident: the British government had just announced that it would pull out its forces from Greece and within the next twelve months it would depart ignominiously from Palestine and India.

The sequence of hurried and humiliating exoduses reflected Britain's economic weaknesses, which been revealed by Keynes during the recent negotiations for a \$3,750 million loan. The money was 'principally required to fund military expenditure overseas' and, he argued, if it was not forthcoming, then 'a large-scale withdrawal from international responsibilities is inevitable'. Or, as he expressed it on another occasion, 'we cannot police half the world at our expense when we have gone into pawn with the other.'[42]

America conceded the loan (the final repayment was made in 2006), cut the outstanding Lend-Lease debt, and fortified its allies with dollars. Greece received \$300 million to train and equip its armed forces and a further \$200 million was advanced to Turkey for the same purpose. Under the 1947 Marshall Aid scheme immense sums were pumped into Western Europe to stabilise shaky economies and reconstruct fractured industries, in particular those of Allied occupation zones in Germany. Big cheques were accompanied by a pledge to wield the big stick: the Truman doctrine committed his country to the worldwide containment of Communism.

Four years after Fulton, British power was looking increasingly threadbare and transient. Britain could barely take the strain of holding the line in the Mediterranean and the Near and Far East as it had done between 1940 and 1942. Quite simply, it lacked the clout, as had been spectacularly proved by its flight from Palestine and its failure to keep the lid down on nationalist agitation which flared up in Persia and Egypt during 1950.

Splutter of Musketry:

Small Wars, 1950–1951

In October 1951, Churchill, now aged seventy-seven, was again Prime Minister. During the general election, his party had campaigned on knife-and-fork domestic issues, such as housing, but he delivered a rousing imperial fanfare with an undertaking to restore the nation's greatness. During the past six years, Britain 'had fallen from the high rank we have won' and our enemies 'rejoice to see what they call "the decline and fall of the British Empire"'.[1] Once in office, Churchill would reverse this process.

The British Empire had plenty of enemies in 1951. Farouk had assumed the role of a patriot king and added his voice to popular demands for Britain to leave its bases in Egypt. His ministers tore up the 1936 Anglo-Egyptian Treaty and the Canal Zone came under virtual siege. Egyptian workers walked out, there were acts of sabotage and terrorism, and anti-British demonstrations. Nationalists were also taking to the streets and shouting anti-British slogans in Persia, where the newly elected Prime Minister, Dr Muhammad Mussadiq, had just endorsed the nationalisation of the Anglo-Iranian Oil Company [AIOC].

Churchill also inherited two anti-Communist wars from Labour. One was against the guerrilla army of the Malayan Communist Party, and the other was being waged in the name of the United Nations against Communist North Korea, heavily supported by men and matériel from China. Since June 1950, substantial British and Commonwealth land, air and naval forces were deployed in defence of the ideological and territorial integrity of South Korea, although the brunt of the war effort was borne by the United States. The conflict was an unwelcome distraction for Britain, since it diverted its already stretched forces from the Middle East and it wrecked Labour's efforts to balance the budget.

For Churchill, the Malayan and Korean conflicts were the

realisation of the vision of the Empire and Commonwealth getting to grips with Communism. He was, however, sorry that the 'First Commonwealth Division' in Korea had not been named the 'Empire and Commonwealth Division'.[2] Four months after becoming Prime Minister, he spoke proudly of six British divisions 'resisting the communist menace or other forms of communist inspired disorder in the Middle and Far East'.[3] He assumed, as did many pundits in Whitehall and Washington, that anti-British agitation in the Middle East was fuelled by Soviet subversion.

Paranoia about Russia's clandestine activities was understandable. During 1949 the balance of power in the Cold War had shifted dramatically: Russia had tested its first Atomic bomb and Mao Zedong had defeated the remnants of Chiang Kai-Shek's armies and taken control of China. In Indo-China the Communist insurgents were giving the French a rough time, and in Malaya the British had yet to secure the upper hand in a jungle campaign.

Operations in Malaya were part of the Cold War and were undertaken by British, Commonwealth and Imperial units. British regulars and national servicemen fought alongside Australian, New Zealand, Fijian, East African contingents, locally recruited units, and Dyak headhunters imported from Sarawak and North Borneo to hunt down the partisans in the forests. To counter accusations that Britain was fighting an old-style campaign to perpetuate imperial rule, the war was labelled an 'Emergency'. This euphemism was not inappropriate since Britain had promised that Malaya would become independent after the fighting had stopped, but only on terms that would not jeopardise British strategic and economic interests, which ruled out any arrangement that would have included Communist politicians.

Malaya was Britain's most valuable colonial asset. Its rubber and tin exports earned Britain about £170 million a year in much-needed dollars. American demand soared after 1950, when it adopted the policy of stockpiling essential raw materials in preparation for a war with Russia. The price of rubber more than doubled to £1,200 a ton, which was a stroke of luck for an impoverished Britain since it meant that the Malayan administration footed a substantial part of the bill for the war.

*

The Korean War was the result of a gamble, nervously undertaken by Stalin after his meeting with Kim Il Sung in March 1949. North Korea's 'President for Eternity' was promised Russian assistance for an invasion of South Korea.[4] The fighting began in June 1950 and within six months had got out of hand, with the United Nations forces colliding with half a million Chinese sent by Mao to rescue Kim Il Sung's retreating army.

The question of what to do next placed an enormous strain on Anglo-American relations, which had repercussions for Churchill when he came to power. Throughout 1951 there was a possibility that America would resort to Atomic bombs to redress the imbalance of manpower in Korea. This prospect frightened the cabinet and the Chiefs of Staff, not least because an atomic offensive against China could easily lead to a world war in which American bases in Britain would be the targets for Russian Atomic bombs. There was also resentment about the furtive way in which America handled the wider questions about the circumstances in which they would resort to an atomic offensive, and their target priorities.

Britain insisted in a say in these decisions. At the end of 1950, an anxious Attlee flew to Washington to dissuade Truman from complying with General MacArthur's request for an atomic attack on troop concentrations on the Chinese–North Korean border. The President was unconvinced, and irritated by the 'Limeys' meddling in American strategic decisions. In April 1951 he ordered the components of two bombs to be flown to the American base on Guam.[5] They remained there in readiness for possible use against the troops that were massing just beyond the Russian border with Korea. The British Chiefs of Staff looked on in trembling impotence. They dreaded MacArthur being offered a 'blank cheque' so that he could fight what Air Marshal Sir John Slessor called 'a big war' against China.[6] The tension subsided once Truman dismissed MacArthur and signalled that, for the time being, the United States would fight a conventional war in Korea. This did not prevent the new commander-in-chief General Mark Clark from asking for a strategic aerial offensive against China and a blockade of its ports.[7] There were further jitters in Whitehall since this strategy would endanger Hong Kong.[8]

Disputes over grand strategy during the Korean War were an awkward reminder that Britain was a subordinate partner whose views could be overridden if they contradicted what the administration judged to be in America's best interests. Churchill took office against a background of residual huffiness in Washington about the 'restraint' which Britain had attempted to impose on America's strategic options in Korea.[9]

The positions of the two powers were reversed during the Persian crisis in the summer of 1951. Washington urged caution, while the mood in Whitehall was hawkish and plans were being drawn up for an amphibious assault on Abadan, which was fittingly named 'Operation Buccaneer'. There was a snag: the buccaneer lacked a cutlass. The demands of the Korean War had overextended the Royal Navy and all that was immediately available was HMS *Mauritius*, which was ordered to Basra despite fears that it might be shelled as it steamed up the Shatt-al-Arab.[10]

A single cruiser was a token of British fury at the Persian parliament's decision, taken in April 1950, to nationalise AIOC's Abadan refinery and take control of the country's oil production. For Mussadiq, the Prime Minister and leader of the Nationalist Front Party, this coup was an overdue and well-deserved retaliation for all the slights and injustices his country had suffered at British hands for the past forty years. He was a fervent nationalist with a mercurial temperament and given to tearful outbursts which embarrassed British and American diplomats who thought he was mad. They (and Churchill) speculated as to whether he was being egged on by Russia, although Mussadiq was a landowner, a member of Persia's traditional ruling elite, and a conservative. He did, however, welcome support from the Tudeh, Persia's Communist Party, to maintain his parliamentary majority.

The AIOC was a perfect target for nationalist animus. It was a grasping corporation that had squeezed Persia, safe in the knowledge that the strong arm of Britain would protect it from the anger of its hosts. The company paid the Persian government a niggardly 13 to 15 per cent of its annual revenues, which, in 1950, totalled £100 million, whilst ARAMCO delivered Ibn Saud half its income. Eighty-five per cent of AIOC was owned by the British government and its American sales earned dollars for Britain. Britain stood to lose, but so did Persia, for the oil revenues comprised over 40 per cent of its annual income. Mussadiq's response was to ask for subsidies from Britain and the United States to stave off an economic crisis.

Attlee's government settled for a war of economic attrition. During the summer, Persian assets were frozen, British administrators and technicians were evacuated from Abadan and the refinery ceased production. It was hoped that a sharp fall in revenues would compel Mussadiq to accept Britain's offer of placing the matter before the International Court of Justice at The Hague. Dean Acheson, the Secretary of State, was relieved, for he had predicted that British troops coming ashore at Abadan would give Russia an excuse to slip back into northern Persia. Every international dispute now had a Cold War dimension.

The Persian crisis was debated in the Commons at the end of July. Skirting around the fact that a lack of resources had ruled out a military response, the Foreign Secretary, Herbert Morrison, reminded members that the country had to tread carefully, or risk international (i.e. United Nations) criticism of 'our allegedly imperialist designs'. Churchill offered no solution to the crisis, but used it as a stick with which to beat Labour, invoking its record of appeasement and surrender, that included the 'winding up' in Palestine, which had left Britain loathed by both Arabs and Jews.

This was a prudent tactic, although those on the right of his party (and some Labour MPs) were baying for Persian blood. In the early days of the crisis, Churchill pleaded for calm and urged his backbenchers to 'show great moderation and caution'. During discussions in the shadow cabinet as to whether or not British technicians should be withdrawn from Abadan, he warned against rash belligerence. With a general election likely to occur, he did not wish to be branded a warmonger.[11] This did not stop the Labour mouthpiece the *Daily Mirror* from asking the question: 'Whose finger on the trigger?' Churchill replied that it was preferable not to have a 'fumbling' one.

Churchill was suppressing his visceral desire to give the Persians a hard knock. When he visited Washington at the close of the year, he told Acheson that, if he had been in power, 'there might have been a splutter of musketry' heard in the oilfields.[12] This was braggadocio, but it brought hurrahs from many of his backbenchers and the editorial columns of the *Daily Express* and the *Daily Telegraph*. The jingoes did have a point, for there was a growing feeling in Whitehall that prevarication with Persia was bound to embolden the Egyptians to the point where they might dare to nationalise the Suez Canal.

34

A Falling from Power?
Atom Bombs and Arabs, 1951–1955

When he re-entered Downing Street, Churchill was convinced that he could still bend the world to his will, just as he had endeavoured to do between 1940 and 1945. His mental resolve remained strong, but his physical vigour was being eroded; he had a minor and then a major stroke in the summer of 1953, but, remarkably, he recovered within eight weeks. From time to time, his colleagues noted that his concentration drifted and he persisted in his old vice of tangential diversions. During the Bermuda summit in December 1953, he complained to his doctor that his intellectual stamina had faltered in the face of the intransigence of John Foster Dulles, President Eisenhower's Secretary of State. 'Dulles is a terrible handicap,' he grumbled. 'Ten years ago I could have dealt with him. Even as it is I have not been beaten by the bastard. I have been humiliated by my own decay.'[1]

The impossible task of making Dulles see reason was a small part of Churchill's grand design which, if it succeeded, would have fulfilled his hope that his 'last innings' would match, or even surpass his wartime performance. His aims were roughly the same as they had been then: to resist an expansionist power in the grip of a cruel ideology (Russia), to restore British power through a close partnership with the United States, and to conserve the British Empire. Churchill was also straining after a new goal, world peace, which, he told voters in 1951, he wanted to be his final 'prize'.[2]

Winning it was a matter of desperate urgency, for Churchill's fascination with science and war was as strong as ever and he grasped the immense destructive power of nuclear weapons. He pored over the forensic details of the human and physical consequences of the nuclear bombardment of cities provided by official scientists, which convinced him that it was imperative to secure a peace between the West and the East. A nuclear war could be averted by the revival of the wartime precedent of frequent, high-level summit meetings. Through the force of his personality, Churchill could again direct history, which was why he was in Bermuda enduring Dulles's sermons on Russian Communism.

New problems resisted old panaceas. The world was changing in ways that Churchill found bewildering and disturbing: after a cabinet meeting in September 1952, Macmillan noted in his diary that the Prime Minister 'although as brilliant as ever, ... is lost (perhaps we all are) in this strange post-war world, at home and abroad'.[3] Faced with the alien and unpredictable, Churchill became increasingly prone to contrast a bleak present with that golden age of his imagination which had been terminated in 1914. Fond memories of the glories of Empire and the Pax Britannica peppered his conversations and, as we will see, he sometimes contemplated applying its remedies to current problems. Churchill's nostalgia was selective and contrived, in so far as it overlooked the fact that his lost age had had its own fears and woes. In 1912 Churchill had agonised about the naval race and an impending European war; in 1952 he was disturbed by the nuclear arms race and the likelihood of an infinitely more destructive global war.

There were new actors on the international stage, small and middling nations whose voices were heard in the United Nations. Its membership grew from 55 in 1945 to 76 in 1955 and the newcomers included Pakistan, Burma, Israel and Indonesia, all former colonies. The pace of decolonisation and the general application of the newly created doctrines of universal human rights were being regularly discussed by the general assembly between 1951 and 1955. The airing of these subjects had implications for all the imperial powers, in particular Britain where the Foreign Office treated the United Nations as a moral forum whose opprobrium had to be avoided at all costs.

This was the reason why, in March 1954, Eden, the Foreign Secretary, overruled Churchill's proposal to send a 'punitive expedition' against Yemeni tribesmen who were making cross-border raids into the Aden Protectorate.[4] This was what would have happened in the age of the Pax Britannica, but in the new world such palliatives as the gunboat and the expeditionary force smacked of 'colonialism' and invited international censure. Washington too was critical of tough policies that were bound to upset non-aligned countries and which were also a bonus for the Soviet propaganda machine. Operations against the Mau Mau in Kenya were exploited for all they were worth with polemics that represented the insurgents as freedom fighters against imperial oppression. Taking their cue from the Communist *Daily Worker*, Soviet propagandists likened British forces to Hitler's SS.[5]

Throughout his life, Churchill had striven to preserve Britain's moral prestige, which he regarded as integral to national greatness. He was determined that it should not be sullied, either by the misconduct of Britain's servants, or those of its ally, the United States. In August 1952, he protested to Truman about America's resort to napalm bombing in Korea and he dissociated Britain from its use in 'crowded areas'.[6] During the Bermuda conference, he 'strongly resisted' President Eisenhower's proposal for an atomic attack on North Korea if it reneged on an armistice signed five months before.[7]

Churchill's intolerance of needless brutality in war extended to operations in Kenya, which outraged his sense of decency and humanity. In a private interview with the liberal Kenyan politician Michael Blundell in December 1954, he spoke candidly and tearfully about 'a horrible situation' which was 'getting Britain into a very bad odour'. It was abhorrent that a nation proud to be 'the home of culture, magnanimity of thought, with all the traditions of our country and democracy' should have sunk to such depths.[8] Yet he did little to dismiss or rein in panicky officers and proconsuls who had discarded their moral compasses on the grounds of military expediency. Had he expressed his disgust publicly, he would have discredited his own party, the reputation of the Empire and those who ran it. Details of the outrages that had so distressed Churchill were withheld from the British people for over thirty years and some remained deliberately hidden for a further thirty.[9]

Britain's nominal adherence to high ethical principles enhanced her international standing. Moral rectitude complemented the former instruments of British power – the Royal Navy and the Empire. In the years before and immediately after the war, Churchill had condemned what he saw as the erosion of the two constituents of this power and lamented his inability to save them. He returned to this theme in April

1954, when he told his cabinet colleagues how he had just received a gift from a pair of Chelsea pensioners who had served alongside him in the Malakand campaign, fifty-seven years before. 'What a period of time', he exclaimed, 'and what a falling from power.'[10]

This was true in atavistic Churchillian terms: the Grand Harbour at Valletta was no longer crowded with battleships and Bengal lancers no longer guarded the British legation in Tehran. Yet, Churchill and his ministers were busy preparing for Britain to begin an energetic climb up the ladder of power: the development of a Hydrogen bomb. Nuclear weapons were the mid-century equivalent of the dreadnought; the more a nation possessed, the more it was respected and feared. The United States and Russia had made the running in the nuclear race, followed by Britain and, during the next three decades, China, France, Pakistan, India, South Africa and Israel joined the field.

Churchill had been amazed when, soon after he took office, he first discovered the details of Britain's atomic programme, which must count as one of the best-kept state secrets of all time. His wonderment was blighted by dismay, for the files revealed that America had excluded British scientists from its own atomic research and that Washington had ignored requests for the inclusion of Soviet submarine and mine-laying bases in the list of America's priority targets.[11]

This indifference offered a vital clue as to why Attlee's government had proceeded to develop an A-bomb. It was a sharp reminder that the United States could never be wholly relied upon to deploy its own nuclear weapons to defend Britain, which, as a host to USAAF bases, was a prime target for a Soviet attack. Hitting them would be, in Churchill's own words, a 'bull's eye' for Russian bombers.[12] Nevertheless, with typical sentimental naivety, he imagined that, if asked, the United States would give Britain some Atomic bombs for her protection. He also had faith in the gentleman's agreement made at Quebec in 1943 which had given Britain a say in America's post-war atomic research. Eight years after, he discovered that the Americans were not the gentlemen he had supposed them to be when he read that they had refused permission for the British to test their prototype A-Bomb in the wastes of Nevada.

Churchill accepted the principle of an independent atomic arsenal and, in December 1951, he approved the test of Britain's Atomic bomb in the Monte Bello Islands, off the western coast of Australia. It was successfully carried out in October 1952 and the RAF received its first consignment of nuclear warheads the following year. One of the alternative test sites had been British Somaliland and subsequent nuclear tests were carried out in the Gilbert and Ellice Islands.

In April 1952, the cabinet agreed to the large-scale manufacture of nerve gas at a secret factory at Nancekuke in Cornwall. Within two years it was expected to be producing fifty tons a week and the Canadian government had agreed to trials of the gas in areas with arctic conditions similar to those of Russia.[13] At considerable cost and with Commonwealth cooperation, Britain was acquiring the armoury of a modern superpower.

Britain's future nuclear strategy relied upon airfields within the Empire. In June 1954 it was decided that, in the event of a Chinese thrust southwards into South-East Asia, Britain would respond with the tactical bombing of military targets inside China. The Chiefs of Staff insisted that 'Nuclear weapons should be used from the onset' against China, which then possessed none.[14] The attacks were to be launched from the RAF base at Tengah near Singapore. V-Bombers stationed at Akrotiri in Cyprus were earmarked for nuclear raids on targets in the southern Russian industrial heartlands. If this base was rendered unusable, these aircraft would be dispersed to airfields in Bahrain and Oman, which were still part of Britain's unofficial empire.[15]

Churchill may have brooded over the shrinking of British power, but his government's nuclear projects were more than ample compensation for past losses. The junior partner was recasting itself as a junior superpower. Atomic and later Hydrogen bombs defended Malaya from the Chinese and Britain from the Soviet Union, while what remained of the Empire was about to be rejuvenated through programmes of accelerated social and economic growth in Africa. Churchill's pessimism about the decay of national greatness was misplaced.

His moping over crumbling power was, however, justified by events in the Middle East, where Britain's former empire of influence and intimidation was expiring. In Egypt and in Persia, the nationalists were in the ascendant and growing more audacious in their demands. In October 1951 the Egyptian government demanded an immediate evacuation of the Suez Canal and full control over the Sudan. At home a knot of Tory backbenchers and the right-wing press clamoured for a vigorous reassertion of British power. Churchill was sympathetic and his fury erupted during informal ministerial discussions in mid-December:

[Churchill] made a tremendous attack on the Egyptians late at night ... Rising from his chair, the old man advanced on Anthony with clenched fists, saying in the inimitable Churchill growl, 'Tell them that if we have any more of their cheek we will set the Jews on them and drive them into the gutter, from which they should never have emerged.'[16]

There was another outburst in this vein at the end of January after a skirmish between British troops in Ismailia and an Egyptian police detachment in which fifty of the latter were killed. The Cairene mob went wild, set fire to those twin symbols of British supremacy, Shepheard's Hotel and the Turf Club, attacked British commercial premises and murdered British subjects. Churchill denounced all Egyptians as 'degraded savages', whose violence was proof that their country 'cannot be classified as a civilised power'. 'How different it would have been', he added, if the Labour government 'had not flinched at Abadan', conveniently forgetting that he had been in favour of moderation towards Persia.[17]

During January and February 1952, Macmillan noted that whenever the subject of Egypt cropped up at cabinet meetings, the Prime Minister's moods were 'black', 'growly' and 'rather obstinate and intransigent'. He was particularly displeased, when, on Eden's advice, the cabinet rejected a proposal to place an embargo on Egypt's sterling reserves for as long as anti-British demonstrations continued.[18] Churchill's belligerence infected his personal secretariat, who wanted the Foreign Office to administer a 'whiff of grape shot' to bring the Egyptians to heel.[19] The Suez Group, a knot of diehard Tory MPs, including Enoch Powell, formed in May 1951 and spoke the same language in the Commons.

A knockout blow against Egypt appealed to the national ego, but it would have risked the lives of British civilians in the country, who, the War Office argued, could not have been rescued before the onset of the fighting.[20] Churchill disregarded this warning and, a year later, he assured Eisenhower that British forces could prevent 'a massacre of white people'.[21]

The Prime Minister was on the warpath and in Whitehall staff officers were kept busy planning a *coup de main* to seize control of Egypt, just as Britain had done in 1882. It was called Operation Rodeo and its success depended upon a land, air and sea assault against Alexandria and a dash to Cairo, all to be accomplished within four or five days. Serious hitches emerged, however: there were shortages of landing craft and men, and there was every likelihood that the Egyptian army would resist the invasion.[22] The soldiers' hearts lay with the nationalists, as was amply proved in June 1953 when a knot of officers led by General Muhammad Neguib and Colonel Abdul Gamal Nasser deposed King Farouk and declared a republic. Nevertheless, Churchill, again sparing with the truth, told Eisenhower that little resistance could be expected from the Egyptian army.[23]

Despite his initial bombast, Churchill was anxious to find an escape route from the Egyptian quagmire that would avoid a war. The United States offered one. It had to be cajoled into taking a visible part in the defence of the Middle East, which, among other things, meant a garrison of American marines on Egyptian soil. This was one of the proposals Churchill took with him when he flew to Washington in December 1953. The Americans were not fooled; once their forces appeared in Egypt, their country would be identified with British imperialism, which was the last thing they wanted. As one congressman tartly observed, Churchill was desperate 'to get his country tied as closely as possible to the United States. What other hope has he?'[24]

Churchill had travelled to Washington confident that his personal magic could somehow resurrect the wartime alliance, but his hosts were of a different mind. His 'powerful and emotional declaration of faith' in Anglo-American cooperation was dismissed by Truman with the remark 'Thank you, Prime Minister. We might pass that on to be worked out by our advisers.'[25] Churchill persevered; in August 1952, when he was soliciting American help over the Persian crisis, he told Truman that: 'I thought it might be so good if we had a gallop together such as I often did with F.D.R.'[26] Truman's administration had no desire to bet on a jockey whose mount was ready to be put out to grass. In the same month, Acheson concluded that 'it is no longer safe to assume, automatically, that Britain can and should be considered the principal protector of Western interests in the Middle East'.[27] This duty would now pass to America, although the transfer of power was bound to be fraught since it required Britain to endure humiliation at the hands of the Egyptians and to reaffirm its subordination to the US.

Tensions and quarrels proliferated. Differences over the conduct of the Korean War and Britain's attitude towards Egypt were so rancorous that it was feared that the United States Navy might refuse to cooperate during the Royal Navy's exercises in the Mediterranean.[28] American approaches to Pakistan for an alliance were opposed by the Foreign Office, which considered them an unwarranted trespass on Britain's traditional sphere of influence.[29]

Churchill's optimistic faith in American altruism did not extend to his cabinet, nor to the right wing of his party. Eden's wartime hostility towards America and its motives was hardening. He could never bring himself to act the part of a junior partner in an unequal relationship and he chafed against this subservience. On his return from Washington in January 1952, he remarked that the Americans 'are polite, listen to what we have so say; but make (on most issues) their own decisions'.[30] Sir Evelyn Shuckburgh, Eden's principal private secretary, was of like mind, accusing the Americans of always placing their national interests ahead of Britain's. 'Having destroyed the Dutch empire, the United States are now engaged in undermining the French and British Empires as hard as they can.'[31] Macmillan, now Minister for Housing, shared these sentiments. In October 1952 he reflected on the 'mixture of patronising pity and contempt' with which the Americans treated Britain. They lacked any generosity of spirit and 'undermine our political and commercial influence all over the world'.[32] All this was true and reasonable, since it was right and proper for American politicians and bureaucrats to protect and advance their own national interests before all others.

This was heresy for Churchill and he ignored it. In February 1953 he told Eisenhower that: 'Anthony and I are resolved to make our cooperation with the United States effective over the world scene.'[33] 'Never be separated from the Americans' were his last words to his ministers before he left office on 5 April 1955.[34] The experience of the past four years of constraints and rebuffs had not shaken his faith in the United States.

Eden's doubts about America were important, for he was Churchill's heir-apparent, and, like Prince Hal, he was impatient to enter his inheritance. Like the physically infirm but mentally alert King Henry IV, the Prime Minister was apprehensive as to whether his successor had the qualities required to fulfil his duties. Eden sensed this lack of confidence and so disagreements between him and Churchill over policy towards Egypt and the United States were laced with an often thinly disguised personal animosity.

Churchill's faith in the Anglo-American accord suffered further blows after the election of Eisenhower in November 1952. He privately feared that a war was now 'more probable', which was understandable given that Ike's Secretary of State John Foster Dulles was an inflexible Cold War zealot.[35] Their ambition was the 'rolling back' of Soviet and Chinese power through a concerted political, economic and propaganda offensive in Asia and Africa. Europe's Asian and African empires were an obstacle which both Eisenhower and Dulles were determined to heave aside.

The latter was perfectly suited for this enterprise: he was a Baptist for whom the defeat of Communism was a religious duty (he once described himself as a 'Crusader') and he was utterly indifferent to British sensitivities and interests. The time had arrived for Britain to toe the line, as he bluntly explained to Eden in May 1954:

... the United States was eager to beat the Communists at their own game and so sponsor nationalism in the independent colonial areas, which was in accordance with our historic tradition, but that they were restrained from doing so by a desire to cooperate with Britain and France in Asia, in North America and in the Near and Middle East.[36]

A shocked Eden quite reasonably concluded that the Americans wanted Britain out of Egypt as fast as possible and that, in the long term they intended 'to run the world'.³⁷ Perhaps so, but it would be a world without empires.

Churchill thought Dulles a rebarbative bore with dangerous, warlike fixations. Worse still, his anti-imperialist prejudices made him a substantial obstacle to the re-establishment of the old Anglo-American *entente*. Nonetheless, with the persistence of a discarded wooer, determined to reignite the embers of a past love, he proceeded to court Eisenhower. All would come right if only Churchill could press his suit in person, and so he proposed a meeting between himself, Joseph Laniel the French Prime Minister and Eisenhower in Bermuda, where he chose a hotel with a golf course to keep the President happy. This conference was postponed after Churchill's stroke in June 1953 and finally convened in December.

During 1952 and 1953 Churchill found that Eisenhower had nothing to offer Britain but that cheapest of all political commodities, goodwill.³⁸ In private, the President was exasperated by what he called Churchill's 'childlike' belief that all the world's problems could be solved by the resuscitation of the wartime Anglo-American partnership.³⁹ Like Roosevelt, Eisenhower considered the Prime Minister a Victorian in his attitude to Britain's place in the world. As for Egypt, Eisenhower and Dulles hoped that Britain would depart with as little fuss as possible.

Once British servicemen had returned home, the State Department would be free to negotiate an anti-Communist alliance between Egypt, Turkey and the Arab kingdoms. This Middle Eastern counterpart to NATO would be led and funded by the United States, which would replace Britain as the dominant regional power. Egypt would be the fulcrum of this new bloc and the CIA had already identified and was making friends with the country's new power-brokers, a clique of radical nationalist army officers who would soon oust Farouk.⁴⁰ The coup prompted a fresh appeal from Churchill for 'moral support', which would make it easier for Britain to impose terms on the new Egyptian 'dictatorship'.⁴¹

None was forthcoming, for Washington wanted Egypt's rulers on its side; their friendship would underpin America's informal empire in the Middle East. Unlike its British predecessor, it would not be burdened by historic resentments or be tainted by racial *hauteur*. Work on this enterprise started almost immediately after Farouk had begun his exile in the fleshpots of the Riviera. Senator Adlai Stevenson visited Egypt in June 1953 and everything he witnessed convinced him that British obduracy and arrogance were the glue that bonded the nationalist movement, and that it was impossible for Britain to defend the base in the face of local antipathy. The answer was to bribe Egypt into becoming an active ally of the West.[42] Dulles also visited Egypt, presented Neguib with a pearl-handled revolver inscribed 'from his friend Dwight G. Eisenhower', and returned home with the same conclusions.

Churchill continued to object strongly to being hustled out of Egypt. In February 1953 he told Eisenhower that 'we are not going to be knocked about with impunity', but he admitted that British interests in Egypt had shrunk since Indian independence and that the security of the Canal might not be worth the 'immense expense' of the base.[43] It no longer represented value for money and its strategic importance may have been exaggerated.[44] Nevertheless, being pushed around by the 'feeblest nation alive' still rankled.[45]

The strategic and financial rationale for leaving Egypt was strong and this, together with the refusal of the United States to countenance Britain's staying, forced Churchill's hand. Alternative bases were proposed and evaluated by Whitehall analysts. Possibilities included Malta, Cyprus and Gaza and, controversially in the light of its relations with the Arab world, Israel.[46] It was agreed that the West's security would not be jeopardised by Britain's departure from Egypt. Whether or not the Egyptian government was capable of running the base, or whether it would ever permit Britain to reoccupy it in an emergency, remained unanswered questions.

These uncertainties became irrelevant in March 1954, when the United States tested the first Hydrogen bomb. Its blast shattered old strategic shibboleths and rendered huge bases like that in Egypt redundant. In June, after nearly two years of bad-tempered negotiations, Britain finally agreed to evacuate the Canal Zone with the proviso that its forces could return in the event of a war with Russia or an invasion of Egypt. There was a small consolation prize in

Egypt's renunciation of its claim to sovereignty over the Sudan, which became independent in 1956.

One of the more worrying elements of the extended Egyptian crisis had been the fear that an emboldened Egypt might follow Persia and nationalise its largest economic asset, the Suez Canal. During the early 1950s, oil consumption in the United States and Western Europe had rocketed, Middle Eastern fields were meeting the increased demand and their products passed through the canal. Yet, while the United States was keen to enlist nationalist movements like that in Egypt into the ranks of the Free World, it had no truck with the nationalisation of major economic and strategic assets.

This was what had happened in Persia, which, since the summer of 1951, had been embroiled in a row with Britain over the nationalisation of the AIOC's operations. The deadlock was creating political problems: Persia was suffering severe economic difficulties of the kind that Communist parties were adept at exploiting and Dr Mussadiq was willing to accept political support from the Communist Tudeh Party.

The Truman administration was convinced that the British government was psychologically incapable of cutting a deal with Mussadiq, since it still viewed the Middle East and its inhabitants through a late-Victorian imperial prism. It distorted reality and left Britain hopelessly myopic in the face of new realities. In August 1952, Henry F. Grady, the United States ambassador in Tehran, publicly declared that, despite their recent experiences in India, Burma, Ceylon and Egypt, the British still retained the 'colonial' attitude of Queen Victoria's reign. They failed to understand the new passions and aspirations of the independence movements in Persia and Egypt and clung to the belief that these could be forced to 'their knees' by financial and political pressure.[47] Eisenhower and Dulles would have agreed.

As with Egypt, Churchill looked to America for a lifeline to haul Britain out of the Persian morass. In August 1952, he told Truman that America should not allow its 'greatest friend' to be 'indefinitely blackmailed' by Mussadiq.[48] The President responded with an offer of a $10 million dollar gift to Persia, agreed that the dispute had to be settled by international arbitration, and suggested that a new oil company should take over from the AIOC on terms that were more generous to the Persians.

The Eisenhower administration took a different view, which was coloured by its anti-Soviet paranoia. Allen Dulles (brother of John Foster) the new head of the CIA pored over analyses of the political and economic turmoil within Persia and convinced himself and his masters that it was vulnerable to a Communist takeover. This could be prevented by a *coup d'état* that would topple Mussadiq and install a government under Shah Muhammad Reza Pahlevi with army and conservative backing. British secret agents had been engaging in the undercover recruitment of anti-Mussadiq elements, and the idea appealed to Churchill, who had always been fascinated by the world of intelligence and clandestine operations.

It was left to the CIA to hand out sheaves of dollars to anyone who would take to the streets and bawl anti-Mussadiq slogans and to engineer mutinies in the Tehran garrison. In August 1953 Mussadiq was overthrown. Churchill was later thrilled to hear an account of the coup from the man who masterminded it, Kermit Roosevelt, a grandson of Theodore. Its subtitle might have been 'By Wealth and Stealth'. A government-in-waiting was ushered in, headed by Shah Muhammad, an autocrat who played the part of America's regional strong man for the next twenty-six years.

Persia had been saved for the West, its oil flowed again and America was on its way to establishing a well-funded hegemony across the Middle East. The 1954 Baghdad Pact was formed, an alliance of Turkey, Iraq, Persia and Pakistan. Egypt remained aloof; its ruler Nasser, who had came to power in 1953, was a headstrong, vain and charismatic nationalist who dreamed his country would take its place as the powerhouse and leader of Arab nationalist movements throughout the region. He sharply rejected Dulles's offers of American patronage and cash in return for an alliance. Britain retired to the periphery of the Middle East, taking responsibility for the external security of Aden and the Persian Gulf sheikhdoms, all of which were now providing oil for the West.

*

Between 1951 and 1955, Churchill had to be compelled to preside over the dismantlement of Britain's informal empire in the Middle East. It had become a rickety structure, but he hoped that America would appreciate its value and assist with repairs. The Truman and Eisenhower administrations favoured demolition on the grounds that Britain was discredited and the mindset of its politicians and diplomats was anachronistic. Churchill would dearly have loved to have unleashed the bombers, warships, landing parties and parachutists on Persia and Egypt, but he was enough of a realist to accept that, however loudly the lion roared, it needed America's permission to pounce. He hoped that this might be forthcoming if only he could resurrect his wartime intimacy with Roosevelt. Neither Truman nor Eisenhower wanted a relationship that had been appropriate for its time but not the Cold War. Both felt that Churchill was a relic of the past, steeped in a late-Victorian, imperial formaldehyde.

The Third British Empire, 1951–1955

While Britain's unofficial empire in the Middle East was in the throes of a terminal malady, its territorial empire was on the threshold of a new era. In June 1952, Macmillan told the country that it had the choice between 'the slide into a shoddy and slushy socialism' or 'the march to the third British Empire'.[1] Six months before his resignation, Churchill gave his blessing to new designs for Parliament Square which would provide 'a truly noble setting for the heart of the British Empire'.[2]

Its façade was deceptively impressive. During the winter and spring of 1953 to 1954 the Queen had made a progress through her dominions and colonies. The newsreels showed her being greeted by dancers and gorgeously bedecked elephants in Ceylon, where she spoke of the Commonwealth as 'a wide family of nations' whose sense of kinship was its strength. There were more native dancers in Uganda, flag-waving crowds and fulsome loyal addresses from her subjects of all races and colours. As the royal yacht *Britannia* steamed towards Malta it was joined by an armada of warships from the Mediterranean Fleet. Throughout, the newsreel commentaries pointedly referred to the 'Commonwealth' rather than the 'Empire' and deployed the language of brotherhood rather than sovereignty.

Commonwealth trade had expanded since the war: in 1955, the dominions and colonies took 45 per cent of Britain's exports and provided 53 per cent of its imports. Bauxite from the Gold Coast, diamonds from Sierra Leone, copper from Northern Rhodesia and rubber and tin from Malaya earned Britain dollars. The future looked promising as ambitious development programmes were implemented to develop infrastructures and exploit existing resources. Of the 1,200 new recruits to the colonial civil service in 1953, there were 500 engineers, town-planners and education officers and 211 geologists and forestry officers.[3]

There were thirty-five dependent colonies in 1951 and the government was making plans to prepare some of them for autonomy. The qualifications for independence were economic self-sufficiency, sound finance, and a cadre of experienced, dedicated and honest politicians, jurists and administrators. No one was certain just how long the process would last, although a cabinet report of 1954 predicted that the Gold Coast, Nigeria, Sierra Leone, Tanganyika, Uganda, the Central African Federation (Nyasaland and Northern and Southern Rhodesia), the West Indies and Malaya would be fit for self-rule by 1975 at the earliest. In 1955 the United Nations Trusteeship Commission suggested that Tanganyika should become independent in 1980. There were, however, notable exceptions: Malta, Cyprus and Aden would be retained as strategic bases and Kenya's current tensions precluded a timetable for independence. If everything went according to Whitehall's schedules, then the colonies would advance slowly and methodically along a well-mapped road that would end with them as independent democracies within the Commonwealth.

The mechanics of reshaping the Empire did not particularly concern Churchill, who, in spirit, had rejected the principles behind them. Commenting on the progress towards self-government in the Gold Coast, he thought that it was 'crazy' to give the vote to 'naked savages'.[4] He was, however, willing to leave colonial policy to others and concentrate what he now recognised to be his depleted energies on Anglo-American relations and the Cold War.

Both impinged on colonial policy. The Eisenhower administration treated the shedding of colonies as clearing the decks for the Cold War, and given the fact that East–West relations were becoming more and more fractious, this process had to be accelerated. Colonies had not only to be guided towards responsible government but measures had to be taken to guarantee that once it was achieved they joined the right side. Washington had always been nervous about Communist infiltration of nationalist movements, which could only be resisted if the West was unsullied by 'colonialism' with all its implied racial prejudices. In June 1954, Congressman Powell told the House of Representatives that 'colonialism' was 'a nasty word, a word that we Americans should be ashamed to speak of in connection with any part of the earth with which we are connected'.[5]

Britain's approach to the problems of decolonisation was applauded in some quarters as a model of wisdom and prudence. In May 1954, the anti-imperialist *Time* raised a cheer:

Britain conspicuously has proven its ability to learn from defeat, to loosen the bonds forged by gunboat and ledger, and to command the loyalty of many of its subjects through freedom instead of force.

It would be foolhardy for America to demand overhasty decolonisation that would 'morally weaken' Britain and France.[6] During a Senate debate on the future of Indo-China, one speaker praised the way in which dominions such as India and Pakistan were attached to Britain through the Commonwealth, and wondered whether France could profitably adopt such a system.[7] Yet there was frustration in Washington over India's conspicuous neutrality in the Cold War, coupled with Nehru's tendency to pontificate about colonialism. It was hoped that money might tempt India on board and American aid rose from $29 million in 1954 to $118 million in 1955.

India's non-alignment was a bugbear when it came to the winding up of the British and French empires in the Far East and replacing them with a reliable anti-Communist regional bloc. It was urgently needed in the early 1950s, since China was supporting the Viet Minh in Indo-China and, to a far lesser extent, the Malayan Communist partisans. The latter had shown an extraordinary resilience, including a capacity to take heavy casualties, but by the end of 1952 the local commander-in-chief and high commissioner, General Sir Gerald Templer, reported that they were 'on the run'.[8] Nevertheless, it was feared that a French defeat in the north would have a 'disastrous effect' on Malayan morale, which was becoming more and more buoyant during 1953 and 1954, thanks to Templer's political and military strategy.[9]

Templer was a brilliant commander who impressed Churchill. The Prime Minister promised the general that he could have all that he wished for, although adding, 'never use it'. Templer's objective was to convince Malayans of all races and religions that: 'This is our country.'[10] Their country first had to be rid of the Communist threat and, simultaneously, to prepare to become a democracy in which no race felt excluded. Europeans had to shed their 'club' mentality and embrace those whom they had long kept at arm's length. Templer's strategy was part political and part military. He aimed to win 'hearts and minds', which could only be achieved by proving that the forces of the Crown were invincible; the population had to be more frightened of British forces than they were of the partisans. The result was a war of attrition in which Commonwealth forces had reduced their opponents to a scattered, demoralised army of 3,000 fugitives by 1955. The political outcome was an independent Singapore, which became the Far East's counterpart of medieval Venice, and Malaysia, which comprised the Malayan sultanates, Sarawak and North Borneo.

While Britain was regaining Malaya, the French were losing Indo-China. The endgame had started early in 1954 with the siege of Dien Bien Phu and its garrison of 30,000 French and Indo-Chinese troops. Eisenhower and Dulles favoured intervention and there was talk of using nuclear weapons, but Congress insisted that France should pledge itself to grant independence to Indo-China and that Britain should provide some troops. There was a flurry of exchanges in which Churchill and Eden urged restraint on Dulles and pointed him towards a negotiated settlement. It was during one such meeting that the Prime Minister famously remarked that 'jaw jaw' was better than 'war war'.

British participation in the Indo-Chinese war was pure folly, as Churchill explained to his physician:

It is no good putting in troops to control the situation in the jungle. Besides, I don't see why we should fight for France when we have given away India. It would have given me pleasure to fight for Britain in India. We think we can hold Malaya even if Indo-China falls.[11]

His observations on India aside, Churchill had been right to keep Britain out of what the Americans later and painfully discovered was an unwinnable struggle against the national aspirations of the Vietnamese, who preferred to die in huge numbers rather than replace a French master with an American stooge.

On 7 March 1954 Dien Bien Phu surrendered just as the peace negotiations began in Geneva. Eden performed the diplomatic game with consummate finesse, a sulky Dulles refused to shake hands with the Chinese Foreign Minister Zhou Enlai, and the French agreed to withdraw from Indo-China. Partition was accepted, but Washington feared that the Communist north would ultimately dominate the country and so made overtures to the fiercely anti-Communist Ngo Dinh Diem, who, it was hoped, would hold the pass in South Vietnam.

Hard-line American Cold Warriors were dismayed by Britain's performance over Indo-China and there were mutterings about appeasement. One congressman suspected that Churchill and Eden had been constrained by British public opinion, which was to an extent true, and laid the blame on the British Labour Party. 'The Socialists' were, he claimed, 'starry-eyed and naive to believe that you can do business with Communists'.[12]

The comparison with the Socialists might have amused (or peeved) Churchill, but he sincerely believed that the present Cold War antipathies were approaching a pitch in which the odds against a hot war were narrowing. If the snarling stopped and the biting began, then Washington would reach for its nuclear weapons. It had threatened to do so in Korea and Indo-China and the Chiefs of Staff felt certain that a nuclear offensive in the Far East would lead directly to a global war.

For this reason, Churchill stepped up his pleas for a summit conference. Stalin had died in March 1953, which Churchill saw as an opportunity for making a fresh overture to the Soviet Union. Eisenhower and Dulles were unconvinced and rejected the Prime Minister's proposals; there would be no second Tehran or Yalta and no opportunity for Churchill to display his conciliatory talents. Ultimately, he was proved right, for the processes of *détente* and rapprochement that ended the Cold War in the late-1980s were largely the result of a sequence of high- and medium-level summits.

The problems created by the Mau Mau insurrection in 1952 were, for Churchill, an unwelcome distraction from the pursuit of his grand international designs. It was a messy and brutal affair whose potential to blight the reputation of the Empire worried Churchill. The roots of the conflict lay in the conflicting land hunger of Kenya's white settlers and the Kikuyu. With its grisly paraphernalia of witchcraft, sexual aberration and brutality towards the young and old, the Mau Mau movement (it called itself revealingly 'The Land Freedom Army') aroused extremes of dread and revulsion among its enemies, the whites and those Kikuyu who stayed loyal to the government. In essence, the Mau Mau was a peasant *jacquerie* that could and did inflict a mass of wounds on its enemies, but it lacked the organisation, manpower and weaponry to defeat them. Nevertheless, the rebels were dogged and operations against them dragged on until November 1956.

Hysteria marked the earliest phase of the war and skewed the judgements of the authorities from the top downwards. The new governor Sir Evelyn Baring was a conventional career administrator who succumbed quickly to panic and remained in its grip. When he arrived, the new local commander General Sir George Erskine was astonished by 'the absence of an offensive spirit' among officials.[13] His ancestors had been Lowland lairds, which may help to explain his disdain for the settlers, of whom he wrote: 'I hate the guts of them all, they are all middle-class sluts.'[14] Churchill had secretly given him the authority to declare martial law. He never saw fit to use it, but he did find himself having to impose rudimentary discipline on his subordinates. In June 1953 he issued a general order against the 'beating up' of suspects, which blemished the reputation of the armed forces and deterred Mau Mau fighters from surrendering.[15]

The hideous nature of the Kenyan counter-terror was exposed in a flow of reports to the Colonial Office during the winter of 1952 to 1953. Four hundred and thirty prisoners had been shot dead while escaping (including six shot while attempting to get out of police cars) and one suspect had committed suicide by throwing himself into a burning hut.[16] Torture was commonplace and endorsed by magistrates who treated native lives as worthless. Reserve Police Officer Keats and Sergeant Reuben of the Kenya [i.e. white] Regiment were given fines for torturing to death a Kikuyu missionary teacher. The magistrate, R. A. Wilkinson, explained his astonishing leniency on the grounds that the accused had been under extreme pressure.[17] In his bland and self-satisfied memoirs, Colonial Secretary Sir Oliver Lyttelton referred in passing to 'one or two isolated incidents of atrocities' which, like the magistrate, he blamed on strain and 'panic' by 'men of low intellectual capacity or low personal courage'.[18] Some details of the counter-terror filtered through to London and there were awkward questions in the Commons.

Churchill took the line of least resistance with occasional well-intentioned detours. He stopped the random impounding of cattle as a collective punishment on the grounds that beasts of the guilty and the innocent would be rounded up.[19] He also queried one of Baring's brainwaves, the introduction of draconian penalties against fire-raisers. 'I see no objection to making arson a capital offence, but I should like to know exactly what "incendiary materials" means. Fourteen years for possessing a box of matches would not go down well.'[20]

Britain could, Churchill believed, find a way out of its predicament in Kenya. Like the Cold War, it could be resolved through a meeting of the chief protagonists. Reasoned debate between men who wanted peace had worked in the past; contentions between Britain and the Boers and Britain and the Irish nationalists had been settled around conference tables. Churchill had played a key part in both settlements and he believed that the formula could be applied to Kenya. As he told Michael Blundell, the Kikuyu were 'not the primitive, gutless people we had imagined'. Their resistance had proved that they were 'savages armed with ideas' and they could only 'be brought to our side by just and wise treatment'. If a Mau Mau spokesman could be found, Churchill even offered to meet him in person.[21]

A potential leader was 'General China', who was caught and sentenced to death. During the debate on whether the sentence should be carried out, Churchill expressed his misgivings about hanging 'men who fight to defend their native land'.[22] General China was reprieved, but there were no negotiations and, in all, just over a thousand insurgents were hanged. Churchill, now visibly ageing and weary, resigned himself to taking the line of the least moral resistance. Lyttelton and Baring continued with the policy of killing what Churchill had called 'ideas' by hanging those who believed in them.

*

The Mau Mau uprising had serious repercussions for British policy elsewhere in Africa. Inevitably, there were fears that the hidden hand of Communism was behind the rebellion and that it was active elsewhere. Little hard evidence emerged, beyond the fact that there was a body of African nationalists who regarded socialism as the way ahead for their countries. An intelligence analysis of 1948 thought that Marxism appealed to the 'educated and vocal classes' who were already hosts to an 'anti-white jealousy'.[23] In 1954, the constitution of the Northern Rhodesian African National Congress [ANC] pledged the party to a 'democratic socialist society' and the banishment of 'capitalist exploitation'.[24] Meanwhile Communist literature was circulating in the Copper Belt.[25]

From 1954 onwards, MI5 reorganised and intensified its operations in Africa with an eye to uncovering Communist activities and the FBI offered help with the surveillance of American black activists with African connections.[26] There were some very dark corners in this murky world of espionage: in 1954 Colonial Office officials suspected the CIA of supplying arms and cash to EOKA terrorists in Cyprus who were demanding the island's merger with Greece.[27] Given America's current obsession with the swift termination of 'colonialism', this was plausible.

In Britain, a watch was kept on the political activities of colonial and non-white Commonwealth students (there were 29,000 in 1960) many of whom gravitated towards the left of the Labour Party.[28] This was reasonable, in so far as it was official policy to attract and cultivate African politicians who would become tractable and reliable rulers of their countries and, of course, Cold War allies.

There were plenty of alarms as firebrand, populist leaders praised the example of the Mau Mau as one to be emulated. 'If Africans had the arms that the Europeans in the country had,' declared one senior official of the Northern Rhodesian ANC, 'there would be civil war by now.'[29] Like the rest of his party, he was fighting against the proposal by Churchill's government to create a Central African Federation, an economically viable state embracing the predominantly black colonies of Nyasaland and Northern Rhodesia and Southern Rhodesia with its white settler community. The Africans feared that they would be dragooned into a state in which the whites would dominate in the way they did in South Africa.

Churchill resigned from office during the prolonged bickering that marked the history of the Central African Federation, which finally fell apart in 1963. His views chimed with those of a Southern Rhodesian delegate who told the 1953 Lancaster Gate conference that his fellow whites were protecting 'the British way of life and western civilisation' and were united by 'an intense loyalty to the country and the crown'. British Africa slipped through Churchill's fingers: he objected to policies designed to turn colonies into self-governing dominions, but did nothing to impede them. For Britain to have dug its heels in, as France did in Algeria and Portugal would do in Angola and Moçambique, would have meant costly and bloody wars of repression, possibly more Kenyas.

The conflict in Kenya, where the rebels were 'killing white men' and their 'stooges' was approvingly invoked by Dr Cheddi Jagan, the leader of the British Guianan [Guyana] People's Progress Party, which secured a narrow majority in the assembly elections in May 1953. Its sympathies, methods and objectives were distinctly Communist and, on gaining power, Jagan demanded the creation of a 'People's Police' and control of school syllabuses. A strike by sugar workers at the beginning of September added to the governor's fears that public order was on the verge of collapse. The Colonial Office, the State Department and the CIA took fright: American fears of a Communist or neo-Communist toehold in the Caribbean overrode any misgivings about 'colonial suppression'. The traditional mechanisms of imperial coercion were activated: two warships were ordered to the capital, Bridgetown, a battalion of British troops came ashore and the governor suspended the constitution.

Churchill endorsed these measures, taken while he was recuperating from his stroke. His faith in Britain's imperial mission remained absolute. He defended it in 1954, when Eisenhower pleaded with him to speed up decolonisation, which was now a matter of urgent political expediency. According to the President, the West was being 'falsely pictured as the exploiters of people, the Soviets as their champions'. In the past he had agreed with Churchill that there were many people unready for responsible government and, if it was prematurely granted, they would fall prey to Communism. Nevertheless, Ike argued, there was 'a fierce and growing spirit of nationalism' that could never be quenched, but could be advantageously channelled.[30]

Churchill refused to be hectored and repudiated Eisenhower's notion of colonialism. It had been and remained a desirable and beneficial process of 'bringing forward backward races and opening up jungles'. 'I was brought up', he continued, 'to feel proud of much that we had done.' Moreover, he mischievously added, 'I am a bit sceptical about universal suffrage for the Hottentots even if refined by proportional representation.'[31] This response was not to the liking of the President, nor would it have pleased many of the Empire's subjects.

What Churchill had failed to comprehend was that the British and, for that matter, the French and Portuguese empires, had now become highly desirable prizes in the Cold War. In its early phases, this contest developed into a struggle for the succession of the old European tropical empires. Both the United States and the Soviet Union wanted their swift dissolution and were doing all in their power to bring this about. The upshot would be the creation of independent, often impoverished states which, by various methods (chiefly bribery), could be lured into the American or the Russian camps. The formula had worked in Persia, which became America's ally, but not in Egypt, which attempted to distance itself from the two superpowers. Churchill's part in this process was that of a bewildered and sometimes resentful onlooker.

The Prime Minister's old racial prejudices re-emerged during cabinet discussions of amendments to the 1948 British Nationality Act which had been created to strengthen Commonwealth solidarity. It also permitted immigrants from the dominions and colonies to settle in Britain; to start with most were from the West Indies and included men and women who had served in the forces and worked in the factories during war. Numbers rose from 3,000 a year in 1953 to 42,000 in 1955. Churchill was perturbed and feared that if the flow was unchecked the incomers would be 'resented by large sections of the British people'. The upshot might be what he distastefully called 'a magpie society'.[32] The subject of immigration control disappeared into the Whitehall digestive system, where it remained for the final two years of Churchill's premiership. That nothing was done was a further indication of the decay of his old willpower and energy; events flowed over him as they did when the subject of decolonisation came up in the cabinet.

ENVOI

Then music drooped. And what came back to mind
Was not its previous habit, but a blind
Astonishing remorse for things now ended
That of themselves were also rich and splendid
(But unsupported broke, and were not mended) –

Philip Larkin, *The March Past,*
25 May [Empire Day] 1951

On 4 April 1955, Churchill celebrated his final day in office by entertaining Queen Elizabeth II to dinner at Downing Street. Afterwards, he gallantly guided Her Majesty to her car and opened the door; he was wearing full court dress with all his medals. Plainly visible in the photographs are those for the Malakand Campaign and Omdurman.

The imperial sentiments that had stirred his imagination on these battlefields had remained with him, but so too had the quintessential dilemma of Empire. Was the process of bringing progress and civilisation to those who lacked them compatible with their coercion?

There was another troublesome conundrum for a humane man deeply attached to the Whiggish notion of a Britain as a nation defined by its people's freedom. Was it possible to balance this with imperial rule?

Churchill had always thought it was; early in 1945 he declared that: 'Without freedom there is no foundation of Empire; without Empire there is no safeguard for our freedom.' The Empire's part in the war justified the last statement, but the rhetoric of the first obscured its ambivalence. Freedom was rationed in large parts of the Empire and for the last ten years of his political career, Churchill wished it to stay so. Too much would be dangerous, not only for Britain but those it emancipated. Withholding it was, in the words of a Sierra Leone nationalist: 'repugnant to the United Nations Charter and absolutely un-British'.[1]

Winston Churchill died just after eight o'clock on the morning of 24 January 1965. He was ninety-one and had been in a coma for a fortnight. The obituaries were ready and the great and the good had drafted their encomiums. Preparations had been made for a lying-in-state and a funeral modelled on that of an earlier national saviour, the Duke of Wellington. The British have always had a knack for state pageantry, and Churchill's obsequies struck the right balance between martial pomp and sombre remembrance.

National grief was measured, thoughtful and nostalgic. At home (and abroad) minds turned to the Second World War. Pride in what, in 1940, Churchill had famously exalted as Britain's 'finest hour' was still vibrant. Yet victory had brought him disappointments. As an historian who drew immense intellectual and political nourishment from history, he had portrayed the war as a further test of the will and stamina of the British nation and had hoped, vainly, that it would emerge stronger than ever as it had after the wars of the eighteenth and early nineteenth centuries. He had misjudged events: 1945 was not 1815. Britannia no longer ruled the waves and the Empire, which after Waterloo had been poised for expansion, was beginning its slow progress towards extinction.

The all-too-obvious eclipse of British power was an embarrassment to the luminaries who had gathered in London for the funeral. They praised Churchill the parliamentarian, the democrat, the orator, the generous-hearted paladin of liberty and the historian. Their valedictions concentrated on his courage and resolution, the qualities that defined his wartime leadership. Ex-President Eisenhower praised him as the embodiment of the defiant and ultimately triumphant will of Britain, or, as a French obituarist expressed it, *'L'incarnation de l'Angleterre indomptable'*.[2] Listeners to the BBC World Service added their own, often deeply moving, tributes to Churchill. 'I owe him life,' wrote a German Jew, an Albanian who had been imprisoned in Dachau thanked his 'liberator', and a New Zealand woman recalled Churchill as 'our rock'.[3] His old antagonist Lord Attlee hailed him as the 'greatest Englishman of our time', a judgement endorsed by the 2002 BBC poll in which Churchill was voted the greatest Englishman of all time.

Then and after, eulogists were reticent about Churchill's lifelong and profound passion for the British Empire. It was a taboo subject that was either tactfully overlooked, or touched upon briefly. *Life* magazine mentioned his 'enduring' belief in 'colonialism' (a dirty word in 1965) and his wartime assertion that 'we mean to hold our own'. In a crabby editorial the *New Statesman* berated him for his resistance to 'the inevitable process of imperial devolution'. Speaking on the BBC, Sir Robert Menzies exalted the man he had once called a 'warmonger' as 'a great Commonwealth statesman'. The Canadian Prime Minister Lester Pearson was closer to the truth when he described Churchill's warmth towards the 'old' Commonwealth and his lack of it towards its successor, which now included former African and Asian colonies.

One new Commonwealth leader, Indian Prime Minister Khrisna Menon, was graciously prepared to forget past acrimony and ordered flags to be flown at half-mast across his country because of Churchill's 'respect and regard for India' and his wartime leadership. These virtues, it seemed, more than compensated for his animus towards Indian nationalism and his prodigious efforts to thwart it.

That once incorrigible beater of the imperial drum, the *Daily Express*, denied Churchill's imperialism by claiming that he had always been a British rather than an imperial 'patriot'. *The Times* concurred and dismissed the suggestion by a hard-left MP that Churchill had been 'a gallant and romantic relic of the eighteenth-century imperialism'. No reasons were advanced to refute what was a perceptive judgement which would have pleased Churchill, for whom the older and younger Pitt were heroes.

The trouble was that Churchill had outlived the imperial ideals he had cherished. Imperialism had long passed out of fashion and was now widely demonised. Colonialism had become a crude umbrella term for the oppression of the weak by the strong, which had justified itself by bogus theories of biological and racial superiority. The latter, combined with mass murder and enslavement, were the outstanding features of the empires of Germany, Japan and Italy, whose overthrow had, ironically, been Churchill's greatest achievement. The British people no longer thought of themselves in Churchillian terms as an imperial race predestined by genetic and moral character to rule and remake the world. A feeling was growing, strongest among the young and in certain academic circles, that the imperial experience was one of submission on one side and oppression on the other. Churchillian pride in Empire was evaporating.

Churchill's Empire too had reached the point of extinction. Under the impetus provided by Harold Macmillan (Prime Minister between 1957 and 1963) the machinery of imperial dismantlement went into top gear and nearly all Britain's remaining Asian, African and West Indian colonies became independent. The illusion of power survived and was promoted by Macmillan in what he thought to be a revival of Churchill's Anglo-American wartime partnership. It was, he boasted, akin to the relationship of ascendant Rome to declining Greece, with the old power guiding the new.

National greatness was reinvented on what was imagined to be a residual respect for Britain's past record. This fantasy was summed up by the cliché that Britain could 'punch above its weight', even though on an international Queensberry scale it had become a winded, middleweight pug in a world dominated by two fit and beefy heavyweights, the United States and the Soviet Union.

The special relationship with the United States which, Churchill wrongly imagined, would somehow sustain the Empire, has continued to flourish. It survived the end of the Cold War and remains the key component in Britain's pretensions to global influence, a substitute for Churchill's steadfast dominions, maritime supremacy and loyal colonies. In its present mutated form, this relationship involves British soldiers fighting on old imperial battlegrounds in the Middle East and Asia to defend America's informal empire. Churchill's balance of altruism has now swung away from the United States towards Britain.

BIBLIOGRAPHY

Abbreviations

BL: British Library
Bod.Lib.: Bodleian Library
CRC: Churchill–Roosevelt Correspondence
CV: Companion Volume
CWP: Churchill War Papers
DAFP: Documents of Australian Foreign Policy
DBFP: Documents of British Foreign Policy
DRFP: Daily Review of Foreign Press
IOR India Office Records
IWM: Imperial War Museum
MEC: Middle East Centre
NCO: Nuffield College, Oxford
NLS: National Library of Scotland
RHL: Rhodes House Library

Unpublished

Bodleian Library, Oxford
  Asquith Papers
  Bonham Carter Papers
  Lennox-Boyd Papers
  Macmillan Papers

Nuffield College, Oxford
  Cherwell Papers

British Library
  India Office Records: Mss Eur 124, 125, 264
  Imperial War Museum

H. T. Lydford Papers
Middle East Centre, Oxford
Lampson, Diaries
Sir Edward Spears Papers

The National Archives, Kew
Adm [Admiralty] 1; Adm 137; Adm 199; Air [Air Ministry] 8; Air 9; Air 20
Cab [Cabinet] 16; Cab 21; Cab 44; Cab 45; Cab 104; Cab 121
CO [Colonial Office] 129; CO 291; CO 323; Co 537; CO 723; CO 733; CO 825; CO 875; CO 926; CO 967; CO 968; CO 1015
Defe [Ministry of Defence] 4; Defe 5; Defe 13
DO [Dominions Office] DO 35
FO [Foreign Office] 141; FO 202; FO 371; FO 954
HO [Home Office] HO 45
KY [MI5] 1; KY 3
Prem [Prime Minister's Office] 3; Prem 11
TS [Treasury Solicitor]
WO [War Office] 32; WO 106; WO 141; WO 157; WO 161; WO 193; WO 203; WO 216; WO 220; WO 236; WO 325; WO 875

National Library of Scotland, Edinburgh
Sir Aylmer Haldane, Diary

Rhodes House, Oxford
Colonel Richard Meinertzhagen, Diary
Welensky Papers

Internet
Roosevelt Papers
Franklin Roosevelt Library Archive
Mackenzie King, Diaries
General Joseph Stilwell, Diaries
The Suspension of the British Guiana Constitution, 1953 (Declassified Documents)
http//www presidency
US National Archives: Record of the Office of Strategic Services
Truman Papers

Published

The place of publication is London unless stated otherwise.

P. Addison, 'The Political Beliefs of Winston Churchill', *Transactions of the Royal Historical Society*, 5th Series, 30 (1980).

P. Addison, *Churchill: The Unexpected Hero* (2005).

J. R. Adelman, *Prelude to Cold War: The Tsarist, Soviet and United States Armies in the two world wars* (Boulder, Colorado, 1988).

M. F. Aiger, 'On the Brink of Civil War: The Canadian Government and the Suppression of the 1918 Quebec Easter Riots', *Canadian Historical Review*, 89 (2008).

Lord Alanbrooke, *War Diaries 1939–1945*, ed. A. Danchev and D. Todman (2002 ed.).

R. Aldrich, 'Imperial Rivalry and American Intelligence in Asia, 1942–46', *Intelligence and National Security*, 3 (1988).

The Empire at Bay: The Leo Amery Diaries 1929–1945, ed. J. Barnes and D. Nicholson (1988).

D. Anderson, *Histories of the Hanged: The Dirty War in Kenya and the End of Empire* (2005).

C. M. Andrew, *Secret Service: The Making of the British Intelligence Community* (1986 ed.).

C. M. Andrew, 'Churchill and Intelligence', *Intelligence and National Security*, 3 (1988).

C. M. Andrew, *Defence of the Realm: The Authorised History of MI5* (2009).

C. M. Andrew and A. S. Kanya-Forstner, 'The French Colonial Party and French Colonial War Aims, 1914–1918', *The Historical Journal*, 17 (1974).

S. R. Ashton, 'Keeping Change Within Bounds', in ed. M. Lynn, *The British Empire in the 1950s: Retreat or Revival* (2006).

The Earl of Avon, *The Eden Memoirs, I, Facing the Dictators* (1962); *II, The Reckoning* (1965).

C. Barnett, *The Collapse of British Power* (1972).

C. Barnett, *The Audit of War* (1980).

I. F. W. Beckett, *The Army and the Curragh Incident* (Army Records Society, 1986).

R. L. Beisner, *Dean Acheson: A Life in the Cold War* (Oxford, 2006).

C. M. Bell, 'The "Singapore Strategy" and the Deterrence of Japan: Winston Churchill and the Admiralty and Force Z', *English Historical Review*, 116 (2001).

T. Bennett, 'The Celluloid War: State and Studio in Anglo-American Propaganda Film Making, 1939–1941', *International History Review*, 24 (2002).

A. Best, 'Intelligence and Diplomacy and the Japanese Threat to British Interests 1914–41', *Intelligence and National Security*, 17 (2002).

A. Best, 'The "Ghost" of the Anglo-Japanese Alliance: An Examination into Historical Myth Making', *The Historical Journal*, 49 (2006).

G. Best, *Churchill and War* (2006 ed.).

R. Blake and W. Roger Louis eds, *Churchill* (Oxford, 1993).

D. Bloxham, *The Great Game of Genocide: Imperialism, Nationalism and the Destruction of the Ottoman Armenians* (Oxford, 2005).

J. M. Blum, *V was for Victory: Politics and American Culture during World War II* (New York, 1976).

M. Blundell, *So Rough a Wind: The Kenya Memories of Sir Michael Blundell* (1964).

M. Blundell, *A Love Affair in the Sun: A Memoir of Seventy Years in Kenya* (1994).

H. Boog, ed., *The Conduct of Air War in the Second War; An International Comparison* (New York, 1992).

M. Boot, *The Savage Wars of Peace: Small Wars and the Rise of American Power* (New York, 2002).

A. Boyle, *Trenchard* (1962).

H. W. Brands, 'The Cairo-Tehran Connection in Anglo-American Rivalry in the Middle East, 1951–1953', *International History Review*, 11 (1989).

British, French and Chinese Nuclear Weapons: Nuclear Weapons Databook, 5, ed. R. S. Norris, A. S. Burrows and R. W. Fieldhouse (Boulder, Col., 1994).

J. P. Brits, 'Tiptoeing along the Apartheid Tightrope: The United States, South Africa and Apartheid', *International History Review*, 27 (2005).

M. Burghleigh, *The Third Reich: A New History* (2001 ed.).

H. C. Butcher, *Three Years with Eisenhower: The Personal Diaries of Henry C. Butcher, USNR* (1946).

D. Butler and A. Sloman, *British Political Facts, 1900–1979* (1980).

The Diaries of Alexander Cadogan, 1938–1945, ed. D. Dilks (1971).

C. E. Callwell, *Field-Marshal Sir Henry Wilson: His Life and Diaries* (2 vols, 1927).

D. Cameron Watt, *How War Came: The Immediate Origins of the Second World War, 1938–1939* (1989).

H. Cecil, 'British War Correspondents and the Sudan Campaigns of 1896–98', in ed. E. Spiers, *Sudan: The Reconquest Reconsidered* (1998).

M. Chaii-Kwan, 'A Reward for Good Behaviour: Bargaining over the Defence of Hong Kong', *International History Review,* 22 (2000).

Lord Chandos, *The Memoirs of Lord Chandos* (1962).

J. Charmley, *Churchill: The End of Glory* (2002).

J. Charmley, *Churchill's Grand Alliance: The Anglo-American Special Relationship 1940–1957* (1995 ed.).

J. Charmley, 'Splendid Isolation to Finest Hour: Britain as a Global Power, 1900–1950', *Journal of Contemporary History,* 18 (2004).

Randolph Churchill, *Winston Churchill: Youth, 1874–1900,* I (1967).

Companion Volume I, parts 1 and 2 (1967).

Randolph Churchill, *Winston Churchill,* II, *The Young Statesman, 1901–1914* (1967).

Companion Volume II, parts 1, 2 and 3 (1969).

Randolph Churchill and Martin Gilbert, *Winston Churchill,* II, *1914–1916* (1971).

Companion Volume, *Documents July 1914–December 1916,* ed. M. Gilbert.

Winston Churchill, *Savrola: A Tale of Revolution in Laurania* (1900).

Winston Churchill, *Frontiers and Wars* (1962 ed.).

Winston Churchill, *Lord Randolph Churchill* (2 vols, 1906).

Winston Churchill, *My African Journey* (1908).

Winston Churchill, *The World Crisis, 1911–1914* (2 vols, 1923 ed.).

Winston Churchill, *The World Crisis: The Aftermath* (1929 ed.).

Winston Churchill, *My Early Life* (1941 ed.).

Winston Churchill, *Thoughts and Adventures* (1932).

Winston Churchill, *Marlborough: His Life and Times* (4 vols, 1934–8).

Winston Churchill, *Great Contemporaries* (1937).

Winston Churchill: *The Second World War* (6 vols, 1948–54).

I, *The Gathering Storm* (1948).

II, *Their Finest Hour* (1949).

III, *The Grand Alliance* (1950).

IV, *The Hinge of Fate* (1951).

V, *Closing the Ring* (1952).

VI, *Triumph and Tragedy* (1954).

Winston Churchill, *History of the English-Speaking Peoples* (4 vols, 1954–8).

Winston Churchill, *Winston S. Churchill: His Complete Speeches 1897–1973*, ed. R. R. James (8 vols, 1974).

Winston Churchill, *War Papers*, ed. M. Gilbert (3 vols, 1994–2002).

[Winston] Churchill, *Churchill and Roosevelt: The Complete Correspondence*, ed. W. F. Kimball (3 vols, 1984).

[Winston] Churchill, *The Churchill–Eisenhower Correspondence 1953–1955*, ed. P. G. Boyle (1990).

I. Clark and N. J. Winter, *The Origins of British Nuclear Strategy, 1945–1955* (Oxford, 1989).

M. J. Cohen, 'Mesopotamia and British Strategy, 1903–1914', *Middle East Studies*, 9 (1978).

M. J. Cohen, 'Churchill and the Balfour Declaration', in ed. U. Dann, *The Great Powers and the Middle East, 1918–1939* (1988).

M. J. Cohen, *Churchill and the Jews* (2003 ed.).

The Collective Naval Defence of the Empire, ed. N. Tracey (Navy Records Society, 1997).

J. Colville, *The Fringes of Power: Downing Street Diaries, 1939–1955* (1985).

L. Comber, 'The Malayan Security Service (1945–1948)', *Intelligence and National Security*, 18 (2008).

S. Connor, 'Japanese Troops under British Control', *Journal of Contemporary History*, 45 (2010).

Daily Review of the Foreign Press (published by the War Office in weekly parts, 1916–20).

The Second World War Diaries of Hugh Dalton, 1940–45, ed. B. Pimlott (1986).

ed. U. Dann, *The Great Powers in the Middle East. 1918–1939* (1986).

U. Dann, 'British Persian Gulf Concepts and Emerging Nationalism', in ed. U. Dann, *The Great Powers in the Middle East, 1918–1939* (1986).

J. Darwin, *The Empire Project: The Rise and Fall of the British World System, 1830–1970* (Cambridge, 2010).

D. Day, 'Anzacs on the Run', *Journal of Imperial and Commonwealth History*, 14 (1986).

D. Day, *Menzies and Churchill at War* (Oxford, 1993).

C. D'Este, *WarLord: A Life of Churchill at war, 1874–1945* (2009).

J. A. DeNovo, 'On the Sidelines: The United States in the Middle East between the Wars', in ed. U. Dann, *The Great Powers in the Middle East, 1918–1939* (1986).

De Robeck and the Dardanelles Campaign, ed. M. Halpern, *The Naval Miscellany*, V (Navy Records Society, 1984).

Documents on Australian Foreign Policy, 1937–1949, ed. R. G. Neale, P. G. Edwards and A. Kennedy, IV [July 1940–June 1941] (Canberra, 1980); V [July 1941–June 1942] (Canberra, 1982).

Documents on British Foreign Policy, 1919–1939 (27 vols, 1937–86).

Documents on British Policy Overseas, Series II, IV [Korea, June 1950– April 1951] (1991).

Documents on Irish Foreign Policy, I [1919–1921], ed. R. Fanning, M. Kennedy, D. Keogh and Euan O'Halpin (Dublin, 1998).

J. D. Doenecke and M. A. Stoler, *Debating Franklin Roosevelt's Foreign Policy, 1933–1945* (Lanham, Maryland, 2005).

J. Dougall, *History and the Culture of Nationalism in Algeria* (Cambridge, 2006).

R. M. Douglas, 'Did Britain use Chemical Weapons in Mandatory Iraq?', *Journal of Modern History*, 81 (2009).

A. Draper, *The Amritsar Massacre: Twilight of the Raj* (1985 ed.).

H. Duncan-Hill and C. C. Wrigley, *History of the Second World War: Studies in Overseas Supplies* (1956).

M. H. Dunsterville, *The Adventures of Dunsterforce* (1920).

The Eden-Eisenhower Correspondence, 1955–1957, ed. P. G. Doyle (2005).

D. Edgerton, *Britain's War Machine: Weapons, Resources and Experts in the Second World War* (2011).

R. Edmonds, *The Big Three: Churchill, Roosevelt and Stalin in Peace and War* (1991).

R. Edmonds, 'Churchill and Stalin', in ed. R. Blake and W. Roger Louis, *Churchill* (Oxford, 1993).

P. Elphick, *Singapore: The Pregnable Fortress: A Study in Deception, Discord and Desertion* (1995).

M. Everest Phillips, 'The Pre-War Fear of Japanese Espionage: Its Impact and Legacy', *Journal of Contemporary History*, 42 (2007).

P. W. Fay, *The Forgotten Army: India's Armed Struggle for Independence, 1942–1945* (New Delhi, 1994).

J. Fenby, *Alliance: The Inside Story of How Roosevelt, Stalin and Churchill Won One War and Began Another* (2006 ed.).

N. Ferguson, *The Pity of War* (1997).

N. Ferguson, ed., *Virtual History: Alternatives and Counterfactuals* (1997).

J. Ferris, *The Evolution of British Strategy and Policy, 1918–26* (1989).

Fear God and Dreadnought: The Correspondence of Admiral of the Fleet Lord Fisher of Kilverstone, ed, A. J. Marder (3 vols, 1952–9).

Foreign Relations of the United States: Diplomatic Papers 1940 (4 vols, Washington, 1958).

A. Fort, *Archibald Wavell: The Life and Times of an Imperial Servant* (2009).

T. G. Fraser, 'India in Anglo-Japanese Relations during the First World War', *History*, 62 (1978).

M. Gandhi, *The Complete Works of Mahatma Gandhi* (58 vols, 1958–80).

M. Gilbert, *Winston S. Churchill*, III (1914–1916) (1971).
Companion Volume, parts 1 and 2 (1972).

M. Gilbert, *Winston S. Churchill*, IV (1917–1922) (1972).
Companion Volume, parts 1, 2 and 3 (1977).

M. Gilbert, *Winston S. Churchill*, V (1922–1939) (1976).
Companion Volume, parts 1, 2 and 3 (1979).

M. Gilbert, *Winston S. Churchill*, VI: *Finest Hour, 1939–1941* (1983).

M. Gilbert, *Winston S. Churchill*, VII: *Road to Victory, 1941–1945* (1986).

M. Gilbert, *Winston S. Churchill*, VIII, 'Never Despair' *1945–1965* (1988).

M. Gilbert, *The First World War* (1994).

D. Gilmour, *Curzon* (1995).

B. K. Gordon, *New Zealand becomes a Pacific Power* (Chicago, 1960).

H. H. Grant, *History of the War in South Africa*, IV (1916).

J. C. Grew, *Ten Years in Japan: A Contemporary Record drawn from the Diaries, Private and Official Papers of Joseph C. Grew, United States Ambassador to Japan 1932–1942* (1944).

K. Grieve, 'Haig and the Government, 1916–1918', in ed. B. Bond and N. Cave, *Haig: A Reappraisal 70 Years On* (1999).

P. Guinn, *British Strategy and Politics* (Oxford, 1965).

P. I. Hahn, *Caught in the Middle East: United States Policy towards the Arab-Israeli War* (Chapel Hill, 2009).

M. Hankey, *The Supreme Command* (2 vols, 1961).

Hankey: Man of Secrets, II (1919–1930), ed. S. Roskill (1972).

The Diaries of Oliver Harvey, ed. J. Harvey (2 vols, 1970 and 1978).

J. Haslam, 'Russian Archival Revelations and our Understanding of the Cold War', *Diplomatic History*, 27 (1997).

M. Hauner, *India in the Axis Strategy: Germany, Japan and Indian Nationalists in the Second World War* (Stuttgart, 1981).

M. Hauner, 'One Man against the Empire: The Faqir of Ipi and the British in Central Asia on the Eve of and during the Second World War', *Journal of Contemporary History*, 16 (1981).

M. S. Healy, 'Colour, Climate and Combat: The Caribbean Regiment in the Second World War', *International History Review*, 22 (2000).

P. Hennessey, *Having It So Good: Britain in the Fifties* (2006).

A. Herman, *Gandhi and Churchill* (2009 ed.).

G. C. Herring, *From Colony to Superpower: U.S. Foreign Relations since 1776* (Oxford, 2008).

J. G. Hershbergh and C. Jian, 'Reading and Warning the Enemy: China's signals to the U.S. about Vietnam', *International History Review*, 27 (2008).

F. H. Hinsley, E. E. Thomas, C. F. G. Ransom and R. C. Knight, *British Intelligence in the Second World War*, I (1979).

F. H. Hinsley and C. A. G. Simkins, *British Intelligence in the Second World War*, IV, *Security and Counter-Intelligence* (1990).

L. Hirszowicz, *The Third Reich and the Arab East* (1966).

R. Hobson, *Imperialism at Sea: Naval Strategic Thought, The Ideology of Sea Power, and the First World War, 1875–1914* (Boston, 2002).

G. W. T. Hodges, 'African Manpower Statistics for the British Forces in East Africa, 1914–1918', *Journal of African History*, 19 (1978).

H. C. Hoffman, 'Diplomatic History and the Meaning of Life', *Diplomatic History*, 27 (1997).

H. L. Hopkins, *The Whitehouse Papers of Harry L. Hopkins*, ed. R. E. Sherwood (3 vols, 1949).

J. Horne and A. Kramer, *German Atrocities 1914: A History of Denial* (Yale, 2001).

R. Hough, *The War at Sea* (1983).

I. V. Hull, *Absolute Destruction: Military Culture and the Practices of War in Imperial Germany* (Cornell, 2005).

R. Hyam, *Elgin and Churchill at the Colonial Office, 1905–1908* (1968).

R. Hyam, *Understanding the British Empire* (Cambridge, 2011).

Imperial Policy and Colonial Practice: British Documents of the End of Empire, Series A, I, ed. S. R. Ashton and S. E. Stockwell (1996).

B. Isitt, 'Mutiny from Victoria Vladivostok, December 1918', *Canadian Historical Review*, 87 (2007).

A. Jackson, *The British Empire and the Second World War* (2006).

A. Jahal, 'Towards the Baghdad Pact: South Asia and the Middle East Defence in the Cold War, 1947–1955', *International History Review*, 11 (1989).

L. E. James, *Mutiny* (1985).

L. E. James, *Raj: the Making and Unmaking of British India* (1997).

L. E. James, *Warrior Race: A History of the British at War* (2002).

Japan's Decision for War: Records of the 1941 Policy Conferences, ed. N. Ike (Stanford, Ca, 1967).

C. S. Jarvis, *Arab Command: The Biography of Lieutenant-Colonel F. G. Peake Pasha* (1946 ed.).

K. Jeffrey, *The British Army and the Crisis of Empire, 1918–1922* (1984).

K. Jeffrey, *Field-Marshal Sir Henry Wilson: A Political Soldier* (Oxford, 2001).

The Jellicoe Papers (1893–1916), ed. A. Temple Patterson (Naval Records Society, 1966).

J. Jenkinson, 'Black Sailors in Red Clydeside: Rioting, Reactionary Trade Unionism and Conflicting Notions of Britishness following the First World', *Twentieth-Century British History*, 19 (2008).

E. T. Jennings, *Pétain's Nationalist Revolution in Madagascar, Guadeloupe and Indo-China 1940–1944* (Stanford, Ca, 2001).

G. Jimsey, *Henry Hopkins: An Ally of the Poor and Defender of Democracy* (Harvard, 1987).

R. Johnson, *Spying for Empire: The Great Game in Central Asia 1757–1947* (2006).

M. Jones, 'Up the Garden Path? Britain's Nuclear History in the Far East, 1954–1962', *International History Review*, 25 (2003).

M. Kahler, *Decolonisation in Britain and France: The Domestic Consequences of International Relations* (Princeton, NJ, 1984).

D. M. Kennedy, *Freedom from Fear: The American People, Depression and War* (Oxford, 1999).

P. Kennedy, *The Rise of Anglo-German Antagonism, 1860–1914* (1982 ed.).

G. O. Kent, 'Britain in the Winter of 1940–41 as seen from the Wilhelmstrasse', *The Historical Journal*, 6 (1963).

F. Kersaudy, *Churchill and De Gaulle* (1981).

The Keynes Papers, *I* (1914–1918), ed. P. G. Halpern (Navy Records Society, 1972).

V. C. Kiernan, *European Empires from Conquest to Collapse* (1982).

The Killearn Diaries, 1934–1946, ed. T. E. Evans (1972).

D. Killingray, 'Repercussions of World War I the Gold Coast', *Journal of African History*, 19 (1978).

D. Killingray, '"A Swift Agent of Government": Air Power in Colonial Africa, 1916–39', *Journal of Imperial and Commonwealth History*, 25 (1984).

W. F. Kimball, *The Most Unsordid Act: Lend Lease, 1939–1941* (Baltimore, 1969).

W. F. Kimball, 'Wheels within Wheels: Churchill, Roosevelt and the Special Relationship', in ed. R. Blake and W. Roger Louis, *Churchill* (Oxford, 1993).

M. Knox-Conquest, 'Foreign and Domestic Policy in Fascist Italy', *Journal of Modern History*, 56 (1984).

G. Kudaisya, '"In Aid of the Civil Power": The Colonial Army in Northern India, 1919–42', *Journal of Imperial and Commonwealth History*, 32 (2004).

R. Lamb, *The Failure of the Eden Government* (1987).

M. P. Leffler, *A Preponderance of Power: National Security, the Truman Administration and the Cold War* (Stanford, Calif. 1992).

J. Lonsdale, 'Constructing the Mau Mau', *Transactions of the Royal Historical Society*, 5th Series, 40 (1990).

D. Lloyd George, *The Truth about the Peace Treaties* (2 vols, 1938).

J. Lukas, *Five Days in London, May 1940* (1999).

M. Lynn, *The British Empire in the 1950s: Retreat or Revival* (2006).

M. Lynn, '"We cannot let the North down": British Policy in Nigeria in the late 1950s', in M. Lynn, *The British Empire in the Late 1950s: Retreat or Revival* (2006).

R. F. Mackay, *Fisher of Kilverstone* (Oxford, 1973).

A. L. Macfie, 'The Straits Question in the First World War', *Middle East Studies*, 19 (1983).

A. L. Macfie, 'British Intelligence and the Turkish National Problem', *Middle East Studies*, 37 (2001).

D. Mackenzie, 'A North Atlantic Outpost: The American Military in Newfoundland, 1941–1945', *War and Society*, 22 (2004).

F. MacKenzie, 'In the National Interest: Dominion Support for Britain and the Commonwealth after the Second World War', *Journal of Imperial and Commonwealth History*, 34 (2006).

H. Macmillan, *The Blast of War, 1939–1945* (1967).

A. Mango, *Atatürk* (2000 ed.).

A. J. Marder, *From Dreadnought to Scapa Flow* (5 vols, 1961–70).

A. J. Marder, M. Jacobsen and J. Horsfield, *Old Friends and New Enemies: The Royal Navy and the Imperial Japanese Navy, II, Pacific War 1942–1945* (Oxford, 1990).

E. Mark, 'The War Scare of 1946 and its Consequences', *Diplomatic History*, 27 (1997).

S. Mawby, 'The Clandestine Defence of Empire: British Special Operations in Yemen, 1951–64', *Intelligence and National Security*, 17 (2002).

M. Mazower, *Hitler's Empire: Nazi Rule in Occupied Europe* (2008).

J. M. McCarthy, 'Australia and Imperial Defence: Cooperation and Conflict 1918–1939', *Australian Journal of Politics and History*, 17 (1971).

J. McColgan, *British Policy and the Irish Administration* (1983).

R. L. McCormick, 'Imperial Mission: The Air Route to the Cape Town, 1918–1932', *Journal of Contemporary History*, 9 (1974).

S. McMeekin, *The Berlin–Baghdad Express* (2010).

S. McMeekin, *The Russian Origins of the First World War* (2012).

J. McQuinton, '"Doing the Boys Some Good": The Exemption Court Hearings in North-Eastern Victoria, 1916', *Australian Historical Studies*, 115 (2000).

R. L. Melka, 'Darlan between Britain and Germany, 1940–41', *Journal of Contemporary History*, 8 (1973).

J. H. Meriwether, '"A Torrent Overrushing Everything": Africa in the Eisenhower Administration', in ed. K. S. Statler and A. L. Johns, *The Eisenhower Administration and the Globalisation of the Cold War* (Lanham, Maryland, 2006).

Selections from the Papers of J. X. Merriman, ed. P. Lewson (Cape Town, 1960).

A. Mitchell, *Revolutionary Government in Ireland: The Dáil Éireann 1919–1922* (Dublin, 1995).

Lord Moran, *Winston Churchill: The Struggle for Survival, 1940–1965* (1968 ed.).

R. Moore, 'Where Her Majesty's Nuclear Weapons Were', *Bulletin of the Atomic Scientists*, 57, I (2001).

R. J. Moore, *Churchill, Cripps and India 1939–1945* (1979).

L. P. Morris, 'British Secret Missions to Turkestan, 1918–19', *Journal of Contemporary History*, 12 (1977).

P. Murphy, 'Intelligence and Decolonisation', *Journal of Contemporary History*, 12 (1977).

From the Morgenthau Diaries, III, Years of War, 1941–1945, ed. J. M. Blum (Boston, Mass., 1967).

M. Mukerjee, *Churchill's Secret War: The British Empire and the Ravaging of India during World War II* (2010).

Azzou el-Mustafa, 'La Nationalisme Morocain et les États Unis, 1945–1956', *Guerres Minimalists et Confuts Contemporains*, No. 177 (1995).

R. H. Myers and M. R. Peattie, *The Japanese Colonial Empire, 1895–1945* (Princeton, 1984).

Naval Intelligence from Germany: The Reports of British Naval Attachés in Berlin, 1906–1914, ed. M. W. Seligman (Navy Record Society, 2007).

M. S. Navias, *Nuclear Weapons and British Strategic Planning, 1955–1958* (Oxford, 1991).

K. Neilson, 'The Defence Requirements Sub-Committee and British Strategic and Foreign Policy and the Path to Appeasement', *English Historical Review*, 118 (2003).

A. O. Offler, *Another Such Victory: President Truman and the Cold War* (Stanford, Calif., 2002).

M. W. Oren, *Power, Faith and Fantasy: America in the Middle East, 1776 to the Present* (2007).

K. A. Osgood, 'Words and Deeds: Race, Colonisation and Eisenhower's Propaganda in the Third World', in ed. K. S. Statler and A. L. Johns, *The Eisenhower Administration and the Globalisation of the Cold War* (Lanham, Maryland, 2006).

P. Overlack, 'German Commerce Warfare for the Australia Station', *War and Society*, 14 (1996).

P. Overlack, 'Asia in German Naval Plans before the First World War', *War and Society*, 17 (1999).

R. Overy, *The Morbid Age: Britain and the Crisis of Civilisation, 1919–1939* (2010 ed.).

M. E. Page, 'The War of *Thangata*: Nyasaland and the East African Campaign', *Journal of African History*, 19 (1978).

J. Palmer, *The Bloody White Baron* (2008).

J. Parker, 'Remapping the Cold War in the Tropics: Race, Communism and National Security in the West Indies', *International History Review*, 24 (2002).

D. J. Payton-Smith, *History of the Second World War: Oil: A Study in Wartime Administration* (1971).

M. R. Peattie, 'Japanese Attitudes Towards Colonialism', in ed. R. Myers, and M. R. Peattie *The Japanese Colonial Empire 1895–1945* (Princetown, 1984).

D. A. Percox, 'Internal Security and Decolonisation in Malaya, 1956–63', *Journal of Imperial and Commonwealth History*, 29 (2001).

R. Polenski and Malcolm Ross, 'A New Zealand Failure in the Second World War', *Australian Historical Studies*, 39 (2008).

R. J. Popplewell, *Intelligence and Imperial Defence: British Intelligence and the Defence of the Indian Empire, 1904–1924* (1995).

G. Post Jnr, *Dilemmas of Appeasement: British Deterence and Defense* (Ithaca, 1993).

Chief of Staff: The Diaries of Lieutenant-General Sir Henry Pownall, I, ed. B. Bond.

L. R. Pratt, *East of Malta, West of Suez: Britain's Mediterranean Crisis, 1936–1939* (Oxford, 1975).

J. Prudos, 'The Central Intelligence Agency and the Policy of Decolonisation during the Eisenhower Administration', in ed. K. Statler and A. L. Johns, *The Eisenhower Administration and the Globalisation of the Cold War* (Lanham, Maryland, 2006).

S. Qing, *From Allies to Enemies: Visions of Modernity, Identity and United States China Diplomacy, 1945–1960* (Harvard, 2007).

R. Quinault, 'Churchill and Russia', *War and Society*, 9 (1992).

R. Quinault, 'Churchill and Black Africa', *History Today*, 55 (June 2003).

W. Raleigh, *The War in the Air*, I (Oxford, 1922).

R. Rathbone, 'Police Intelligence in Ghana in the late 1940s and 1950s', *Journal of Imperial and Commonwealth History*, 21 (1993).

D. Renton, *Zionist Masquerade: The Birth of the British Zionist Alliance 1914–1918* (2007).

Review of Foreign Press: Political Press (Published by the Foreign Office, 1920–1).

D. Reynolds, *In Command of History: Churchill Fighting and Writing the Second World War* (2005 ed.).

M. Reynolds, 'Buffers not Brethren, Young Turk Militant Policy in the First World War', *Past Present*, 205 (2009).

R. Rhodes James, *Gallipoli* (1984 ed.).

R. Rhodes James, *Churchill a Study in Failure* (1970).

A. Roberts, 'The Holy Fox': A Biography of Lord Halifax* (1991).

A. Roberts, *Eminent Churchillians* (1994).

G. Roberts, *Stalin's Wars From World War to Cold War, 1939–1953* (Yale, 2006).

E. M. Robertson, *Mussolini as Empire Builder in Europe and Africa, 1922–36* (1978).

D. Rodogno, *Fascism's European Empire: Italian Occupation during the Second World War* (Cambridge, 2006).

W. Roger Louis, *Imperialism at Bay: The United States and the Decolonisation of the British Empire, 1941–1945* (1985).

W. Roger Louis, *Ends of British Imperialism: The Scramble for Africa, Suez and Decolonisation* (2006).

Y. Roi, 'Official Soviet Views on the Middle East, 1919–1939', in ed. U. Dann, *The Great Powers in the Middle East* (1988).

C. G. Roland, 'Massacre and Rape in Hong Kong: Two Case Studies involving Medical Personnel and Patients', *Journal of International History*, 32 (1997).

C. B. Rooney, 'The International Significance of British Naval Missions to the Ottoman Empire', *Middle East Studies*, 34 (1998).

The Works of Theodore Roosevelt (20 vols, New York, 1926).

N. Rose, *Churchill: The Unruly Giant* (1994).

N. Rose, 'Churchill and Zionism', in ed. R. Blake and W. Roger Louis, *Churchill* (Oxon, 1998).

S. Roskill, *Hankey: Man of Secrets* (3 vols, 1970).

V. Rothwell, *Britain and the Cold War* (1982).

V. Rothwell, *War Aims of the Allies in the Second World War: The War Aims of the Major Belligerents* (Edinburgh, 2005).

K. Ruane and J. Ellison, 'Managing the Americans: Anthony Eden, Harold Macmillan and the Pursuit of "Power by Proxy" in the 1950s', *Journal of Contemporary History*, 28 (2004).

B. Rubin, 'Anglo-American Relations with Saudi Arabia', *Journal of Contemporary History*, 14 (1979).

M. Ruotsila, 'The Churchill-Mannerheim Collaboration in the Russian Intervention, 1919–20', *The Slavonic and Eastern European Review*, 80 (2002).

A. Selden, *Churchill's Indian Summer: The Conservative Government, 1951–1955* (1981).

Selections from the Smuts Papers, II [June 1902–May 1910], ed. W. K. Hancock and J. van der Poel (Cambridge, 1966).

M. Sharpe, 'ANZAC day in New Zealand 1916–1939', *The New Zealand Journal of History*, 15 (1981).

E. Shuckburgh, *Descent into Suez 1951–1956* (1986).

J. Singh, *India, Partition and Independence* (2010).

P. Sluglett, *Britain in Iraq: Contriving King and Country* (2007).

C. S. Smith, *England's Last War against France: Fighting Vichy, 1940–1942* (2009).

R. Smyth, 'British African Colonies and British Propaganda during the Second World War', *Journal of Imperial and Commonwealth History*, 14 (1985).

M. Soames, *Clementine Churchill* (2002 ed.).

M. Soames, ed., *Speaking for Themselves: The Personal Letters of Winston and Clementine Churchill* (1998).

C. Somerville, *Our War: How the British Commonwealth fought the Second World War* (1997).

J. Springhall, 'Mountbatten versus the Generals: British Military Rule in Singapore', *Journal of Contemporary History*, 36 (2004).

A. J. Stackwell, 'Leaders, Dissidents and Disappointed: Colonial Students in Britain as the Empire ended', *Journal of Imperial and Commonwealth History*, 36 (2008).

J. W. Stilwell, *The Stilwell Papers*, ed. T. H. White (1949).

W. Stivers, *Supremacy in Oil: Iraq, Turkey and the Anglo-American World* (1982).

N. Stone, *The Atlantic and its Enemies* (2010).

F. A. A. Taha, 'The Sudanese Factor in the 1952–53 Anglo-Egyptian Negotiation', *Middle East Studies*, 44 (2002).

M. C. Thomas, 'Innocent Abroad? Decolonisation and United States Engagement in French West Africa', *Journal of Imperial and Commonwealth History*, 36 (2008).

M. Thompson, *The White War: Life and Death on the Italian Front* (2008).

R. C. Thompson, *Australian Imperialism in the Pacific: The Expansionist Era, 1820–1920* (Melbourne, 1986).

A. Thomson, '"The Vilest Libel of the War?" Imperial Politics and the Official Histories of Gallipoli', *Australian Historical Studies*, 25 (1992–3).

J. M. Thomson, *Russia, Bolshevism and the Versailles Treaty* (Princeton, 1966).

C. Thorne, *Allies of a Kind: The United States, Britain and the War against Japan, 1941–1945* (Oxford, 1980 ed.).

D. R. Thorpe, *Supermac: The Life of Harold Macmillan* (2010).

S. Tønneson, *Vietnam, 1946* (Berkeley, Ca, 2010).

C. Townshend, *The British Campaign in Ireland, 1919–1921: the Development of Political and Military Policies* (Oxford, 1975).

R. Toye, *Churchill's Empire: The World that Made Him and The World He Made* (2010).

The Transfer of Power, 1942–1947, ed. N. Mansergh, II (1972).

T. Travers, *Gallipoli, 1915* (Stroud, 2001).

R. C. Tucker, 'The Cold War in Stalin's Time', *Diplomatic History*, 27 (1997).

H. Ünal, 'Britain and Ottoman Domestic Politics: From the Young Turk Revolution to the Counter-Revolution, 1906–1909', *Middle East Studies*, 37 (2001).

J. W. St G. Walker, 'Race and Recruitment in World War I: Enlistment of Visible Minorities in the Canadian Expeditionary Force', *Canadian History Review*, 70 (1989).

W. K. Wark, 'The Air Defence Gap, British Air Doctrine and Intelligence Warnings in the 1930s', in ed. H. Boog, *The Conduct of the Air War in the Second World War: An International Comparison* (New York, 1992).

P. Warwick, ed., *The Boer War* (1990).

B. Wasserstein, *The British in Palestine: The Mandatory Government and the Arab-Jewish Conflict, 1917–1929* (Oxford, 1999).

W. Webster, *Englishness and Empire* (2005).

O. A. Westad, 'Secrets of the Second World War: The Russian Archives and the Reinterpretation of Cold War History', *Diplomatic History*, 27 (1997).

N. J. White, 'Decolonisation in the 1950s: The Version according to British Business', in ed. M. Lynn, *The British Empire in the 1950s: Retreat or Revival* (2006).

S. White, *Britain and the Bolshevik Revolution: A Study in Politics and Diplomacy, 1920–1924* (1979).

D. Winter, *Haig's Command: A Reassessment* (1991).

W. C. Wohlfirth, 'New Evidence on Moscow's Cold War', *Diplomatic History*, 27 (1997).

E. Zilmo, 'Who Owns Gallipoli? Australia's Gallipoli Anxieties, 1915–2005: Discordant Notes', *Journal of Australian Studies*, 16 (2006).

V. Zubrok, 'Stalin's Plans and Russian Archives', *Diplomatic History*, 27 (1997).

NOTES

PART ONE: 1874–1900

Chapter 1. Jolly Little Wars: Omdurman
1. Spiers, pp. 68–9.
2. Randolph Churchill, *Winston Churchill*, I, 418–19.
3. Randolph Churchill, *Winston Churchill*, I, 407.
4. Randolph Churchill, *Winston Churchill*, I, 360.

Chapter 2. He'll Be Prime Minister of England One Day: A Subaltern's Progress
1. Randolph Churchill, *Winston Churchill*, I, CV, i, 675–6.
2. NLS, Haldane Diary, Ms 12, 274, f.114; Randolph Churchill, *Winston Churchill*, I, CV, i, 675–6.

Chapter 3. A Dog with a Bone: Lieutenant Churchill's Imperial World
1. Winston Churchill, *Speeches*, I, 40.
2. Randolph Churchill, *Winston Churchill*, I, CV i, 617–18.
3. Winston Churchill, *Speeches*, I, 40.
4. NA, WO 106/42.
5. Hyam, *Elgin and Churchill*, p. 490.
6. Winston Churchill, *My African Journey*, p. 55.
7. NA, KY 1/15,90.
8. NA, WO 106/342; Winston Churchill, *Speeches*, I, 61.

PART TWO: 1901–1914

Chapter 4. An Adventurer: Questions of Character
1. Randolph Churchill, *Winston Churchill*, I, 315.

Chapter 5. Humbugged. The Colonial Office, 1905–1908
1. Hyam, *Elgin and Churchill*, p. 42.
2. Winston Churchill, *Speeches*, I, 382; II, 1497.
3. Grant, IV, 558.
4. Hyam, *Elgin and Churchill*, pp. 140–1.
5. Grant, IV, 673.
6. Bod.Lib., Milner, Dep 277, ff. 58–63.
7. NA, CO 291/103, 37.
8. NA, CO 291/103, 105d.

Chapter 6. Tractable British Children: More Native Questions
1. *Hansard*, 5th Series, 154, 214.
2. *Smuts Papers*, II, 244–5.
3. *Smuts Papers*, II, 309, 363–4, 379, 381.
4. Randolph Churchill, *Winston Churchill*, II, 163–4.
5. Kiernan, p. 119.
6. Herman, p. 137.
7. Hyam, *Elgin and Churchill*, pp. 246, 251, 494.
8. Hyam, *Elgin and Churchill*, pp. 411–12.
9. Hyam, *Elgin and Churchill*, p. 405.
10. Hyam, *Elgin and Churchill*, p. 359; Winston Churchill, *My African Journey*, p. 37.
11. Winston Churchill, *My African Journey*, pp. 37–8.
12. Winston Churchill, *Frontiers and Wars*, p. 58; *My African Journey*, p. 41.
13. Winston Churchill, *My African Journey*, pp. 87, 123.
14. Winston Churchill, *My African Journey*, p. 48.
15. Herman, pp. 149–50; NA, CO 291/103, 511.
16. NA, KY 1/15, 53.
17. Winston Churchill, *Speeches*, I, 911.
18. Hyam, *Elgin and Churchill*, pp. 352–3.

Chapter 7. Breathing Ozone: The Admiralty, October 1911–March 1914
1 Randolph Churchill, *Winston Churchill*, II, CV, iii, 1653.
2. Raleigh and Jones, I, 174.
3. Hobson, pp. 217–20; 231–2.
4. Overlack, 'Asia in German Naval Planning', *War and Society*, 14 and 18, *passim*.
5. *Naval Intelligence*, p. 171.
6. Randolph Churchill, *Winston Churchill*, II, CV, iii, 1602.
7. Mackay, p. 403; Marder, *Fear God and Dreadnought*, II, 426, 451, 484, 507.
8. Marder, *Fear God and Dreadnought*, II, 471; Randolph Churchill, *Winston Churchill*.
9. *Naval Intelligence*, pp. 467–8.
10. Randolph Churchill, *Winston Churchill*, II, CV, iii, 1811, 1814, 1865.
11. Marder, *Fear God and Dreadnought*, II, 410–11.
12. Randolph Churchill, *Winston Churchill*, II, CV, 1564–5.
13. Randolph Churchill, *Winston Churchill*, II, CV, iii, 1597.
14. Hough, p 44
15. Kennedy, *The Rise of Anglo-German Antagonism*, p. 376.
16. Winston Churchill, *The World Crisis*, p. 120.
17. Randolph Churchill, *Winston Churchill*, II, 528.
18. Randolph Churchill, *Winston Churchill*, II, CV, iii, 1599.
19. Randolph Churchill, *Winston Churchill*, II, 613–26.

Chapter 8. These Grave Matters: The Irish Crisis, March–July 1914
1. Randolph Churchill, *Winston Churchill*, II, 450; Winston Churchill, *Speeches*, I, 850; II, 1605, 1919.

2. Randolph Churchill, *Winston Churchill*, II, 486.
3. Beckett, *The Army and the Curragh Incident*, p. 74.
4. NA, WO 141/4, III, Fifth Report, 20–1.
5. Beckett, *The Army and the Curragh Incident*, p. 165.
6. Winston Churchill, *Speeches*, II, 2395, 2304.

Chapter 9. *The Interests of Great Britain: The Coming of War, July–August 1914*
1. Winston Churchill, *Speeches*, I, 85.
2. The best and most comprehensive accounts are Martin Gilbert, *The First World War* (1994) and Norman Stone, *World War One: A Short History* (2007).
3. Ferguson, *The Pity of War*, p. 74, quoting NA, Cab 38/19/47.
4. *DRFP*, 17 October 1918.
5. Soames, *Speaking for Themselves*, p. 96.
6. NA, Adm 137/10, 14, 15.
7. NA, Adm 137/10, 21, 25.
8. Randolph Churchill, *Winston Churchill*, II, CV, iii, 1989.
9. Bod.Lib., Bonham Carter, 686, f.284.
10. Horne and Kramer, *passim*, but especially pp. 74–6 and 296–300.
11. For the German army's military philosophy, its origins and evolution see I. V. Hull, *Absolute Destruction: Military Culture and the Practise of War in Imperial Germany* (Cornell, 2005).

PART THREE: 1914–1922

Chapter 10. *A War of Empires: An Overview, 1914–1918*
1. Ferguson, *The Pity of War*, p. 434.
2. Reynolds, 'Buffers', pp. 149, 156, 161.
3. Bod.Lib., Milner, 46, 3–4.
4. Isitt, 'Mutiny', pp. 232–4.
5. Guinn, pp. 192–4.
6. Thompson, *Australian Imperialism*, pp. 203–4; NA, Adm 137/1, 24, 25.
7. Hankey, I, 249.
8. Andrew and Kanya-Forstner, *The French Colonial Party*, p. 87; Strachan, I, 520.
9. NA, Adm 137/97, 63.
10. NA, Adm 137/111, 74–5.
11. Thompson, *The White War*, p. 29.
12. Hull, pp. 239–40, 245–8, 252.
13. DRFP, 11 March 1916; 18 and 28 April 1918.
14. Polenski and Ross, pp. 19–20.
15. Sharpe, 'ANZAC day', p. 161.
16. Aiger, 'On the Brink', *passim*.
17. McQuinton, 'Doing the Boys Some Good', p. 237.
18. St G. Walker, 'Race and Recruitment', pp. 5–6.
19. Winston Churchill, *Speeches*, IV, 2434, 2439.
20. NA, WO 95/83 [10 July 1917].
21. NA, CO 132/296.

22. NA, CO 132/296, Appendix.
23. Jenkinson, 'Black Sailors', pp. 53, 57.
24. Strachan, I, 496; Hodges, *African Manpower*, p. 110.
25. Dougall, p. 44.
26. Winston Churchill, *Speeches*, IV, 2652.
27. Callwell, I, 122.

Chapter 11. I Love this War: The Dardanelles and Gallipoli, August 1914–May 1915
1 Bod.Lib., Bonham Carter, 686, f. 137; Gilbert, *Winston Churchill*, III, CV, ii, 400.
2. Randolph Churchill, *Winston Churchill*, II, 225.
3. Bod.Lib., Bonham Carter, 12, 81.
4. Hough, p. 144.
5. NA, Adm 137/95, 61.
6. Bod.Lib., Asquith, 27, 107–8.
7. Buckinghamshire Record Office, T-A 3/517.
8. The best accounts are R. R. James, *Gallipoli* and T. Travers, *Gallipoli 1915*.
9. Hough, p. 84.
10. Randolph Churchill, *Winston Churchill*, I, CV, 777; Winston Churchill, *My Early Life*, p. 28.
11. See p. 77.
12. NA, Adm 137/95, 114; Adm 137/97, 132, 383.
13. NA, Adm 137/97, 384.
14. NA, CO 323/638, 544, 547.
15. NA, Adm 137/97, 109, 12a, 156, 222, 425.
16. NA, Adm 137/97, 384.
17. NA, Adm 137/97, 213.
18. NA, WO 106/559, 43rd report.
19. NA, WO 157/825, 12 and 18 September 1915.
20. NA, FO 141/1465.
21. NA, FO 141/1465, Notes on Propaganda.
22. Macfie, 'The Straits Question', pp. 60–1, Callwell, II, 264.
23. Macfie, 'The Straits Question', pp. 50–1; Andrew and Kanya-Forstner, *The French Colonial Party*, p. 82.
24. Randolph Churchill, *Winston Churchill*, I, 317.
25. NA, Adm 137/111, 174–5.
26. Bod.Lib., Bonham Carter, 12, 22–3.
27. Macfie, 'The Straits Question', p. 58.
28. NA, Cab 45/217, A1 question 24.
29. Keyes, I, 110; Marder, *From Dreadnought to Scapa Flow*, II, 250–7; Keyes, I, 145n.
30. Bod.Lib., Bonham Carter, 12, 1–3.
31. Bod.Lib., Bonham Carter, 12, 4d.
32. NA, WO 106/1463.
33. Macfie, 'The Straits Question', p. 58.
34. NA, Cab 47/217, C3 question 8.
35. Keyes, I, 293.

36. De Robeck, p. 445.
37. NA, Cab 47/217, 40.
38. NA, WO 106/1519.
39. Bod.Lib., Asquith, 27, 107–8.
40. Bod.Lib., Bonham Carter, 12, 77–80.
41. NA, WO 106/1539.
42. Quoted in Marder, *From Dreadnought to Scapa Flow*, II, 260.
43. NA, FO 371/3657, 526.
44. Hull, pp. 278 and 282.
45. *Round Table*. No. 20 (September 1915), pp. 857–8.
46. Sharpe, 'ANZAC day', p. 83.
47. Zilmo, 'Who owns Gallipoli', pp. 1–2.
48. Quoted in Marder, *From Dreadnought to Scapa Flow*, II, 199.
49. Thomson, 'The Vilest Libel of the War?' pp. 629–31.
50. DAFP IV, 475, 603.
51. Winter, *Haig's Command*, pp. 248, 252.

Chapter 12. *A Welter of Anarchy: Churchill, the Empire and the Bolsheviks, 1919–1922*

1. Dunsterville, p. 28.
2 De Novo, *On the Sidelines*, p. 243.
3. Gilbert, IV, CV, ii, 1180–1.
4. Jeffrey, *Sir Henry Wilson*, p. 234.
5. Bod.Lib., Milner, 29, ff. 2–3.
6. NA, CO 537/835, 6.
7. NA, WO 106/55, 40.
8. Popplewell, pp. 307–8.
9. NA, WO 32/5728, II, 3, 6, Appendix C, 69; Andrew, *Secret Service*, p. 337.
10. NA, WO 157/1263, No. 38, Appendix, iv.
11. BL, IOR, Mss Eur E 264/125, 5, 55.
12. Gilbert, IV, CV, i, 991–2.
13. BL, IOR, Mss Eur 264/54G, 12, 18, 19.
14. NA, Air 1.125/B 11395.
15. BL, IOR, Mss Eur 54G, 32, 33, 46.
16. DBFP, 1st Series, XIII, 439, 457, 459, 563, 667.
17. Johnson, *Spying for Empire*, pp. 236–7.
18. *Hansard*, 5th Series, 139, 2545.
19. White, p. 95; Andrew, *Secret Service*, p. 397.
20. NA, WO 32/5780; WO 106/55, 36; WO 32/5728 which is a synthesis of this material compiled in August 1921; WO 157/1263, No. 23,18, No. 34, 12, No. 48, 14 and Appendix, i–ii.
21. Gilbert, IV, CV, I, 609.
22. NA, CO 537/1735, 16; Gilbert, IV, iii, 1460; *Cohen, Churchill and the Balfour Declaration*, pp. 96–7.
23. NA, KY 3/267.
24. Gilbert, IV, CV, ii, 1178–9.

Chapter 13. Carry on like Britons: Churchill's Russian War, 1919–1921
1. Quoted by Rose (p. 183) from Winston Churchill, *Speeches*, VIII, 7774.
2. NA, Adm 156/179, 482; Adm 156/94.
3. NA, WO 157/121, Report, 17 July 1919.
4. Gilbert, IV, 274; NA, WO 95/5430, 18 August 1919.
5. Gilbert, IV, CV, i, 763, 767; for the mutinies see: NA, WO 158/714 and WO 32/9245.
6. Ruotsila, 'Churchill-Mannerheim Collaboration', pp. 16–17.
7. NA, WO 157/1263, No. 41, 8.

Chapter 14. The Weight of the British Arm: Policing the Empire, 1919–1922
1. Winston Churchill, *Speeches*, III, 3026.
2. *Hansard*, 5th Series, 133, 962.
3. Gilbert, IV, 734.
4. Gilbert, IV, 915.
5. BL, IOR, Mss Eur E 264/10, 402; Gilbert, IV, CV, i, 662–3.
6. Gilbert, VIII, 140.
7. Killingray, 'A Swift Agent of Government', p. 438.
8. BL, IOR, Mss Eur E 264/10, 403.
9. O'Dwyer, p. 289.
10. BL, IOR, Mss Eur E 134/5, 68.
11. Detailed and balanced accounts of the Amritsar affair can be found in A. Draper, *The Amritsar Massacre: Twilight of the Raj* (1985) and N. Lloyd, *The Amritsar Massacre: The Untold Story of One Fateful Day* (2011). In 1999 Queen Elizabeth II officially apologised to the people of India for the blunders of Dyer and O'Dwyer.
12. BL, IOR, Mss Eur E 124/5, 136, 137, 248.
13. BL, IOR, Mss Eur E 264/54G, 22, 33, 38–9, 46.
14. BL, IOR, Mss Eur E 124/5, 131, 248.
15. NA, WO 32/5356, 1A, 61A.
16. NA, WO 32/5356, No. 24/59/D, 29A.
17. NA, CO 537/5324.
18. NA, WO 95/5415 [15th Sikhs].
19. Callwell, II, 239; Gilbert, IV, CV, ii, 1118.
20. Gilbert, IV, CV, ii, 11401.
21. *Hansard*, 5th Series, 131, 1705–1820 for the debate.

Chapter 15. Reign of Terror: Churchill and Ireland, 1919–1923
1. Mitchell, *Revolutionary Government*, p. 24.
2. Winston Churchill, *The World Crisis: Aftermath*, p. 289.
3. Winston Churchill, *Thoughts and Adventures*, p. 219.
4. *Documents on Irish Foreign Policy*, I, 219 [Report of Art O'Brian, Sinn Féin representative in London, 12 December 1920].
5. Winston Churchill, *Speeches*, III, 3021.
6. *Hansard*, 5th Series, 135, 962–3.
7. Mitchell, *Revolutionary Government*, p. 214.

8. Gilbert, IV, CV, ii, 1085.

9. Andrew, *Defence of the Realm*, pp. 145–6.

10. Callwell, II, 291.

11. Gilbert, IV, CV, ii, 1195.

12. Townshend, *The British Campaign*, p. 116.

13. NA, WO 141/44; Gilbert, IV, 455.

14. Townshend, *The British Campaign*, p. 170.

15. *Documents on Irish Foreign Policy*, I, 219.

16. McColgan, pp. 16–17.

17. Winston Churchill, *Thoughts and Adventures*, p. 225.

18. Toye, *Lloyd George and Churchill*, p. 223.

19. Mitchell, *Revolutionary Government*, pp. 326, 329.

20. Mitchell, *Revolutionary Government*, p. 325.

21. Toye, *Lloyd George and Churchill*, p. 223.

22. *Documents on Irish Foreign Policy*, I, 353–4.

23. NA, Air 8/48.

24. *Spectator*, 7 January 1922; *National Review*, LXXIX (March–August 1922), pp. 53, 704.

Chapter 16. *The Possibility of Disaster: The Near and Middle East, 1919–1922*

1. Jeffrey, *The British Army*, pp. 38, 50–60.

2. Gilbert, IV, CV, ii, 937–9.

3. McCormick, *Imperial Mission*, pp. 79, 82, 86, 91.

4. Sluglett, pp. 69–71.

5. NA, WO 157/1309, 5.

6. Bloxham, pp. 139,152, 154; NA, WO 157/1309, Part 3, 1.

7. NA, FO 371/ 3658, 516.

8. FO Review of Foreign Press; *The Political Review*, p. 613 [2 April 1920].

9. Mango, p. 278.

10. Mango, p. 225.

11. Gilbert, IV, 498–500.

12. NA, WO 157/1263, No. 37, App. vii–viii; Mango, p. 313.

13. NA, WO 157/1263, No. 39, App. i–ii.

14. Lloyd George, *The Truth about the Peace Treaties*, pp. 1011, 1015; Mango, pp. 308–9.

15. Bloxham, p. 144.

16. Gilbert, IV, 483.

17. NA, WO 165/85, 30.

18. Douglas, 'Did Britain use Chemical Weapons in Mandatory Iraq', pp. 873–4, 878, 883; Gilbert, IV, 483; Sluglett, pp. 279–280. The gas myth was repeated in 2003 by Robert Fiske in the *Independent*, Tony Benn MP and Greenpeace.

19. Roskill, *Hankey*, II, 201.

20. Wasserstein, p. 97n.

21. *Hansard*, 5th Series, 138, 589.

22. NA, FO 371/3657, 8.

23. RHL, Meinertzhagen, 22 [20 June 1922].

24. RHL, Meinertzhagen, 22 [20 June 1922].
25. Gilbert, IV, 895.
26. RHL, Meinertzhagen, 22 [24 December 1921].
27. Gilbert, IV, 552–3.
28. Sluglett, pp. 42–3.
29. Wasserstein, p. 98.
30. Gilbert, IV, CV, iii, 1430.
31. Gilbert, IV, 207.
32. Boyle, *Trenchard*, pp. 289–390.
33. Sluglett, pp. 186–7, 189–90.
34. RHL, Meinertzhagen, 22, 44–5.
35. Sluglett, p. 92.
36. Callwell, II, 316.
37. Winston Churchill, *Speeches*, III, 3270.
38. Sluglett, p. 67.
39. NLS, Haldane, Ms 20251, 147.
40. *The Times*, 22 September 1922.
41. NA, Air 8/45.
42. NA, Air 8/45.
43. DRFR, 4 January 1918.
44. Wasserstein, pp. 119–20; RHL, Meinertzhagen, 21 [12 February 1919].
45. Winston Churchill, *Speeches, IV*, 3348; Cohen, *Churchill and the Jews*, pp. 77, 79.
46. *Hansard*, 5th Series, 144, 1623–4, 1626.
47. *Contemporary Review*, CXXI (April 1922) p. 436.
48. Gilbert, IV, 541.
49. Winston Churchill, *Speeches*, IV, 3343.
50. Cohen, *Churchill and the Jews*, pp. 54–5.
51. Winston Churchill, *Speeches*, 3263.
52. Wasserstein, pp. 6–7.
53. Gilbert, IV, 562–3.
54. Toye, *Lloyd George and Churchill*, pp. 319–20.
55. De Novo, p. 227.
56. Cohen, *Churchill and the Jews*, p. 91.
57. Gilbert, IV, 618.
58. NA, CO 537/1735, 16.
59. Gilbert, IV, CV, ii, 1385
60. Roskill, *Hankey*, II, p. 245.

PART FOUR: 1923–1939

Chapter 17. *The Will to Rule: The Struggle to Keep India, 1923–1936*

1. Andrew, 'Churchill and Intelligence', p. 181.
2. Gilbert, V, CV, iii, 33; BL, IOR, Mss Eur F 125/160/64, 2.
3. Amery, pp. 48–9.
4. Winston Churchill, *Gathering Storm*, p. 33; Gilbert, V, CV, ii, 222.

5. *The Times*, 13 December 1930.
6. Winston Churchill, *Speeches*, V, 4670.
7. Gilbert, V, ii, 1431–2.
8. *Egyptian Mail*, 11, 14, 18, 22 March 1919.
9. Moran, p. 277.
10. Gilbert, VII, 1226.
11. Gilbert, V, CV, iii, 10n.
12. Hyam, *Understanding the British Empire*, p. 323; Toye, *Churchill's Empire*, pp. 156–66.
13. Soames, *Clementine Churchill*, p. 277.
14. Hyam, *Understanding the British Empire*, p. 322.
15. Winston Churchill, *History of the English-Speaking People*, III, viii.
16. Hyam, *Understanding the British Empire*, pp. 237–9.
17. Moran, p. 395.
18. NA, KY 1/15/1, 141–2.
19. Roberts, *Eminent Churchillians*, pp. 211–14.
20. Gilbert, V, CV, ii, 1358.
21. Gilbert, V, 356.
22. Gilbert, V, CV, ii, 20.
23. Kudaisyam, p. 43.
24. Gilbert, V, 401–2, 411.
25. Gilbert, V, 377; CV, ii, 129.
26. Roberts, *Holy Fox*, p. 34.
27. Gilbert, V, 375, 381, 469; CV, ii, 652.
28. Gilbert, V, CV, ii, 1060.
29. BL, IOR, Mss F 125/160/64, 2.
30. NA, KY 3/251, 23A, 36A.
31. Gilbert, V, CV, ii, 388.
32. Gilbert, V, CV, ii, 537, 549–50, 569.
33. Gilbert, V, 376, 399–400; CV, ii, 222n.
34. Herman, pp. 310–11; Toye, *Churchill and the Empire*, pp. 173–4.
35. Gilbert, V, 596.
36. BL, IOR, Mss Eur F 125/110, 90, 94.

Chapter 18. An Unnecessary War, Part I: The Japanese Challenge, 1931–1939

1. NA, FO 262/1419, 158.
2. Fraser, 'India in Anglo-Japanese relations', pp. 366–7.
3. NA, FO 262/1419, 39, 90, 129, 131–2, 135.
4. Mackenzie King, Diary, 16 August 1943.
5. Hopkins, *White House Papers*, I, 577–8; Thorne, p. 727n. Gilbert, V, CV, ii, 303–7.
6. NA, Adm 1/11062, 14.
7. Gilbert, V, CV, i, 920.
8. Gilbert, VIII, 1505n.
9. Winston Churchill, *Speeches*, V, 4784.
10. Gilbert, V, CV, i, 303; Bell, 'Singapore Strategy', p. 610.

11. Gilbert, V, CV, i, 303, 920.
12. Gilbert, V, CV, i, 1281–2.
13. Ed. Myers and Peattie, Introduction, pp. 39–40.
14. Peattie, in ed. Myers and Peattie, pp. 92–4, 99, 121–3, 125.
15. Gilbert, V, CV, ii, 704.
16. Gilbert.V, CV, ii, 823.
17. Gilbert, V, CV, iii, 16.
18. *Evening Standard*, 27 November 1936.
19. Gilbert, V, CV, iii, 467.
20. *Evening Standard*, 21 January 1938.
21. Grew, p. 249.
22. Everest Phillips, p. 249.
23. NA, FO 371/23752, 46–7.
24. NA, KY 3/251, 32A, 50A, 59A.
25. Winston Churchill, *Speeches*, VI, 6144.
26. BL, IOR, Mss Eur F 125/160/64,10; NA, KY 251/, 36A.
27. NA, FO 371/23572, 266, 274ff.
28. NA, KY 3/251, 61A, 63A; Best, *Diplomacy and Intelligence*, p. 95.
29. NA, FO 371/23571, 256, 259.
30. BL, IOR, Mss Eur F 125/160/64, 2.
31. Everest Phillips, p. 249.
32. BL, IOR, Mss Eur F 125/160/64, 3–4; NA, Adm 1/11062, 10, 11d; Cab 16/209, 8–9.
33. Darwin, *Empire Project*, p. 425.

Chapter 19. An Unnecessary War, Part II: Appeasement, 1935–1939

1. *Imperial Policy*, I, 86–7.
2. Wark, 'Air Defences Gap', *passim*.
3. Winston Churchill, *Speeches*, VI, 5656, 5694, 6151.
4. Hauner, pp. 25, 32, 57–8.
5. Overy, *The Morbid Age*, pp. 271–2.
6. Hauner, p. 310.
7. Cameron Watt, pp. 41, 621.
8. Pratt, p. 3.
9. Knox-Conquest, p. 15.
10. Rodogno, p. 53.
11. Rodogno, pp. 186–9.
12. Gilbert, V, CV, i, 23, 675n, 677.
13. Gilbert, V, CV, ii, 1301.
14. Robertson, *Mussolini as Empire Builder*, pp. 160–1.
15. Winston Churchill, *Speeches*, VI, 5675, 5685.
16. Nicholson, *Diaries*, I, 211.
17. Gilbert, V, CV, iii, 1107.
18. Gilbert, V, CV, ii, 1264.
19. Gilbert, V, CV, iii, 1231, 1375, 1414.
20. Pratt, p. 67.

21. Winston Churchill, *Speeches*, VI, 6099.
22. Cohen, *Churchill and the Jews*, p. 177; MEC, Lampson Diaries, 11 October 1938.
23. NA, KY 3/267/3, 61A.
24. *Imperial Policy*, I, 125–6.
25. MEC, Lampson Diaries, 9, 24 November 1936.
26. MEC, Lampson Diaries, 26 December 1938.
27. NA, KY 3/251, 61A; Hauner, *One Man against Empire, passim.*
28. NA, Air 8/259, Staff Memo [July 1937], 1–2.
29. Hauner, p. 30.
30. NA, FO 371/ 32376.
31. NA, CO 926/1/4.1-4.
32. Pratt, pp. 162–4.
33. Amery, *Empire at Bay*, p. 484.
34. Cohen, *Churchill and the Jews*, p. 174.
35. Gilbert, V, CV, iii, 1505n.
36. Pratt, p. 114.
37. MEC, Lampson Diaries, 28 April 1939.
38. BL, IOR, Mss Eur F 125/160/64, 2.
39. NA, Adm 1/11062, 12.
40. NA, Adm 1/11062, 4; Cab 16/209, 13.
41. NA, Cab 16/209, 20, 45, 50; Pratt, pp. 164, 191.
42. BL, IOR, Mss Eur F 125/160/64m, 1–2.
43. The mindset of the period is brilliantly analysed in Richard Overy's *The Morbid Age*.
44. Soames, *Speaking for Themselves*, p. 391.
45. Charmley, p. 142.

PART FIVE: 1939–1945

Chapter 20. *A War of Peoples and Causes: Churchill as War Leader and Strategist*

1. Gilbert, C, CV, iii, 1578.
2. Lukas, p. 8.
3. E.g. C. Este, *Warlord: A Life of Churchill at War, 1874–1945*, Chapters 42–50.
4. Pownall, I, 333.
5. Roberts, *Eminent Churchillians*, pp. 27–32.
6. Pownall, I, 203.
7. Pownall, I, 42, 45.
8. Gilbert, VI, 684–5.
9. NA, WO 216/5, 1A; Gilbert, VI, 1072–3.
10. Gilbert, VI, 1070–1; Alanbrooke, p. 154 and note.
11. Best, *Churchill at War*, pp. 183–4.
12. Dalton, p. 80.
13. Cadogan, p. 375; Dalton, p. 41 [19 June 1940].
14. Winston Churchill, *The Grand Alliance*, pp. 152–81.
15. Charmley, *End of Glory*, p. 408; Roberts, *Eminent Churchillians*, pp. 152–81.

16. Lukas, p. 117.

17. Hinsley, Thomas, Ransom and Knight, I, 203–4.

18. For Butler's conduct see Lukas, pp. 59–60, 92–3, 120, 202–4.

Chapter 21. *We Felt We Were British: The Imperial War Effort*

1. Mackenzie King, Diaries, 16 August 1943.

2. Somerville, pp. 4, 35.

3. NA, CO 968/9/6, 81.

4. NA, CO 875/7/12, 4–5.

5. NA, WO 106/2866A, Bulletin 5, Appendix A, 3.

6. NA, WO 2866A, Bulletin 2, 1–2; WO 106/2866, Bulletin 24 [August 1942], 4–5.

7. NA, WO 203/2355, Report August to September 1945, 9, 13.

8. Toye, *Churchill's Empire*, pp. 214–15.

9. Somerville, p. 5.

10. Bod. Lib., Macmillan C 278, 169; C 281, 87.

11. Somerville, p. 66.

12. Gilbert, VI, 556n.

13. Healy, *Colour, Combat and Climate*, pp. 73–4.

14. NA, WO 203/2355, Report February to April 1945, 22, 28.

15. NA, WO 106/2866A, Bulletin 2, 1–2.

16. NA, CO 875/7/12, 4.

17. Jackson, p. 185.

18. NA, CO 323/1737/8, 8, 43.

19. NA, CO 926/1/4, 1–3.

20. Roosevelt Papers, Box 2 [Extracts from broadcasts made between 5 and 22 December 1941].

21. NA, CO 129/581/15, 55–8.

22. NA, CO 875/7/6, A 32; CO 875/7/5, 94.

23. Payton-Smith, p. 205.

24. *St John's News*, 4 September 1939.

25. NA, Adm 199/738, 11, 27–8, 92.

26. NA, WO 106/4932, 5A.

27. Payton-Smith, p. 205.

28. Webster, p. 27.

29. Day, *Churchill and Menzies*, pp. 4–5, 13–14.

30. Mackenzie King, Diaries, 7 May 1941; 21 August 1941.

31. Mackenzie King, Diaries, 23 August 1941.

32. Mackenzie King, Diaries, 30 August 1941.

33. Mackenzie King, Diaries, 22 August 1941.

34. Winston Churchill, *Speeches*, VI, 6472.

35. Herman, p. 446.

36. NA, WO 208/804A; WO 208/819, App. D, 35C.

37. NA, WO 203/2355, Report November 1944 to January 1945, 14; WO 203/2355, Report August to September 1945, 5.

38. Gilbert, VI, 1047n.

39. CWP, II, 1124.

40. Amery, p. 367.
41. MEC, Lampson Diaries, 3 and 8 September and 9 October 1939.
42. NA, WO 203/2365/2365, Report May to July 1945, 2; Report February to March 1945, 7.

Chapter 22. A Disaster of the First Magnitude: Holding the Middle East, 1939–1941
1. DAFP, IV, 633.
2. NA, WO 216/5, 1A.
3. CWP, II, 1718.
4. Rodogno, pp. 25–7; Hirszowicz, pp. 87, 90.
5. Avon, *The Reckoning*, p. 126.
6. Churchill, *Speeches*, VI, 6543.
7. I am indebted to the late Neil Hart for this popular assessment of the Duce.
8. CRC, II, 184.
9. NA, WO 193/310, 4A, 14A, 27A.
10. NA, WO 193/279, Washington Embassy to FO, 16 December 1944.
11. NA, Air 8/1748, *passim.*
12. NA, Air 8/550, C-in-C Middle East to FO, 22 May 1941.
13. NA, Air 8/541, 22, 25, 26, 36.

Chapter 23. Supreme Effort: Distractions, Chiefly French
1. NA, Air 9/116, 1–2.
2. NA, Prem 3/188/2, 3.
3. NA, WO 193/222, 1A.
4. Jennings, pp. 15–16.
5. Mazower, pp. 117–18, 120.
6. NA, Prem 3/188/2, 3–5.
7. Hinsley, I, 154–5; Melka, p. 60.
8. NA, Adm 199/1281.
9. CWP, II, 1713.
10. NA, CO 106/2866A, Bulletin No. 1, 1.
11. NA, CO 875/7/6, 57.
12. DAFP, IV, 506.
13. WO 192/222, 1A and n.
14. NA, WO 106/2866A, Bulletin No. 1, 13; CWP, II, 477.
15. MEC, Spears Diary, 11 March 1941.
16. NA, Adm 199/1281, MO 504640; Roosevelt Papers, Box 6.
17. Hirszowicz, pp. 122–3, 129.
18. Hirszowicz, p. 102.
19. NA, Air 8/529, [Note on Changes in the Situation in Iraq, 3].
20. NA, Air 8/549, Churchill to Wavell, 8 May 1941.
21. NA, Air 8/549, Wavell to WO, 11 May 1941.
22. NA, Air 8/549, WO to Wavell, 1 June 1941.
23. NA, Air 8/549, Churchill to Wavell, 8 May 1941.
24. MEC, Spears Papers, Box 1, File 1; Killearn, p. 167.
25. NA, Air 8/550, Wavell to WO, 20 May 1941.

26. NA, Air 8/550, 25.
27. NA, Air 8/550, Naval officer i.c. submarines Malta to Malta Force, 17 June 1941.
28. NA, Air 8/550, Tedder to Chief of Air Staff, 2 July 1941.
29. MEC, Spears Papers, Box 1 [Intelligence assessment, 16 July 1941].
30. Kersaudy, p. 146.
31. NA, Air 8/550, Wavell to WO, 5 August 1941.
32. MEC, Spears Papers, Box 1, File 7.
33. There is an excellent account of the Syrian campaign and its aftermath in Smith, *England's Last War Against France*, pp. 191–278.
34. Gilbert, VII, 647n.
35. CWP, II, 919.
36. MEC, Spears Papers, Box 2, File 7.
37. MEC, Spears Papers, Box 2, File 7.
38. NA, Air 8/550, 27 May 1941.

Chapter 24. Britain's Broke: Anglo-American Exchanges, 1939–1941
1. NA, Air 8/541, 40.
2. Randolph Churchill, *Winston Churchill*, I, CV, I, 600.
3. Gilbert, IV, 122–3.
4. Theodore Roosevelt, I, 3.
5. Thorne, p. 21.
6. Kimball, *Unsordid Act*, pp. 186–7.
7. Bennett, p. 67.
8. Webster, p. 25.
9. NA, WO 208/7892.
10. Winston Churchill, *Speeches*, VI, 6228; CWP, III, 365.
11. Kennedy, pp. 453, 461; CWP, III, 77.
12. Kimball, *Unsordid Act*, pp. 168–70.
13. WO 193/310, 36A.
14. NA, WO 216/150, 34.
15. NA, WO 106/5932, 57A.
16. CRC, I, 140–2.
17. *Hansard*, 5th Series, 370, 255–6, 262; CRC, III, 242–3.
18. *The Gleaner*, 5 April 1941.
19. Jimsey, p. 139.
20. Kennedy, *Freedom from Fear*, p. 450.
21. Kimball, *Unsordid Act*, p 32
22. CRC, II, 221.
23. Kennedy, p. 443.
24. Kimball, *Unsordid Act*, pp. 28, 29.
25. Bennett, *Celluloid War*, p. 84.

Chapter 25. A Shocking Tale: The Singapore Debacle, 1941–1942
1. Gilbert, VI, 346.
2. Gilbert, VI, 346–7.
3. NA, Prem 3/15/2, 29.

4. DAFP, IV, 13, 73.
5. McCarthy, 'Australia and Imperial Defence', p. 20.
6. NA, FO 371/26421, 6.
7. NA, WO 208/951.
8. *Japan's Decision for War*, pp. 26, 65.
9. *Japan's Decision for War*, pp. 26, 56, 77.
10. *Japan's Decision for War*, p. 238.
11. *Japan's Decision for War*, pp. 153, 238.
12. *Japan's Decision for War*, p. 153; Marder, *Old Friends*, pp. 84–5.
13. *Japan's Decision for War*, p. 252.
14. Gilbert, VI, 1256–7; Harvey, p. 53.
15. Thorne, pp. 5–7.
16. Gilbert, VI, 1258–9.
17. Marder, *Old Friends*, p. 23.
18. Marder, *Old Friends*, p. 4.
19. NA, CO 968/9/6, 131; CO 967/7/77, 123.
20. NA, CO 968/9/6, 13, 70, 74, 84.
21. NA, CO 967/7/77, 121, 122.
22. NA, CO 967/7/77, 8.
23. NA, CO 967/7/77, 110.
24. NA, Adm 199/622B; NA, Adm 199/622A, 14.
25. NA, CO 968/9/6, 74.
26. NA, Adm 199/622A, 451.
27. NA, Adm 199/622B, 71.
28. NA, WO 106/2357C, 1A.
29. Elphick, pp. 221, 230.
30. NA, WO 106/2357C, 1A.
31. Marder, *Old Friends*, p. 55.
32. NA, WO 106/2569, 1, 68, 83.
33. Alan Brooke, p. 231.
34. *Evening Post*, 20 February 1942; *St John's News*, 16 February 1942.
35. *East African Gazette*, 20 February, 11, 14 July 1942.
36. NA, WO 106/2866, Report No. 22 [March 1942], 7.
37. *The Times*, 18 February 1942.
38. *Hansard*, 5th Series, 378, 118, 272, 304, 306.
39. MacKenzie King, Diaries, 27 February 1942.
40. *Time*, 23 February 1942.
41. *Time*, 2 March 1942.
42. NA, WO 106/2658, 2, 7–8.
43. NA, Prem 3/152/1, 34–5.
44. NA, CO 968/9/5, 38.
45. NA, CO 875/14/6 [Report of Colonel Marchant, Assistant Commissioner].
46. NA, CO 967/139.
47. Harvey, p. 70.
48. Gilbert, VI, 1273.

Chapter 26. The Dark Valley: Perils and Panic, 1942
1. NA, WO 106/42932, 1A, 4A.
2. Marder, *Old Friends*, pp. 143-4.
3. *Time*, 24 August 1943.
4. Marder, *Old Friends*, p. 88.
5. Gilbert, VII, 118, 122; Cadogan, p. 461.
6. Gilbert, VII, 73-6.
7. NA, WO 208/928.
8. Hirszowicz, pp. 240, 243-4, Hauner, p. 43.
9. Killearn, p. 209.
10. Hirszowicz, p.198.
11. Hirszowicz, p. 219.
12. NA, WO 208/882, 33, 80-1.
13. Hirszowicz, p. 198.
14. NA, WO 208/8/82, 11A.
15. Hauner, *India*, p. 43.
16. Bod.Lib., Macmillan, C 280, 16, 58-9.
17. NA, Adm 199/738, 449, 539.
18. DAFP, IV, 474; Day, 'Anzacs on the Run', pp. 188-9, 197.
19. *Sunday Times* (Perth), 22 February 1942.
20. DAFP, IV, 447.
21. *Melbourne Argus*, 20 February 1942.
22. Moran, pp. 36-7; DAPF, IV, 397, 411, 428.
23. DAFP, IV, 526, 555, 558, 668.
24. Alan Brooke, p. 257.
25. NA, Prem 3/151/2, 38, 42; DAFP, IV, 701, 836.
26. NA, WO 208/929.
27. NA, WO 208/929.
28. *Canberra Times*, 8 May 1942.
29. NA, Adm 199/738, 521; DAFP, IV, 717.
30. Reynolds, p. 299.
31. Adelman, pp. 134, 187-8.

Chapter 27. A State of Ordered Anarchy: India, 1942-1943
1. Gilbert, VII, 209.
2. Gandhi, LXXV, 193, 195.
3. Gandhi, LXXV, 441.
4. Gandhi, LXXV, 5.
5. Gandhi, LXXV, 110.
6. Singh, p. 71.
7. BL, IOL, Mss Eur F 125/77, 7.
8. *Transfer of Power*, II, 3-4.
9. NA, WO 208/792.
10. CRC, I, 402.
11. Winston Churchill, *Hinge of Fate*, p. 209.
12. CRC, I, 447.

13. Hopkins, II, 516–17.
14. Amery, p. 785.
15. Amery, pp. 826, 833.
16. Amery, p. 838.
17. Amery, p. 783.
18. Amery, p. 729.
19. Hopkins, II, 517.
20. Reynolds, p. 337.
21. NA, WO 208/804B, 2.
22. Hopkins, II, 517.
23. http://www presidency: USCB cdu/Frankin Roosevelt pap.
24. Hopkins, II, 767.
25. Reynolds, p. 336: Stilwell, Diary, 17 October 1942.
26. Amery, p. 829.
27. WO 208/792, press reports, *passim*.
28. BL, IOL, Mss Eur F 125/110, 209.
29. *Hansard*, 5th Series, 383, 907, 908, 1342; Amery, p. 832; for the aerial attacks see NA, Air 23/2052.
30. BL, IOL, Mss Eur F 125/110, 210.
31. Amery, p. 832.
32. BL, IOL, Mss Eur F 125/110, 210.
33. NA, WO 208/804B, 2, 5, 7–8.
34. NA, WO 208/1576A.
35. NA, WO 208/812, 2A.

Chapter 28. The Wealth of India: Subversion and Famine, 1943–1945

1. Amery, p. 872.
2. Amery, pp. 1032–3.
3. Winston Churchill, *Hinge of Fate*, pp. 304–5.
4. Thorne, p. 356; Herman, p. 513; Amery, p. 946.
5. http://Pyswarrior.com/Axis propaganda against Indian troops.
6. NA, WO 208/809A.
7. NA, WO 220/560, 1A, 14–15.
8. A. Sen, *Poverty and Famines: An Essay on Entitlement* (Oxford, 1982), M Tauger, 'Indian Empire Crises of World War II', *British Scholar*, 1 (2009) and letters from both authors in the *New York Review of Books*, 24 February 2011.
9. Fort, p. 362.
10. Mukerjee, *Churchill's Secret War*; by training the author is a scientist and she makes further allegations against Churchill in *Harpers Magazine*, 4 November 2010.
11. NCO, Cherwell, F 235/32.
12. Adelman, p. 186.
13. NA, WO 208/809, 25A, 35A.
14. Amery, pp. 933–4.
15. Amery, p. 943.
16. Amery, pp. 950–2; Thorne, pp. 474–5.

17. Moran, p. 193; NCO, Cherwell F 245/4; F 249/7.
18. CRC, III, 117.

Chapter 29. The Flag Is Not Let Down: Churchill, Stalin and Roosevelt
1. Hopkins. III, 765.
2. Thorne, p. 592.
3. Bod.Lib., Macmillan C 278, 169.
4. Gilbert, VII, 1166.
5. NA, WO 193/179.
6. Stilwell, p. 227.
7. Marder, *Old Friends*, p. 340.
8. Mackenzie King, Diary, 3 May 1944.
9. Marder, *Old Friends*, pp. 349–50; CRC, III, 91.
10. Morgenthau, III, 138.
11. Thorne, p. 99.
12. Thorne, p. 106.
13. Stilwell, Diary, 17 October 1942; Killearn, p. 258.
14. Cadogan, p. 462.
15. Stilwell, *Papers*, p. 230; Alanbrooke, p. 478.
16. Haslam, p. 224.
17. Herring, p. 547.
18. Mackenzie King, Diary, 11 August 1943, memo, p. 3.
19. NA, WO 193/295, 3A.
20. Zubrok, p. 297.
21. NA, WO 208/791.
22. NA, WO 193/203, 'Security of the British Empire'.
23. Mackenzie King, Diary, 11 May 1944.
24. Edmonds, *Cold War*, pp. 244, 247.
25. Gilbert, VIII, 6–7.
26. Tucker, *The Cold War*, p. 279.
27. Edmonds, 'Churchill and Stalin', pp. 321–3.
28. Gilbert, VII, 587; VIII, 65, 67, 75, 89.
29. Gilbert, VII, 1205.
30. Gilbert, VIII, 88–9.
31. Hopkins, III, 783; Doenecke and Stoler, p. 55.

Chapter 30. Fraternal Association: America and the Future of the British Empire
1. Oren, p. 451.
2. NA, CO 825/45/9, 88.
3. NA, WO 216/95, 1A.
4. Herring, p. 613.
5. Interview, 30 June 1971 [Truman Library @ nava gov.].
6. CRC, III, 5.
7. NA, CO 967/19, App. 1.
8. Thorne, p. 583.
9. Mackenzie King, Diary, 8 May 1944.

10. Winston Churchill, *Speeches*, VII, 6824.

11. CRC, III, 105.

12. Winston Churchill, *Speeches*, VII, 6918.

13. Winston Churchill, *Speeches*, VII, 6878.

14. Winston Churchill, *Speeches*, VII, 6824.

15. Winston Churchill, *Speeches*, VII, 7302.

16. Bod.Lib., Macmillan C 277, 259.

17. NA, CO 967/18, 48.

18. NA, CO 967/18, 10.

19. NA, CO 967/18, 24.

20. Thorne, p. 279.

21. Herring, p. 562.

22. NA, CO 967/21, 6.

23. NA, CO 967/21, 6.

24. Morgenthau, III, 129.

25. Mackenzie King, Diary, 11 August 1943, memo, p. 2.

26. Aldrich, pp. 14–15.

27. Aldrich, pp. 37–8; US National Archives, Record of the Office of Strategic Services, Box 9, # 23371, # 23375, # 23380.

28. Aldrich, pp. 37–8, 42.

29. NA, WO 106/2899, 78, 83, 85.

30. Gilbert, VIII, 69.

31. Parker, pp. 338–9.

32. Rubin, p. 564.

33. Rubin, p. 259.

34. Oren, p. 418.

35. Rubin, p. 564.

36. NA, CO 733/462, 105.

37. http://www.presidency.ucst/franklin.Roosevelt,pup; Doenecke and Stoler, p. 54, where Churchill's comment is omitted.

38. Macmillan, C 276, 280.

39. Healy, p. 81.

40. Toye, *Churchill's Empire*, pp. 248–9.

41. NA, FO 954/15A.

Chapter 31. Your Lofty Principles: Gains and Losses, 1945

1. Mackenzie King, Diaries, 5 May 1944.

2. Gilbert, VIII, 18.

3. Macmillan, *Blast of War*, p. 507.

4. Harvey, p. 364.

5. Amery, p. 1031.

6. Gilbert, VII, 1232.

7. Amery, p. 1034.

8. NCO, Cherwell, F 242, 5.

9. NCO, Cherwell, F 243, 5.

10. Jackson, p. 39.

11. Edgerton, *Britain's War Machine: Weapons, Resources and Experts in the Second World War* (2011).
12. NCO, Cherwell, F 250, 7.
13. *East African Standard*, 6 August 1941.
14. I am indebted to Rupert Boulting for this account of his father's exchange with Churchill.
15. NA, Prem 3/170/2, 5; Hopkins, III, 71–2.
16. NA, Prem 3/170/2, 57.
17. NA, Prem 3/179/2, 77.
18. Moran, p. 282.
19. Thorne, p. 630; Doenecke and Stoler, pp. 57–8.
20. Tønesson, p. 21.
21. Thorne, p. 633.
22. NA, Cab 44/234, 56.
23. NA, CO 967/15, *passim*.
24. NA, Cab 121/763, 1–2.
25. Roland, *passim*.
26. NA, CO 537/1862, 89–90, 107, 122, 150; TS 26/830, 3; WO 325/5, 1.100, 112. Unlike the Germans, the Japanese have shown little contrition for these and other atrocities committed by their armed forces, nor have they issued any formal apologies.
27. NA, WO 32/11719, 58A, pp. 3, 9.
28. NA, WO 32/11719, 58A, p. 25.
29. Springhall, pp. 638–9.
30. Comber, pp. 130–1.
31. NA, WO 106/2685, 7–8; WO 208/786, Summary No. 13, p. 3.
32. NA, WO 203/2355, Report November 1944–January 1945, p. 1.
33. Thorne, p. 608.
34. Thorne, p. 611.
35. Rothwell, *Britain and the Cold War*, p. 121.
36. Harvey, pp. 363–4.
37. NA, CO 733/462, 69.
38. NA, CO 733/462, 51.
39. NA, CO 733/462, 99–100.
40. Hahn, pp. 17–18.
41. Gilbert, VII, 1052.
42. *Daily Telegraph*, 3 April 2011.
43. Andrew, *Defence of the Realm*, p. 357.
44. Rose, *Churchill and Zionism*, p. 162.
45. Gilbert, VII, 1047–9.

PART SIX, 1945–1955

Chapter 32. Abiding Power: The Empire and the Cold War, 1946–1951

1. Bod.Lib., Macmillan D 7, 85.
2. Bod.Lib., Macmillan D 8, 4.

3. *Hansard*, 5th Series, 432, 18.

4. *Hansard*, 5th Series, 491, 1350-1.

5. *Hansard*, 5th Series, 491, 1363.

6. *Hansard*, 5th Series, 491, 978.

7. Jahal, pp. 416–17.

8. NA, Prem 8/1343.

9. NA, WO 193/303, 4A.

10. Bod.Lib., Macmillan D 8, 82.

11. *The Argus* [Melbourne], 7 August 1945.

12. Bod.Lib., Lennox-Boyd, 3455, 13.

13. Gilbert, VIII, 634.

14. *Hansard*, 5th Series, 495, 1064.

15. Gilbert, VIII, 634.

16. Leffler, pp. 436, 475.

17. NA, Air 20/11516, 1A; Connor, p. 394.

18. Gilbert, VIII, 201.

19. NA, WO 193/303.

20. Gilbert, VIII, 171.

21. Hennessey, p. 102.

22. Roberts, *Stalin's Wars*, p. 308.

23. *Hansard*, 5th Series, 495, 966.

24. Gilbert, VIII, 211, 213.

25. NA, FO 371/62420, U 678, U 176.

26. Hoffman, p. 413.

27. Roberts, *Stalin's War*, p. 311.

28. Mark, pp. 384–5, 401.

29. Mark, pp. 393, 387, 401.

30. Gilbert, VIII, 196.

31. Roberts, *Stalin's War*, p. 309.

32. Tucker, p. 279.

33. IWM, Lydford, HTL 7.

34. Hahn, pp. 21, 68.

35. Leffler, p. 113.

36. NA, Prem 11/292,11; Leffler, p. 324.

37. Clark and Winter, pp. 66–7.

38. NA, Defe 4/44, 96.

39. NA, CO 537/5324.

40. NA, Defe 4/44, 96.

41. Leffler, pp. 143, 551.

42. Roger Louis, *Ends of British Imperialism*, p. 445; Roger Louis and Robertson, p. 464.

Chapter 33. Splutter of Musketry: Small Wars, 1950–1951

1. Gilbert, VIII, 641.

2. *Hansard*, 5th Series, 487, 107.

3. *Hansard*, 5th Series, 495, 201.

4. Tucker, pp. 276–7; Roberts, *Stalin's Wars*, p. 368.
5. Tucker, *passim*.
6. NA, Defe 4/41, 21 March 1951; 6 April 1951.
7. Leffler, pp. 486–7.
8. NA, Defe 4/41, 14 March 1951.
9. NA, Defe 13/58, 13.
10. NA, Adm 1/27285.
11. Bod.Lib., Macmillan D 8, 95, 108.
12. Brands, p. 444.

Chapter 34. A Falling from Power? Atom Bombs and Arabs, 1951–1955
1. Moran, p. 536.
2. Hennessey, p. 177.
3. Bod.Lib., Macmillan D 12, 51–2.
4. Mawby, p. 111.
5. NA, CO 822/461, 31, 68.
6. Gilbert, VIII, 757.
7. Gilbert, VIII, 928; Hennessey, p. 330.
8. Blundell, *A Love Affair*, p. 108.
9. In 2010 a quartet of aged Mau Mau survivors began a suit in the English courts for damages in regard of alleged maltreatment by Crown forces.
10. Bod.Lib., Macmillan D 16, 119.
11. NA, Prem 11/293, 72, 126.
12. NA, Defe 4/44, 57; *Churchill–Eisenhower Correspondence*, p. 148; Hennessey, pp. 144, 148.
13. NA, Defe 3/43, 676.
14. NA, Defe 13/228, 15.
15. R. Moore, *passim*.
16. Shuckburgh, p. 29.
17. W. Roger Louis, *Ends of British Imperialism*, p. 613.
18. Bod.Lib., Macmillan D 10, 42–4, 103, 109.
19. Shuckburgh, p. 76.
20. NA, Defe 4/52, 20.
21. *Churchill–Eisenhower Correspondence*, p. 25.
22. NA, Defe 4/52, 22, 41; Bod.Lib., Macmillan D 10, 76–7.
23. *Churchill–Eisenhower Correspondence*, p. 25.
24. Brands, p. 443.
25. Shuckburgh, p. 32.
26. NA, FO 371/98694, EP 15314/259.
27. Hahn, pp. 75–6.
28. NA, Defe 4/25, 29.
29. Jahal, pp. 426, 429.
30. Bod.Lib., Macmillan D 10, 55.
31. Shuckburgh, p. 63.
32. Bod.Lib., Macmillan, d 12, 54–5.
33. *Churchill–Eisenhower Correspondence*, p. 21.

34. Gilbert, VIII, 1123.
35. Colville, II, 131.
36. Charmley, *Churchill: The End of Glory*, p. 283.
37. Shuckburgh, p. 187.
38. *Churchill–Eisenhower Correspondence*, pp. 32–3.
39. Charmley, *Churchill: The End of Glory*, p. 260.
40. Prudos, p. 35.
41. NA, FO 371/10281, 2.
42. NA, FO 371/10281, 11924/106/53G.
43. CRC, pp. 28-9.
44. Shuckburgh, p. 77.
45. Roger Louis, *Ends of British Imperialism*, p. 614.
46. NA, Defe 4/41, 19 March 1951; Defe 4/52, 36, 42.
47. NA, FO 371/986694, EP 15314/25.
48. NA, FO 371/986694, EP 15314/254.

Chapter 35. The Third British Empire, 1951–1955
1. Ashton, p. 33.
2. Ashton, p. 12.
3. Ashton, p. 12.
4. Toye, p. 29.
5. *Congressional Record*, 100, Part 7, 8667.
6. *Time*, 17 May 1954.
7. *Congressional Record*, 100, Part 2, 1505.
8. NA, Defe 4/58, 168.
9. NA, Defe 4/66, 130.
10. Moran, pp. 387–8.
11. Moran, p. 571.
12. *Congressional Record*, 100, Part 7, 9246.
13. NA, WO 236/88, 5.
14. Toye, p. 296.
15. NA, CO 822/474, 42.
16. NA, CO 822/454, 38, 118, 159, 169, 171, 179, 211; CO 822/474, 20.
17. NA, CO 822/471, 70–1.
18. Chandos, p. 402.
19. Toye, p. 295.
20. Bod.Lib., Lennox-Boyd, 3394, 60.
21. Blundell, *A Love Affair*, pp. 108–9.
22. Toye, p. 298.
23. NA, CO 537/4307, Report 4.
24. NA, CO 1015/1758, 11.
25. RHL, Welensky, 61/6, 10, 12.
26. Murphy, *passim*.
27. Bod.Lib, Lennox-Boyd, 3455, 250–1, Memoirs of Major W. R. 'Bill' Moore.
28. Stockwell, *passim*.
29. RHL, Welensky, 75, 1, 3–4.

30. *Churchill–Eisenhower Correspondence*, pp. 163–4.
31. *Churchill–Eisenhower Correspondence*, pp. 167, 176.
32. Roberts, *Eminent Churchillians*, pp. 215–30.

Envoi

1. Bod.Lib., Lennox-Boyd, 3394, B 31 [28 March 1957].
2. *Revue des Deux Mondes*, 1–4 (1963), p. 316.
3. *The Listener*, 28 January 1965; 4 and 11 February 1965.

INDEX

The author and publisher are grateful to the following
for permission to reproduce photographs:

The Imperial War Museum (pictures: 1. © IWM (ZZZS426F)
3. © IWM (HU 68489) 4. © IWM (CH 4779) 5. © IWM (Q13807)
6. © IWM (Q24861) 7. © IWM (HU 56552) 8. © IWM (Q60172)
9. © IWM (HU 56848) 10. © IWM (HU 89851) 11. © IWM (MOL
FLM 1322) 12. © IWM (HU 63611) 13. © IWM (1505) 14. © IWM (IND
4410) 15. © IWM (K7530) 16. © IWM (HU 69100) 17. © IWM (A5444)
18. © IWM (TR 975) 19. © IWM (E5330) 20. © IWM (CM 774)
21. © IWM (E3593) 22. © IWM (MEM 2179) 23. © IWM (IND 740)
25. © IWM (HU 2766) 28. © IWM (H12752) 29. © IWM (E26640)
30. © IWM (TC 10203) 31. © IWM (A30491) 32. © IWM (TR3224)
33. © IWM (CT42) 34. © IWM (MAU554) 35. © IWM (TR 65682))
PA/PA Archive/Press Association Images (picture 2)
The National Archives (picture 24)
AP/Press Association Images (picture 26)
Time & Life Pictures/Getty Images (picture 27)

Endpaper map of the British Empire, 1922 © *The Probert
Encyclopaedia 2009*